IDEOLOGY, POWER AND PREHISTORY

T0381924

IDEOLOGY, POWER AND PREHISTORY

EDITED BY DANIEL MILLER
AND
CHRISTOPHER TILLEY

The right of the
University of Cambridge
to print and sell
all manner of books
was granted by
Henry VIII in 1534.
The University has printed
and published continuously
since 1584.

CAMBRIDGE UNIVERSITY PRESS
CAMBRIDGE
LONDON NEW YORK NEW ROCHELLE
MELBOURNE SYDNEY

CAMBRIDGE UNIVERSITY PRESS
Cambridge, New York, Melbourne, Madrid, Cape Town, Singapore, São Paulo, Delhi

Cambridge University Press
The Edinburgh Building, Cambridge CB2 8RU, UK

Published in the United States of America by Cambridge University Press, New York

www.cambridge.org
Information on this title: www.cambridge.org/9780521255264

First published 1984
This digitally printed version 2008

A catalogue record for this publication is available from the British Library

Library of Congress Catalogue Card Number: 83–15121

ISBN 978-0-521-25526-4 hardback
ISBN 978-0-521-09089-6 paperback

v

CONTENTS

To my mother (C.T.)
To my father (D.M.)

CONTRIBUTORS

Mary Braithwaite, Department of Archaeology, University of
Cambridge.

Ian Hodder, Department of Archaeology, University of
Cambridge.

Mark Leone, Department of Anthropology, University of
Maryland.

Daniel Miller, Department of Anthropology, University College,
London.

Michael Parker Pearson, Department of Archaeology, University
of Cambridge.

Christopher Tilley, Department of Archaeology, University of
Cambridge.

Alice Welbourn, Department of Archaeology, University of
Cambridge.

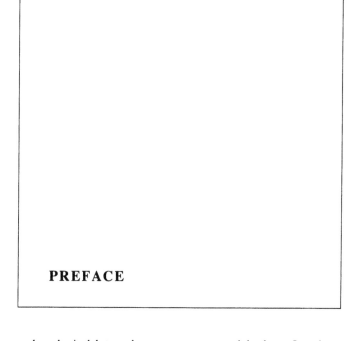

PREFACE

This volume arises out of a symposium held at the third Theoretical Archaeology Group conference, Reading, U.K. in December 1981. Most of the papers are, however, either extensively revised or use quite different examples from the original presentations. All but one of the contributors to this volume also wrote papers for an earlier publication in this series, *Symbolic and Structural Archaeology* (Hodder, Ed. 1982). The ideas that form the focus of this volume were one of a number to be tentatively explored there.

A consideration of ideology and power means that we are no longer able simply to 'read off' the nature of past societies from material evidence. Instead the archaeological record must be understood as actively mediated and manipulated as part of the social strategies of the individuals and groups that constituted a past society. Material culture can be used to express interests and ideas which may very well be contradictory. In order to understand ideology and power successfully a historical, particularist and contextual approach to the evidence is fundamental. This allows us to tackle both the variability and the specificity of archaeological data and contemporary material culture. It makes the past irreducibly the creation of sentient social actors and allows us to come both to a better understanding of it and of ourselves.

We recognise that this is only one of a number of attempts, at present being conducted, which seek to reorientate the nature of archaeological theory and practice. We are grateful for any interest and criticisms that have been given to us in the past from people working with similar or very different problems. In particular we should like to thank other members of the Cambridge Seminar Group who have not contributed papers here, and all those who at the conferences, in seminars and in coffee rooms have stimulated the development of these ideas. Our warmest personal thanks must go to those people who worked so hard to contribute to the book and were patient enough to put up with us as editors.

April 1983   Daniel Miller and Christopher Tilley

PART ONE

Theoretical perspectives

Chapter 1

**Ideology, power
and prehistory:
an introduction**
Daniel Miller and
Christopher Tilley

This volume is first shown to form part of a larger dialogue arising from some critiques of the dominant models in archaeological theory. In particular, it is part of an attempt to credit people and society in prehistory and material culture studies with the same abilities as we credit ourselves, rather than reducing them to the passive recipients of external forces. Two general discussions then follow, a summary is given of some approaches to the concept of power, and in particular a description and critique of Foucault's recent work on this topic is used as the basis for developing a working model of power. A model for the critique of ideology is developed through the examination of three examples. Firstly Marx's critique of the bourgeois conception of the political economy, secondly Marx's own labour theory of value, and thirdly the implications of three recent critiques of Marx's work. From these are derived some general characteristics of a working model for the critique of ideology, which differs in a number of respects from the original example of Marx's writings.

A problem in archaeology has always been that its method has provided the dominant metaphor for its interpretation. Before all else, archaeology has been about discovery. It is as quest and search that archaeology first commanded and now continues to fascinate its wide audience. This is encapsulated in the image of the archaeologist finally clearing a way through the last of the jungle to reveal the ancient ruined city, or burrowing through placid fields and orchards to uncover the unsuspected evidence of antiquity. In recent times the urge to discover has become a more fine-grained, refined ambition to locate all that might have been missed by the grand dig, to note the small seeds, the ghosts of wooden walls, the first clearance of trees.

All archaeologists take pride in the achievements of this exploration, in the idea, continually affirmed, that the future promises new pasts. Such is the attraction of these discoveries that, prior to a relatively recent rise in self-consciousness, exhibited in the 'new archaeology', it was held that the results of these investigations were comparatively self-evident as facts about the past. There had, however, always been those who questioned the nature of interpretation, and this questioning grew rapidly in the 1960s as a sustained critique of simple discovery, in favour of the development of a theoretical structure, which was expected to give a systematic basis to interpretation that might match the increasingly sophisticated and systematic methods being used in excavation and the laboratory analysis of remains (Clarke 1973).

This shift in the discipline, and the particular direction which it took, put the emphasis on a critique of the archaeologist as discoverer, and addressed the nature of the societies which were being investigated only in a limited fashion. Again it was method that dominated, although in this case the 'procedure' of interpretation. It was the models and hypotheses, held by the archaeologists, and their inductive or deductive qualities, that were seen as the centre of interest, and it was at this level that a restructuring of the archaeologist's approach from mere discoverer to interpreter was held to be necessary. Although the debate was apparently at the level of epistemology and the nature of the archaeologist as scientist, in practice it also had implications for the implicit model of what was being discovered (Miller 1982a, p. 86; Tilley 1982, p. 30).

In so far as the nature of the past in general, and the characteristics of the archaeological record in particular, were discussed in an explicit fashion, this was primarily through consideration of sampling biases (e.g. Mueller Ed. 1975). A realisation developed that archaeological remains were not direct reflections of past activities but were distorted by differential preservation, discard and curation patterns etc. (Schiffer 1976). The assumption behind this work was that when such natural and cultural transformation processes could adequately be taken into account, the archaeological record would be straightened out and the nature of the past could then be 'read off' more easily. The logistics of such an approach tended to result in one factor being held constant, and that was the image of the creator of the archaeological record. The model of ancient peoples emerged as similar to the rigid frame of behaviourist agency and its contingent deterministic response. This in turn led to a focus by some on factors that could be held 'constant', such as in the study of bones, rather than cultural artifacts (Binford 1978).

This volume continues the debate about the models held by archaeologists. The focus of attention, however, is not on the models archaeologists have erected purportedly to explain artifactual evidence, but rather on models held with regard to the creators of this past. A direct implication of ascribing an active intelligence to past peoples, as opposed to a passive stimulus-response conception, is that the remains we recover are to be interpreted as creations by people in accordance with their representation of the natural and social world. This is not a determin-

ant response but an active intervention; the social production of reality. This represents a radical shift in perspective in the direction of making the past *human*. It is a perspective that respects the agents that created what we find and grants them the same abilities and intentions that we would credit to each other as sentient social beings. It is also a recognition of the importance of taking into account the conceptions we hold of our own society which inevitably mediate our understanding of the past. The images created from a positivist perspective of passive agents reacting as 'game theory' subjects or as playing out 'roles' contingent on external pressures is a precise image of the same science that gives technical control its dominant place in our own society, serving to bolster up asymmetries of power and dominance (see chapter four below, p. 38). It is almost as though the ascription of the connotations of savagery, of minds less able to rise above their confrontation with the environment, now exorcised in discussions of contemporary society, is still preserved in relation to the past. In cultural evolutionary theories, societies are treated like football teams with labels on their backs. They compete in the adaptive stakes – ground rules for the game laid out *a priori* – before any analyses start. The assumed need of societies to adapt to externally induced socioenvironmental stresses or internally developed pathologies (Flannery 1972, Gall and Saxe 1977), becomes a differential measure of success. Some societies develop to the status of civilisations and reach the top of the league while others are relegated to the lower divisions of bands and chiefdoms. To use such a framework is not a normatively neutral process. It is to measure, to compare, to order the sequences according to definite criteria, time and place, and in doing so to pass judgement. It seems preferable to grant to all *Homo sapiens sapiens*, the abilities and characteristics we would wish granted to ourselves.

The present volume also continues a dialogue held between a number of workers in the field of prehistory, historical archaeology and general material-culture studies. It is a dialogue that began with a dissatisfaction with the dominant trends developing in archaeology during the late 60s and early 70s. The kind of archaeology espoused directly invited a response because of its unusually didactic and self-conscious form and tone. The history of the 'new archaeology' is instructive and it is important that lessons are learnt from it; that the undoubted advances made during the period in analytical techniques are preserved and are reflected in contributions to this book but that something of what now seem to be its shortcomings, should also be borne in mind. Part of the nature of this dissatisfaction has been discussed in detail by Ian Hodder in the introduction to *Symbolic and Structural Archaeology* (Hodder Ed. 1982a). There, the emphasis was on the misconceptions and limitations of functionalist assumptions that aligned with the didactic epistemology, and this theme is continued in Hodder's contribution to this volume.

The dissatisfaction arose with a number of interrelated elements forming the 'project' of the 'new archaeology', specifically:

(a) The uncritical acceptance of a positivist epistemology as the best means to gain knowledge of the past, taking this to be something different from empiricism rather than a form of it (e.g. Hill 1972).

(b)   As a direct concomitant of the former, a stress on functionalism and reduction of explanation to the need of human populations to adapt to an environmental milieu.

(c)   A behaviourist emphasis considering the archaeological record mainly in terms of biological directives; a calorific obsession (e.g. Zubrow 1975).

(d)   The labelling of any approach which asserted the primacy of social relations, cognition and intentional dispositions as 'paleo-psychology' which was consigned to the unsubstantiated realm of pure speculation.

(e)   A failure to consider the social production of archaeological knowledge.

(f)   An emphasis on the conservative values of stability and equilibrium deemed to be the norm, and a lack of attention to conflict and contradiction.

(h)   A reduction of the analysis of social change to the elucidation of external factors impinging on the social system.

(i)   A belief by some in mathematisation as the goal of archaeology; the attempt to reduce past social systems to a suitable equation (e.g. Gunn 1975).

A lesson might be learnt from the manner in which the 'new archaeology', despite its assertions to the contrary, may have in certain respects acted to continue previous traditions. Archaeology may be held to tend towards 'fetishism'; this idea as used in critical approaches suggests that relationships between people may be represented as though they were relationships between objects. Archaeology has always tended in this direction because of the nature of its evidence, which is primarily a world of objects. The history of archaeology has been a struggle between the representation of its evidence as signifying human subjects and as signifying types of object. In much of the earliest archaeology the relationship between these two was seen as relatively straightforward. The goal of archaeology was knowledge about past peoples. The artifact was the signifier, the subject who made and used them the signified, and the symbolic process was direct. For example, during that period when diffusionist models were paramount, the signifier might be a group of similar artifacts observed to spread over a given area, and the signified would then be a prehistoric people who were assumed to have moved over this same area.

The tendency in archaeology has been towards a fetishism in which little account is taken of the supposed signified, the result being that the process becomes subject to an inverse transformation. Concern becomes increasingly directed towards the artifacts themselves, that is, the stone tools, ceramic sherds or to faunal remains, and the prehistoric record is visualised primarily in terms of artifacts. In effect, the peoples or cultures become labels for similar artifacts or subsistence patterns: the subjects of the past have become the signifier, the label, while the evidence have become that signified.

Archaeological fetishism is, then, the tendency towards this inversion of the major symbolic process necessitated by any

attempt to interpret the past. Such tendencies exemplified by the virtual ascription to ceramic styles of an ability to reproduce further 'generations' of ceramic styles without reference to human agency have been noted and criticised in the past by Brew (1946) and Thomas (1972).

The history of the 'new archaeology' repeats, in part, this process. In its initial conception it set out to restructure archaeology along the alignment presupposed by its principal form of legitimation: the study of past peoples. In particular it called for a renewed approach to the study of the processes of social change. In articles such as 'Archaeology as Anthropology' (Binford 1962) the call was for a return towards anthropology and a direct reference to the peoples of the past. This legitimation was pronounced at a programmatic level throughout the period. In practice, however, a similar inversion continued. The rise of computer-aided statistical methodologies, and an internal focus on strategies such as sampling, led to a still stronger stress on the artifact as artifact. A major difference from the previous traditions was the reticence in ascribing a label that had pretensions to a prehistoric people. Taken as a subsumption of observed variability, this 'normative fallacy', as it was termed, was to be avoided. Increasingly concern focused on the variability of the artifact. That which was theoretically signified, namely people of the prehistoric past, tended to be eliminated, or reduced to the status of passive adaptors to environmental shifts, to await the time when more refined methods would somehow allow for their treatment as more active agents.

A line of thinking which certainly attracted many adherents to the 'new archaeology' was its optimism, that archaeology could be anthropology. The old view of a ladder of increasing difficulty of inference (Hawkes 1954), in which work was thought to be virtually impossible beyond the initial technological and economic rungs, was summarily rejected. However, the methodology and epistemology adopted for climbing higher directly precluded much success. The social and symbolic 'rungs' were only dealt with insofar as they could be reduced to effects of the economic and technological. The pessimism of normative archaeology was recreated but in a different manner; the top 'rungs' of the ladder became merged with those at the bottom, which on *a priori* and possibly expedient grounds, were again asserted as primary.

This is the background to the dialogue of which this volume forms a part. Much of our dissatisfaction was with the elimination of the proper signified of prehistory. This relationship with past peoples is always a symbolic one, mediated by archaeological remains, and it was appropriate that the concern with the return of people into prehistory should coincide with the espousal in anthropology of a concern with the symbolic process in the development of structuralism and semiotics. This was directly relevant to the key problem of archaeology. At the time when these approaches were impinging upon the search by the archaeologist for a more appropriate means to conceptualise the past, these ideas had themselves developed in a series of directions that made them more suitable for archaeological appropriation. The original structuralism of Lévi-Strauss could never have served such a purpose since it retained much of the more mechanical approaches of the sciences in its ever-present tendency towards formalism.

One important development in structuralist studies was an articulation with an increasing interest in the legacy of materialist approaches. This encouraged an emphasis on diachrony which had very positive results for its application to archaeology (e.g. Friedman and Rowlands 1977). Another influential shift within social theory developed from a disavowal of the more mechanical side of both structuralist and Althusserian structural-marxism, towards a concern with agency and strategy. This is evident in the work of social theorists such as Giddens (1979) and anthropologists such as Bourdieu (1977). The extensive influence of both of these trends will be evident in the papers in this volume.

From these perspectives has arisen an interest in the critique of ideology as an approach to material-culture studies and in particular to prehistory. This is an approach that presupposes an active construction and representation of the social world by past peoples, but which maintains a critical attitude to the analysis of these practices. This project has to confront several problems, relating to the conceptualisation of human society, if it is to avoid regressing in the manner of similarly optimistic and radical reappraisals of the possibilities of prehistory. In restoring the concern with agency in prehistory, we should not relapse into the kinds of individualist and psychological models of human behaviour which characterised some earlier forms of archaeology (e.g. Collingwood 1956, Hawkes 1968), and have been subject to the weight of criticism of all the succeeding traditions. This involves a positive use of advances in social theory and anthropology that have moved towards a non-reductionist model of human agency compatible with the coarse-grained scale of the archaeological enterprise. Indeed, Marx, who has provided the inspiration for many of the ideas used in this volume, played a crucial role in his insistence that human agency was understandable only as it was historically constituted by social relations.

This implies a critical approach to the concept of intention. Where intentions are discussed by Leone (chapter 3), and Miller (chapter 4), it is to show that although the agents must be allowed to have some understanding of their own world, as often as not their intentional actions have led to consequences that were the very opposite of those intentions. The major dimensions of social conflict and contradiction revealed by analysis often cross-cut the supposed concerns attributed to intention. In no case is individual intention of itself the cause of observed patterns. Terms such as 'strategy' and 'representation' have meaning only in relation to the development of institutions and social relations. It is essential that any recourse to peoples as agents of prehistory maintains a conception of society commensurate with these strictures.

The second means by which we can avoid regressing into the older form of fetishised archaeology is by setting our studies of prehistory directly alongside historical archaeology and studies of contemporary material culture which use comparable theoretical models to analyse analogous situations. In the trajectory of the dialogue of which this volume forms a part, there are three major elements in the overall research strategy. Firstly there is research into the articulation between interpretations of the past and the social and political context of the present. These include studies of the manner in which the past is represented (Leone 1978), the form taken by archaeology in different social contexts (Miller 1980), and the implications of the social theory that pertains to these debates (Tilley 1981, 1981b, 1982a). These researches come alongside a growing interest in the implications of critical theory. Working with models of social action which seem plausible and pertinent in the analysis of our own actions as interpreters may break down the distance that otherwise allows the emergence of implausible mechanised and fetishised models of past peoples.

The second research emphasis is towards the analysis of contemporary societies, and the application of these models to the study of material culture. This has in the past, included studies of the creation and maintenance of spatial boundaries (Hodder 1979, 1982b), architecture (Donley 1982) ceramics (Braithwaite 1982, Miller 1982), the disposal of rubbish (Moore 1982), and mortuary practices (Parker-Pearson 1982). These have been carried out in both industrial and non-industrialised societies. A contingent interest is in the general development of material culture studies, including the critique of the covert role played in the reproduction of asymmetry in age and gender (Hodder 1982c, Miller Ed. 1983). By placing these studies alongside one another, as in this volume, the prehistoric material may be directly equated with the interpretation of living societies. This does not mean that archaeology cannot go beyond other branches of anthropology. On the contrary, it is precisely intended that it does so since the relationships between these elements are dialectical not parasitic. The archaeological record is used to indicate the subtle and active role played by material culture, and this in turn leads to attempts to 'excavate' the underlying strata of meaning formed by material culture in the modern world. Archaeological materials are usually temporally extensive and may reveal major shifts in the symbolic position held by similar artifacts in relation to ideology over time. Of the three studies in the second section of this volume, only one is conceived of as essentially synchronic, the other two are concerned with the changing denotation of ideologically informed practices, as they are confronted by different social contexts or alternative material representations.

Symbolic and Structural Archaeology (Hodder Ed. 1982a) was an exploratory volume communicating a disquiet and a set of possibilities for change. It related to a number of themes and maintained a diverse range of responses. Although many of the contributors are the same, this volume is not a sequel, which would have had to comprise a series of works on a number of interrelated topics. Rather, the present volume picks up and emphasises only a single theme, the critique of ideology, which was explicitly discussed in only two papers in that volume (Shanks and Tilley 1982, Shennan 1982). It is hoped that the present volume represents a relatively coherent set of discussions. This is not to say that the authors adopt similar approaches, or are in agreement with one another. On the contrary, the volume retains a variety of interpretations as to the most important implications of these ideas for archaeology and material culture studies. There is, however, a set of core problems to which all of the papers relate. These concern the duality of the symbolic relations between past artifacts and past peoples, that is how the artifacts signified for the people who used them in the past and how the artifacts signify that process in turn for us, and how this process is mediated by power and the objectification of power. The area of debate is over how material practices give rise to conflicts in interest and to the nature of the role played by the material world in the representation and alteration of these practices. Having indicated the background to these concerns, we now examine the two concepts that provide the major instruments of the subsequent critical analysis; power and ideology.

Power

Discussions of power in social theory have tended to polarise according to a number of specific conceptual oppositions. Power has been conceived as *either* a property predicated on the actions of individuals, *or* as being a feature of collectivities. It has been regarded as the intentional, dispositional capacity of individuals to realise their objectives, or a structural feature of social systems. Power has been regarded as something which is either possessed or exercised and as being solely a negative, repressive phenomenon or a positive, productive element in social life. Concomitantly most theorists have worked from fairly narrow definitions connecting power with force or coercion (e.g. Mao's aphorism that power grows out of the barrel of a gun) or the capacity of agents to impose sanctions for non-compliance with their wishes by others: 'the chance of a man or a number of men to realise their own will in a social action even against the resistance of others' (Weber 1968, p. 926). Alternatively power has been conceived as being legitimate authority circulating in the social system in a manner equivalent to money (Parsons 1963), or as a generalised media of communication (Luhmann 1979). Lukes associates power *ipso facto* with clashes of interest: 'A exercises power over B when A affects B in a manner contrary to B's interests' (Lukes 1974, p. 27), while to Poulantzas (1973) power arises from structurally determined class relations. Needless to say all this work has been based on conceptions of political practices in contemporary western societies. An alternative line of approach has been to erect elaborate typologies of different types of power, rather than relying on restrictive definitions. Attempts have been made to distinguish carefully between force, coercion, manipulation, persuasion, influence and authority, legitimate or illegitimate power (e.g. Lasswell and Kaplan 1950, Wrong 1979).

In the position taken in this chapter we wish to avoid conceptual splits between on the one hand, viewing power as either individualist/collectivist, in terms of possession/exercise, involving restricted definitional statements, and on the other hand, the erection of contentious and almost infinitely extendable typologies. Two senses of the noun power may be distinguished, *power to* and *power over* (Benton 1981, p. 176). By *power to* we refer to power as an integral and recursive element in all aspects of social life. *Power over*, by contrast, can be specifically related to forms of social control. While *power to* can be logically disconnected from coercion and asymmetrical forms of social domi-

nation and does not, therefore, imply *power over*, the latter sense of the noun power must always involve *power to*. At a very broad and general level both of these senses of power indicate an irreducible link between power as a capacity to modify or transform, referring to the ability of human subjects to act in and on the world and in definite relationships to each other. Power enables agents (individual or collective) to significantly and non-trivially alter, or attempt to alter, the conditions of their existence and the outcomes of determinate situations in specific social and material contexts.

Foucault (1977, 1980, 1981) has attempted, more convincingly than any other contemporary social theorist, to dispel the notion that power is inherently negative or repressive. This is the idea that power is a monolithic and unitary mechanism, or sets of mechanisms, that can 'do' nothing but say no; to deny, to constrain, to set limits, to prevent the actualisation of human potentialities in one way or another. Foucault's work maintains a clear break between traditional ways of conceptualising power in either Marxist or non-Marxist traditions. Both Marxist and 'liberal' views of power have tended to deduce it in one form or another from the economy. Power tends to be treated as a concrete possession analogous to a commodity which can be wielded, transferred, seized or alienated. The 'juridico-discursive' conception of power (Foucault 1981, p. 82) involves the propensity to analyse power relations in terms of the language and imagery of the law. Power is conceived as a concrete possession of individuals. The partial or total cession of this power of the part of individual subjects allows sovereignty or political power to be established.

In classical and revisionist Marxist conceptions power tends to be treated as a function of the economic. In other words power is related back to the mode of production and solely conceived in the role in which it plays in the maintenance of the social relations of production, linked in discussions of the capitalist mode of production with class domination. The *raison d'être* of political power is located in the economy as a determinant in the last instance (Althusser 1971, Poulantzas 1973, pp. 99–105).

In both positions, whether power ultimately arises from a 'contractual cession' or an economic base related to class interests, it is simply conceived as flowing from the top to the bottom of the social order, from the superstructural political forces (classes, state apparatuses or individual decision makers) who possess it and exercise it on subjected populations in either an overt or a covert manner. Foucault has effectively challenged the negative conception of power intrinsically associated with such positions:

It is defined in a strangely restrictive way, in that, to begin with, this power is poor in resources, sparing of its methods, monotonous in the tactics it utilises, incapable of invention, and seemingly doomed always to repeat itself. Further, it is a power that only has the force of the negative on its side, a power to say no; in no condition to produce, capable only of posting limits, it is basically anti-energy. This is the paradox of its effectiveness: it is incapable of doing anything, except to render what it dominates incapable of doing anything either. (Foucault 1981, p. 85).

Power, rather than being simplistically conceived in terms of possession and/or a repressive role in inhibiting agents from fulfilling objectives, life-chances etc., should be conceived as having two sides or faces. On the one hand, power has a directly productive effect in social life and, on the other, a negative side linked to social control, hence the importance of the distinction introduced above between *power to* and *power over*.

Foucault stresses that power subjects bodies (people), not to render them passive, but as active beings. For example, the relationship of power to sexuality since the seventeenth century has not been just as a repressive mechanism pushing sexuality into the background, setting limits to it and controlling its forms and modes of expression (something we may be 'liberating' ourselves of now). The relationship has been productive of an ever increasing discourse and knowledge of (hence power in relation to) sexuality which has both denied it and extended, intensified and elaborated, its forms and practices. Because historically sexuality has become an object of analysis, surveillance and control, this has also directly engendered an intensification of individuals' desire for, in and over their bodies. In one sense power makes individuals what they are, it produces the social reality and the objects of discourse in which the individual is situated. To understand this requires a particular conception of the articulation between power and knowledge. Power produces both domains for its exercise and the reality in which it operates: 'power produces knowledge (and not simply by encouraging it because it serves power or by applying it because it is useful) . . . there is no power relation without the correlative constitution of a field of knowledge, nor any knowledge that does not presuppose and constitute at the same time power relations' (Foucault 1977, 27). Knowledge is a condition of possibility for power relations, a knowledge which is not so much true or false, as legitimate or illegitimate in terms of power strategies. Power creates and causes to emerge new objects of knowledge and bodies of information.

Accepting this conception of power as being both positive, and linked with the production of knowledge, we need to situate it in relation to social actions and practices.

Foucault's position can be briefly sketched as follows. By power Foucault does not mean, (i) institutions or mechanisms that ensure the subservence of the citizens of a particular state, (ii) forms of subjugation characterised by legitimate authority rather than coercion, (iii) class domination. These are the 'terminal forms' that power takes, rather than its locus or source. For instance, the state is conceived in terms of the overall strategies and effects of power. It is the effect of institutions and procedures and social establishments which themselves define the manner in which power is exercised. Power is not a unitary phenomenon, instead there are 'micro-powers' situated throughout the society. Power is to be found in specific institutions (hospitals, prisons, schools etc.), factories, state apparatuses, families, interest groups – in all social forms – but is never exactly located in them. Power operates and emanates from a multiplicity of centres via a variety of mechanisms. Power is never possessed by individuals or institutions but it is exercised by them. It is not appropriated for specific purposes hence to ask 'who holds power?' and 'what is the source of this power?' is neither relevant nor necessary. It is 'the moving substrate of force relations, which by virtue of their inequality, constantly engender states of power . . . the name that one attributes to a complex strategical situation in any particular society' (Foucault 1981, p. 93). A strategy is not possessed or formulated by any particular individual or state apparatus, but is a combination of a multiplicity of force relations arising throughout society characterised by their positioning, forms, techniques etc. Power is omnipresent in the social body.

All individuals and groups exercise power and are subject to its exercise. Power is not in some way external to definite types of social relations (economic, sexual, religious etc.) but part and parcel of them. Power comes from 'below' rather than 'on top' (state power) and forms a general matrix for social life. Where there is power there is also resistance or a plurality of resistances. The exercise of power sets up these resistances to its effectivity and these are its irreducible opposite.

Power relations, Foucault claims, are both intentional and non-subjective (1981, p. 94). From where, then, does intentionality arise? Power in Foucault's terms has a certain rationality because it is exercised with a series of aims and objectives. These are not attributable to any particular agent but arise 'anonymously' in the social body from the local situations or micropowers in which they first appear. The rationality of power is characterised by the 'tactics' it uses. These tactics become connected to one another from the local micro-level at which they are first inscribed and end by forming comprehensive systems the logic and aim of which is clear whilst not being attributable to any inventor (1981, p. 95).

Contemporary western societies are portrayed in *Discipline and Punish* as being disciplinary societies. Discipline is one of the main techniques of power. It provides the primary mode of social subjection. Discipline is located in a wide variety of institutional forms (schools, prisons, the army, the police, hospitals, factories). Is it surprising then, Foucault asks, that prisons resemble factories, schools barracks and hospitals (Foucault 1977, p. 228). Discipline 'makes' individuals, it creates subjects because it is the result of a power that regards individuals as both the objects and instruments of its exercise. Discipline also has the effect of normalisation and corrects deviations from the norm. Power is exercised via careful observation and surveillance, by the comparative measure from the norm, hence the insane are more individualised by discourse than the sane, the patient more than the healthy, the child more than the adult. By comparing individuals by a continuous assessment in the form of examinations, collated medical reports, etc., discipline asserts a normalizing judgement. The norm around which power is exercised is, in the terms of Foucault's analysis, a real material and physical relation. There is little space for any consideration of ideological control. Foucault's conception of power-knowledge opposes the concept of ideology as either being a discourse opposed to science or as a feature of the social world, involving the 'management' and representation of reality. His insistence on the positive, productive characteristics of contemporary power apparatuses, linked with the contention that the power-knowledge relation leads to a politics of truth, is the precise opposite of the Frankfurt school's critique of ideology (Foucault 1980, pp. 131–3; Gordon 1980, p. 237).

Notwithstanding the novelty of Foucault's analysis and the many insights to be gained, it cannot be accepted in toto for the following reasons: (i) accepting that power should not be conceived as a property belonging to an individual agent or a collectivity, power is still attributable to individuals and agents. This is neither a delusion nor a theoretical error and Foucault's conception of power fails to specify on what sort of basis this attribution can be made. Having ruled possession of power out of court, Foucault does not seem to consider this problem further. (ii) To suggest that power strategies have an object and a purpose but at the same time are still non-subjective is contradictory. Intentions may only be properly conceived as being attributable to human subjects or groups of individuals. Power strategies, as Foucault conceives them, like social systems can have no goals or objectives, but who then do they serve? (iii) To make resistance the irreducible opposite to power is to suggest that resistance is always present in relations of power, and to ignore ideology. Why should there be resistance to power if it is ideologically misrepresented, or is actually non-repressive, i.e. for the general good, unless one is to say that resistance to power, whatever its forms, is an existential part of human nature. (iv) To fail to attribute power to agents is also to fail to realise that power conveys definite psychological and material benefits: prestige, access to resources etc. Even if power cannot be possessed by agents, prestige and resources can as an effect of the operation of power be attributed to them. (v) Foucault's analysis tends to depoliticise power relations and the effect of political struggles in contemporary societies is left unanalysed.

Drawing on Foucault's analysis we conceive *power to* as a component of all social interaction and as a feature embedded in all social practices. This power draws upon and creates resources. Viewed at perhaps the most abstract level it can be regarded as a dispositional capability, neither possessed nor exercised or controlled by any particular agent or collectivity, but as a structural feature of social systems, which is only manifested through its effects on individuals, groups and institutions.

Power can be logically separated from either exploitation or social control, i.e. its effects need not necessarily promote repressive control. It is not a resource, something which can be used, but operates and produces effects through the resources drawn upon by social actors in their interrelationships with each other and an environmental milieu. Power, conceived as a dialectical moment in interaction, draws upon and creates resources and is present through its effects; on this basis it may be attributed to individuals, groups, institutions etc., who benefit from it.

These resources may be either material or non-material. By material resources is meant control over coercive media, possession of the means of production, raw materials etc. These are extrinsic resources drawn upon in power relationships. By non-material resources we refer to knowledges, skills, competences etc. These are intrinsic to individual social actors or collectivities. Resources are not dormant features but are actively produced through the material and symbolic praxis of agents. All power relationships are dependent upon access to an asymmetrical distribution of resources.

As such, power should be conceived as a positive force intimately involved in the production, reproduction and transformation of the social order and what counts as social reality (knowledge in and of the world). Power, then, as a component of praxis, involves the capacity to transform, to produce specific effects and outcomes as a result of the interaction of human subjects with their environment, involving necessarily 'the realisation of teleological positings' (Lukács 1980, p. 9).

Power over is the accomplishment of effects which can only be realised by an agent (individual or collective) through the agency of others. This means power enables an agent to get another agent to do/not to do something they would otherwise do/not do and this may be directly contrary to the objectives of the agent over whom this power is exercised. *Power over*, except in the limiting case of a bound prisoner, always involves a dialectical relationship between the power 'holder' and those upon whom power is exercised, as agents always have some resources, mental or material, to resist the exercise of power. Power relationships thus exhibit a dialectical asymmetry and will always be contingent. The effects produced by power are rarely, if ever, assured (Hindess 1982). Unintended effects may be produced and the outcome of a power relationship cannot be simply deduced by a process of adding up resources on either side.

In determinate social situations, where social control and exploitation are a regularised feature of life resulting in the differential restriction of life-chances for the majority of social agents, the production and maintenance of this control is likely to be both ineffective and unstable in the long run if the only resort to bolster control is by means of physical force or the threat of the use of such force in the form of coercive sanctions. The social order must be legitimised and the principles upon which control is based justified. One of the most powerful means of achieving this is the active production of a normative consensus naturalising and misrepresenting the extant nature of asymmetrical social relations so that they appear to be other than they really are. Ultimately all forms of power, whether analysed in terms of authority, persuasion or other related terms, can be reduced to either physical force (or its threat) or manipulation, where this power must produce its effects through the agency of others. This is because the use of power to further the objectives of specific interest groups will almost always entail the reproduction of the effects of this power for its own sake. The securing of this power is either irrelevant to, or more usually, directly contrary to, the interests and objectives of those subject to it.

Lukes' self-styled 'three-dimensional' conception of power stresses the importance of the ideological legitimation of the social order in which the effects of power may be analysed in part in terms of successfully misrepresenting social reality so that those subjected to power are largely unaware that this is contrary to their interests: 'A may exercise power over B by getting him to do what he does not want to do, but he also exercises power over him by influencing, shaping or determining his very wants' (Lukes 1974, p. 23). This raises a whole series of problems. Firstly, the conception is based on the classical view that ideology is false consciousness which involves an empiricist conception of knowledge. Secondly, as Lukes views the exercise of power in all cases as being contrary to the interests of those subjected to it, the problem arises as how to determine the real or objective interests. This latter problem has been discussed at length (McLachlan 1981; Benton 1981, among others). Exactly how are an agent's interests to be conceived? Given that an agent's wishes, desires, actions etc., may be systematically manipulated by the active distortion of social reality on the part of those in positions of power, are his/her interests actually what the agent thinks or believes his/her interests are? Might there be a significant difference between an agent's 'objective' interests (i.e. discursively formulated) and 'real' interests? Real interests here refer to what the agent's interests would actually be if that agent were situated differently in relation to the material and social conditions of his/her existence. Does this mean that power is in this sense legitimate? Can power be used to affect an agent in opposition to his/her 'objective' interests but in accordance with what are supposed to be that agent's 'real' interests, and if so is this not a manifesto for totalitarianism? The nub of the problem is that given ideological forms of manipulation of the social order, in what manner will real interests of agents be determined? This problem can only be adequately resolved in relation to a detailed consideration of the nature of ideology. This is taken up below, but that discussion is predicated upon a notion of power as discussed here, which may be summarised by the following points:

(1) *Power to* is an integral element in social life, a component of all social practices, an existential part of human existence and can be disassociated from social control and domination, characterised by *power over*.

(2) Power may have some of its conditions of existence in the economic base, e.g. systems of labour exploitation but is not simply an affect of the economic.

(3) Power is both productive of knowledge and non-material resources, and a negative repressive element bolstering social inequalities.

(4) Power is dialectically related to resources, to operate it draws on these resources and in turn reproduces them.

(5) Power is not unitary, it cannot be tied down to a single essence or form.

(6) At one level power is neither possessed nor exercised but is a structural feature of the social totality only manifested at its point of constitution in social action and intereaction through its effects.

(7) Power is attributable to individuals, groups etc., not as possession but in terms of the effect of its exercise producing a structured asymmetry of resources.

Ideology: the approach

In focusing on the concept of ideology as a means of altering our perspective on the nature of the past, we have to hand a term that has developed over a considerable period and undergone many changes of meaning. Its history and development are succinctly presented by Larrain (1979). Most recently the notion of ideology has undergone a shift from being a relatively crude tool for the investigation of dominant interests and their legitimation, to becoming a much more subtle and sophisticated technique in the hands of anthropologists such as Bourdieu, or the social theorists following the Frankfurt school, in which the complex interplay of images and strategies are teased out and related to competing interests.

The scale of these interests is that of social convention and collective representation analysed at the level of observable variability. Ideology works, however, with somewhat different assumptions from the more traditional anthropological notion of culture with its dominant Durkheimian model of collective representation. The critique of ideology emphasises differences in interest and conflicts in representation, for a variety of groups within a society. The most fruitful arena of debate today is probably the feminist critique, that has moved from the more blatant examples of male dominance, to the more subtle forms of the reproduction of gender asymmetry as naturalised in the everyday and mundane features of the modern world.

The critique of ideology has been applied in the critical analysis of a range of problems. Current developments in anthropology are often directed at a much more fine-grained analysis than that which is intended here. The problematic addressed in this volume is more at the scale of the longer periods and larger regions that form the framework of most archaeological enquiries. One effect of this breadth of scale and also the sheer variety of social formations to which this critical analysis might be applied, is that it seems reasonable, at this stage, to develop a very broad reading of the concept of ideology itself. For example, we might use a general model of a group linked by interest, rather than attempting to specify what those interests might be, which is left to the specific application of the model to the historically contingent subject of analysis. Much of the debate over ideology is concerned with its precise application to the analysis of contemporary society. This development of a detailed 'archaeology' of capitalism may, however, be less useful as a guide, than the original inspiration from which the model derives.

The concept of ideology developed here is quite distant in a number of ways from that which is presented by Marx. Nevertheless, it is the case, that Marx's work represents the base-line from which virtually all subsequent discussion has developed. The present analysis returns to this base-line, but in a slightly unconventional manner. The discussion will focus, not upon what Marx and subsequent authors have said about the concept of ideology itself, although Marx's comments will be touched upon, but rather Marx's writings will be used to exemplify in themselves what such a concept might come to mean in practice. By not attempting to synthesise the vast literature that has grown up since, it is hoped to avoid much of what has become a convoluted and sometimes rather sterile debate, in favour of argument by example.

Specifically the investigation will revolve around a core aspect of the three volumes of Capital (which is also its opening section), that is Marx's 'labour theory of value'. This is not out of direct concern for that particular theory, but rather because it has become the prime example for a number of approaches to the nature of ideology. There will be three parts to this investigation. In the first instance the focus will be on the bourgeois conception of value as characterised by Marx, which is close to his own, more explicit model of ideology, as illustrated in other sections of Capital and in his earlier writings. Secondly, the investigation will turn to the concept of ideology as exemplified by his own presentation of the labour theory of value, and thirdly the investigation will turn to that which is implied by critiques of this theory.

Marx's labour theory of value

A clear presentation of the labour theory of value is found in the opening section of volume one of *Capital*. Marx can best be understood as positing a set of categories that are conceived of as relationships rather than entities (Ollman 1971, p. 13). He begins by presenting a series of dichotomies differentiating the concept of *value* from that of *use-value*. He argues for a twofold characterisation of labour. (a) The division of labour results in many different and specific kinds of work that in turn create the variety of objects. This specific labour produces the use-value of those objects. (b) These objects are also the product of abstract labour, i.e. that labour in general which has gone into their production, whatever its specific form. It is by embodying this abstract labour, that the object has value. Marx states: 'We see then that that which determines the magnitude of the value of any article is the amount of labour socially necessary, or the labour-time socially necessary for its production . . . Commodities, therefore, in which equal quantities of labour are embodied, or which can be produced in the same time, have the same value' (1974, p. 47).

The use-value of an object is directly observable as the potential utilitarian use to which it may be put; its value, by contrast, is an abstract attribute that is not immediately evident. Value only becomes clear when we consider exchange. Marx argues that exchange between objects is a very different phenomenon from that which is usually presented. He notes that in order to exchange objects as commodities, they have to be reduced to an equivalence, i.e. their value. It is because they all embody quantities of labour-power, which gives them their value, that they may be seen as commensurate and exchangeable. Marx states: 'It is the expression of equivalence between different sorts of commodities that alone brings into relief the specific character of labour-creating value, and this it does by actually rendering the different varieties of labour embodied in the different kinds of commodities to their common quality of human labour in the abstract' (1974, p. 57).

In a series of stages, Marx shows how this abstract equivalence becomes in the capitalist economy transformed into money. Money therefore acts not only as a standard for price, but also: 'It is a measure of value inasmuch as it is the socially recognised incarnation of human labour' (1974, p. 100). This argument is relatively straightforward, but its implications for the workings

of the highly complex political economy of capitalism occupies Marx for the weighty three volumes of Capital. The entire work is, however, a continuation of the same argument. Marx attempts to demonstrate systematically how a whole range of terms used in economics are in fact based upon the social relations of production. He argues for example that it is not in exchange that profit is produced as claimed, since 'Circulation, or the exchange of commodities, begets no value' (1974, p. 161). To obtain value the capitalist must find something that creates value and is available for sale. He therefore depends on the labour power that he can purchase. Since the workers cannot obtain the tools or machines needed to translate their work into commodities, they are forced to sell themselves to the owner of the means of production. The capitalist therefore obtains surplus value, by all the work the labourer does over and above that necessary for the reproduction of his or her own labour, that is the feeding of the family, or if all the family are put to work, then merely the feeding of the individual.

As Marx delves into the different forms these relations take, the argument, although of the same nature, becomes more complex. In the second and third volumes Marx shows how many other economic terms, such as rent or a variety of forms of capital, may be revealed as transformations of value. The pivot of the analysis remains the socially necessary labour to produce a commodity at a given level of the productive forces. The form of this analysis indicates the material connections that bind these various aspects of the capitalist process. There are also connections of another form in the manner in which these processes are represented, both the representation by the capitalist (Mepham 1979) and the analysis of Marx (Ollman 1971) must be understood as structured discourse.

Of the three perspectives from which this argument may be analysed for an understanding of the workings of ideology, the first, and that which Marx himself had in mind when he writes about the concept of ideology, are the actions and contingent beliefs held by the bourgeois and repudiated in his argument. In the bourgeois scheme of things, these same economic categories which Marx reveals as stemming from value, are taken as real in themselves. For them, there is no such category as abstract labour value. For the capitalist it is indeed exchange which produces profit. On most of the points of the above argument, the perspective of the bourgeois and that of Marx are quite contradictory. For Marx, abstract labour produces value which allows for the existence of money, for the capitalist it is money that produces equivalence between commodities and that labour may in turn be measured against. For the ordinary capitalist, use-value and price, are the only 'value' of concern.

The essential difference between the perspective taken by Marx and that of the bourgeois is brought out in a section of *Capital* termed the 'fetishism of commodities'. In this section Marx explains, how it is that what ought to be obvious appears not to be seen. It is 'because the relation of the producers to the sum total of their labour *is presented to them* as a social relation, existing not between themselves, but between the products of their labour' (Marx 1974, p. 77). The bourgeois model of the political economy makes sense as a relation between things in terms of prices and profits and exchange, in which people meet in terms of their relationship with commodities, i.e. as owners or sellers, but it makes no sense as an account of the relationship between people. Rubin argues therefore that 'the theory of fetishism is, per se, the basis of Marx's entire economic system, and in particular of his theory of value' (Rubin 1972, p. 5).

The bourgeois model of the world is essentially their representation of what is taking place from the point of view of their interests. Marx makes clear that it is this point of perspective that is crucial in explaining why the world appears to them as it does. An example is the nature of exchange. To the ordinary non-capitalist buyer or seller, an exchange will usually appear as commodity–money–commodity, for example they obtain money by selling their labour power and with that money, purchase a commodity. To the capitalist, however, who may be part of precisely the same exchange but is entering and leaving at a different point the process may present itself as money–commodity–money.

If this representation of the political economy by the bourgeois is taken as an example of the bourgeois ideology, its characteristics start to emerge. Clearly it is a representation of the world that is in the interests of and from the perspective of the bourgeois. The second important attribute is that it is not merely an abstracted theory, on the contrary it is a description of how the capitalist does indeed work. 'The circulation of things – to the extent that they acquire the specific social properties of value and money – does not only express production relations among men, but it creates them' (Rubin 1972, pp. 10–11). Representation is of importance not as mere presentation, but because the subject attempts to reproduce the world in the image from which it is understood and apprehended. The capitalist goes about his or her daily work calculating profit, planning investment precisely in accordance with the bourgeois ideology of relations between things. The emphasis in *Capital* is on the origin of ideology in the opacity of the phenomenal form of everyday action (Mepham 1979, see also his discussion of the mystification of the wage form pp. 153–5).

The next attribute of the bourgeois representation as ideology is that it has a moral foundation. Marx most often presents details of the bourgeois conception (that is the ordinary capitalist as opposed to the academic theorist), when he illustrates how the capitalist is attempting to legitimate the continuation of the status quo in opposition to some reform measure proposed in government such as the factory acts. Two features are of importance here. (a) The bourgeois account is not taken as a defensive constructed representation, but, on the contrary, is assumed to be the natural and unquestionable order of things. This character of naturalness is the first legitimatizing property of the representation. It is obviously reinforced by the extent to which the bourgeois has succeeded in creating the world in the image of this representation. (b) The bourgeois represent their world as in accordance with a set of principles centred on the concept of individual liberty: every individual is free to work to his or her

own advantage, and it is essential that the government be prevented from curbing this liberty of the individual.

Another aspect of this bourgeois representation is what it ignores, and that is the possibility of another perspective emerging because of the emergence of a class in contradiction to itself. While this model is from the perspective of and in the interests of the bourgeois, it is contradicted from that of worker, the proletariat. While it is legitimated by the freedom of the bourgeois to exploit, it is contradicted from the simultaneous further deprivation of the proletariat, who have become free only to sell their labour power, and create slaves of themselves. It is important to note that ideology is not equated with the entire actions, beliefs or representations of the world held by a given group. It is only when those representations are generated by a conflict of interests and an assymmetry of power that is in turn reproduced through these representations that we confront the phenomenon of ideology (Larrain 1983, p. 15).

Our initial concept of ideology can then be summarised as it is exemplified by the bourgeois representation of the political economy. Ideology is the representation of the world held by the dominant group in the society, and is also the rationale which guides their everyday actions. It is a representation that accords with the interests of that group and that emanates from the perspective of that group. It centres on its model of the political economy but includes a moral legitimation of the whole of society. It is contradicted by the existence of an exploited group whose interests it does not represent. It may therefore be seen as mystifying in that it makes appear as natural and correct that which is partial, and that it makes appear as coherent that which fails to acknowledge the contradictions it encompasses. Finally it is characterised by both deriving from and being a representation of the material world, and it is the dialectical relation between these two; representation and action, in actual material practice, that is comprehended by Marx's own profound concept of praxis.

Ideology in Marx's account of capitalism

The second account of the concept of ideology may be taken by focusing, not on what Marx takes to be the bourgeois representation, but rather as is exemplified by Marx's own account. Marx presents his work as a scientific discovery. In a preface he compares himself to a physicist, who has recovered the elementary and simple basis of the money-form. The basis of the discovery is the differentiation of value and use-value based on the twofold character of labour as abstract and specific. For Marx then, his discovery was as a recovery of something real from beneath the bourgeois representation, which was a mystification that served to hide this reality. It may be noted that Marx talks of mystification rather than illusion, the concept of ideology appears to have a reality for Marx based on two realms, the material and the ontological. The material reality of ideology that conceives of it as distortion of something that has a material base, is clear in Marx's earlier writings about ideology itself: 'men developing their material production and material intercourse, alter, along with their real existence, their thinking and the products of their thinking. Life is not determined by consciousness, but consciousness by life' (Marx and Engels 1970, p. 47).

Marx never appears to have allowed for a totally autonomous ideological realm. The further claim is made for his own analysis of the workings of the political economy, which is contrasted with ideology, in part as science, (though not to be confused with 'bourgeois' science which is itself ideological). 'Hitherto men have constantly made up for themselves false conceptions about themselves, about what they mean and what they ought to be' (Marx and Engels 1970, p. 37). Marx notes that the bourgeois representation will still be an adequate model for bourgeois action even after this discovery. He states: 'The recent scientific discovery, that the products of labour, so far as they are values, are but the material expressions of human labour spent in their production, marks, indeed, an epoch in the history of the development of the human race, but by no means, dissipates the mist through which the social character of labour appears to us to be an objective character of the products themselves' (1974, p. 79). If then we accept the claims made directly by Marx about his own work in relation to a definition of ideology, there are two additional attributes to be considered. Firstly, the material base of ideological thought, such that a systematic if distorted linkage might be expected between the organisation of production and the dominant ideology, as was clearly the case for the bourgeois ideology, and secondly that such ideology might be revealed by scientific analysis. It is of interest however, to compare the claims put forward by Marx for his ideas, and that which is exemplified by their form and usage.

On closer consideration, the 'discovery' by Marx of the nature of value appears to be of a very different order from that kind of discovery in the natural sciences which he is claiming here as his model. The difference between Marx's account and the bourgeois account, is essentially a difference in perspective. Marx has quite literally a different point of view. He understands the political economy from the point of view of the relations of production as experienced by the labourer, while the bourgeois do not regard the political economy from the perspective of relations of production at all, but only as a relation between things, a mystification that applies also to the worker. It is in effect a different construction based on a different subject.

Rubin (1972) argues that it is the sociological aspects of Marx's work that have been least understood. Marx was not primarily concerned with the quantitative analysis of prices and capital, although he was clearly attempting to give his works a veneer of positivist science. This however, covers what is essentially a systematic attempt to recentre the perspective of representation. The crux of the Marxist concept of value is that it defines all other economic categories from the point of view of the social relations of production. It is these relations that give rise to the conflict of interest that is the class struggle. In many ways, what Marx achieved is easier to comprehend with the rise of structuralist and post-structural analysis (Sturrock 1979), which developed first on the analysis of the internal relations of the text, and then emphasised the relations between the text and its subject

(e.g. Ollman 1971). The work of Barthes and Foucault illustrate how texts are representations from the perspective of interest and power and the ways in which such de-centering can be achieved (e.g. Barthes 1977, pp. 32–51, 142–8; Foucault 1981, pp. 3–12).

This analysis of the centre or the subject of activity is brought out most clearly in the concept of alienation as discussed in Marx's earlier work (which emerges as that of the fetishism of commodities in the argument of *Capital*). In *The German Ideology*, it was shown how the direct imposition of a set of ideas and ideals by those whose interests dictated these ideas upon other groups in society, resulted in the alienation of those other groups. 'Just because individuals seek *only* their particular interest, which for them does not coincide with their communal interest, the latter will be imposed upon them as an interest "alien" to them, and "independent" of them, as in turn a particular "general" interest' (Marx and Engels 1970, p. 54). The clearest example of this sense of alienation is precisely the fetishism of commodities, where their own social relations are made to appear to them merely as relations between the products of their labour. The extent to which groups were prevented from gaining access to means by which they could objectify, and thereby come to have an understanding of, their social relations, was taken up by later writers.

This relationship of alienation and reification is a clue to the effective role of Marx's own theory as perceived by Marx and as realised by Marxism. Prior to Marx's writings, the proletariat are faced with a dominant ideology that is developed from the interest of the class that exploits them. Marx's concept of the proletariat's own set of beliefs at this stage is unclear and will be discussed below, but what is clear is that Marx having redefined the political economy from the perspective of the proletariat, wished that perspective to become the consciousness of the proletariat. There is, therefore, in Marx's own writings a number of attempts to predict Marxism even before it had arisen, as for example, in the Manifesto where he talks of the spectre haunting Europe, and in the quotation above about the epoch-making role of his own discovery. Marx is projecting a self-avowedly critical theory, one whose new understanding was intended to change the consciousness of people and thereby effect revolutionary action. If, therefore, Marx's own writings are taken as a model for, rather than against, ideology, it would be suggestive again of the extent to which that consciousness though indeed rooted in the materiality of the relations of production as its base, could nevertheless be intended to play a minor part in itself altering (or re-centring) the world in the direction of its own image, in a similar manner to the bourgeois ideology it is intended to counter. Once more it is a representation that aims towards the reproduction of the world in its image.

This takes the argument to a third stage. The workings of the model of ideology were first exemplified by Marx's account of the bourgeois model of the world. It has now been shown how Marx's own account may also be analysed as a re-centring of perspective, that itself may be a form of the workings of ideology, and further, that in its use by the early Marxists as a model of the transformation of consciousness, this alteration of perspective becomes a key element in the model. A problem that manifests itself at this stage is the question as to the relationship between ideology and science. The relationship between these two terms has been a focal point of discussion in recent years. Just as positivist philosophers have made claims to the effect that positivism is the only means to gain truth and genuine knowledge of the world, Marxist philosophers have made similar claims, branding all types of analysis, with the exception of Marxism (theoretical practice), as being distorted representations (theoretical ideologies) of the reality of the social (see especially Althusser and Balibar 1970, p. 58ff). There seems little point in attempting to recover quite what Marx did or did not mean. What is of more interest is to discover how useful his specific analysis may be as a foundation for all applications of the model of ideology. A survey of some critical accounts of Marx will lead to the final stage in constructing a model of ideology, in which his work comes to serve as a model for critical analysis, but is not credited with the kind of status as a science that some readings have ascribed to it.

Critiques of Marx

The first critique comes from Cutler et al. (1977–8), who engage in a systematic revaluation of the argument of *Capital*. They do so from the sympathetic stance of wishing to formulate a critical account of the working of modern capitalism, but the feeling that to do so, demands a genuinely critical account of Marx's own critique of the capitalism of his day. In effect, they appear to reject a good deal of the detailed content of Marx's argument and many of the implied claims as to what the argument represents. For example, in their preface, they suggest of the notion of value which is the key factor in Marx's account, that it 'effectively limits any conception of circulation based on credit money, limits the role of finance capital to the redistribution of the surplus value already produced and silences the discussion of the range of determinants of industrial capitalist profits' (1978, p. 3). The details of their specific analysis may be found in the first chapter. They are certainly not the first to reject the specific analysis of the workings of the economy and in particular the conception of money and prices. The work by Sraffa (1972) on the production of commodities by means of commodities, is accepted by some as achieving a more satisfactory formal account. They also reject Rubin's defence of the theory of value, although they acknowledge the importance of his focus on the qualitative and sociological aspects of Marx's work as exemplified in the theory of commodity fetishism. They note with reference to Rubin and others, however, the failure by Marx to achieve a satisfactory reading of use-value in its relation to demand, and indeed the problem of consumption in general.

This critique of Cutler et al. although one of the most systematic examples, obviously does not exhaust the problems of Marx's account. It seems likely that in future years the present impact of microchip technology and the focus this brings on contemporary attempts to virtually eliminate labour from manufacture, may suggest further revisions of the basis for advanced

capitalism. It is important, however, to specify the implications of such a critique. It does not seem that the questionable nature of any attempt to take Marx's account as 'scientific', in any way affects the actual historical importance of his critique, any more than the questionable and partial account of the bourgeois, limited their ability to exploit. Such criticisms do, however, make implausible an opposition between Marxist 'science' and either ideology or bourgeois economics as 'non-science', and they therefore aid in the present project of using Marx himself as an example of the concept of ideology, in which ideology is related to interest rather than opposed to reality.

The second critique focuses on two points, the actual nature of past ideologies as exemplified in different periods, and an equally important question as to the nature of the consciousness of those groups who are subordinate in a society. Abercrombie et al. (1980), investigate several historical periods and the contemporary situation, to question the validity of any assumption that the beliefs of the dominant group do pervade the subordinate group as suggested in *The German Ideology* (see above). They argue for example, that in West European feudalism the most developed systems of legitimation, such as that of honour, were effective as a coherent logic for the organisation of the nobility but were of little relevance and were little known by the peasantry. They note that during specific periods there have been competing ideologies, for example, the existence today of a subordinate but developed working-class consciousness in Britain, which may not be associated with the whole of that class, but is the point of identification and representation for a portion of it. Investigations of practices that oppose dominance have been the subject of a number of recent studies in contemporary Britain, by the Centre for Contemporary Cultural Studies (Hall et al. Eds., 1976) on youth subculture, and by Cohen on the Notting Hill carnival (1982).

On this issue of competing ideologies, the Abercrombie critique is quite compatible with the model of ideology that has been presented here. This model has stressed the extent to which ideology works as a coherent model for effective action with its associated legitimation by the dominant group, but also that it may be faced with the beliefs and practices of any other group that recognise their own interests as in conflict with that dominant group. This point is stressed by Braithwaite (chapter 7). In many ways Marx himself, at least as exemplified by his work, is not responsible for the emphasis on a model of false consciousness, which often came to be seen as the deliberate mystification of subordinate groups as an instrument of hegemony, that was developed by later writers on ideology. Marx may have seen the mystificatory and thereby alienating effect of ideology as emerging more as a byproduct of the need by the dominant group to maintain a coherent view in the face of conflict and contradiction that arise from competing interests. Larrain argues, that for Marx 'Ideology is a solution in the mind to contradictions that cannot be solved in practice' (1979, p. 46).

The third critique is still wider than the previous two and is most prone to analyse Marx himself as the producer and product of ideology. Baudrillard (1975) makes the, at first surprising, claim that Marx was a conservative in his analysis, rooted in the very assumptions of the political economy that he claimed to be criticising. Marx's analysis rested on the primacy of labour, he saw people as primarily constituted by their labour, and it is this belief that Baudrillard argues is evidence for the extent to which Marx was influenced by the work ethos of the German, puritan and capitalist ethic of his time. Marx is accused of making a fetishism out of labour. Man is labour, history is of labour, and objects only have value by reason of the abstract labour they represent. Labour becomes a universal preoccupation, as the measure of all people and all things. For Marx 'the transformation of nature is the occasion of its objectification as a productive force under the sign of utility' (1975, p. 45). Baudrillard criticises this ethnocentric functionalism and its application by anthropologists such as Godelier to other societies in what he regards as an inappropriate manner. As such, the ideological struggle that Marx undertakes is embedded within a wider ideology that he fails to acknowledge or criticise. 'Marx makes a radical critique of the political economy, but still in the form of political economy' (1975, p. 50).

The main thrust of Baudrillard's argument is towards that which Marx by his narrow focus thereby missed, which may be termed 'the political economy of the sign'. The focus on production ignored the effect of consumption, the way in which the meaning of the objects produced, themselves reproduce, the relations of domination and subordination. Baudrillard himself produces a critique of the notion of use-value which is the mirror image of the original critique of value conducted by Marx (1981, pp. 132–42). This critique, which examines use-value as a fetishised form derived from the abstracted notion of utility, helps to provide a basis for the analysis of the relationship between commodity and consumer as well as producer. This is crucial to an analysis of ideology as a form of representation. 'In order for the system to be reproduced there must be not simply the reproduction of labour power but the continuous reproduction of the code' (Poster 1975, p. 9). Baudrillard is clearly influenced here by writings in structuralism, which uncover the subtle ways in which relations of power are embedded in everyday forms of discourse. 'This manipulation, that plays on the faculty of producing meaning and difference, is more radical than that which plays on labour power' (1975, p. 122). Such a critique need not be considered unduly idealist, as the code is found to be constituted in the material conditions of everyday life. The key question then becomes: 'Who controls this code?'

A working model

As indicated earlier, the discussion of the concept of ideology has remained at a fairly general level, both in terms of the implications drawn from the examples, and in the lack of any specific analysis of the nature of the groups to whom a given ideological stance is ascribed. The terms that have been used to describe the notion of ideology include ideas, ideals, beliefs, and representations. These are all suggestive of cognitive and normative forms, ways in which models of the world are held by the sub-

jects. They might appear to act at an autonomous and idealist level above the material world, that is they legitimate and comment, but do not appear to act of themselves. Yet balanced against these implications have been comments on the manner in which these same concepts are models generated by material conditions, which may only emerge in practical action. This was found, for example, in the case of bourgeois consciousness. The term praxis has been emphasised in Marxist theory because Marx above all scholars illustrated the importance of this constant dialectic between thought and action. It is closely related to terms such as structuration (as used by Giddens 1979), and reproduction, which again focus on the dynamics of this dialectic process between representation and action.

The second major theme in the analysis of ideology is coherence. All beliefs and representations are partial in that they focus on only a limited number of the relations between the factors that bear upon us. They are selected dimensions upon which we hang our understanding of the world. Bloch (1975) and other anthropologists who use structuralist techniques to analyse ideological modes, have shown the tendency to coherence and formal organisation that are characteristic of the more explicit modes of representation. Religion, honour, kinship, and other normative models that have been used to legitimate dominant groups will have these properties. There is usually a continual move towards coherence not only in the internal structure of the model itself but between it and the social practice it legitimates.

Three examples have been described in order to derive a general model of ideology, that is ideology represented by bourgeois practice, Marxist analysis and critiques of Marx. The work of Marx remains the dominant example, and in this we have in most respects followed Larrain (1979, 1982). We have not attempted to survey or consider in detail the implications of the massive body of social theory and critical practice that has emerged since. Larrain (1979), Sumner (1979) and CCCS (1978) provide broad overviews of a number of the influential accounts that drew on Marx's analysis. An important recent contribution to the debate by Althusser (1971; 1977) is discussed by Shanks and Tilley (1982, pp. 130–1). From the above examples we may derive the following characteristics of a critique based on the model of ideology:

(1) Society is analysed in terms of the different and often conflicting interests held by groups within it. For Marx, these stemmed from the relations of production, but other sources of conflict are compatible with this model. In the model held by Marx, however, the material base for these ideas is stressed, as Larrain suggests: 'The origin and function of ideology have to do with a limited material practice which generates ideas that misrepresent social contradictions in the interest of the ruling class' (1982, p. 15).

(2) A given group in society attempts, in so far as it has the power to do so, firstly to understand and secondly to represent its interests in its creation of the cultural world. This representation also constitutes a transformation of the world in the direction of those interests.

(3)   Such representations tend to exhibit certain properties (see Shanks and Tilley 1982, pp. 131–4):–

   (a)   They tend to represent as universal that which may be partial.

   (b)   They tend to represent as coherent that which may be in conflict.

   (c)   They tend to represent as permanent that which may be in flux.

   (d)   They tend to represent as natural that which may be cultural.

   (e)   They tend to formalise, i.e. present as dependent upon its own formal order, that which might otherwise be subject to contradiction.

(4)   As a form of power ideology may supplement coercive means of maintaining social control, which can never of themselves be completely effective.

(5)   Ideology is therefore not to be equated with all social practice, but only with that which is generated by and tends to reproduce conflicts in interest.

(6)   Although critical studies tend to focus on the ideology of dominant groups, these are always opposed by subordinate groups, which can overcome both coercive and ideological controls.

As developed in the above discussion, ideology and power are inextricably bound up with social practices; they are a component of human *praxis*, by which is to be understood the actions of agents on and in the world, serving as an integral element in the production, reproduction and transformation of the social. Because ideology and power are components of praxis they are manifested in its material products, and are thus open to archaeological investigation.

The purpose of this introductory section has been to situate our approach in relation to other positions taken in contemporary archaeological theory, and to provide some conceptual groundwork for the papers that follow. The second section of this volume consists of three papers dealing with contemporary and historical materials which are relatively accessible for study. All three papers deal with the material world and thereby form a bridge between the theoretical exposition of the present chapter and the four detailed studies of European prehistory which make up the third section. In the fourth and concluding section of the book, the results of these studies are considered together. The problems of the application of these ideas to the study of long-term social change, and their general relevance to archaeological materials, topics which have not been discussed in this introduction, are emphasised there, using the examples of the specific case studies presented in this volume.

Acknowledgements

DM would like to thank Mike Rowlands for critical comments on parts of this paper and Rickie Burman and Susie Gilbey for their help.

References

Abercrombie, N., Hill, S. and Turner, B. (1980) *The Dominant Ideology Thesis*, Allen and Unwin, London

Althusser, L. (1971) 'Ideology and ideological state apparatuses', in L. Althusser, *Lenin and Philosophy and Other Essays*, New Left Books, London

Althusser, L. (1977) *For Marx*, New Left Books, London

Althusser, L. and Balibar, É. (1970). *Reading Capital*, New Left Books, London

Barthes, R. (1977) (Ed. S. Heath) *Image-Music-Text*, Fontana, London

Baudrillard, J. (1975) *The Mirror of Production*, Telos Press, St Louis, Mo.

   (1981) *For a Critique of the Political Economy of the Sign*, Telos Press, St Louis, Mo.

Benton, M. (1981) ' "Objective" interests and the sociology of power', *Sociology* 15 (2), 161–84

Bloch, M. (1977) 'The disconnection between rank and power as a process', in J. Friedman and M. Rowlands Eds., *The Evolution of Social Systems*, Duckworth, London

Brew, J. (1946). 'The use and abuse of taxonomy', in *The archaeology of Alkali Ridge, Southern Utah* (*Papers of the Peabody Museum*, 21)

Binford, L. (1962) 'Archaeology as anthropology', *American Antiquity* 28, pp. 217–25

   (1978) *Nunamiut Ethnoarchaeology*, Academic Press, New York

Bourdieu, P. (1977) *Outline of a Theory of Practice*, Cambridge University Press

Braithwaite, M. (1982) 'Decoration as ritual symbol: a theoretical proposal and an ethnographic study in southern Sudan', in I. Hodder Ed., *Symbolic and Structural Archaeology*, Cambridge University Press

Centre for Contemporary Cultural Studies (1978) *On Ideology*, Hutchinson, London

Clarke, D. (1973) 'Archaeology: the loss of innocence', *Antiquity* 47, pp. 6–18

Cohen, A. (1982) 'A polyethnic London carnival as a contested cultural performance', *Ethnic and Racial Studies* 5, pp. 23–42

Collingwood, R. (1956) *The Idea of History*, Oxford University Press

Cutler, A., Hindess, B., Hirst, P. and Hussain, A. (1977–8) *Marx's Capital and Capitalism Today*, 2 vols. Routledge and Kegan Paul, London

Donley, L. (1982) 'House power: Swahili space and symbolic markers', in I. Hodder Ed., *Symbolic and Structural Archaeology*. Cambridge University Press

Flannery, K. (1972) 'The cultural evolution of civilisations', *Annual Review of Ecology and Systematics* 3, pp. 399–426

Foucault, M. (1977) *Discipline and Punish*, Vintage Books, New York

   (1980) *Power/Knowledge*, (C. Gordon Ed.). Harvester, Hassocks

   (1981) *The History of Sexuality*, Penguin, Harmondsworth

Friedman, J. and Rowlands, M. (1977) 'Notes towards an epigenetic model of the evolution of civilisation', in J. Friedman and M. Rowlands Eds., *The Evolution of Social Systems*, Duckworth, London

Gall, P. and Saxe, A. (1977) 'The ecological evolution of culture: the state as predator in succession theory', in T. Earle and J. Ericson Eds., Exchange Systems in Prehistory, Academic Press, New York

Giddens, A. (1979) *Central Problems in Social Theory*, Macmillan, London

Gordon, C. (1980) 'Afterword' in M. Foucault, *Power/Knowledge*, Harvester, Hassocks

Gunn, J. (1975) 'An envirotechnological system for Hogup Cave', *Antiquity* 40, pp. 3–21

Hall, S., Clarke, J., Jefferson, T. and Roberts, B. Eds. (1976) *Resistance through Rituals*, Hutchinson, London

Hawkes, C. (1954) 'Archaeological theory and method: some suggestions from the old world', *American Anthropologist* 56, pp. 155–68

Hawkes, J. (1968) 'The proper study of mankind', *Antiquity* 42, pp. 255–62

Hill, J. (1972) 'The methodological debate in contemporary archaeology:

a model', in D. Clarke Ed., *Models in Archaeology*, Methuen, London

Hindess, B. (1982) 'Power, interests and the outcomes of struggles', *Sociology* 16 (4), pp. 498–511

Hodder, I. (1979) 'Social and economic stress and material culture patterning', *American Antiquity* 44, pp. 446–54

    Ed. (1982a) *Symbolic and Structural Archaeology*, Cambridge University Press

    (1982b) *Symbols in Action*, Cambridge University Press

    (1982c) *The Present Past*, Batsford, London

Larrain, J. (1979) *The Concept of Ideology*, Hutchinson, London

    (1982) 'On the character of ideology: Marx and the present debate in Britain', *Theory, Culture and Society* 1, pp. 6–22

Lasswell, H. and Kaplan, A. (1950) *Power and Society*, Yale University Press, New Haven, Conn.

Leone, M. (1978) 'Time in American archaeology', in C. Redman et al. Eds., *Social Archaeology: Beyond Subsistence and Dating*, Academic Press, New York

Luhmann, N. (1979) *Trust and Power*, Wiley, London

Lukács, G. (1980) *The Ontology of Social Being: Labour*, Merlin Press, London

Lukes, S. (1974) *Power: A Radical View*, Macmillan, London

Marx, K. (1974) *Capital*, Lawrence and Wishart, London

Marx, K. and Engels, F. (Ed. C. Arthur) (1970) *The German Ideology*, International Publishers, New York

McLachlan, H. (1981) 'Is "power" an evaluative concept?', *British Journal of Sociology* 32, pp. 392–410

Mepham, J. (1979) 'The theory of Ideology in Capital', in J. Mepham and D. Rubin Eds., *Issues in Marxist Philosophy*, vol. 3. Harvester Press, Brighton

Miller, D. (1980) 'Archaeology and Development', *Current Anthropology* 21, pp. 709–26

    (1982a) 'Explanation and social theory in archaeological practice', in C. Renfrew, M. Rowlands and B. Segraves Eds., *Theory and Explanation in Archaeology*, Academic Press, New York

    (1982b) 'Structures and strategies: an aspect of the relationship between social hierarchy and cultural change', in I. Hodder Ed., *Symbolic and Structural Archaeology*, Cambridge University Press

    Ed. (1983) 'Material Culture Studies: THINGS ain't what they used to be', *Royal Anthropological Institute Newsletter* 59

Moore, H. (1982) 'The interpretation of spatial patterning in settlement residues', in I. Hodder Ed., *Symbolic and Structural Archaeology*, Cambridge University Press

Mueller, J. Ed. (1975) *Sampling in Archaeology*, University of Arizona Press, Tucson, Az.

Ollman, B. (1971) *Alienation*, Cambridge University Press

Parker-Pearson, M. (1982) 'Mortuary practices, society and ideology: an ethnoarchaeological study', in I. Hodder Ed., *Symbolic and Structural Archaeology*, Cambridge University Press

Parsons, T. (1963) 'On the concept of political power', *Proceedings of the American Philosophical Society* 107, pp. 232–62

Poster, M. (1975) 'Translator's introduction' in J. Baudrillard, *The Mirror of Production*, Telos Press, St Louis, Mo.

Poulantzas, N. (1973) *Political Power and Social Classes*, New Left Books, London

Rubin, L. (1972) *Essays on Marx's Theory of Value*, Black and Red, Detroit

Schiffer, M. (1976) *Behavioural Archaeology*, Academic Press, New York

Shanks, M. and Tilley, C. (1982) 'Ideology, symbolic power and ritual communication: a reinterpretation of neolithic mortuary practices', in I. Hodder Ed., *Symbolic and Structural Archaeology*, Cambridge University Press

Shennan, S. (1982) 'Ideology, change and the European Early Bronze Age', in I. Hodder Ed., *Symbolic and Structural Archaeology*, Cambridge University Press

Sraffa, P. (1972) *Production of Commodities by means of Commodities*, Cambridge University Press

Sturrock, J. (1979) *Structuralism and Since*, Oxford University Press

Sumner, C. (1979) *Reading Ideologies*, Academic Press, London

Thomas, D. (1972) 'The use and abuse of numerical taxonomy', *Archaeology and Physical Anthropology in Oceania* 7, pp. 31–49

Tilley, C. (1981a) 'Conceptual frameworks for the explanation of socio-cultural change', in I. Hodder, G. Isaac and N. Hammond Eds., *Pattern of the Past*, Cambridge University Press

    (1981b) 'Economy and Society: what relationship?', in A. Sheridan and G. Bailey Eds., *Economic Archaeology: Towards an Integrated Approach*, B.A.R., Oxford

    (1982) 'Social formations, social structures and social change', in I. Hodder Ed., *Symbolic and Structural Archaeology*, Cambridge University Press

Watson, P., LeBlanc, S. and Redman, C. (1971) *Explanation in Archaeology: an Explicitly Scientific Approach*, Columbia University Press, London

Weber, M. (1968) *Economy and Society*, volume 2, Bedminster Press, New York

Wrong, D. (1979) *Power: its Forms Bases and Uses*, Basil Blackwell, Oxford

Zubrow, E. (1975) *Prehistoric Carrying Capacity: A Model*, Cummings, Menlo Park, Calif.

PART TWO

Ideology and power in the present and historical past

Chapter 2

Endo ceramics and power strategies
Alice Welbourn

The process by which children come to accept the gender-specific associations of everyday objects are considered. The eight basic forms of the Endo ceramic assemblage are described, as used in everyday and in ceremonial contexts. The central role played by some pots in the wedding ceremonies reveal certain associations that may account for the pattern of decorative treatments of the assemblage. Pottery serves both to separate but also to mediate between the spheres of activity and interpretation represented by the two genders. This analysis is reinforced by a consideration of the use of broken pots and raw clay. The pottery forms can thus be related to the assimilation and ritual legitimation of the social order, and in particular, of male dominance. However, both the muted and practical power of women must be considered.

Introduction

The dominant theme of this book is to investigate the kinds of relationships which exist between ideology, representations of power and material culture. In this chapter these relationships will be illustrated by means of a specific case study concerned with the use of pottery by a predominantly agricultural group in Kenya. As will be demonstrated one of the main themes of this study is the suitability of the theoretical approaches advocated (outlined in Chapter 1) to a society divided not by social *classes* but in terms of sex and age, factors which while being *presented* in a specific social form, are nevertheless overtly given a biological justification.

The Endo

The Endo are the northernmost group of many sections which together form the tribe known as the Marakwet. The Endo group lives on the western wall of the Great Rift valley of Kenya, East Africa. They inhabit the lower slopes of the Cherangani hills in Rift Valley province. Their fields and the animals which the people tend are located in the plains of the Kerio valley below the settlements. The Marakwet tribe is one of nine or more such tribes of a linguistic group known as Kalenjin. As is the case with the other sections the Endo practise patrilocality and patrilineal inheritance. The society is strongly clan-based and clan allegiance determines each man's place of abode, his area of fields, access to water, grazing rights and the inheritance of all these assets. A man remains with one clan for life. A man's wife, in contrast, moves from her father's to her husband's clan on marriage. Her clan of origin, and of her own mother, then maintain strong ties through marriage and thereby form multi-generational allegiances between different clans in the area.

Sexual division of daily activities

From birth, a child's sex is acknowledged by all adults through specific name-giving ceremonies which vary according to whether the child is male or female. As a child grows up it gradually learns to distinguish between areas and activities which belong predominantly to the world of its mother and those associated with its father. At home it watches its mother and other women involved in food preparation and child care, and, as the child grows older and ventures down into the valley it sees its father and other men at the animal shelter tending the animals. The child also sees men clearing and burning new land for cultivation and women digging and weeding the fields for millet, maize and cassava. Again, the child sees the men maintaining and rechannelling the traditional artificial watercourse which belongs to each clan and traverses the hillside to the valley below. These artificial channels provide all the necessary water for domestic activities, for watering the fields and supplementing the river supplies for the animals. The maintenance of these water channels is fundamental to the survival of the Endo agriculture since rainfall is seasonal but unreliable. The organisation of this maintenance forms an integral part of a man's clan responsibilities and the supply of water is basic to the women's work both at home and in the fields.

As the child grows up, therefore, it sees the social context of these everyday activities and observes the objects associated with each activity and, furthermore, experiences these activities and objects through participation. Children help their mothers to carry water from the channel or gather wild vegetables and fruit to supplement the diet and scare off the birds when the crop is ripening. They also assist their fathers by helping to herd the goats, sheep and cows during the day. Small boys begin to beg older ones to make bows and arrows for them so that they may learn to shoot at trees and rats. Small girls start to help older ones to feed the babies and to care for them while their mothers work in the fields. In these mundane and unstructured forms socialisation takes place.

However, there are several everyday activities in which children do not participate – male preparation of beer made with honey taken from wooden beehives and the attendance of women at childbirth and during post-natal care. These activities are deemed unsuitable for children and they are excluded. They only begin to be allowed access to this adult knowledge after having undergone circumcision and initiation ceremonies through which they gain new status as young male and female adults. It should be clear from what has been said above that by the time they participate in these ceremonies they are already fully aware of the values and activities associated with their sex and, by extension, with objects which are sexually specific. It was, in fact, traditional practice for children to marry straight after their ritual seclusion in the initiation ceremonies.

Ceramics

There are eight basic vessel forms in the Endo assemblage (Fig. 1). Each of these pots has a specific use and, strictly speaking, their use should not be interchangeable, indicated by the fact that each pot has a specific name. In practice, however, the three smaller pot forms are quite regularly interchanged. The large, *vertically* lugged pot is known as *terroban*: literally 'pot of harvested food'. This pot is used solely by women to cook millet, finger millet and, nowadays, maize and cassava. The latter two crops, being recent introductions, tend to be more frequently cooked in aluminium pans, also a recent introduction. The two indigenous crops are almost invariably cooked in the traditional cooking pot. Since men are never involved in cooking plant foods these pots remain in the hands of women only. The large *horizontally* lugged pot, *kabebkwa*, is used solely by the men to brew traditional honey beer or *kipketin*. Honey is gathered from beehives which have been constructed by men and placed in high trees. The preparation of honey beer is a carefully executed process carried out entirely by men. The *kipketin* is used as an

Fig. 1. The Marakwet-Endo pot assemblage.

TERRE MA'		
(MORR BO TERR)		
TERROBAN	KOSUM	KABEBKWA
FOOD	WATER	HONEY
TERRONGIYON	TERRO SAGAT	KABEBKWA
VEGETABLES	MEDICINE	MEAT

integral part of the blessing of those people undergoing ceremonies: boy's name-giving ceremonies and marriage ceremonies for instance. The oldest *men* of the group are executors of these blessings. The *kipketin* and, by extension, the pot in which it has been brewed are objects associated with the male world and male power. Children see *kipketin* being made but take no part in making it and have virtually no experience of the *use* of *kipketin* since they do not attend ceremonies prior to initiation.

The third large pot in this group, having *no* lugs, is the water pot, *kosum*, used to store water and keep it cool for drinking and washing. *Kosum* stands on the floor of the woman's kitchen hut and is used by all members of the family. Water is collected, morning and evening, from the artificial watercourses by the boys and older girls of each family, and is used from the *kosum* for the needs of the entire family.

There are three smaller pots: a smaller version of the women's cooking pot; a smaller version of the men's beer pot and a medicine pot. The first is called *terrongiyon*: 'pot for vegetables'. Various edible green-leaved plants grow naturally both in the valley and on the mountainside slopes near to the settlements. These are collected regularly by the children and older girls, forming a normal part of the diet. They are eaten particularly with meat and are cooked in this small pot which possesses vertical lugs. The second pot is a smaller version of the men's beer pot, known as *kabebkwa*, and is used for boiling meat. The Endo herd cows, sheep and goats and this animal husbandry, as mentioned above, is a male domain. The men spend most of the day at the shelter of their animals and most frequently roast goat meat. At home, however, they use the small *kabebkwa* pot if they decide to boil it. Meat is the only cooked food which men can be seen to cook for themselves. The third small pot is known as *terro sagat* and is characterised by a low degree of morphological regularity, contrasting with the other vessels. Usually it resembles *terrongiyon* and could be used either for vegetables or for medicine when initially purchased. It often has no lugs at all or can even look like the small *kabebkwa*.

Ceremonial pots and the final wedding ceremony

The pots discussed so far are in regular, everyday use. The two large pots used in ceremonies are unfamiliar and this serves

to accentuate their importance, just as the presence of familiar everyday objects, in unfamiliar contexts makes their importance stand out. Individuals are thereby made aware of the ritual nature of the activities taking place. Material culture is used to enhance and underline the boundary between the sacred and profane aspects of social existence. By this means each individual is made more conscious of the new knowledge which is being imparted. The pattern of childhood learning (of observation and participation) is being recreated. Only through having attained the correct age is the individual allowed access to a new status within society and the experience of unfamiliar elements of the material culture assemblage that accompany this change of status.

Two pots, known as *terre ma'* and *morr bo terr* are used during the ceremony of *tum nyohoe* or the 'full, complete wedding ceremony', which is the fourth and final wedding ceremony which a couple perform. Although the ceremony is secret and cannot be fully described here, its basic symbolic principles can be discussed. Other objects, besides the two large pots mentioned above, are gioven special uses in the other wedding and the initiation ceremonies and it is only by attending these ceremonies that the special uses of these objects become known by participants. The final wedding ceremony admits a couple, especially the man, to the ranks of seniority and leadership within the group. He becomes entitled to join the group of elders responsible for ultimate decision-making for the entire community. In order to perform the ceremony the couple officiating must have an established family and, traditionally, some of their children had families of their own. The provision of food and drink for everyone for the four days' duration of the ceremony necessitates a sizeable accumulation of supplies beforehand.

The two pots are covered with cowhide and *terre ma'* has four or six knobs around its rim and can hold up to twenty-five litres of *kipketin*. *Morr bo terr* is used as an additional container for extra supplies of alcohol and is neither as large nor as central to the ceremony as *terre ma'*. *Morr bo terr* means 'calf of pot' while *terre ma'* means 'pot of fire'.

Part one of the third day

It is the third of four days of *tum nyohoe* (see Fig. 2) and maize-beer drinking and a food-grinding ceremony have occupied

Fig. 2. Tum nyohoe day three. Sequence of events.

WOMEN'S SECRET MEETING INSPECTION OF GOAT ENTRAILS	"TERR"– MEN'S MEETING AND DISCUSSION	"TERR"– MEN'S SECRET CEREMONY	"KOSUM"– DANCING AROUND KOSUM
BEFORE DAYBREAK	8 a.m.	MID-MORNING	AFTERNOON

the first two days. After dawn of the third day the elders of the clan congregate at the house of the groom, assembling in his compound to have a discussion. This is a most solemn occasion and the most serious issues facing the clan are frequently referred to 'terr'. This meeting is named after the pot which will be used at it. The discussion concentrates on issues which endanger the continuity and purity of the clan – namely unnatural deaths, girls eloping or being raped, purity rites for mothers of twins who are thus deemed to be too fertile, and other similar concerns.

Part two of the third day

The ceremony continues by banning all women who were previously listening to the discussion from the general compound area. A secret ceremony now ensues confined to the men of the clan who have already themselves undergone this ceremony. This ceremony, like all those before it, emphasises the superiority of the participants in relation to juniors who are excluded and it also emphasises sexual divisions within the clan group. This part of the ceremony will be further discussed below, after outlining the activities taking place in the afternoon.

Part three of the third day

Around noon the *terre ma'* which has been standing in the middle of the compound is removed and late in the afternoon it is replaced by *kosum*, the water pot. Men and women then dance around this pot in an anti-clockwise direction, from the husband's clan, his mother's clan, the wife's father's clan and her mother's clan. Senior women, i.e. those who have already undergone this ceremony, anoint the neck and shoulders of the pot with castor oil, which they also use to anoint themselves and the bride and groom. The bride has an inflated goat-intestine around her neck and the groom wears a woman's goatskin dress. The goat was killed before dawn in a secret women's ceremony and its entrails are inspected before *terre ma'* is brought out and the men's morning ceremony can begin. The bride, groom and everyone else also have *sinanderr* (ceremonial leaves) in a garland round their necks. On the ground are strewn *sinanderr*, the remains of a ring of leaves which encircled the *terre ma'* and the whole compound in the morning. The dance-ring is eventually taken over by the visiting female relatives of the wife, while her male relatives continue drinking maize beer with her husband's male relatives. The dancing and anointing of women, pot and husband continue nevertheless.

Discussion of part two of *tum nyohoe*

The *terre ma'* plays a central symbolic role for the Endo in this ceremony. It represents at once several different concepts. In this one pot is presented and represented the male universe of patrilocality, animal husbandry, irrigation-maintenance, the social importance and allegiance of the clan and the access to power which *kipketin* brings through honey-production, brewing and blessing. The pot acts as the container of *kipketin*, the honey beer, produce of the male world of bee-keeping and the ritual medium for blessing at ceremonies. It is also the male balance of fertile liquid for female-produced milk. The actions taking place

in this ceremony are secret so more details cannot be given, but these themes are the ones upon which actions are based. The men enact and recreate for themselves the power of their universe by means of their actions around the pot in this ceremony. The meeting 'terr' begins as a platform for discussing and resolving matters affecting the security of the clan against impurity, in particular the impurity which can pollute them through the actions of *women*. The pot in this ceremony is indeed a central force and focal point for re-establishing the order of the men's universe and, by extension, the whole known symbolic world.

The symbolic value of everyday pots

Whilst none of the everyday pots is so central to a ceremony as *terre ma'*, from an understanding of the wedding ceremony and from general observations of the use of these pots, as well as comments which some people, mainly men, are prepared to make about them it becomes clear that a framework of order underlying the use of the ceramics runs parallel to the social order.

Returning first to *terroban* and *kabebkwa*, the cooking and the brewing pot, respectively, it can readily be seen from the description of their uses (see above) that the former belongs very much to the female world of cereal-food preparation and the latter to the male world of bee husbandry and honey-beer brewing. But what of the smallest three pots, *terrongiyon*, *terro sagat* and *kabebkwa*? These may be conceptualised as smaller representatives of the world of adult activities. In the same way that pre-pubescent children share sex-role based activities such as herding, child care, bird scaring the uses of these smaller pots are less specifically defined than the uses of the larger ones. However, it is apparent that, within the terms of such a conception, the water pot *kosum* presents a problem. This pot is large and of the same order of volume as *terroban* and *kabebkwa* yet it is not confined to a gender-specific activity. How is this anomaly to be explained?

The decoration of the pots provides a strong insight. The women who make these pots describe different surface areas in terms of their own bodies, namely the mouth, ears, neck, chest and stomach. A clear link is made between pots and people: *eet* are ears and handles, *got* is mouth, *gat* is neck, *tagat* is chest, *mor* is stomach and *kel* is legs or base (Fig. 3). If it is suggested to them that pots might resemble people they laugh and deny it. Men, however, are ready to admit that the vertical lugs on the large cooking pot are like the long, stretched, ears of a woman wearing heavy earrings and that the horizontal lugs on the beer pot are like the shape made by the wooden cross-studs which Endo men used to wear in their ears. By contrast the women only give 'functional' explanations: a vertical lug is easier to tip sideways on the fire and a horizontal one is easier for picking up a pot and pouring.

The decoration on the pot surface consists of 'roulette' indentation, made whilst the clay is wet with a twist of grass, folded like a piece of corn dolly. This is the only decoration and is used to decorate all the pots. Although exceptions may *occasionally* be found, the general rule to which all potters adhere is that there should be *no* decoration around the neck of *kosum*, the handleless water pot. Apart from this exception decoration on all everyday pots normally covers *got*, *eet*, *gat* and *tagat* with no decoration on *mor* or *kel*, the reason being offered for this being that it would be rubbed off in use. *Kosum*, then is the only pot in the series with equivalent volume with no handles and the only one with no decoration on *gat*, its neck. The women's explanation for this is that it is to mark out the difference between *kosum* and other pots and that this is traditional.

An examination of human decoration clearly shows what is being indicated. The immediate way in which a stranger can tell whether an Endo female has completed circumcision and become an adult is to look at her ears. If she is an adult she wears a ring of heavy blue beads in each ear. These are presented to her during her seclusion and she receives them with great pride. Although now Endo men rarely wear earrings they used to have distinctive earrings, usually horizontal in form to distinguish their status from boys. Endo women wear a variety of neck-ornaments: beads, iron rings and shells and, again, although few men now wear neck-ornaments they used to have quite distinctive neck-ornaments contrasting with those of the women. Consequently necks may be seen to be an important part of the body for establishing identity, status and individuality. As we have seen types of jewellery and earrings worn serve to demarcate and separate men, women and children. It is said that the wearing of leaf garlands (*sinnander*) around the neck is a sign of individual position and attainment. The manner in which animals wear a bell round their necks to emphasise their ownership by someone and to help them to be found if they stray is reflected in the wearing of bells round the neck by women who have suffered disaster with child-deaths. Connected with this feature is the fact that a woman starts to wear iron rings around her neck from the end of her circumcision seclusion until death. The number of these rings tends to show a strong correlation with seniority. If someone were to catch hold of her by these rings the act would be considered a grave personal insult. References are made to people's necks quite frequently in ceremonial songs. Thus body-decoration on the ears and of the neck distinguishes between male and female in a very clear way.

Kosum – the ceremony of the water pot

Kosum, then, is the pot which exhibits no sex-specific attributes: it has no handles – no ears – to distinguish it and it is undecorated on its neck. In short it is a neutral pot, betwixt and between, relating neither to the male world nor to the female in its appearance whilst its use refers to both. The explanation lies in the nature of *kosun*, neither male nor female yet related to both worlds. If this ambiguity causes some kind of overlap or discontinuity in the social order the pot would be 'betwixt and between' and concomitantly 'hedged about with ritual' (Douglas 1966). This is precisely what is happening here.

Tum nyohoe is the fourth and final major step of the wedding process. The other three stages concentrate first of all on the suitability of both lineages; secondly upon the mother and the expected child; thirdly on the husband and his peer group. The fourth ceremony acts as a reconciliation of both sides and forms the last major rite of passage. The men become elders and partake in the decision-making of the seniors while the women, once their milk-flow has formally finished, may now start to use castor oil to bless others. The final transformation has officially been completed and future access to power by adults is dependent on their progeny. For example men and women are able to mark themselves out with ritual headdresses once their children start to mature and are circumcised and married.

Looking again at *kosum* we find that this is the only pot of the series *not* used in a transformation process. Raw cereal is *transformed* into food with the addition of water and heat in *terroban*. Raw honey is *transformed* into mead with the addition of water and yeast in *kabebkwa*. Both these pots can be stored in the wickerwork *sana* above the fireplace, or in the storage space in the roof. *Kosum*, on the other hand, always rests on the floor with water in it. It does not need to be kept warm nor in storage-parts of the house. *Kosum* is covered with ash to make it water-tight when it is first being prepared for use. When women put ash on themselves this signifies infertility, non-sexuality, suicide, and in the compound rubbish-piles ash cannot be mixed with chaff and goat dung for fear of pollution (chaff is the surplus from cereals cooked by women, dung is the surplus from animals tended by men and dead fire must not pollute either).

Terroban, in contrast, need not be made water-tight with ash. Instead castor oil is wiped inside, forming a hard crust when the pot is used on the fire. The sticky nature of honey performs a similar role on the inside surface of the *kabebkwa*. Castor oil is thicker than water, it will not dry out and dryness is associated with hunger. Castor oil is used to soften the goat skins which are worn. It is also used to anoint the bodies of young men and women during their initiation ceremony marking the childhood/adulthood transformation. The women and the husband are treated in the same way at *tum nyohoe*. Castor oil is essentially a female medium of blessing but at initiation and again at *tum*

Fig. 3. Schematic drawing of a pot.

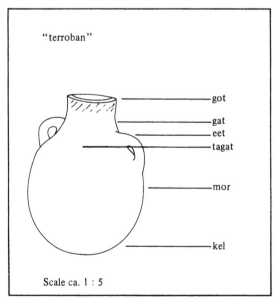

"terroban"

got

gat
eet
tagat

mor

kel

Scale ca. 1 : 5

nyohoe the man adopts the female goat skin clothing and receives the female blessing of castor oil. *Kosum* is described by men in *tum nyohoe* as the women's pot; *terre ma'* is not for them. *Kosum* stands then in opposition to *terre ma'* in the ceremony. On the other hand *kosum* receives the same treatment as the husband: it is anointed with castor oil along with all the women so in this ceremony *kosum* symbolically embraces both male and female qualities.

Terre ma' and *tum nyohoe*

The evidence outlined above suggests a reassessment of the role of *terre ma'* in the ceremony. It becomes obvious that *terre ma'* represents discontinuities in the social order. Its representation of the male world can also be seen to reflect the presence of the female world. This situation is analagous to that which pertains in households *conceptually* headed by a man, legitimised by means of clan inheritance, but practically run by the man's wife.

It was mentioned above that *terre ma'* is only produced once the entrails of a goat have been inspected and declared to be of good omen. This goat may be male or female and has been slaughtered early in the morning at a secret women's ceremony. Goats are *anomalous* animals. In some contexts they may be considered as extensions of the female world within terms of male ownership. In others they are viewed as extensions of male husbandry and male labour. In this context the sex is irrelevant because the goat is produced from the women's secret ceremony reminding the men that both their power and actions are still dependent on the maintenance of harmony and order between the sexes. The *terre ma'* as well as *kosum* can thus be understood as embodying the combination of male and female belief and activity within society. The juxtaposition of these pots in this ceremony maintains the outer male view of social order and distinctive male/female boundaries. Deeper inquiry reveals that a balance of interdependence must be ritually maintained between the two sexes.

Other uses of pots

Broken pottery has uses and pots are not thrown away. A pot, once broken, does not become categorised as 'rubbish', contrasting with the treatment of ash, chaff, goat dung etc. Broken pots can lie ignored for years in and around compounds. This seems to suggest a conception of permanence in relation to pots. This idea may be strengthened through the reasoning that pots are always stored and used within the confines of the compound. They are not used to transport anything from one place to another. That is the role of calabashes.

Pots therefore represent a form of permanence in the compound and may symbolise the permanence and long life of the occupants and the lineage. Broken pots are called '*materr*' and have three uses: (a) as roof-top guards (b) as vessels for water to ward off evil (c) as guards to protect water-channels. On the whole pots on top of houses and grain stores tend to be vertically handled pots. There do not seem to be any clear rules as to which pots should be used for this purpose except that *kosum* is never

used. The pots are only placed on houses and grain stores but not on smiths' shelters or animal shelters. Hence they are associated with the home, the dwelling area and places where both male and female activities take place but not in exclusively male domains. The tops of the houses and grain stores have a central apex-stick known as *sorrei*. On the death of the male head of the compound the *sorrei* is lowered to face at an angle into the valley for four days and the pot through which it is placed removed. Endo men state that the *sorrei* represents the presence of the male in the house, at the pinnacle of the family. It is tempting to suggest that the pot, through the neck of which the *sorrei* projects represents the female presence in the compound. Whether or not this is the case it certainly represents a conception of permanence in the compound. The removal of this pot for the four days of mourning represents the absence of the former order. Its replacement after mourning and the return of the *sorrei* to a vertical position indicates the continuation of life in the compound after the death of its head. In this respect it is interesting to observe modern alternatives to pots on roofs, i.e. metal cans and bowls; neither calabashes or wooden objects have been substituted for pots. Modern objects imported into the area tend to represent a certain permanence through the expenditure involved in their acquisition and the resultant prestige gained in their possession. Although wood and calabash would not rot or be broken their conceptual position as use objects remains distinctive from pottery. Calabashes are vessels of transport and wooden objects are associated with beer drinking and animal husbandry which are both male pursuits rather than household activities.

The second use of broken pots is to hold water into which *pi po gonyin* – literally people with eyes – may look to dissolve the harm they may cause someone. They are placed by doors for strangers to use, as a protection for the household. The third use of broken pots is to place a large broken vessel by the head of a water-channel and therefore to protect the well-being of the entire clan. These pieces of pottery were originally supposed to contain medicine, but do so no longer.

I could receive no specific explanations from either men or women for any of these three uses apart from to follow the customs of the ancestors. The functional explanation given for the broken pots on the roof is to stop the rain coming in and spoiling the thatch and the contents of the loft. We can observe, however, that *all* pots are connected with water, both those in use and broken ones. Some form of permanence, and therefore of protection is suggested in the use of broken pots in these contexts.

By studying the use of clay, the raw medium of the pots, it is easier to understand the relationship between pots and water. While clay mixed with dung is used as a medium of protection and stability, clay from termite-mounds is used to celebrate the completion of life-crisis rituals. Pure clay seems to be the medium used for protection during periods of uncleanliness and transition. Its raw untreated state is regarded to be appropriate for use by initiates in seclusion huts, by mothers just after birth, and by warriors in battle. It would appear that people during vulnerable stages need to be protected by a layer of something neutral protecting them against the outside world and the potential danger of their situations. The clay at the same time reflects the pollutive nature of their condition, by being dirty and soaking up the dirt, sweat and pollution of their bodies. The coating of clay emphasises simultaneously the dirt and delicacy of their transient state, ensuring eventual transformation from this state in the subsequent washing process. The physical washing away of the clay from their bodies, which always follows, reflects and re-enacts the conceptual washing away of the pollution of the transient state. When they emerge fresh, clean, finished with the clay, they are also transformed: new adults, mothers of named children, warriors absolved from the pollutive state of harming human life. The initial administration of clay and the subsequent body washing is an essential part of these transformations.

As explained above *kosum* is not used for rooftops, the reason given by the potters being that the *neck* of *kosum* is too wide. However, once *kosum* is broken, restrictions on its conceptual position seem to be lifted in the sense that, apart from its absence on house roofs, *kosum* pieces are not specifically excluded from other uses. The ideas which lie behind the uses of broken pots are not clear-cut. Nonetheless because of the use of clay and water on *bodies* in the process of transforming people from one state to another and the connections between pots and people's bodies which have been discussed above the following hypothesis is put forward. All pots but *kosum* are used with water to *transform* one substance into another (cereal into food, honey into beer, flesh into meat, bark into medicine: the natural into the cultural). All these transformations take place with the pot/water association. These common, everyday juxtaposition- and transformation-processes find parallels in the use of clay and subsequent washing with water in transformations of human states. Pot is transformed clay. Pots and water represent transformations of humans, clay and water. The broken pots are used to protect houses against rain-damage, good people against evil, and protect water-channels for people.

The protective support which clay and water both give to humans in transformation has been translated into protective support against everyday danger and pollution. Broken pots are the medium for this support, but *kosum* would not be an appropriate pot to protect the house, which represents the male and female adult worlds. Once the pot is broken into smaller pieces its sexual ambiguity is no longer a threat and an issue – its neck and lack of ears are no longer obvious. Furthermore if pots involved in a transformation-process are treated in a different way from *kosum* we can explain why *terrosagat* does not play a part in any ceremony. Although it lacks handles it is used on the fire to transform bark into medicine and both men and women have knowledge of these medicines. The pot is small and males and females of all ages use medicine. Even the smallest children have had experience of a social transformation in their name-giving ceremony. *Terrosagat* represents no specific sex but it is still used to transform substances in an equivalent manner to the way in which young children do non-gender-specific tasks. So the pot does not need to be isolated, nor does its position need to be resolved by ritual, because it is a vessel of transformation it reflects the actions with which it is associated.

Conclusion

Children learn from an early age what their position in everyday life should be, determined by the activities deemed appropriate to their sex and age. Their position in society, while reinforced by everyday life has already been determined for them at a very early age by the ritual of the name-giving ceremony. This ceremony distinguishes between boys and girls in a number of significant ways: for boys honey beer is used, for girls milk and for boys a metal tool for making beehives is used, for the girls a wooden cooking stick. Even at birth women in the village smear their faces with clay in spots for boys ('because boys stay in one place') and all over for girls ('because girls may go anywhere'). So from birth it is ritually established that 'boys are permanent' and 'girls are temporary' i.e. it is the boys who will inherit their fathers' fields, animals, settlement-area and access to water. It is to the boys that the powers of household and ritual leadership will pass. Although nothing is specifically said about this to the children the everyday sexual division of labour and responsibilities makes it clear to them that this is the way things are. Children see new wives come to live in the area, they see older sisters leaving to live elsewhere and they recognise that they are related to other people in the settlement through their father. They have to go to another village to visit their mother's relatives. The children learn this through observation and accept it as given and by the time of initiation they consciously adopt these traditions. The use of material objects in these rituals enhances and reinforces the significance and importance of the ritual passage, especially when many of these objects have everyday uses. The ritual legitimation of the social order is reflected and reinforced by the everyday legitimation of repeated use.

What ritual means do the men employ to establish their superiority, control of land-ownership and inheritance, in a situation in which everyday life depends at least equally if not more, on the labour-input of women? The men succeed in maintaining their position by setting up a series of structural oppositions which if not specifically expressed are always underlying principles in their world view. Men are the spokesmen and it is they who meet formally and have public discussions. The given outer, expressed view of the world is a male one. They are in charge of the ceremonies and it is old men who give the blessings with honey beer. They run the 'ritual shows'. There are some secret female ceremonies, at which men are not present. But men are there, for example, outside the hut while the ceremony is proceeding inside. The reverse is never true. Women never assist at ceremonies which are solely male. Hence men set themselves in opposition to women by assuming public ritual control. The possibility that women, by contrast, might be in control of private or everyday life is never discussed. Day to day existence is 'functional', ordinary, mundane. This is also reflected in the way in which men and women differ when speaking about themselves and their environment. Throughout the discussions of the pots it was women who gave the practical explanations while the men were willing to grant a conceptual explanation. This distinction is also made in the *tum nyohoe* ceremony in which the ritual pot, *terre ma'* was identified as a men's pot while the mundane,

everyday *kosum* water pot was referred to as the women's pot. As
a more general extension of this line of argument we can recognise
the structural opposition set up in this ceremony between honey
and water, fertility and neutrality, culture and nature. Earlier in
the paper it was mentioned that honey can be interpreted in the
wedding ceremony as the male balance to female milk. In the
final ceremony the formal end of a woman's reproductive life is
being marked and so milk is not used. Water is for the women.
The men's cultural creation of fertility continues while the
women's natural creation of fertility ceases: men's lives are
permanent, women's lives are temporary.

It is by means of setting up specific structural oppositions
that men produce and reproduce their control:

Men	: Women
Permanent	: Temporary
Symbolic	: Functional
Ritual	: Everyday
Terre ma'	: *Kosum*
Honey	: Water
Culture	: Nature
Fertile	: Neutral

The assumption of the validity of these oppositions legitimises the
men's assertions of power and leadership. And the ultimate
control lies in the hands of the elders since they are the only men
who, by virtue of their age have knowledge of all the ceremonies.
But if men have all the power why must they keep reasserting it in
these ceremonies? It is precisely because the power which they
have is based solely on conceptual divisions. In everyday social
practice the role of women as producers and reproducers is
indispensable and therefore potentially powerful. Thus as we saw
with *kosum* and *terre ma'* , where both pots represent a variety of
both male and female concepts, the reality of the situation is
misrepresented by the men's theoretical concepts. Men's view of
women is indeed entirely conceptual, even though women move
house and clan and it is these movements which provide the
multi-generational links between different clans. Even though a
woman's reproductive powers come to an end it is her former
powers which have enabled her husband to achieve his status.
Even though the milk which a woman produces for her child is a
natural product the food which she feeds it as everyday sustenance
has been culturally produced by her. Although men are in charge
of young people's ritual progress through life, women are in
charge of the socialisation of their children in daily affairs. Even
if women prefer to give functional explanations for how things are
this does not mean they are less 'true'. The superiority of men can
be seen therefore to be based very strongly on their conceptual
view of the world.

What then is the women's view of male supremacy and
progress through life? What power do women exert in their lives?
As we have seen women play a far stronger role in mundane
contexts than in the symbolic, ceremonial, ritual realm. Women's
ways of doing things are through everyday actions rather than
public expression. Women no doubt accept men's assertions of
control to a certain degree because that is what they have been

brought up to know and accept. Beyond this lies a woman's
muted power, so distinctive from that of her husband, playing an
integral part in her life. The hours invested by women in routine
labour throughout the year far exceed those of the men who, by
contrast, have seasons of peak activity and slack periods. Women
are preoccupied each day with food preparation, wood collection,
child care and countless other tasks. They control basic sustenance and their muted strength has a great practical power.
Although it is not overtly acknowledged it is certainly present (S.
Ardener 1978, pp. 20–30).

Furthermore women, through their reproductive powers
have yet another practical hold on society. It is only women who
can ensure the continuation of the men's clan and it is of great
significance, therefore, that the secret women's ceremony which
precedes the men's ceremonies at *tum nyohoe* is of a sexual
nature. Only through the women celebrating this muted power
can the men's public ceremony of power legitimation proceed.
Even though their milk supply has ended, they now have castor
oil, with which men at ceremonies are always blessed. Men
acknowledge the threat which woman's sexuality can bring to
them by discussing women's malpractices at the start of the
ceremony.

Finally the worlds of men's ritual power in Endo society
and of the practical power of women are brought together by the
use of material objects to mediate these spheres. Material culture
has been shown to represent the 'balance' of power in society,
both through its regular use in the mundane world and its special
use in the ritual world. Both spheres of use are important. They
complement each other and act as constant reassertions of the
roles played out by women, men and children:

> Goods are neutral, their uses are social; they can be used as
> fences or bridges (Douglas and Isherwood 1978, p. 12).

Acknowledgements

This research was made possible by the permission of the Office of the
President of Kenya, to whom I am most grateful. My fieldwork would
have been impossible without the help of Samuel Kipsirimbi and Jakob
Tirimbi. The Catholic Mission at Chesongoch were extremely supportive
and the Carsons of Kapsowar Hospital were also most kind in their
generosity. The help and encouragement of Sheena Crawford, Linda
Donley and Michael Mallinson were at all times gratefully appreciated.
Richard Leakey, my supervisor in Kenya gave me his kind support and Dr
Ian Hodder, my supervisor at Cambridge, has consistently helped me
tremendously. My final thanks must go to the people of Sibow village and
of Endo location, Elgeyo-Marakwet for their endless warmth and
generosity during my stay with them.

References

Ardener, S. Ed. (1978) *Defining Females*, Croom Helm. London.
Douglas, M. (1966) *Purity and Danger*, Routledge and Kegan Paul,
London
Douglas, M. and Isherwood, B. (1978) *The World of Goods*, Penguin,
Harmondsworth

Chapter 3

**Interpreting ideology in
historical archaeology:
using the rules of
perspective in the
William Paca Garden in
Annapolis, Maryland**
Mark P. Leone

This chapter focuses on the manner in which ideologically informed representations serve to naturalise the arbitrary nature of the social order. The construction of an eighteenth-century garden is shown to employ a number of means towards this aim. Through the use of classical quotations and the development of a concept of precedence with juridical associations, the garden presents a particular rationalisation of time, which also denies its own transient nature. Its geometry and optics exemplified in its use of perspective, serve towards a controlled rationalisation of space. Overall the garden not only acts as representation but also works as an instrument for the close experimental observation and control of nature. The garden and the segmented and ordered form of Georgian architecture can be related to the contradictions of a society proclaiming freedom and independence but maintaining a system of slavery. The deliberately planned wilderness garden exemplifies such contradictions.

The eighteenth century in Tidewater Virginia and Maryland is today the subject of intensive, rigorous, and multidisciplinary research. There are few areas in the United States where there is more work done by creative people using materials from the past. Historians, architectural historians, folklorists, and historical archaeologists are all producing studies which offer the first new ideas on Chesapeake society since the turn of the century and which are giving the area an historical importance rivalling that long claimed for New England. The Chesapeake is being endowed with a deeper historical identity.

Understanding of the founding and growth of American civilization in the Chesapeake has been furthered by social his-
torians, through the application of basic concepts of anthropology (Breen 1976; Tate and Ammerman 1979). Architectural historians and folklorists have used social history and structuralism from Chomsky's linguistic theory to analyse Chesapeake buildings (Glassie 1975). Historical archaeologists have drawn from the fields of cultural ecology and settlement-pattern theory, to study the region's colonial remains. There has been some use of critical theory, but by far the greatest combination of ideas used to comprehend Chesapeake society in the seventeenth and eighteenth centuries is the quantitative, genealogically precise social history which takes the anthropological concept of culture and describes the anonymous, the statistical, the customary, and the vernacular in order to produce a more comprehensive view of a past society than has hitherto been available.

Virtually all of these studies (with full citations) have been used in the most recent and powerful synthesis of the Chesapeake, *The Transformation of Virginia 1740–1790* (1982a) by Rhys Isaac. He uses symbolic analysis of the kind most closely associated with Clifford Geertz to interpret a tightly controlled and widely inspected body of archival, archaeological, and decorative arts data. Isaac's analysis is important here because it allows us to pinpoint the theme of this essay. Using Isaac as a foil, I hope to show the contribution which may follow the application of critical theory to data from material culture, including historical archaeology. This may prove useful both because Isaac makes little use of archaeology (despite his familiarity with the basic materials) and because historical archaeologists, whose data often come from societies in which capitalism was evolving, rarely employ any of the variants of Marxist theory which could contribute to an interpretation of archaeological data.

The critical approach used here concentrates on the concept of ideology put forward by Shanks and Tilley (1982, pp. 129–54) and derived largely from their critique of Althusser (1971, pp. 127–86). I derive my understanding of the concept also from my reading of Lukács (1971, pp. 82–222). The concept of ideology used throughout this essay therefore contains two points. The first is that ideology, being neither worldview nor belief, is ideas about nature, cause, time, and person, or those things that are taken by a society as given. Second, these ideas serve to naturalize and thus mask inequalities in the social order; ideas, such as a notion of person, when accepted uncritically, serve to reproduce the social order. Ideology's function is to disguise the arbitrariness of the social order, including the uneven distribution of resources, and it reproduces rather than transforms society.

Ideology takes social relations and makes them appear to be resident in nature or history, which makes them apparently inevitable. So that the way space is divided and described, including the way architecture, alignments, and street plans are made to abide by astronomical rules, or the way gardens, paths, rows of trees, and vistas make a part of the earth's surface appear to be trained and under the management of individuals or classes with certain ability or learning, is ideology. Ideology is the ordering of time as well, and the mechanical measures of time, whether these be prehistoric henges, premodern sundials, or clocks. They are the material culture of the ideology of time. The ideology of time in capitalism cuts up daily activity into fragments which appear more rational and which thus become more controllable. Similarly, when time past is cut up and called precedent, it may be easier to control the present, for in the kind of society which looks to history as a guide for actions taken in the present, a continuum with the past may be made to appear inevitable when it is actually arbitrary. Thus, the class or interest group which controls the use of precedent does so to insure its own interests. It is in this sense that the classic Marxist writers have said that history tends to be written for class purposes.

Forms of ideological representation may be found in discussions of nature, or cause, or of matters considered obvious and inevitable. Ideology has been discovered in archaeological contexts through analyses of prehistoric astronomical markers and observatories (Thorpe 1981), and European Neolithic tombs (Shanks and Tilley, 1982, pp. 129–54), and may very likely be found amid all those items archaeologists have for so long lumped under labels like ceremonial objects or style. Such objects and configurations of objects often appear to have little or no adaptive and utilitarian function but, when taken as manifestations of ideology, may be shown to function in such a way that they reproduce unequal distribution of resources, while masking this process in actions taken as given. This is as likely to be true in ranked precapitalist societies as in the later and more familiar capitalist societies.

Rhys Isaac presents a bountiful amount of material on eighteenth-century Virginia. My own interpretation of his work, mediated by the concept of ideology and using archaeological and archival data from eighteenth-century Annapolis, Maryland, is stimulated by Isaac's work and is intended to complement it.

Rhys Isaac argues that between 1740 and 1790 in Tidewater Virginia, the social hierarchy became more and more rigid with the planter-gentry isolating itself on the top of a pyramid which was becoming ever more shaky. With wealth and the sources of its prosperity becoming ever more constricted as a result of English control over the colonial economy and the continued long-term decline of tobacco prices, those with wealth constructed, with an undetermined degree of consciousness, a local order which acted to maintain control over what they possessed. The result was a tight hierarchy with little access to the premier places from below or from outside. Since the top of the hierarchy had little or no support from the English Crown, there was no defense from Britain for the erosion of their economic position. And since the underpinning of the society from within was based on a large number of slaves and an ever larger number of impoverished whites, the base of the society was shaky indeed. Isaac comes to two conclusions as a result of this position. The one of general interest is that the planter-gentry made common cause with the poorer whites of the colony to claim independence from the English Crown, which of course resulted in a new government, the United States, which was controlled by property-holders. Isaac argues that such a coalition of property-owners, from largest to least, acted to preserve the standing social order for the short run. All this was done in the name of liberty, in places like Virginia and Maryland. Isaac's second conclusion, and the one of interest here, is that as the hierarchy in Virginia became more and more threatened, it sought greater and greater control, which was expressed as the Georgian order. The Georgian order or style included behavior as well as material culture. Indeed, it was a cohesive way of thought. The operative principle within Georgian thought has been expressed by James Deetz (1977). It is organized around the bilateral symmetry or the segmentary dividing of life, its functions and things, into parts arrayed into a hierarchy of isolated elements. This segmentation was expressed throughout the material environment, as in houses, windows, doors, and place-settings. But when it was imposed on nature, as in gardens, vistas, systematic observations of the stars, winds, tides, and native peoples, the segmentation quickly became confused with nature itself. And the system of segmentation, ordering, and even grading toward hierarchy was mistaken as itself being natural and discovered within nature. This segmentation and its confusion with nature, as in gardens and astronomical observations, had the impact of making the social world, which was similarly arrayed, appear to be unquestionable.

Isaac argues that in the presence of colonial Virginia's incomplete institutions, the Georgian order was an attempt at creating a set, controlled, rational-appearing, and unemotional mentality which gave planters control over all society in an era of increasing disorder. Incompleteness included the absence of precedent as a form of reasoning when making decisions, frequent use of expediency to govern, and the emotional emptiness of Anglicanism, as well as the weakness coming from this combination.

Isaac interprets Virginian taste and style as including the use of architecture, interior design, furniture, decoration, silverware, dress, dance, as well as manners as Georgian space. Georgian distance (Isaac 1982b). Georgian refinement is the compartmentalization necessary to preserve the economic and political hierarchy which was being so steadily compromised by the rise and the close interaction of formerly distant classes, now newly threatening the established classes through religious revivalism and revolutionary sentiment (1982, pp. 303, 305, note 7).

Isaac is not saying that Georgian ideas are manifested in architecture, silverware, and manners; nor is he saying that Georgian style passively reflects the breakdown of a creaky economic and political order. He is saying, though, that the material culture – place-settings, table manners, etiquette, individualization and privatization achieved through doors, distance, chairs, hyphens, wings, place-settings, and gardens – all created the inhibitions, withdrawal, and isolation needed to prevent any attack on the established order (1982a, p. 308). The concept of ideology adds to his discussion the question of the naturalization of the Georgian style, through its shrouding by contemporary discussions of natural philosophy, astronomy, Isaac Newton's theories, observations of the weather, plants and soil conditions. These all served to remove the arbitrary Georgian conventions from challenge by making them appear to be derived from nature or antiquity. With this construction it is possible to ask: who could fail to believe that those who systematically observed nature were not also those who should define and discuss a more natural or God-given political order? The same inevitability was created when the elite recited history, for who could fail to believe that those who knew the stars and plants and the ancient deities from Jupiter to Mars should not also be in charge of handling the historical precedents of their own society in the form of law. Those who knew how the natural order worked and those familiar with the long gone and esteemed ancient political orders should surely be the same to head the current order. Thus the scientific equipment, books, observations, the ancient history, the classical and Biblical allusions are not the product of the idle time of the rich, or of arcane interests, or of cultivated and rare intellect; rather these activities placed hierarchy and control in nature and history, making hierarchy and distance appear inevitable. When this logic, which is the ideology of class in Virginia and Maryland, was believed, society was reproduced intact. This logic was most likely to appear when the existing hierarchy could be most easily challenged. Thus, Georgian style in Virginia, and most likely in other places, not only expresses hierarchy but also disguises it. The disguise is composed of the ability to make aspects of nature and the human past look as though they are organized into commensurable orders and units with those of the observer. The disguise hides the arbitrariness of the social order and, when believed and acted on, perpetuates that order.

Isaac points out that the Georgian order grew more definite as the challenges to it grew in strength. As the American Revolution approached, the Georgian order came to its fullest expression. When the Revolution was over, and its effects on the mobility and growth of American society were fully felt in the early nineteenth century, and when those planters who had controlled the American Revolution died, the Georgian world – anything but mobile and expansive, or in ideological terms, libertarian and democratic – died also. The ideology of permanent hierarchy ended with the old planter gentry as did its Georgian style. The coincidence of their demise is indicative of the importance of Georgian style within the culture. Isaac correctly sees the Georgian order as a behavioral effort to control economics and politics. My addition has been to suggest that the effort to control worked by placing the order in nature and history in order to remove the effort from challenge. When the order died and the Georgian style ceased, its material culture and referents ceased too.

An extension of this example of the operation of ideology, when it creates equivalent divisions in natural realms, also involves the use of citations from the past. When the past is used as precedent for action taken now or to meet current conditions, it may be appropriated for current use. As the eighteenth century wore on, the past became a more pressing concern and a subject of ever more precise description in Virginia and Maryland. This was true of plants, plantations, native peoples, individuals, and political units. Isaac does not explore this development but it is an extension of his idea and may be explained using the notion of ideology. In making regular and divisible observations on nature, like wind or the movement of the planets, these, once compiled, became a guide to knowledge for the present and future of these same phenomena. The behavior of plants observed regularly and precisely, when published, formed a compendium predicting regular behavior. Precise and uniform observations created an even, unbroken flow from past to present thus making the two seem continuous. Earlier observations had been qualitative and irregular, often regarding nature in America as freakish or inferior to what was then known. The new factor which appeared by the mid eighteenth century was the regular collection of data, made by systematic observations, with predetermined comparability, uniformity of recording, often on charts and tables, having even flow over intervals. Whether these observations were on heat, rainfall, yield of fields, plants, seasons, sizes, or shadows and light, they composed an even set of lapses, which once observed, provided what appeared to be a rational basis in nature for current and future practice. Such behavior became ever more current in America as the eighteenth century wore on.

When applied to mid eighteenth-century human affairs, the compilation of even observations occurred through the building of precedent, and there are three or four important developments in analogous uses of the human past. Philip Vickers Fithian, a young Presbyterian minister from Princeton, New Jersey, kept a diary (1773–4) in Tidewater Virginia where he was tutor for a year to Robert Carter's children. He observed himself as well as his surroundings. He deliberately recorded his own spiritual development; he used his diary to watch himself change.

His own self-observations were intended to form a precedent for and measure of his change. He created his own history out of regular, even, comparable units of observation on himself and his society.

'I shall collect together and write down what I have been doing in the last year. But will my life bear the review? Can I look upon my actions and not blush? And shall I be no less careful, or have no better success, in the prosecution of my duty the year to come . . . ?' (Farish 1943, p. 61). We do not know how Fithian actually used his careful observations, but with his diary we can see the beginning of a natural history of self-observation.

A second example of interest in data from the past that developed in the eighteenth century involved classical history. Many writers and diarists cited classical Greek and Roman authors and frequently read both. Eighteenth-century diarists were familiar with the ancient texts and with the Renaissance uses of the ancient world and employed these as adornments to their own world. But even so, the classical texts were not so much understood as they were recited, and they were not compared to each other, nor were used to understand classical society. Antiquity was not as precisely observed, described, compared, or subjected to activities like those imposed on the natural world. Virginia and Maryland may have differed from Italy or England in this way, for the American elite did not handle antiquity nearly as rigorously as it handled observations on nature. Thus, the citations to the classical world, whether they were in diaries or in gardens expressed as urns, statues, or terraces, are likely to be best seen as an early and undeveloped appearance of universal history and its potential for use as precedent. In 1709, William Byrd notes: 'I rose at 5 o'clock and read in Homer and a chapter in Hebrew' (Wright and Tingling 1963, pp. 16–17). And on another day in 1739, 'I rose about 6, and read Hebrew and Greek' (Woodfin 1942, p. 121). The entries referring to the classics are all episodic and virtually never mention why he read them, what he thought of them, or how he connected them with his own life. If such reading was to be used as precedent, we do not have ready access to the process nor do we have enough information to tell whether he understood the ancient writers' meaning. All we know is that he was familiar with the texts.

By the 1750s and 1760s in Maryland, there may be a greater understanding of the context of classical citations than there had been earlier in Virginia, and here we may see the development of precedent. *New Principles of Gardening* by Batty Langley was published in 1726 and was found in Annapolis, Maryland in several libraries. It was probably used in the construction of several of the formal gardens found there which feature classical citations (*Charles Carroll letterbook*). The following quote dates from the 1720s, but if used at all in Annapolis, would have had meaning in the 1760s and 1770s.

Principle XXVII. There is nothing adds so much to the beauty and grandeur of gardens, as fine statues; and nothing more disagreeable, than when wrongly plac'd; as Neptune on a terrace-walk, mount, etc. or Pan, the god of sheep, in a large basin, canal, or fountain. But to prevent such absurdities, take the following directions.

For open lawns and large centers:

Mars, god of battle, with the goddess Fame; Jupiter, god of thunder, with Venus, the goddess of love and beauty; and the Graces Aglaio, Thalia, and Euphrosyne; Apollo, god of wisdom, with the nine Muses . . .

For woods and groves:

Ceres and Flora; Sylvanus, . . . and Ferona, goddess of the woods; Actaeon, a hunter, whom Diana turn'd into a hart, and was devoured by his own dogs; Eccho, a virgin rejected of her lover, pined away in the woods, for sorrow, where her voice still remains, answering the outcries of every complaint . . .

For fruit-gardens and orchards:

Pomona, goddess of fruit, and the three Hesperides, Eagle, Aretusa, and Hisperetusa, who were three sisters that had an orchard of golden apples kept by a dragon, which Hercules slew when he took them away . . .

For small paddocks of sheep, etc. in a wilderness [garden]: Morpheus and Pan, gods of sheep; Pates, the shepherd's goddess; Bubona, the goddess of oxen; and Nillo, a famous glutton, who used himself to carry a calf every morning, until it became a large bull, at which time he slew it with his fist, and eat him all in one day . . . (Langley 1726, pp. 204–6).

Some of the original attributes of the gods and *dii minores* are understood, although there is no information to show how they might have been used as precedent for modern conditions.

A third area which shows how material from the past was beginning to be handled as precedent, and thus provide a guide for the present, is law. Isaac described early eighteenth-century Virginian law as an *ad hoc* mixture of provincial enactments and uncertain applications of English law (1982a, p. 199) which led to confusion and continual but useless appeals to England. No such conditions prevailed later in the eighteenth century in either Virginia or Maryland. The use of precedent, including familiarity with English law, and the capacity to use these to win a case, all developed. Some Americans even received training at the Inns of Court. The units of the past, in this case law and its logic, were codified, compared, situated in different contexts, and given different meaning depending on use. This part of the past, whose origins and earlier cases had no direct tie to the world of the colonial experience, was handled in the same way as the natural world; it was given regularity and compared in even units so that it could be used to meet undefined but pressing circumstances.

The citation of precedent became important in Maryland because the use of English law became a means of containing the proprietary government (Lois Carr, personal communication). English law and citation of precedent may have been one way in which Marylanders created a past for their own use. Marylanders defended living situations by placing them in history, using legal precedent as the vehicle, thus making the origins of current practice difficult to question. This practice may have been a different form of naturalizing the condition of those in control, including whatever inequalities composed their condition, but it is analogous to the even subdivisions seen in the creation of natural philosophies and a natural order.

I would now like to turn to Annapolis, Maryland, and to a

famous, re-created eighteenth-century garden there, in order to explore further the rationalization of the past. The hypothesis offered is that the garden represents the use of the past as a set of precedents which appear so natural and convincing that they eliminate doubts about the extant social order, thus perpetuating it at a time of its own weakness. The garden, then, may be an expression of ideology in which the ordering of plants and historical objects in space may provide a key to the beginning of the use of past as precedent. Precedent in nature and precedent in law would serve to make its owner's place at the top of the hierarchy appear fixed and deserved.

The garden under consideration (Fig. 1) was built, along with the house, in the 1760s by William Paca, one of the Signers of the Declaration of Independence. The house is a large, five-part Georgian mansion with a two and a half storey central block separated by hyphens from one and a half storey dependencies on either side. The house was altered in the nineteenth and twentieth centuries, when it was turned into a hotel, but it was never destroyed completely. The house and its immediate grounds were excavated and fully reported by Stanley South (1967). The two-acre garden, which is at the back of the house, was buried and partially destroyed when the house was turned into a hotel. It was excavated by Bruce Powell (1966), Glenn Little (1967), and Kenneth and Ronald Orr (1975).

On his marriage William Paca became a wealthy man and shortly afterwards he had his house and garden designed and laid out professionally. The garden as it stands now is a reconstruction and is the product of documentary research and archaeological excavation. A fraction of the garden, including two outbuildings, are portrayed in a coeval painting. In addition there are some references to it by people who noted some of its features when they visited it before it disappeared. In addition, there are similar gardens in Annapolis and surrounding states to facilitate comparison. Such gardens exist at the Ridout and Carroll houses in Annapolis, the Mount Clare Mansion in Baltimore, Mulberry Fields on the Potomac River, and Middleton Plantation in South Carolina. In other words there are enough known, dated, and surviving examples to provide extant proof of a genre of landscape. There are also garden books which were used in Annapolis and in the colonies generally to guide in the construction and maintenance of all aspects of making a great garden. Such gardens were largely ornamental, but probably also contained a kitchen garden. The gardens were symmetrical, were walled either with built or planted materials, often contained exotic and imported plants, and had built terraces – frequently five – descending in an even series to some natural or constructed focal point, thus controlling the view. The descending terraces and controlled lines of sight indicate that the garden was thought of as a volume, not as a flat space.

The Paca House is a Georgian mansion and its facade and floor plan are bilaterally symmetrical, although not perfectly so. If bisected, the two halves of the facade or floor plan look alike even though in the case of this floor plan they are not mirror images of each other. It is likely that the characteristics which Deetz suggested (1977) are associated with this style, namely ideas of the person as individual, the afterlife as a specific reward

for personal behavior in this one, privacy, segregation of everyday life's different activities from each other, and segregation of the members of the family, also apply to this example of Georgian style and life.

The Paca House garden is also Georgian in style. It has a central axis dividing it into two parts using a straight, broad path which descends through four sets of steps as it goes away from the house. Even though in this case the axis is not down the exact middle of the garden, the visual effect is one of equal division. The steps lead a person physically and visually down over five brief slopes or terraces which fall away from the house. The terraces are similar to each other and create the same effect as when looking at a Georgian façade, Georgian window, or floor plan: bilaterally balanced symmetry. The reconstruction shows formal plats or parterres on each terrace, balanced sets of urns on pedestals, and in general, the complete predictability of one side given a look at the other. This is so despite the fact that the halves and compartments created by the axis are not of equal dimensions. There is certainly enough archaeological and comparative evidence to justify the balanced symmetry.

Authors like Miller (1733), Langley (1726), and LeBlond (1728) prescribed the kind of careful measurements and geometrical forms, plants, ponds, fountains, mazes, grass plots, groves, arbors, and the general dispositions of all items needed in gardens. They described the precedents which should be observed in order to maintain a successful and ongoing garden, including knowledge of local soil, wind, and flora. It is this knowledge which is common to Landon Carter, George Washington, and Thomas Jefferson. It is knowledge based on the past behavior of plants and winds, animals and clouds, which have been uniformly and continuously divided, labelled, and recorded. The theory and practice of gardening are based on closely controlled past performance and may demonstrate elements of Georgian segmentation imposed on nature, and on nature's past. Consequently, the garden may be a clue to how events from the past could be ordered; this marks the arrival of universal chronology or universal history.

The systematic use of past plant and weather behavior to plan and predict is made up of minute observation of many small items like past plant and weather performance and is the same process that is used in the creation of a systematic law. This process may be comparable to subdividing the human past when it is made into precedent. The building of legal precedent occurred in the later eighteenth century at a time when those who depended on the law in Maryland were most vulnerable from the Crown, the proprietary government, and from the classes below. The tie to the garden may be as follows: just as precedent inserted into law allowed the established order to protect its own position by making that position appear historically valid, so that same social position seemed to be more fixed when it appeared to be served by optical, astronomical, and geometrical phenomena displayed in the garden's *allées* and vistas.

It is useful at this point to look at the rules for building pleasure gardens in order to see how perspective, which is the link to precedent, was developed. The rules may support the hypothesis that the garden is ideology, and includes at least the

Fig. 1. The William Paca garden, Annapolis, Md. Overview of the William Paca Garden, as now reconstructed. The outlines of the Garden, including basic subdivisions, are archaeologically derived. The parterres are conjectural, as are the positions of most of the plantings. The pond's shape is archaeologically valid. The Garden slopes from left to right a total of sixteen and one-half feet.

Drawing prepared by Barbara Paca, courtesy of historic Annapolis, Inc.

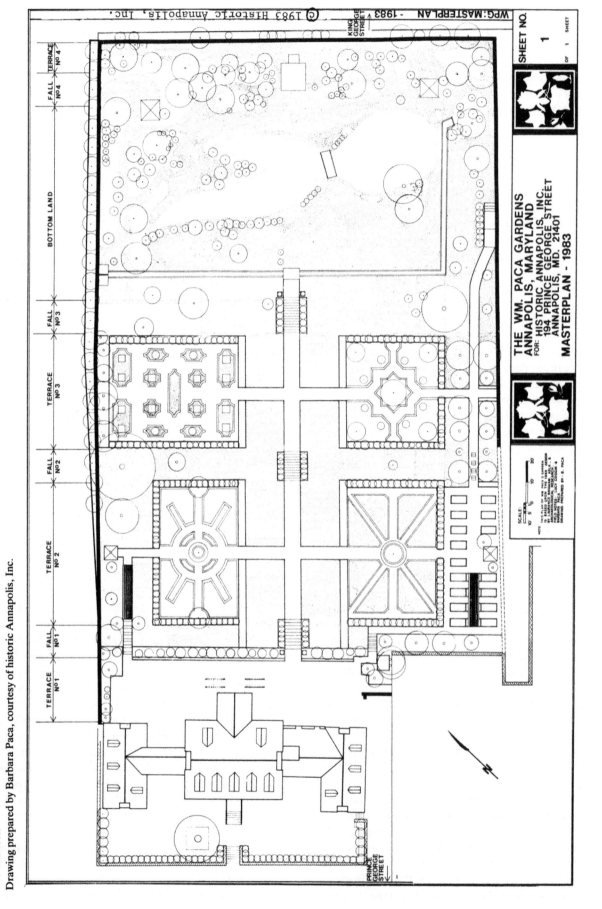

beginnings of the modern ideological constitution of the past. There are two areas in which it is possible to see garden building as naturalizing a specific attitude to the past. The first involves the initial rules for planning a garden's future. The planning is based on observations of wind and weather, shade and soil, and is often then set out as principles.

Before the design of a garden be put in execution, it ought to be considered what it will be like in twenty or thirty years time, when the palisades are grown up, and the trees are spread: for it often happens, that a design, which looks handsome when it is first planted, and in good proportion, becomes so small and ridiculous in process of time, that there is a necessity either to alter it, or destroy it entirely, and so plant anew (Miller 1733, 'Garden').

To follow this advice, Miller relays an experiment in natural history carried out by Dr Stephen Hales who modelled his work on Isaac Newton's scientific methods. Miller goes on:

the incomparable Sir Isaac Newton has not only shortened the geometrician's work, by his wonderful discoveries in abstract mathematics, but has also taught us, by his own practice, how to make and judge of experiments and observations with the utmost accuracy . . .

'The author [Reverend Dr Hales] having covered, with milled land, a garden plot, in which a sunflower was growing, so as to leave only one passage for air to communicate, and another to pour in water to water the plant, made several curious experiments upon it.

'1. That the plants which weighed about 3 pounds, perspired about 30 ounces in a 12 hour day, in the month of July, 1724, but in a warm night it perspired only 3 ounces, and nothing in a cold night . . .

'2. That as the area of the surface of the leaves was equal to 5616 square inches; and the area of roots only to 2286 square inches, the water or moisture imbibed by the roots to supply the perspiration at the leaves, must move faster in the roots than through the leaves, in the proportion of 5 to 2. But in the stem, whose transverse section was one square inch, faster than in the leaves, in the proportion of 5616 to one. (Miller 1733, 'Vegetable Staticks').

We know that Washington and Jefferson made and recorded regular observations on a wide variety of phenomena in their respective gardens (Klapthor and Morrison 1982, pp. 156–60). We do not know whether William Paca did the same, since most of his papers have been lost, but it would not be out of character since he built two large and varied landscape gardens in his lifetime. But whether he did or not is immaterial, for the age dictated careful observations like these, and Paca and his peers saw gardens as a way of thinking concretely about natural philosophy. They experimented with nature by grouping, segmenting, grafting, breeding, and transplanting, and they linked these activities with similar observations on sunlight, fire, soil, weather, and water. They ordered nature and built a past for it.

The second area in which it is possible to see garden building as naturalizing a specific attitude to the past by using the idea of perspective is in garden geometry. Hedges tall and short, clipped trees, geometric patterns in the parterres which enclose flowers, and exotic plants imported from their native areas, rows of evenly planted trees, the regularly cut-back edge of the forest, all define the treatment of plants by shaping or moving them in conformity with geometrical definitions.

If we take the whole garden, it may be seen as an exercise in optics, or in the regular study of vision and light. The terraces in the Paca garden descend evenly downward to a pond and then beyond to a focal point which is a mount with a miniature temple topped with a winged Mercury. The terraces carry the axis downward toward the distant point. If one stands at the door of the main house or at the head of the path, or somewhere lower on the median, one realizes the garden is not flat but a volume attempting to operate like a Renaissance painting: to create a different distance from what actually exists between viewer and object. There are explicit directions for this. First: 'In a fine garden, the first thing that should present itself to the sight should be an open level piece of grass . . . There ought always to be a descent from the house to the garden . . . On the opposite side of the gravel walks may be borders four feet wide for flowers, which will sufficiently answer the purpose of parterres; and if from the back of these borders there are evergreens planted in such a manner, as to rise from the borders gradually, so as to form an evergreen slope, it will bound the prospect very agreeably; and where there are any objects worthy of sight, or distant prospects to be obtained, there should be the vistas left.

'The principal walk must be in the front of the house, and should extend from the grass-plat next the house, to the end of the garden: if they be very wide, the sides should be turfed next the borders, and at the ends they may be terminated by a fosse [ditch] to continue the view' (Miller 1733, 'Garden').

To build a terrace the gardener might employ principle 'XXVII. The proportion that the base of a slope ought to have to its perpendicular, is a three to one, that is, if that perpendicular height be ten feet, its base must be thirty feet; and the like of all others' (Langley 1726, p. 201).

The manipulation of space in order to create perspective is made precise in principle:

XV. That all walks whose lengths are short, and lead away from any point of view, be made narrower at their further ends than at the hither part; for by the inclination of their sides, they appear to be of a much greater length than they really are; and the further end of every long walk, avenue, etc. appears to be much narrower than the end where you stand.

And the reason is, that notwithstanding the sides of such walk are parallel to each other, yet as the breadth of the further end is seen under a lesser angle than the breadth of that part where you stand, it will therefore appear as if contracted, altho' the sides are actually parallel; for equal objects always appear under equal angles, Q.E.D. (Langley 1726, p. 196).

The garden is therefore a three dimensional setting, manipulated to create illusions of distance through the use of perspective. The basic pattern used to create perspective in the Paca garden is terracing; this is made to descend to a distant place, which is in turn made to appear more distant through the illusion created by the systematic lowering of the bottom plane. Rows of evergreens are planted along the line of sight, and although they are parallel, assist in making the distant views appear further away. At Mulberry Fields (constructed 1755, gardens predate 1814) the fence lines of the field below the terraces are opened out as one goes away from the house. This has the effect of bringing the Potomac River much closer than the mile away it actually is. The illusion created by the application of the rules of perspective corresponds to that involved in Renaissance painting, where mathematical rules were used to create distances between objects which were not in reality distant. These mislead the eye through their creation of an image of reality. Depending on how the rules were used, objects could appear further away or closer as the artist desired, or 'in perspective'. These are the rules, used with a degree of precision in eighteenth-century gardens, that made objects like a river, pond, or temple appear further away or closer than they actually were.

The gardener deals explicitly with geometry and with optics. Slightly less explicitly, he deals with the rules for creating illusions using space, so he is concerned with fooling the eye or with misrepresentation. Now, if ideology is also a misrepresentation of reality and serves to misrepresent the conditions of existence, what unequal human relationships are naturalized through the garden? Since the garden is manipulated space, is there some cultural practice represented in it which is, as a consequence, placed in nature so that it seems inevitable and beyond question? Just as the citation of precedent grew to protect the established social order, so also gardens took optical, astronomical, or meteorological phenomena and ordered them in such a way that they appeared to naturalize the social hierarchy. They displayed their principles in the allées, vistas and parterres of their gardens.

The link between the optical illusions using garden space and the development of precedent in law is best explained by John Rowe, who correctly placed the origin of the idea, which he referred to as 'perspective distance', in the Renaissance. Rowe defined perspective distance as an understanding about time as well as space, not just about painting (1965, pp. 1–20). Rowe placed the origin of seeing things in the perspective of both space and time inside the assumption that other peoples on the globe and other eras of history were separate, had their own integrity, and were worth knowing as such. This idea Rowe called perspective distance, and placed its origins in the Italian Renaissance. With its advent in the thirteenth century, classical antiquity was acknowledged to be dead, not continuous with the present, and other cultures to be quite different and not necessarily versions of those living. Knowledge of the distant eras in space and time was possible through direct observation of the foreigners or the remains of the dead societies. Both were acknowledged to be apart from the viewer; separate but internally consistent. Just as mathematical rules used in painting could make what was close appear more distant, so the assumption that other spaces and

other times were not continuous with one's own but were separate and internally consistent, allowed them to be brought closer and to appear to be seen as wholes.

The Paca garden probably attempted to control sight by using the optical illusion of perspective. The garden handled distance in space and it may also have handled distance in time because there are references to antiquity at the ends of some vistas. And of course the garden was very likely built out of handbooks, themselves based on compilations of past behaviors of plants, etc.

Given that the Paca garden may illustrate growing control over the notion of perspective, applied to time as well as space, then one of the end points of such a development is the emergence of universal history and evenly segmented time. This did not appear fully developed in America until the nineteenth century, but the development of an ability to use perspective in gardens and precedent in law were probably its beginnings. They are part of the regular use of events set in uniform time. Describing universal time is not my goal here. Rather my concern is a fragment of it; the construction of events from the past in an orderly, segmented pattern as both chronology and precedent. This includes the practice of placing evenly segmented units backward to include all past events, which is what perspective looks like when applied to the past.

If this development can be seen in the Paca garden, then why would it be there? We know that William Paca was descended from planters, was tied to merchants, and was a successful, and later, a famous lawyer. He came to teach law in later life. William Paca's surviving records show his involvement in an urban, mercantile, profit-oriented economy, which used some wage labor, rent, and interest on lent capital. They also reveal a society preoccupied with law and its basis in precedent (Stiverson and Jacobsen 1976). Paca was a lawyer by training and continual practice; it was his profession and he handled many cases early in his career, attended the Continental Congress, was Governor of Maryland three times and a federal judge. His skill in law and ability to influence others through its practice was a matter of note. 'Paca's contributions to the *Maryland Gazette* [the chief newspaper in Annapolis] during the controversy [over state support for the established church] were brilliantly conceived and argued, and they established him in the judgment of one historian as the ablest constitutional lawyer of the province at the time . . . Paca [showed] brilliant insights and remarkable powers of logic.' Further, 'Paca preferred fighting injustice and oppression by constructing finely argued newspaper essays that traced constitutional precedents and appealed to man's natural rights . . . ' (Stiverson and Jacobsen 1976, p. 62).

The environment in which Paca practiced as lawyer, writer, representative, governor, and judge was, moreover, one of economic and political change. Annapolis was a merchant town, Maryland a maritime colony with an extensive trade with Europe and the Caribbean. It was an area which was in rebellion over taxation and tariff; it was an economy based on massive use of credit, struggling to calculate interest, with finding efficient ways of book-keeping and accounting, and with periods of staggering devaluation and inflation. The whole problem of tying money and profit to time lapsed and space travelled was faced in the later eighteenth century and saw, among other economic changes, several experiments with printing new monies (Papenfuse 1975, pp. 62, 67, 95, 131–4, 207, 232, 234). Paca was not born to wealth; he married into substantial amounts of it. He grew up and lived in economic circumstances where everyone around him was faced with serious economic fluctuation and political change.

Then, to add conflict to instability, there was the problem of slavery. Paca owned over one hundred slaves himself (Stiverson and Jacobsen 1976, p. 92). Yet he argued so strongly for freedom that he 'quarrel[ed] with the Constitution . . . [which] he felt . . . did not adequately safeguard individual rights, and many of the guarantees he sought – particularly freedom of religion, freedom of the press, and legal protection for those accused of crimes . . . ' (Stiverson and Jacobsen 1976, p. 91). This argument occurred before the Bill of Rights was written and added to the U.S. Constitution.

The major contradiction we see in Paca's life, and which arose at the time of the Revolution, was between a slave-holding society and one proclaiming independence in order to promote personal freedom and individual liberty. The contradiction has been highlighted and analyzed often. It is of some significance here because it reveals the internal pressures building within the society which helped to provoke the alliances behind the Revolution and the later social upheaval in the American Civil War. Paca lived in a time in which fundamental social contradiction – slavery and individual freedom, in principle for all – was dealt with temporarily and the tensions were well enough disguised that society remained stable for at least Paca's generation.

The contradiction hidden by the quest for a fixed natural order, whether in law or nature (i.e. formal gardens, astronomy, or natural philosophy) is that between slavery for others and freedom for themselves. Slavery involved 'fratricidal conflict, prisoners of war [in Africa], the horrors of oceanic travel, land-lords, overseers, and taskmasters . . . undeserved suffering, imbrutement, lawless domination, patrollers and spies, sexual assault, kangaroo courts . . . branding irons and chained feet . . . insults . . . the auction block . . . The freedom sought and won by white Americans for themselves was intended to prevent slavery for themselves since they saw themselves becoming at the hands of Great Britain no better than "hewers of wood, and drawers of water". The plight of the colonials between 1764 and 1776 bore a striking resemblance to that of the Afro-Americans during the heyday of the Transatlantic traffic in human beings' (Okoye 1980, pp. 20–1). Given this, Isaac argues that the growing economic and political closeness of slaves and owners provoked the Revolution, which had the impact of temporarily preserving the sought-for distance between the classes. Thus the Revolution and all its natural philosophy and Georgian style, some of whose physical manifestations have been treated here, acted to gloss over the growing double contradiction: liberty was won to prevent conditions which seemed like enslavement to whites, but was not to be extended to blacks who were essential in preserving hierarchy, economic as well as racial. These are the conditions of the time of

the garden and are behind the contradictions it was very likely built – although not necessarily consciously – to mask. That is why the garden, and the Georgian order in general, are ideology.

In the Paca garden we can see that space was manipulated to create a perspective, and the rules embodied in creating true perspective provide a clue to Paca's and his era's perception of time. The material references to classical antiquity compose an index to some notion of the past in the garden, while the use of garden books shows clear use of precedent. Given the link between the use of perspective in Paca's garden and his deep and successful immersion in law, the garden may naturalize perspective which is the principle that ties them together, and thus the garden may have substantiated the cultural segmentation of space and time. Perspective allows one to view space and time in measurable interchangeable segments; and this is how universal space and time link Mr Paca's garden to his law, Annapolis' workers to their hours, capital to interest, ships at sea to weeks travelled and thus to profit and loss (Gurevich 1976, pp. 240–1).

The division into equal units of space, work, travel time, lending time, the turning of past into precedent, all preface a full development in the next decades, 1790–1870, of quantified treatments of virtually all of society. From nature, precision moved to the past, and then into the workplace and credit house, and then into all the divisions of industrializing society. Indeed such universalization helped to create the divisions into which society was stratified. The divisions and the statistics bringing them to life may be seen fruitfully as part of ideology.

'In the 1790s, inventories of descriptive facts about society were touted as providing an authentic, objective basis for ascertaining the common good. Complete possession of the facts, it was hoped, would eliminate factionalism and allow government to rule in the best interest of the public. Further, collections of social data were thought to constitute the proper scientific proof that the new experiment in republicanism did indeed benefit all citizens. By 1820 . . . avid collectors of statistics had come to recognize that distinctions and divisions in American society legitimately existed and had to be reckoned with. The particular distinctions they made – for example, between agriculture, commerce, and manufacturing – they regarded as inherent in the social order; empiricism, they insisted, was objective and value-free. But of course their empiricism was freighted with unacknowledged values. The kinds of things they did not count and calculate in 1820 – for instance, the number of slave-owners, black mortality, the incidence of crime, female illiteracy . . . ' are an illustration of how segmentation, quantification, and precision can create society and hold it intact (Cohen 1981, p. 55). All this is ideology and is seen in an early way in the 1760s garden and its associated activity – the division and subdivision of cultural space and time and making it appear as though the divisions were actually derived from nature or antiquity through the use of the idea of perspective.

As American society evolved in the later eighteenth century, or was transformed, as Isaac puts it, substantial stress appeared in the social order, and if the hypothesis in this paper is an appropriate vehicle for organizing the data, then we might expect ideological activity to intensify throughout the eighteenth century. Certainly that is what happened by extending precision into all aspects of the social order, as seen above. But we would also expect to find elements of this ideological activity in material culture. And we do.

The specific version of the hypothesis in this paper acknowledges the contradiction of Paca's substantial inherited wealth, based in part on slavery, and his passionate defense of liberty. It can be argued that if liberty were realized, his position was likely to be compromised. To mask this contradiction, to make it appear to disappear, to prevent its becoming a conflict, his position of power was placed in law and nature. This was done both in practising law and in gardening, through the citation of precedents, which is a segmentary view of space and time made available through the use of the laws or rules of perspective. One would predict then that the more the contradictions of the social order became manifest, the more intense the ideological activity would be. This is plainly seen in the back third of the Paca garden.

The far one-third of the Paca garden is a so-called wilderness garden, the only one known to have existed in prerevolutionary America. As opposed to rectangular symmetry, the far third consists of a pond with curved edges looking like a fish, crossed at an odd angle by a Chinese style bridge, and contains meandering paths, scattered clumps of bushes, trees, and small half-hidden buildings. The wilderness garden, sometimes called a Romantic garden in Victorian times, is thought to represent a freer and more spontaneous approach to nature, but the Paca garden appears by the 1760s and probably represents neither freedom nor spontaneity. My hypothesis would be that the introduction of the arcane geometry of a wilderness garden should serve as an index to greater mystification of the roots of the social order.

Lévi-Strauss, following B. Karlgren, a Sinologist, has pointed out that elaborated curvilinear designs and arabesques 'represent the formal survival of a decadent or terminated social order. [They] constitute, on the esthetic level, its dying echo' (Lévi-Strauss 1963, p. 265). Curvilinear designs may occur in a wide range of art forms, from painting, architecture, to rugs and gardens. Such design is not usually associated with the Georgian style, but when it is, it should not appear as mysterious as Lévi-Strauss has left it. Curves are composed of segments made up of arcs, circles, eggs, hyperbolas and other regular, segmented, strict geometrical forms. They are no less regular than lines and angles. They order nature in a different way but they order it nonetheless. The key is that they create the illusion of openness, flow, motion, and continuity, not predictable end.

'The usual method of contriving wildernesses is to divide the whole compass of ground, either into squares, angles, circles, or other figures, making the walks correspond to them; planting . . . trees [so as to seem] promiscuously without order . . . ; for as these parts of a garden should, in a great measure, be designed from nature, so whatever has the stiff appearance of art, does by no means correspond therewith . . . Walks [should] have the appearance of meanders and labyrinths, where the eye cannot discover more than twenty or thirty yards in length; and the more the walks are turned, the greater pleasure they will afford' (Miller

1733, 'Wilderness'). This is from one of the gardening books used in Annapolis.

Such design uses the geometrical organization of plants which naturalizes the changes in the social order to maintain a continuity. The order of Tidewater society faced a fundamental dilemma in the 1760s and 1770s of upholding traditional authority and supporting popular sovereignty. The wilderness garden may be an intensified effort to implant in nature and arithmetic the twists and turns of the ideology which was so constructed that the order of traditional society was maintained in the presence of substantial pressures to open the hierarchy and promote mobility. Even though it was probably built with the rest of the garden, it serves like the mazes in other American formal gardens: it creates the illusion of flow and movement but is in fact the rigid control over spontaneous movement.

The formal garden was not an adornment, the product of spare time; it was not for food and still less for idle fashion. It was a place for thinking and for making the observations which were essential to economic and social life. It was not passive; it was very active, for by walking in it, building it, looking at it, admiring and discussing it, and using it in any way, its contemporaries could take themselves and their position as granted and convince others that the way things are is the way they always had been and should remain. For the order was natural and had always been so.

Acknowledgements

An earlier version of this paper was presented in a symposium 'Is Structuralism Possible in Historical Archaeology?', organized by Anne E. Yentsch at the 1982 annual meeting of the Society for Historical Archaeology.

I am grateful for the long, patient, and generous help in describing landscape restoration, and the William Paca Garden in particular, given me by Mrs J.M.P. Wright, Chairman of the Board of Historic Annapolis, Inc. and Chairman of the William Paca Garden Committee. Barbara Paca provided many of the references to and much of the information on eighteenth-century gardening. Dr Lois Green Carr provided helpful information and Jean Russo gave the paper a careful, sympathetic reading. Lisa Morton patiently and carefully guided me through the files on the garden at the William Paca Garden Visitors' Center in Annapolis, Maryland. Jacquelyn Winter did all the typing. Historic Annapolis, Inc. generously provided complete access to its files and resources for this essay and without its help and permission the research would not have been possible. Any errors of fact or interpretation are my responsibility alone.

Rhys Isaac's essay (1982b), 'Terrain, Landscape, Architecture, and Furnishings: Social Space and Control in Old Virginia' was read at a symposium *History and Anthropology in the Colonial Chesapeake* organized by this author, and much of the inspiration for this essay comes from his. Ann M. Palkovich explained much of the material on perspective, depth of field, and their geometry. Elaine G. Breslaw introduced me to the Tuesday Club papers and the world view of eighteenth-century Annapolis. Garry Wheeler Stone clarified Mulberry Fields.

References cited

Althusser, Louis (1971) 'Ideology and Ideological State Apparatuses', in *Lenin and Philosophy*, pp. 127–86, Monthly Review Press, New York

Breen, T.H. Ed. (1976) *Shaping Southern Society*, Oxford University Press, New York

Charles Carroll Letterbook (1760), September. Hall of Records, Annapolis, Maryland

Cohen, Patricia Cline (1981) 'Statistics and the State: Changing Social Thought and the Emergence of a Quantitative Mentality in America, 1790–1820', *William and Mary Quarterly*, Third Series, 38: 1, pp. 35–55

Deetz, James F. (1977) *In Small Things Forgotten*, Doubleday, Garden City, New Jersey

Farish, Hunter Dickenson Ed. (1943) *Journal and Letters of Philip Vickers Fithian, 1773–1774, Plantation Tutor of the Old Dominion*, Colonial Williamsburg Inc., Williamsburg, Virginia

Glassie, Henry (1975) *Folk Housing in Middle Virginia*, University of Tennessee Press, Knoxville

Greene, Jack P. Ed. (1965) *The Diary of Colonel Landon Carter of Sabine Hall, 1752–1778*, vol. 1, The University of Virginia Press, Charlottesville, Virginia.

Gurevich, A.J. (1976) 'Time As a Problem of Cultural History', in Paul Ricoeur Ed., *Cultures and Time*, pp. 229–45, The Unesco Press, Paris

Isaac, Rhys (1982a) *The Transformation of Virginia 1740–1790*, University of North Carolina Press, Chapel Hill

(1982b) 'Terrain, Landscape, Architecture, and Furnishings: Social Space and Control in Old Virginia', Paper read at the twenty-second annual meeting of the Northeastern Anthropological Association, Princeton, N.J.

Klapthor, Margaret Brown and Morrison, Howard Alexander (1982) *G. Washington, A Figure Upon the Stage*, Smithsonian Institution Press, Washington, D.C.

Langley, Batty (1726) *New Principles of Gardening*, Bettsworth and Batley, London

Le Blond, Alexander (1728) *The Theory and Practice of Gardening*, Bernard Lintot, London

Lévi-Strauss, Claude (1963) 'Split Representation in the Art of Asia and America', in *Structural Anthropology*, pp. 245–68. Basic Books, New York

Little, J. Glenn, II (1967–8) 'Re: Archaeological Research on Paca Garden. November 8, 1967, May 24, 1968. Letters on file, William Paca Garden Visitors' Center, Annapolis, Maryland

Lukács, Georg (1971) 'Reification and the Consciousness of the Proletariat', in *History and Class Consciousness*, M.I.T. Press, Cambridge, Mass.

Miller, Philip (1733) *The Gardener's Dictionary*. Printed for the author. London

Okoye, F. Nwabueze (1980) 'Chattel Slavery as the Nightmare of the American Revolutionaries'. *William and Mary Quarterly*: Third Series, 37: 1, pp. 3–28

Orr, Kenneth G. and Orr, Ronald G. (1975) 'The Archaeological Situation at the William Paca Garden, Annapolis, Maryland: The Spring House and the Presumed Pavilion House Site. April', Typescript on file, William Paca Garden Visitors' Center, Annapolis, Maryland

Papenfuse, Edward C. (1975) *In Pursuit of Profit: The Annapolis Merchants in the Era of the American Revolution, 1763–1805*, Johns Hopkins University Press, Baltimore, Maryland

Powell, B. Bruce (1966) 'Archaeological Investigation of the Paca House Garden, Annapolis, Maryland. November 16, 1966', Typescript on file, William Paca Garden Visitors' Center, Annapolis, Maryland

Rowe, John H. (1965) 'The Renaissance Foundations of Anthropology', *American Anthropologist*, 67, pp. 1–20

Shanks, Michael and Tilley, Christopher (1982) 'Ideology, Symbolic Power and Ritual Communication: A Reinterpretation of Neolithic Mortuary Practices', in Ian Hodder Ed., *Symbolic and Structural Archaeology*, Cambridge University Press

South, Stanley (1967) *The Paca House, Annapolis, Maryland*. Unpublished ms., Historic Annapolis, Inc., Annapolis, Maryland

Stiverson, Gregory A. and Jacobsen, Phebe R. (1976); *William Paca, A Biography*. Maryland Historical Society, Baltimore, Md.

Tate, Thad W. and Ammerman, D.L. (1979) *The Chesapeake in the Seventeenth Century*. Norton and Co., New York

Thorpe, I.J. (1981) Anthropological Orientations on Astronomy in Complex Societies. Paper read at the Third Theoretical Archaeology Conference, Reading, U.K.

Woodfin, Maude H. Ed. (1942) *Another Secret Diary of William Byrd of Westover, 1739–1741*, The Dietz Press, Richmond, Virginia

Wright, Louis B. and Tingling, Marion Eds. (1963) *The Great American Gentleman William Byrd of Westover in Virginia. His Secret Diary for the Years 1709–1712*, Putnam's Sons, New York, G.P.

Yentsch, Anne E. (1982) Letter on Spring House Excavations, William Paca Garden. 15 March, on file, William Paca Garden Visitors' Centre, Annapolis, Maryland

Chapter 4

**Modernism and suburbia
as material ideology**
Daniel Miller

This chapter illustrates how the critique of ideology can be used for the study of material objects by reference to the familiar contemporary built environment. An outline is given of the Frankfurt School's model of the relationship between science and technology, and ideological control. It is then shown how modernist architecture fulfils the expectations derived from the model. Modernism cannot, however, be understood in isolation, but only in relation to other major traditions to which it is opposed. In Britain an important alternative tradition is the suburban semi-detached house. By examining the contrary values and ideals represented in these two traditions, the complex ideological underpin-nings of the apparent meanings of the constructed world are revealed. One class of people are shown not only to objectify their interests in their own housing but to construct that which objectifies the values to which they are opposed, in such a manner, that they are able to make the consumers of these images appear as though they were the producers. Finally a parallel is drawn between the nature of authority revealed in this analysis and that of the four archaeological examples developed in the following chapters.

Introduction
This chapter is intended as a bridge between Chapter 1 in which an attempt is made to build a working model of ideology, and the archaeological uses made of that concept in the third section of this volume. It is devised on the lines of an old archaeological adage: when in doubt start from the best known and then work towards the least known. In this case the least known and most problematic is the archaeological record. The problems of its interpretation are notorious, so that it would seem unwise to apply the ideas developed in Chapter 1 immediately

to them. The model of ideology was derived from the discussion of written texts, and before there can be any hope of applying these ideas to archaeological remains, a process of translation has to be effected from the textual to the material. The goal is an application to prehistory where the evidence is exclusively material.

The process of translation between these two modes of discourse, may be aided by attempting an initial examination of evidence that is well known, familiar and accessible. Such a study would give us some conception of the insights to be gained and the pitfalls to be avoided in any application to the more intractable subject of conventional archaeology. The material which seemed best to fit this requirement was the modern built environment, which is already the subject of extensive research and interpret-ation. The question to be put to this material is whether it seems that something approaching what in Chapter 1 has been described as a model for a critique of ideology may be applied to it.

Any application of the concept of ideology demands an initial characterisation of the general categories of peoples' interests and forms of power that appear to fit that particular, historically constituted subject of analysis. In this case we are dealing with advanced industrial capitalist and 'socialist' societies. The specific nature of any proposed candidate for 'ideology' will be particular to those societies, and will not be amenable to any direct translation at this level to archaeological research. Archaeologists working in the analysis of quite different societies may focus on very different relations based on, for example, lineage or gender. In order to remain comparable, however, this account will retain the same generalised coarse-grained perspective suggested in Chapter 1, foregoing the subtleties and sophistications of the modern 'ideology critique' for the older tradition of generalised 'dominant' or alternative ideologies that may characterise a broad sweep of time-periods and geographic areas.

The first step in this exercise is to discover a candidate for the critique of contemporary society from the perspective of ideology. None of the forms that were specifically discussed in Chapter 1 are acceptable. Criticisms were given there of both the bourgeois and the Marxist concepts of social relations, and in any case, both were applied to the nineteenth century. The present century has seen radical and rapid changes in society, both the creation of the socialist bloc and the development of new kinds of capitalism, and it would be quite surprising if these earlier works could provide more than a model for today's social theory. We are looking therefore, for something in a similar tradition of critical analysis, but highly revisionist with respect to Marx's critique.

Such a candidate may be located in the concept of ideology formulated by the Frankfurt school, a group of German social theorists who were particularly active in the 1930s but who have been most influential, along with the more recent writings of Marcuse and Habermas, in the 1960s. Not only has the tradition of social theory they represent presented a sustained analysis, but their current reputation may be an indication of the revealing properties of that analysis. The roots of this critique are somewhat older, and that aspect with which I am concerned here goes back at least to Max Weber. Weber took certain forms of representation of the world to be characteristic of capitalist society as he saw it, and these were contrasted with other societies and their belief-systems. In particular he focused on subjects such as rational calculation, bureaucratic control, and organisational forms modelled on science. He devoted much of his surveys of various societies to those aspects of their belief-systems that he felt may have accounted for the development, or lack of development, of this 'outlook' on the world. This idea of a dominant form of representation in modern society was refined as a critical theory and a more polemical critique of the modern state by members of the Frankfurt school. Examples of this critique include the well known polemic of Marcuse *One Dimensional Man* (Marcuse 1964) and the article by Habermas 'Technology and science as ideology' (Habermas 1970).

In brief, the argument is as follows. The key to modern society is science. The scientific age replaces the industrial age. Science consists of the domination of nature and its control by people. Nature is no longer seen as something to be adapted to, but something that is itself adapted to our use. Nature is controlled and, by and large, a human-made environment replaces the natural environment, as a more predictable and controlled context for life. We come to understand and appropriate the world around us and make it serve our will. To do this requires a certain attitude towards the world, one that Weber tries to capture in his concept of purposive rational action. This is an attitude in which technical control is the goal of knowledge, and furthermore comes to constitute knowledge. Knowledge thereby becomes restricted to that which is controllable. Only that which can be directly sensed, tested or predicted is knowledge, any speculation beyond this is not real knowledge. Direct testing becomes the criterion by which something can be said to be known. This is the basis of positivism in its various forms. This belief comes to permeate all branches of academic knowledge. These tendencies are by no means unique to the modern period but this century has seen a marked acceleration in their growth.

The same principles come to dominate the forms and relations of production. Value becomes less plausibly related only to labour, and becomes linked more to technical knowledge and science. The microchip creates new commodities, often with a minimum of human labour, and the hierarchy of productive relations becomes based more on professionalism and technical ability than on the older criterion of business capital. Planning and organisation in bureaucracy and management increase in importance, and social relations become increasingly transformed into relations of technical control. Through this sequence, science, as the domination of nature by people, becomes increasingly the model for the technical domination of people by people. This attitude leads to a further stress on objectivity and control, and a suspicion of anything which cannot be assimilated easily into such. This leads in turn to what is known, in crude terms, as the fact–value dichotomy. Politics also becomes assimilated, as judgment of political ability becomes based more on apparent technique than value. Governments become elected for their promises in relation to their technical control of the economy, and their ability to run a complex network with the minimum of disruption. Efficiency in the state becomes paramount over social values, and again it is technical ability that becomes political legitimation. Bureaucratic control may become increasingly immune to the fluctuations of particular political regimes.

This in brief is the model. It has many variations, and many applications to the particular analysis of particular societies, but at this coarse level it best fits the model of ideology sought, because of the following attributes. It is a perspective or representation of the world that is being ascribed to interest. It controls what can be known because it controls what knowledge is, it is the dominant force in the organisation of production, and is also the basis for the legitimation of the dominant groups in society. It underlies the apparent basis of power. One of the points of this critique is that it applies equally well to various extremes of those political affiliations which are more usually taken to be the ideological base of society, but which from this perspective may be largely mystifications. Thus the Frankfurt school see these critical ideas as applying both to the societies that have an apparent legitimation of individual liberty and opportunity in the 'west', and to the apparent legitimation of socialist equality and communal enterprise in the 'east'. The critique works below the level of these supposed dominant ideals. As ideology, they are not part of a contrast between real and ideal, they are both representations and also descriptions of the way societies actually work – their observable material relations. Unlike some conceptions of ideology no such divisions are accepted. The Marxist concept of praxis, in which conception and action are in continual dialectical tension, is implicit in such a critique.

The question of just how pervasive this ideology as representation and guide to action in a given society becomes, is a matter for specific analysis of specific societies. Whether it represents merely that which education attempts to inculcate and organisations to implement, but is relatively restricted in terms of the mass of population, or whether it pervades all conceptions of reality, might be determined in part from a study of the forms in which it is represented. In the following examination of one element of this expression, we may be able to gauge, in part, the extent of relevance of this critique.

In order to investigate the extent to which such an ideology may be identified within the material world, a subject must be found in which these ideas might be implicated. Of the surrounding material world, it is the built environment that most dominates our everyday patterns of living, and it is therefore to architecture that we might first look to find evidence for a material expression of dominance, embodying these principles. Within the built environment we would look for developments that appear to coincide with the development of this ideology and of modern science. Obviously there would be no point in investigating architecture that belonged to a previous period. Secondly, a clue might be found in a style of architecture that transcended the apparent political and national boundaries, as do the principles that we are looking to see embedded within it.

That architecture might be capable, as material production, of the direct representation of a set of dominant ideals and principles as to the nature of society, might be suggested by studies of other areas and places. One of the best known attempts at such an enquiry was that of the art historian, Panofsky. He posited a particularly close relationship between the architecture of the high gothic and the then prevalent scholasticism. Many of the explicit structural relations that scholasticism sought as an understanding of the world were to be found in the equally explicit form of the gothic cathedrals and their dominant and evident architectural principles. In his short survey Panofsky (1957) provides a series of such parallels. Other studies that have investigated such relationships include a study of folk housing in middle Virginia by Glassie (1975) using the technique of structural analysis, and studies of Indian architecture – addressed both to the traditional temple city under a theocratic regime (Piper 1979), and to the planning of urban centres such as Delhi as a representation and instrument of colonial power (King 1976). A recent book edited by S. Ardener (1981) examines the way in which the use of space reproduces a particular aspect of power relations, that of gender.

Anthropological studies that are concerned with the relationship between ideology and the built environment may develop much more detailed and sophisticated approaches to this relationship, as found in the work of Bourdieu (1971). A particularly clear example of the possibilities of such an analysis may be found in a recent study of the relationship between Islam, ideology and the organisation of space (Gilsenan 1982, Chapters 8 and

9). These last studies, however, go much beyond the relatively gross level of analysis that is being attempted in the following exercise. They may represent models archaeologists would ideally ascribe to, but at present they are the limits of understanding of the full resources of anthropology engaged in a parallel search and may not be the most appropriate immediate reference points.

Architectural modernism

An obvious candidate for the material expression of ideology as described above is found in architectural modernism. Modernism is represented in a large part of that architecture which has grown up in the period of concern. It did not exist prior to the development of the modern form of this ideology and is therefore coincident with it. It is closely associated with change itself. Furthermore, another term for modernism has been the 'international style'. The office blocks and municipal housing in which this style is often found have become so ubiquitous that we would not know from an examination of the buildings whether we were in Moscow, Rio or Sydney. These attributes of modernism are uncontroversial. What is more difficult to interpret is what, as a group of buildings, this movement represents, what image of the world, what ideals and relations might be implicated in them. Such an investigation is aided, however, by the large quantity of writings on precisely this theme, and from the observable patterns within the range of the buildings themselves.

To commence this review with an investigation of the relevant writings, rather than with the buildings themselves does not mean we will be reduced at the end to mere subjective intention. It will be argued later that there is other, material evidence, that can be utilised. Further, there are reasons that will be presented for supposing the movement to be much larger than its apparent ideals and intentions, as declared by its practitioners. The ideology modernism represents may often have subverted these declared intentions, and worked rather in favour of an overarching dominant reference that establishes the conventions through which meaning is generated. Nevertheless it is helpful that there exists a surprising consensus in the writings of architects, authors and critics about what appear to have been the explicit models of modernism, which may then be compared with its results.

Most of this discussion refers not to the mass of actual modernist buildings, but symbolises the movement with respect to certain individuals and schools that are seen as having played a key role in its development. The general mass of buildings are viewed as in part derived from, or developed from, these leaders. Furthermore, the emphasis is on modernism as style – the façade, the appearance, the evident 'messages' of the architecture – rather than on morphology. This is not to say that the argument is addressed to the reflection of ideology in appearance, as opposed to the actual realisations of the social controls through morphology, since, as will be made clear, the suggestion is that the form and appearance of the buildings are themselves effective instruments of ideological control and are therefore to be understood as active interventions, not mere reflection. An analysis of morphology might lead in very different directions and to different confrontations.

These architects and schools reduce, in much of the literature, to a single example of each. Le Corbusier, a Swiss architect who has been highly influential from his early work in the 1920s through to his final work in the 1960s, stands for the architects. The Bauhaus which operated in Germany in the 1920s and 1930s teaching architecture, art and applied crafts such as furniture and which included Hans Meyer and Walter Gropius as its directors, stands for the schools. Most histories of modernism do not begin with these figures but, much earlier with the critical writings and work of William Morris (e.g. Pevsner 1960). It is, however, these two that are taken as having provided the dominant flavour to modern architecture. Neither can be taken as simple homogeneous inspirations, both had periods, inconsistencies, and in the case of the Bauhaus the diversity of its constitutive individuals. The key period for the development of modernism is the 1920s (see Frampton 1980, for a general history). There were major precursors: in Germany the Deutsche Werkbund; in Holland a movement centered on the journal *De Stijl*; and in the United States the work of Sullivan and Frank Lloyd Wright, but it was Le Corbusier and Bauhaus who in the 1920s became the symbolic figureheads of the movement. Thereafter a modernist building might be loosely categorised as Le Corbusian (of a given period) or Bauhausian, and this was sufficient to give an impression of its style as modernist. There have been numerous developments of modernism, but almost all had some link with one or other inspiration. In Britain, after successive waves of European influence, a home-grown style termed New Brutalism developed, inspired by the later work of Le Corbusier and particularly by a residential block built by him in Marseilles, while in the sixties came the residential tower blocks also popularised in Europe by Le Corbusier. Modernism itself was not, however, a fashion that came and went. It is at present (with its offshoots such as post-modernism) still the dominant and growing trend of world architecture, and it has thereby increasingly been able to stand for what our urban environment has become.

A survey of what might be represented in this movement reveals a surprising degree of unanimity between the various relevant writings. These include the often substantial publications of the actual architects such as Sullivan, Le Corbusier and Gropius (for a period the director of the Bauhaus). There are also the various historians of the movement ranging from the more positive (Pevsner 1960, Banham 1960) to the more critical (Frampton 1980 and Tafuri 1976). Equally, there are commentators, again ranging from positive (e.g.Gardiner 1974) to negative, including the recent sceptical journalism of Tom Wolfe (1982) and the more sustained humanistic form of critical commentary by Mumford (1975). I have made considerable use of the various publications of the Open University on the history of modern design and architecture, and particularly of a compendium of original sources under the title *Form and Function* (Ed. T. and C. Benton 1975). While there may be some agreement as to what modernism represents in these writings, what differs is their attitude to those ideals, and their opinions as to their effects.

The qualities which modernism is taken to represent group around several key, frequently used, terms and the relationship between them. These are 'Objectivity', 'Rationality', 'Formalism', 'Honesty', 'Functionalism', 'Science' and 'Machine Aesthetic'. These terms are matched by certain observable features of the buildings themselves that, in their presence and relationships, indicate the style. These include the dominance of straight lines both for the sides of the building and the flat roof, the use of steel, glass and reinforced concrete as opposed to brick, stone and slate, the attempt to reveal the structural features of the building on its external face, exposing the frame to view, the lack of any additional decorative facade and often the comparative height of the buildings as against other styles. These attributes make up a clearly polythetic category, and given the sheer numbers of related buildings in the modern world, gradations between it and virtually any other prominent style of architecture may be expected.

The first striking relationship between an ideal and the architecture refers to the goals of science. Modernism has continually pushed in the direction of the limits of technical ability, as the tallest, biggest, most awe-inspiring style. As such, it is, along with the space race and the microchip, one of the most evident symbols of the dominance of human beings over nature. The geometric lines of modernism clearly emphasise their opposition to the curves and convolutions that dominate our surrounding natural environment.They represent, therefore, in a brash manner, the replacement of nature with science. This goal has been ascribed to its founders, as in Tafuri's comment that, 'form assumes the task of rendering authentic and natural the unnatural universe of technological precision. And since that universe tends to subjugate nature totally in a continual process of transformation, for Le Corbusier it is the whole anthropo-geographic landscape that becomes the subject on which the reorganisation of the cycle of building production must insist' (1976, p. 126).

The language and ideals of science are appropriated as principles and values. Le Corbusier developed the early stages of his ideas through an approach he called purism. A stated principle of purism was that 'a work of art should induce a sensation of mathematical order, and the means of inducing this mathematical order should be sought amongst universal means' (Benton 1975, p. 89). For Le Corbusier there was to be a scientific system ranging from the smallest modular block from which buildings were 'composed', to the grant plan seen most clearly in his scheme for a city of three million in which the imposition of pattern and geometry over the landscape stands out clearly as a predominant aim.

The explicit legitimation of such work was not often based upon the connotations of the concept of science itself, but rather on that principle which was held as characteristic and essential to the scientific attitude. The key word here was 'objectivity'. The movement that dominated modernism before it was taken over by Le Corbusier and Bauhaus was termed 'Sachlichkeit' or 'The new objectivity'. It was still a major principle several decades later. Banham says of a movement prominent in the 50s: 'Any discussion of brutalism will miss the point if it does not take into

account brutalism's attempt to be objective about "reality" '
(1966, p. 47).

Left to itself as a term, it is hard to know quite what 'objectivity' might mean as a principle of architecture. Its sense develops through its relationship with other terms in this network, such as rationality and honesty. These ideas were already clearly spelled out by Sullivan in 1896 in an article called 'The tall office block artistically considered'. He states that: 'We can succeed in modernising the appearance of things by carrying out the simple intention to be strictly rational, by following the principle of rejecting without exception all forms and ornamentation which a modern factory could not easily manufacture and reproduce' (Benton, p. 18). This statement served two compatible forms of legitimation which in turn were to relate to the principles of 'functionalism' and 'machine aesthetic'.

Rational architecture was that which assimilated the newly developed methods of production and the increasing dominance of factory-based machine-production techniques. Le Corbusier was enthusiastic about what he called the 'mass-production spirit' (Winter 1977, p. 324), the result of which is evident in his buildings. Frampton says of one of his styles: 'The Ville Radieuse type seems to have been orientated towards more economic criteria, that is towards the quantitative standards of serial production' (Frampton 1980, p. 178). For Mies van der Rohe also the aim was 'to generate a culture of simple logical building amenable to refinement and open in principle to the optimum utilisation of industrial technique' (Frampton 1980, p. 237). These statements must be set beside the actual history of the buildings. It was not in fact that modernism was the best consumer of new technical achievements. Where new technical possibilities, as applied for example to the kitchen or bathroom, appeared of clear benefit, these were absorbed quickly and easily in a mass-produced form into the whole profession, neither merely nor particularly into modernist style buildings. Mumford notes that, 'functionalism came forward as a fact long before it was appraised as an idea' (1975, p. 155). It was rather the explicit desire to pronounce on these possibilities as ideals expressed through the architecture that modernism projected. Mumford noted that, 'much of what was masked as strict functionalism or as austere rationalism during the last generation in architecture was in fact a sort of fetishism; an overevaluation of the machine' (1975, p. 157).

The relationship between this functionalism and the equally prominent formalism is curious, since at first glance they might be thought of as contradictory principles. In practice they were not only compatible but mutually reinforcing, because functionalism related far more to the association between architecture and production than between architecture and consumer. Mass production itself is clearly an encouragement to formalism using a modular technique and prefabricated sections. Where other styles used individualist façades to mask such trends in the technology of the profession, modernism proclaimed the modular ideal. In so far as functionalism was supposed to address the 'functions' of the buildings, that is the needs and requirements of the users, this was developed as a utopian rather than a sociological strategy, at an abstracted academic level. Most prominent was

the academic left utopianism found in the constructivist movement in the Soviet Union and in the Bauhaus ethos. These principles had a major impact on Soviet building after the revolution but seem to have gradually declined until under Stalin the architecture reflected no more of a collectivist spirit than that current in the West (Frampton 1980, Chapter 19). As described by Tafuri in his book *Achitecture and Utopia*, 'modern architecture has marked out its fate by making itself, within an autonomous political strategy, the bearer of an ideal of rationalisation in which the working class is only effected in the second instance' (1976, p. 181).

The left principles were commonly a mystification giving legitimacy to what, in effect, was a much stronger and more direct appeal to the architects, that worked through a series of interlocking prestige systems and whose goal lay in the models of art. The architects continually appear to be looking over their shoulders to the artists and the developments in abstraction. Le Corbusier also worked as a painter. Artists such as Klee and Kandinsky were associated with the Bauhaus alongside architects such as Gropius and Mies van der Rohe. Here were the principles that determined the direction taken by the network of associations. One of the most fundamental associations was based in the adage 'Form follows Function', but this only made sense if tied to a corollary that beauty, in turn, follows function, and it is this part of the network that is represented in the 'machine aesthetic' that dominated the modernist movement. Bruno Taut stated as his third principle of the new movement in 1929: 'beauty originates from the direct relationship between building and purpose, from the natural qualities of the material and from elegance of construction' (Benton 1975, p. 171). This stemmed from the deepest roots of modernism in the ideals espoused by William Morris, who affirmed that the form–function relationship should be one of 'honesty' and it was honesty that ensured beauty. The Bauhaus proclaimed in the words of its director, Gropius, that 'we want to create a clear, organic architecture, whose inner logic will be radiant and naked, unencumbered by lying façades and trickeries; we want an architecture adapted to our world of machines, radios and fast motor cars, an architecture whose function is clearly recognised in the relation of its forms' (Benton 1975, p. 124).

These principles had an obvious impact upon the appearance of the buildings that they inspired, by vehemently attacking that which had been traditional about the external appearance of a building and replacing this with a clear new principle. What is opposed is ornament. Ornament was that which made up a façade in its colloquial as well as literal sense. It was this that served to hide the structure of the building. Movements such as Art Nouveau and Art Deco were hiccups in opposition to this general trend away from ornamentation rather than true elements of it (Pevsner 1960). Note the strength of opposition in Gropius' words above, which are taken to still further extremes in the earlier (1908) statement by Loos that 'the evolution of culture is synonymous with the separation of the ornamental from the functional' (Benton 1975, p. 42). Loos equated ornament with crime. In the place of ornamentation should be the honest declaration of structure and materials, the keynote of the brutalist philosophy. Mies van der Rohe went so far as to put fake metal beams on the outside face of a skyscraper when he was, for structural reasons, unable to reveal the encased beams within. The person viewing from outside had to be able to 'see' how the building was made and of what.

Such a policy once again creates another link in the network, this time back to formalism, since it was always decoration and ornament that played a large part in distinguishing various styles. When buildings are reduced to mere plain structural models, a homogeneity inevitably tends to result. The most important result of this trend is towards what Tafuri (1976) calls the 'absolutely asemantic quality' of modernist architecture. In effect, such buildings come to mean nothing other than their own modernist principles, having no external reference. They are formalist in their rejection of context, be it social or geographical. The glass and concrete blocks tell us nothing about whether they are designed for offices or as a hotel, whether we are in Indonesia or South America. This lack of reference makes the category that modernism represents much more flexible. It has none of the 'pragmatic' constraints of most material categories that may be generated initially through formalism but distort towards their particular context. As such, modernism may be associated with that kind of ritualised authority that Bloch (1977) noted uses formalism as a protection from evaluation. It attempts to gain an abstraction and a closure that is beyond critique.

It will be evident by now that modernism effected, in written principle and visual effect, one of the most potent instruments of what the Frankfurt school claims to be the ideology of our age. The buildings represent the largest and most dominant artifacts of our daily experience, either individually or as new city-centres. These artifacts represent science in attempting to impinge on our consciousness as the limits of technical ability and as 'unnatural' imposed geometry. The 'distance' they exhibit is equally a distance from nature, a distance from the human scale and a distance from the irregularity that indicates the individual interpretation of social convention. They thereby equate in practice and as material constraint that which the Frankfurt school have related in social theory. The rationality represented in their austere modular forms is that of technical ability and universalism abstracted away from the pragmatic contextual rationality of ordinary human strategy.

The ability of modernism to encompass the ideology of technical control as a duality of control over the environment and control over people, is fostered by its permeation through the design not only of buildings but also the objects and decoration of its interiors. An example is the often quoted control over the users of Mies van der Rohe's best known office block in New York, where the use of blinds and objects next to the external face of the building is controlled lest it interfere with the image of the whole 'monument' to the outsider. More effective were the Soviet 'super-communes' with their educative intention in reorganising the pattern of daily living with shared corridors, bathrooms and canteens, until they were abandoned under consumer opposition (Frampton 1980, Chapter 19). A model of effectiveness was the 1904 Larkin building by Frank Lloyd Wright, built for a mail-order firm and rationally planned right down to the desks, as noted by Duffy: 'The seat hinged to the clerical desk restricts freedom of movement, saves space, is entirely rational, and effectively expresses the degradation of the clerk' (1980, p. 268). A degree of parallelism between the effect of appearance, of morphology and of interior is evident.

Ideology was not the mere reflection or product of technology, the new forms could always have been decorated, and assimilated without difficulty, as occurs in a genuine vernacular tradition, and as is imitated in the post-modernist style. It was always intended and evidently succeeds in doing more than this. As Breuer noted in 1934, 'The origin of the Modern Movement was not technological, for technology had been developed long before it was thought of. What the New Architecture did was to civilise technology. Its real genesis was a growing consciousness of the spirit of our age' (Benton 1975, p. 181). This is a constant theme of Mumford, who caught the implications in his critique of modernism's principal prophet: 'The monotony of Le Corbusier's favoured forms has expressed the dominant forms of our age, the facts of bureaucratic control and mechanical organisation equally visible in business, in industry, in government, in education' (Mumford 1975, p. 119). What modernism attempted was to render these principles as the natural environment of our daily life. Interaction with them becomes habit, a naturalising context as noted by Benjamin (1973, p. 142), in which progress and shock become expected and assimilated in an anaesthetised and accepting world, which sees those elements of our society that modernism represents as an inevitable condition of existence.

The evidence given here for a connection between building style and ideology has been mainly presented in the form of quotation and written comment. A set of photographs might have been included as a supplement, but in practice these buildings may be viewed from any urban centre today. As such they provide the best evidence for the effectiveness of their embodiment of these principles. There is a separate range of studies which explores how deeply they have penetrated, as a style, particular domains of the building industry. A volume edited by King (1980) provides some historical background, including chapters on the modernist dominance in areas such as hospitals, lunatic asylums, prisons and office blocks. Schools have been radically altered. The first influential example of brutalism in Britain was a school at Hunstanton in Norfolk in 1954 by the Smithsons, and now much copied (Banham 1966, p. 19). This range of institutions is particularly instrumental as an effective carrier of authoritarian principles, even when teachers and other consumers attempt to preserve their traditional patterns despite the inconvenience of the new structure. The architecture of such institutions has become an important exemplifier of the nature of discipline and power analysed by Foucault and described in Chapter 1 (e.g. Foucault 1977).

In new schools and office blocks today, modernism has become nearly ubiquitous. Their impact is equally strong in large-scale, government-built housing projects, again often quoted as exemplary schemes in the architectural literature. The 'alienation' that Marx noted had permeated through to the home as the property of other than its inhabitants, is now forcibly expressed in a style and scale, that being far from the compass of the family or individual, magnifies further this theme. The major point is that in no sense are we dealing here with some academic and esoteric set of ideas that at an abstract level assimilated ideology as representation. Though modernism may have started in such a manner, it has now become the most obvious transformation towards a new representation by people of their own environment, in the last few decades. It is not a reflection but an instrument; the housing projects express a control over their own inhabitants who have no means of transforming that environment in accordance with their own understanding and their own interests. This point would be still more evident in an analysis of morphology as opposed to this consideration of façade and appearance.

The final aspect of modernism that I wish to discuss is the way in which it reflects upon intention. Archaeologists have often cautioned against the hope that prehistoric remains might reveal representation, on the basis that intention is not to be found with the trowel. The scale at which the concept being explored here operates is, however, not to be reduced to individual intention. Figures such as Le Corbusier and Bauhaus are symbols of something that goes far beyond any particular group, as indicated by the sheer extent of its development and the variety of contexts that assimilated it. Indeed one of the most instructive elements of the history of this movement are the several ironies that become apparent when intention is investigated.

Morris, as recognised by Pevsner and others, was the founding figure of many of these ideas; his opposition to what he saw as dishonesty in style was an inspiration adhered to ever after. In a number of respects the political implications of modernism as social control also find their precursors in other styles and trends in the nineteenth century such as Georgian architecture as a representation of culture against nature (Glassie 1975), or the internationalism of the neo-classical. The interesting feature of Morris' role here is that no figure of the last two centuries has been more vehement in his opposition to the machine and to everything that modernism in fact effected, and yet Morris in his opposition to the machine created the style which was later taken as most indicative of the machine age. Wolfe (1982) takes great delight in showing how the very people who paid for many of these new buildings in America actually had an intense dislike of them and of the idea of having to work or live within them. It is hard to find any popular base for the willingness to spend fortunes on such buildings. It is hard to locate the educationist or teacher or pupil who did not need 're-education' to adjust to the glass and concrete formal masses they were to teach in. If there was an explicit moral principle it was most often socialist. The Bauhaus in particular and the Soviet architects favoured these buildings as an educational instrument of socialist thought. It is this association that has led to the idea that modernism is an expression of egalitarian ideals, which will be questioned below. In fact the same style was used in fascist regimes, and these same Bauhaus architects built the major monuments to monopoly capitalism in Manhattan using essentially the same architectural plans.

Exported Soviet realism, as in the much praised High Point buildings of Highgate, London, are now the preserves of the upper middle classes. It is only the architects who consistently strove after these goals as 'architectural' ideals. The extent of their acceptance demands a more complex analysis.

The actual implementation of modernist architecture depended upon a series of interlocking strategies and prestige systems. Within the architectural profession, the drive to increasing abstraction and progress linked into prestige competition is evident in their own writings. In turn, the implications of the large scale modernist buildings as technical achievements made them most suitable as prestigious developments. These might take the form of competition between big business in New York or between local British councils in new housing development, and new city centres, or towards purer forms of revolutionary expression in the Soviet Union. The specific forms of these prestige systems and emulatory patterns are contingent, although their link to rapidly developing fashions in material forms is a product of the nature of such systems (Miller 1982). What is important is that the fundamental expressive quality of the architecture, in relation to the possibilities of technical ability and rational efficient control, were those favoured by the corporations and bureaucracies that employed the architects in every one of these situations.

The above account of modernism as an architectural style seems to fit, in most respects, the model of the underlying authoritarian nature of the contemporary state as outlined by the Frankfurt school. As such it points towards the critique of ideology as outlined in Chapter 1 and as it might be used in archaeological research. It retains the coarse-grained level of large scale alterations in the manner in which human society represents its own form in its material products and in this case in its production of the material environment. Most of the discussion presented would now be regarded as architectural history. The debate within the profession has moved on to a post-modernism, one of whose main aims was to provide the more contextually defined reference, the 'pragmatics', that had been denied in modernism. In practice, the additional deliberately imposed vernacular has been still more desocialised (Habermas 1982). In contrast another style, known as 'high-tech', has developed as the still more explicit metaphor of science and scientific control. Post-modernism in turn is now viewed as dated, and the fashions continue. I would suggest, however, that the general form of architecture that this chapter has so far been concerned with might well subsume many of what the architects take to be distinctive and even opposing styles, in the overall impression of modernistic architecture which the public retains.

This general trend is towards an architecture which expresses technical control, in which the relationship to nature is implicated in the relationship between people exemplifying, but also acting to maintain, relations of dominance and control. Following the Frankfurt school this may be taken as the 'dominant ideology' for our time. Certain cautions were expressed, however, in Chapter 1 as to the possible limitations of this concept as an approach. One of these took the form of a question as to the actual extent to which these ideals maintained a hold over the general population of a given society, but this would require investigation in the individual and contingent circumstance. Recently, there has been a growing literature on the evidence for groups opposing the dominant images in contemporary British society, but these have focused mainly on minority groups such as youth subcultures (e.g. Hall et al. Eds. 1976). One of the most important details about modernism is that most of the new buildings actually constructed have, at least in Britain, never been modernist in style. The division between modernist and non-modernist is most closely associated with, though clearly not always exactly consistent with, the distinction between building at the scale of the individual, residential group as against buildings at a larger scale. What, then, is represented by this distinction, and what explains the persistence of the non-modernist, which in Britain is dominated by the tradition of the suburban semi-detached?

The analysis of suburbia must be carried out alongside an examination of the extent to which modernism is in fact a pervasive feature of current building. Since the development of structuralism, we are alerted to the possibility that the impact of dominance might be expected to be found beyond its own immediate reproduction, since the effect of a new alignment in a semantic space is inevitably to alter all other concepts that share this space and that are redefined in relation to it. Our evidence for the effect of modernism is therefore only in part the extent of its application, and should also be sought in the reaction of other non-modernist architectural styles to it.

Housing in Britain: the high rise block

This review will concentrate on the evidence from Britain this century. The reason for narrowing the focus is that while the modernist style is precisely the 'International' style; most alternative architectural traditions are often best known as local or national. These are more diverse styles, which have assumed the referential load rejected by modernism. Britain differed from many comparable areas in Europe and the United States in two main respects. Firstly at the time of the advent of modernism, a far smaller percentage of its population was living in apartment flats and, secondly, there grew up an unusual degree of governmental control of building. If we lower the scale of architecture being considered, we find the more particular connotations of these building styles varied greatly. In the United States, for example, the history of the apartment block is quite dissimilar to that of Britain. In a review history, Hancock (1980) notes the early importance of such blocks, and their use at all levels of society, becoming an additional instrument in the growth of spatial segregation by wealth, colour, and most recently, age, as well as a common stage in the developmental cycle of the domestic group. In the United States, government subsidy for building has, contrary to its claims, been mainly for the middle and wealthy classes and only in a relatively smaller degree towards welfare building. The dominant images of apartment blocks may be those of the luxury prestigious blocks, as for example in Lakeside Chicago or Manhattan, which may offset the alternative image of the mass tenement estates.

In Britain a different history has resulted in different associations. Although there are many modernist luxury hotels, modernist blocks have mainly been associated with public housing and business concerns. The history of one of the most prominent features of the modernist style, the high rise apartment block, is instructive (Ash 1980, Sutcliffe Ed. 1974). In the initial mass development of low flats three and four storey high in the 1930s, such flats tended not to take up the modernist image and, being at a relatively high rental, were only rarely used for mass housing of the poor (Ravetz 1974). The major impact on British residential housing came with the remarkable rise and fall of the popularity of the high rise flat in the 1960s. Cooney (1974) shows how local councils and central government were drawn into the development of this form of housing, in which their own rivalry for prestige became linked with that of the architects, as also (but later) were private developers. Ash (1980) documents the result of this shift in policy. In 1964 only 7% of the population lived in apartments, although the figure was over 50% for some European countries. The British government, however, not only was responsible for over half the building output but, by the use of subsidies, could effect major changes of building policy in a comparatively short time. Seen as a method of rapid slum-clearance, a shift to subsidies for such high rise blocks had immediate results. Although such flats were 50% more expensive per square foot than ordinary two storey houses, impoverished councils such as Glasgow built them in quantity, because the large government subsidies made them effectively cheaper. This last example was despite the fact that the 1960s were a time of major population-decline in Glasgow and easing of pressure on the land (Smith 1974). The early 1960s saw an ever-increasing percentage of new accommodation of this form, rising to a peak in 1966. The decline of this same style, partly due to public pressure especially following the partial collapse of a block at Ronan Point in 1968 and the removal of subsidies had a dramatic effect leading to the virtual ending of high rise building by 1970.

The point of the high rise is that they, like the lower but equally oppressive estates in areas such as Liverpool (Kirkby) and Manchester (Hulme) with their 'streets in the air' (a claim of the Smithsons), represent an evident arm of state control over the individual. One critique remarked on their alienating properties, seeing them as the architectural equivalent of the filing cabinet (Smith 1974, p. 237). In this case the effect of their morphology is clearly echoed in the equally mechanical style. So blatantly was the style of these estates opposed to the aspirations of their occupants that the results were bound to have an impact on the main housing market. In a sense this effect was not an attribute of modernism itself, the reaction was equally strong to the terraced estates that preceded them. All such government housing had preserved in its form a mark of the faceless homogeneity and unalterable facade that was a direct material representation of the control over the occupant. Since, however, it was the state sector which adopted modernism for residential accommodation, the style took on a new reference.

There were two main areas in Britain in which modernist styles had a major impact: one was the context for the controlling environment, which includes not only the major business premises, but the new blocks for civil service and government departments, hospitals and schools. This might be an instrument of the central government but is equally prominent in the new city centres, built at notorious expense by local councils. The other was the mass of residential housing which was imposed by government. It is in opposition to these two areas that we can best understand the dominant styles of the owner-occupied sector, which still constitutes the majority of British housing.

The suburban tradition

Burnett provides an overall history of suburban housing and concludes: 'In reviewing the history of the middle-class house it is at once obvious that no revolutionary change in preferred housing type occurred over the last century and a half. The ideal continued to be a detached or semi-detached house in a suburban or semi-rural setting' (1976, p. 309). Some minor adjustments occurred in the semi-detached ideal; the present dominant style with its red tiled roof, outside woodwork painted white, and casement windows, seems to have emerged with the development of Golders Green (a suburb of north-west London), after the building of the underground station in 1907, (Jackson 1973), and then spread rapidly over the new suburbs. It remains, however, a continuation of this strange form of housing, a Victorian compromise that allowed for tradesmen to come around the back, and for costs to be kept low while still preserving the appearance of the detached house.

So striking is this conservatism that it demands some explanation. In reviewing the literature on private housing during the period, it becomes increasingly clear that we are faced not with a simple vernacular tradition that persisted regardless of the impact of new forms of architecture, but rather that this conservatism might itself be understandable in precisely the context of an opposition to the new style and the particular areas of housing that it was being applied to. The suburban tradition was quite varied. It included the better terraces, often with bay windows and sash fittings; some influence of the garden cities, which provided a quite different and, from the consumer point of view much more acceptable, form of government housing. There was also a low, often single-storey style which was seen as a 'Scandinavian' look. What all of these had in common was that, in direct opposition to modernism, they depended on decoration and facade. The literature constantly stresses that it was decoration rather than quality which often sold the house, and therefore was of prime concern to the private builder. 'External appearance assumed great importance for it often made the sale: there had to be the strongest possible contrast with the drab, uniform terraces of the inner city streets, a little show, and a hint of the country cottage . . . All attention focused on the superficial; decorative features were paramount' (Jackson 1973, p. 145). It was appearance not quality that mattered. Burnett notes: 'Too often as in the thirties, the detailing was merely crude and clumsy, stuck on to a standard design to give a spurious individuality and,

perhaps to make it abundantly clear that no local council could have authorised such idiosyncrasy' (Burnett 1976, p. 298). Burnett also notes a general trend over the last century – standards in council houses improved and private housing became smaller. This meant that the desire to differentiate grew all the stronger. 'As the size and structure of the two types of dwelling came closer together, it became ever more important to accentuate the identity of the private house by such symbols as distinctive façade and front garden. The occupier himself could further 'personalise' the external appearance of the house in ways not open to the council tenant' (Jackson 1973, pp. 295–6). Conservatism in building style is an element of this relationship, since the state had appropriated in modernism the language of change.

A clear example of this emphasis on contrast is the expansion of owner occupation amongst the working class in the 1930s, when modernism was starting to make an impact in some sectors. Wilkins, surveying the suburban boom in 1934–5, finds there were two main concerns that dominated their appearance and opposed any modernist influence. Buyers wanted a conventional traditional style that did not look 'odd' and, 'in any case, they didn't want their home to look like their place of work, and the building they worked in, was inevitably given an up to date modern image' (Wilkins 1976, p. 79). Secondly, they did not want anyone to mistake their property for a council house, which meant an emphasis on the bay window, the recessed porch and any attributes with which the council houses were not provided. Such an opposition may well have been greatly strengthened by the full appropriation of the modernist style for residential accommodation by the state in the high rise episode of the 1960s.

When one turns to the question of facilities, the mystificatory nature of modernist claims are all the more evident. Modernism was advocated as the inevitable adaptation in style to the new function of the house, and yet, in the recent history of housing, we find the adoption of all the new advantages of the modern age – the indoor bathroom, the electrical appliances, the new-technology kitchen – in a whole range of architectural styles. It was the number of power points that was of importance not the form of the façade (Forty 1975). Not only were such developments compatible with a range of styles, but the effective inertia in the state of architectural aspirations of the consumer appears almost as an affront to the enormous changes in the facilities and functions available to them.

The opposition to modernism may be related to a resultant recontextualisation of the values of the suburban community. A spirited defence of this kind of housing, generalised as the suburb of 'Dunroamin', has recently been published by Oliver et al. (1981). They point out that although this is the form of housing occupied by half the country's population, it has, from its inception, been subject to a torrent of abusive invective from the establishment and particularly from architects. It was condemned as an unremitting homogeneous sprawl, emphasising the most vulgar taste, and expected to turn into slums within a short time. It was said to produce its own alienation and isolation for its inhabitants. This argument was heavily one-sided: 'The printing presses were on the side of the Modernists, when the invective was let loose, but the symbols through which Dunroamin could communicate its values were expressed in the building itself' (1981, p. 157). The authors attempt to interpret the values being expressed in the houses. They see the houses in part as a reaction to the Victorian terrace, the factory, the modernist style and the municipal housing estate, but also see them as a positive affirmation of home, family, stability and individualism (1979, p. 157).

The dominant mode of expression of these values was through their art of ambiguity. Even the language of description betrays this. There are 'the *half* timbered walls of the "*semi*-detached" homes for the "*middle*" classes set on *sub* urban estates' (1981, p. 78). Their position between town and country was emphasised by the extensive use of parks and trees in which to set this urban form. This assertion of a middle way, an abhorrence of what they saw as extremes, allowed for considerable individual expression within this middle area. The suburbs are in fact much less homogeneous than the council estates. The do-it-yourself tradition of individually adapting the buildings adds to an already conscious attempt by the builders to make neighbouring pairs of semis differ in facade, in response to demand. The decoration and furnishings are typically a massing together of various styles and images, and the dominant theme is again multivalency. In organisation they represent the informal 'pragmatics' that is opposed to formal order. The authors argue, with some justification, that it is precisely the ambiguity of the style, the jumble of 'tudorbethan' and art deco, that so affronted the critics, a classic response from the makers of categories to the unplanned and uncontrollable. Ambiguity becomes dirt (Douglas 1966).

The authors of Dunroamin suggest that suburbia has been the most successful housing form of recent history in that there is very little evidence of the isolation and alienation suggested by its critics. They see its success as demonstrated not just in the continuing demand for this type of housing but in the high levels of satisfaction recorded for its inhabitants. The suburbs as they point out are not merely an arena of aspirations, they are also symbols of having 'arrived'. The suburbs have proved responsive to individual expression and have given its inhabitants the stability they demanded. It is hard to deny that the last few decades have been a boom period for the British middle classes.

It would be only too easy to conclude from the success of Dunroamin that the houses represent a justification for the values they express. This is certainly the message of the authors. In particular they echo the idea of its inhabitants that they demonstrate the 'vision of the free individual as against that of the egalitarian community' (1981, p. 121). In this, they represent the general political argument that the failure of state housing and intervention is evidence of the failure of an egalitarian and community ideal. It is at this point that we may turn back to the critique of ideology and the forms of mystification and naturalisation that ideology may employ. Several such processes may be seen at work in this case. Firstly, the individuality of the private housing is contrasted with the communal spirit of the housing estate. It should be clear, however, from the earlier part of this chapter, that state architecture and modernism represent nothing of the kind. There is no evidence that the communities which

inhabit these estates either had any say in their design and construction or would regard them in any sense as the expression of their community. There is nothing 'egalitarian' about them since they were demonstrably imposed on the people who live in them by a hierarchical bureaucracy, and align in style with the office block. What they express are principles of technical control and authority. This has however, been transformed by conservative ideologies and represented as the superiority of individualism over egalitarianism. A transformation which is very clear in the attitudes of the authors of Dunroamin.

A second mystification is the representation of partial interests as the interests of the community as a whole. Suburbia is the housing of a distinct class, the middle class, and is dependent for its success on the various means at the disposal of the middle class, which include financial resources, transport, communications and a general ability to utilise certain facilities now available to them. It is very doubtful that the community represented in the sociological studies of Young and Willmott (1957) could be transplanted into such an environment and react in the same fashion. This would demand not only an equality of resources but also an identity of interests and values. That is to say that, as ideology represents interests, so the suitability of its material manifestations demands an identity of interests also. This normative demand relates not only to class but also to family. The housing form is directed towards the ideologically 'complete' nuclear family, and has never been responsive to the actual demography of the British population, to the elderly or the single parent.

The real nature of the ideology represented by suburbia is however, only apparent when we look for the actual implications of the contrast between it and the housing estate, through which a contrast between classes has become not reduced, but accentuated in recent times. The major contradiction emerges when we ask who has been responsible for the building of the estates and the appropriation of modernism. The answer lies not in a given political category – the international style as we have seen has been taken up by every part of the political spectrum. Modernist state architecture in Britain was promoted by precisely the kind of individuals who inhabit the suburbs and in some cases the larger fully detached houses. These acts were committed, however, in their other capacity as bureaucrats, decision makers and controllers of finance. The real contradiction of modern housing is of a more profound form than even the conflict between classes. It expresses the conflict between the two aspects of the same individuals in the modern world, on the one hand acting as agents of large scale institutions and on the other hand acting in relative autonomy. The same individual may choose a semi-detached for his or her family and a modernist housing estate as an agent working within the state. This is the irony that Wolfe makes so much of in his attack on modernism. It is part of the 'tragedy' of modern objectification analysed at the turn of the century by Simmel (1968), in terms of the autonomy of the creations of culture.

Habermas has recently noted the importance of the tradition modernism represented as a response to the gulf that had opened between form and function, given the massive changes in production in the nineteenth century. He sees it as having been a necessary response to the growing 'neurosis' that had developed (1982, p. 12). In his emphasis he is attempting to defend this tradition against the kind of neo-conservatism that espoused the critique of modernism and supported neo-vernacular tendencies in post-modernist architecture. Modernism did not, however, resolve this 'neurosis' which lies deeper in the kind of structural divisions that Simmel noted. Thus what has been often glossed here as 'peoples', 'classes', 'values' and 'interests' derive their form and meaning from the problematic nature of modern culture itself. This, when examined over a longer time-period can be seen to transcend the political stances held by those who have taken part in the debate and practice of modern architecture.

The present situation indicates the complexity of ideological constructions. On the one hand, many of those who live in detached and semi-detached houses by and large feel that this style of housing constitutes a successful environment for them. The people who live in council housing estates by and large feel that these are disastrous, especially when they have adopted a modernist appearance and high rise morphology. One group has managed to produce an environment in accordance with their interests, the other has not. The values that are expressed in suburban housing are of individuality and tradition, linked to conservatism. These values do not, however, exist as aspirations in the abstract. They are in the main, not developed as coherent in themselves, but are identified in their opposition to another set of values, which are seen as communal and egalitarian and are linked to the authoritarian practice. It is here we may detect another twist to the cycle of ideology.

The values expressed in suburban housing depend not only upon their isolated presence, but also on the form in which the values they are opposed to are constructed. It is clearly in the interests of the maintenance of these values to control also the dominant representation of the values to which these are opposed. The structure of the modern British state means that those who value that which is represented by the suburban tradition also control the style of the office blocks, the factories and the state housing. By using modernist style and high rise morphology for this last group, an association is established between this sector and the ideal of change with its opposition to the traditional. The buildings being modular and not being amenable to alteration by the individuals who inhabit them, they can also be associated with the communal values and egalitarian principles. Most important they may then be associated with the authoritarian principles that these buildings represent. In this manner, we have a material construction which in itself suggests that communal and egalitarian values are closely associated with authoritarian prctice and with a radical break from traditional values. This effectively denies any attempt by an inhabitant of these estates to suggest that communal values may actually themselves represent a measure of that tradition which they value and deem to be opposed to authoritarian principles. In effect, the people who manifest authority in their practice have managed to disassociate themselves from this practice of authority and

associate it rather with the very people who are controlled by the authoritarian act.

It is this contradiction which in part explains the failure of the so called neo-vernacular, one of the major post-modernist styles. This was a deliberate attempt to retain some of the referential qualities of an architecture not designed by architects, but within planned projects. Habermas associates it with the neo-historicism of modern conservatism (Habermas 1982, p. 14). In this change we may detect a shift in the mechanism of ideology. Previously ideology worked through naturalisation, in which a relatively strong expression of authoritarian principles attempted to constitute the local environment to the extent that it appears as the natural order of things. The shift is back to a new mystification, in which most of the morphological elements of the estates are retained, but the detailing is now hidden in a façade that is supposed to represent a more responsive look. In practice, this neo-vernacular is still an imposed styling, which expresses the role of the architect as an instrument of authority.

As indicated earlier, the scale of this analysis crosscuts the declared intentionality of the social actors. The people involved in these contradictions have ascribed to a variety of political objectives, the right and left have been fairly equal in their approval of the modernist constructions described (and now in their disapproval). The contradiction analysed is evident in that which is manifested in the buildings themselves and the observed choices made in residential patterns of the people involved. The activities which appear 'instrumentalist' in analysis need not be equated with intention of the social actors. The nature of these contradictions is found not only in the area of buildings. Raymond Williams suggested in his analysis of the media in 1961 that it was quite common for the group who most loudly condemned what they claimed was the 'vulgarisation' of culture in 'mass' or 'working-class' culture, to include the very people who created much of the 'mass' culture in their image of that class (Williams 1961).

Conclusion

For the archaeologist it is the excavated analogy of the actual patterns of building styles which provide the evidence for the kinds of relationships under consideration. This chapter began with the analysis of textual evidence, through which many of the ideals of the modernist architects were expressed. It is evident, however that the buildings themselves are equally eloquent and may even deny the declared intentions of their builders. The materials used in the façades, the plate-glass sheets and chromium steel, the masses of reinforced concrete, the extent to which these express externally and oppose any form of ornamentation are signs of modernism. The geometry of the buildings, their straight lines, their modular form and their size complement the messages of their materials. When the discussion turned from modernist to suburban housing, the evidence became still more dependent upon the appearances of the housing. No comparable analysis of written texts is possible since there are few architects who are prepared to declare the values which they see expressed in this form.

A critical analysis of modern architecture works in a manner not dissimilar from archaeological interpretation. It is the material correspondences between the worlds of business, state offices and the housing estate, and in turn their architectural opposition to suburbia, which provide the basis for the critique. In this chapter, as in the archaeological cases of Chapters 5–8, the analysis depends on the uncovering of evidence for authority, and for the control of that which is represented in the material environment, and its effects upon society. At first glance, the differences in analysis may seem enormous, and indeed the historical context in which the analysis is set is dissimilar in the extreme from the examples set in prehistory. Nevertheless there are structural parallels in the use of the concept of ideology to uncover the mode by which authority is constituted.

In the chapters based on archaeological evidence, the emphasis is on the way in which the relationships between people gain their asymmetrical form by reference to an authority exemplified in the relationships between people and the super-natural, whether this be the authority of the lineage or that of deities. The contemporary analysis does not rely on a relationship to the supernatural, but there are linkages at a structural level between the mechanism by which authority is constituted and implemented. Institutionalised authority depends upon the establishment of values which are beyond the scope of individual people and indeed oppose the scale of the individual. Authority is usually, therefore projected in a ritualised mode, involving a scale beyond the individual generation and often a power that transcends the individual experience. Hierarchical relationships between people are thereby manifested as relationships between a person and something that transcends their own individuality. The sense in which lineage or religious forms of representation are 'institutionalised' in the practices observed by archaeologists may be related to the modern institutions from which this metaphor is derived. The institutions of authority in the contemporary state also work in a manner by which they oppose themselves to the scale of the individual and deny the people by whom they are constituted. In the four archaeological examples presented in this volume this 'institution' is cosmological, grounded in ritual practice, whereas in the contemporary case the institution takes a material form and is grounded in practical social relations. Despite their obvious differences, they are similar in that both become the basis and the metaphor for concepts of authority, the dominant models by which the notion of authority is understood and made legitimate.

Acknowledgement

I would like to thank Rickie Burman and Rickie Burdett for their comments on this paper.

Bibliography

Ardener, S. Ed. (1981) *Women and Space*, Croom Helm, London

Ash, J. (1980) 'The rise and fall of high rise housing in England', in C. Ungerson and V. Karn Eds., *The Consumer Experience of Housing*, Gower, Farnborough

Banham, R. (1960) *Theory and Design in the First Machine Age*, The Architectural Press, London

Banham, R. (1966) *The New Brutalism*, The Architectural Press, London

Benjamin, W. (1973) 'The work of art in the age of mechanical reproduction', in *Illuminations*, Fontana, London

Benton, T. and Benton, C. (1975) *Form and Function*, Crosby Lockwood Staples, London

Bloch, M. (1977) 'The past and the present in the present', *Man* 12, pp. 278–92

Bourdieu, P. (1971) 'The Berber house or the world reversed', in J. Pouillon and P. Maranda Eds., *Échanges et Communications*, Mouton, The Hague

Burnett, J. (1976) *A Social History of Housing*, David and Charles, Newton Abbot

Cooney, E. (1974) 'High flats in local authority housing in England and Wales since 1945', in A. Sutcliffe Ed., *Multi-storey Living*, Croom Helm, London

Douglas, M. (1966) *Purity and Danger*, Routledge and Kegan Paul, London

Duffy, F. (1980) 'Office buildings and organisational change', in A. King Ed., *Buildings and Society*, Routledge and Kegan Paul, London

Forty, A. (1975) *The Electric Home*, Open University Press, Milton Keynes

Frampton, K. (1980) *Modern Architecture: A Critical History*, Thames and Hudson, London

Gardiner, S. (1974) *Le Corbusier*, Fontana, London

Gilsenan, M. (1982) *Recognising Islam*, Croom Helm, London

Glassie, H. (1975) *Folk Housing in Middle Virginia*, University of Tennessee Press, Knoxville

Habermas, J. (1970) 'Technology and science as ideology' in *Towards a Rational Society*, Beacon Press, Boston

  (1982) 'Modernism and post-modernism', *9H* 4, pp. 9–15

Hall, S. et al. (1976) *Resistance through Rituals*, Hutchinson, London

Hancock, J. (1980) 'The apartment house in urban America', in A. King Ed., *Buildings and Society*, Routledge and Kegan Paul, London

Jackson, A. (1973) *Semi Detached London*, Allen and Unwin, London

King, A. (1976) *Colonial Urban Development*, Routledge and Kegan Paul, London

  Ed. (1980) *Buildings and Society*, Routledge and Kegan Paul, London

Marcuse, H. (1964) *One Dimensional Man*, Routledge and Kegan Paul, London

Miller, D. (1982) 'Structures and Strategies: An aspect of the relationship between social hierarchy and cultural change, in I. Hodder Ed., *Symbolic and Structural Archaeology*, Cambridge University Press

Mumford, L. (1975) *Architecture as a Home for Man*, Architectural Record Books, New York

Oliver, P., Davis, I. and Bentley, I. (1981) *Dunroamin: the Suburban Semi and its Enemies*, Barrie and Jenkins, London

Panofsky, E. (1957) *Gothic Architecture and Scholasticism*, World Press, New York

Pevsner, N. (1960) *Pioneers of Modern Design*, Penguin, Harmondsworth

Piper, J. (1979) 'The spatial structure of Suchindram', *Art and Architecture Research Papers*, 17, pp. 65–80

Ravetz, A. (1974) 'From working class tenement to modern flat: local authorities and multi-storey housing between the wars', in A. Sutcliffe Ed., *Multi-storey Living*, Croom Helm, London

Simmell, G. (1968) *The Conflict in Modern Culture and other Essays*, Teachers College Press, New York

Smith, R. (1974) 'Multi-dwelling Building in Scotland 1750–1970', in A. Sutcliffe Ed., *Multi-storey Living*, Croom Helm, London

Tafuri, M. (1976) *Architecture and Utopia: Design and Capitalist Development*, MIT Press, Cambridge, Mass.

Wilkins, B. (1976) 'The owner occupier boom in domestic architecture', in T. Faulkner Ed., *Design 1900–1960*, PETRAS, Newcastle upon Tyne

Williams, R. (1961) *Culture and Society*, Penguin, Harmondsworth

Winter, J. (1977) 'Le Corbusier's technological dilemma', in R. Walden Ed., *The Open Hand*, MIT Press, Cambridge, Mass.

Wolfe, T. (1982) *From Bauhaus to Our House*, Jonathan Cape, London

Young, R. and Willmott, D. (1957) *Family and Kinship in East London*, Routledge and Kegan Paul, London

PART THREE

Ideology and power in prehistory

Chapter 5

**Burials, houses,
women and men in
the European Neolithic**
Ian Hodder

A summary of the main approaches to the study of megaliths reveals how recent processal work that relates them to general principles fails to deal with the specificity of their variability, and their particular historical context. A systematic comparison between central and western European megaliths and central European long-houses in the 5th and 4th millennia reveals eight points of similarity. It is suggested that the tombs represent a transformation of the houses. This may be understood in relation to a transformation in the productive base and social organisation of the period. The specific form of the houses is related to the marking out and naturalisation of the position of women, and the importance of lineages at a time when labour was the key factor in the productive system. When the scarcity of land becomes predominant over the scarcity of labour, the emphasis changes from the domestic context of the home to the mediating properties of the supernatural expressed in the tombs, for control over the lineage. The evidence for Central and Atlantic Europe is compared.

The history of research on the megalithic monuments of western Europe provides a clear illustration of the deleterious effects of the split between historical and processual approaches in archaeology. In this paper, some of these effects will be illustrated, but then, using essentially the same material, an alternative approach will be examined. A perspective that treats the evidence as ideologically informed representations can resolve the previous dichotomies and indicate the potential in the study of prehistoric social relations. Initially the Neolithic tombs and monuments were seen as caused by a spread of megalith builders or of the megalithic idea (Montelius 1899; Childe 1925, 1957; Crawford 1957; Daniel 1958). For example, Piggott (1965, p. 60) saw the adoption or propagation of the collective chambered tombs linked to a spread of new religious ideas, and the link between megaliths, frameworks of ideas and world pictures continues to be stressed by, for example, Kinnes (1981, p. 83). Recently, however, some archaeologists have criticised this use of historical and distributional arguments and have suggested that the occurrence of megaliths cannot simply be explained in cultural terms (for example, Chapman 1981, p. 72). In some of these more recent works there has been a tendency to be concerned mainly with generalisations, such as the use of megaliths as markers of territory, or of social and economic tensions. This has had the effect of removing megaliths and neolithic burials from their historical context in western Europe, and from the domain of the ideological, by which I refer to meaningful social action and negotiation within specific historical contexts.

Several writers have emphasised the role of Neolithic megalithic monuments in western Europe as social centres (Case 1969; Fleming 1972, 1973; Reed 1974; Kinnes 1975; Whittle 1977; Jarman, Bailey and Jarman 1982). Specifically reacting against diffusionist arguments Renfrew (1976) has suggested a social role for the tombs as territorial markers in segmentary societies. A central question posed concerned the restricted occurrence of megaliths on the 'Atlantic façade' – western Europe (France, Britain, Spain, Portugal, Netherlands), northwest Europe (Scandinavia and north Germany), and the western Mediterranean (south France, Italy and the west Mediterranean islands). Renfrew suggested that territorial markers were needed in this area because of greater population stress which itself had two sources. First, the westward spread of the Neolithic was halted by the Atlantic coast such that birth rates had to be cut back as population reached its saturation point. Excess population could no longer split off and expand westwards. The resulting social stress was further aggravated by a second factor, the existing high levels of hunter-gatherer-fisher populations in the rich coastal and estuarine regions. These two conditions led to the building of tombs for the ancestors to act as foci for equivalent segmentary units.

Chapman's (1981) anti-diffusionist arguments are based on an hypothesis suggested by Saxe (1970) and Goldstein (1980) and it is claimed that interment in cemeteries or monuments will emerge in periods of imbalance between society and critical resources. Late Mesolithic cemeteries, Neolithic central European cemeteries, and the megaliths of western Europe are seen as related to increasing territorial behaviour and the use and/or control of crucial but restricted resources.

The first problem with such arguments is that it appears difficult, if not impossible, to identify social stress or restricted resources in the general terms used by Renfrew and Chapman. In reference to Renfrew's argument there is no evidence that demographic stress was greater in Atlantic Europe than in central Europe. There is good evidence of concentrated Mesolithic occupation in areas which do not have megaliths (for example Geupel 1981, and in southeast Europe, Srejovic 1972). The adoption of agriculture in western Europe was often different from that in central Europe (there is evidence for slow and gradual adoption in Britain, and in south France where cereals were not cultivated until well after the first animal domesticates) and the rate of population growth (if any proves to have occurred) is unknown. Certainly there is no evidence for higher population-densities in western than in central Europe. Indeed, during the period of megalithic monument construction (approximately 4th to 2nd millennia BC), much of the clearest evidence we have of 'filling-up' of the environment and dense occupation comes from central Europe (Kruk 1980; Sielman 1972; Meier-Arendt 1965). Chapman recognises this fact and suggests that both the megaliths of western Europe and the inhumation cemeteries of central Europe are like responses to an imbalance between society and critical resources. But how is one to recognise territorial behaviour and the use and control of restricted resources? Almost by definition, all societies and all animal species have such characteristics. Certainly, following Meillassoux (1972 – adequately criticised by Woodburn 1980), one of Chapman's own sources, one would expect all agricultural societies to have a need to control restricted resources.

But it is not so much the lack of evidence of social and economic stress, territoriality and restricted resources that is my concern here, and I will be using the same sources of evidence in the interpretation to be offered in this paper. Rather, the second and more important criticism concerns the weak link between burial, megalithic monuments and the processes described. In Renfrew's model, it is not at all clear how megalithic monuments helped to control the birth rate. Any marker or inhumation cemetery could have functioned as a focus or as a symbol of the ancestors. Chapman's arguments are very general and his hypothesis is described as being as relevant to Lepenski Vir, where burial under houses is referred to as indicating formal disposal areas (1981, p. 75), as to inhumation cemeteries and megalithic monuments. It is even implied that a role similar to formal burial is played by enclosed habitation sites (*ibid.*, p. 78). As Kinnes (1981, p. 86) remarks, 'a central place for any social group might be a mortuary site: equally it could be any other structure, boulder or tree'. In both Renfrew's and Chapman's and in other work of this type, the megalithic monuments lose most of their specificity. Megaliths are seen as indicating more social stress and acting as better foci than other types of burial, and in the Saxe and Goldstein model, the formal burial is seen as legitimating control of resources by reference to the ancestors. But large enclosed settlements, significant points in the physical landscape, distinctive portable artifacts or enclosed urned cremation cemeteries might have done equally well. The megalithic monuments have not really been explained at all.

Closely linked to this second point is a third, that no attempt is made in recent, 'processual' studies, to account for the form of the megalithic monuments themselves (see, however, Fleming 1973). While there is great variation in type of monument, most authors cite general similarities in passage and gallery graves and associated art and ritual which occur in many, if not all, the various areas where Neolithic megalithic monuments are found. There are round mounds, rectangular and trapezoidal mounds. There are earthen and stone barrows, timber and stone chambers.

There is often, but not always, evidence of multiple interments, excarnation of the bodies prior to burial in the tombs and of careful arrangement of the bones. The facades of the tombs are often elaborate, and are associated with high artifact densities while in many cases, few artifacts are found within the tombs. The tombs are often orientated in specific directions. Widespread similarities are not just a late phenomenon but occur at an early stage, for example at Hoedic and Teviec. All this detail, and much more, is lost in the cross-cultural, processual approach that has been applied recently. The explanations provided have been inadequate because there is a disproportionate amount of information that has to be left aside.

The processual studies of Renfrew and Chapman and the others cited above have been widely accepted and discussed, but in view of the criticisms above it is argued here that alternative explanations must be sought. The inability of recent interpretations to account for the megalithic monuments of western Europe derives, in this author's view, from the artificial split made in archaeology between history and process. It will become clear in this article that a previous generation of archaeologists attracted by the megalithic problem (such as Childe, Clark, Daniel, Piggott), but dubbed diffusionist, historical or even culturalist by processual archaeologists were concerned with megaliths as megaliths. They did consider the monuments in their own right within a specific historical context. They attempted to explain the shape, orientation and content of the tombs and the tomb ritual. However inadequate their results, the meaning of the tombs and monuments themselves was considered. More recently archaeologists moved to an opposite and more extreme position in which the meaning of the tombs, what they signified in a particular historical context, was entirely disregarded.

This reaction against a consideration of specific cultural meaning necessarily led to a failure of the attempts at a processual and functional explanation. The processual explanations could not cope with the richness of information relating to the things to be explained. Since one had no idea what, for example, the shape of the tomb meant in its particular historical context, one could have absolutely no idea of how it might have functioned. Even if one was content only to explain the fact that megaliths existed, there could again be no successful outcome. It can *never* be possible to 'test' the hypothesis, or support the analogy, that the tombs functioned as territorial markers or legitimated rights to resources without also having some hypothesis concerning the meaning of the tombs in the society and time period concerned. The tombs and monuments of the Neolithic in western Europe had symbolic associations and meanings and this meaningful context must be considered if we are to understand how they worked within social processes. But equally, archaeologists working within an historical and cultural framework had limited success because symbolic meaning was discussed with limited reference to social process, function and legitimation. It is the divide between the consideration of history and particular symbolic meanings on the one hand and the consideration of process and function on the other, a divide set up and encouraged by the 'new archaeology' of the sixties and seventies (Hodder 1982a),

which has held back explanation in archaeology. The problem of the megaliths of western Europe is just one example of the difficulties that have arisen. Any rigorous and adequate explanation must allow that symbolic meaning and social process are actively and recursively related and must apply integrated social models.

In particular, the dichotomy set up between meaning and function had the effect that ideology became a problematic area of enquiry which could have no successful issue. There has, of course, been a recent increase in attempts made within a processual framework to discuss ideology and legitimation, and the hypothesis of Saxe concerning the use of burial to legitimate access to resources, and applied by Chapman to European Neolithic burials, is an example of such developments. But, as already indicated, such a framework tends to relegate ideology to an epiphenomenon of the assumed primacy of functional contingencies and does not adequately consider the particular symbolic meanings of the monuments and rituals. The Saxe hypothesis not only presents a relatively passive view of society, but also, and more clearly, it disregards the cultural context so central to ideology and ideological functions. When individuals act socially, and represent their actions to others, they necessarily do so within a framework of meaning, and this framework is relative and historically constructed. Without consideration of the cultural context one cannot hope to understand the effects of past social actions.

While a number of recent articles have examined megalithic monuments as symbolic and as socially active, legitimating internal social strategies (Shennan 1982; Gilman 1976; Tilley 1981; Shanks and Tilley 1982; Hodder 1982b), they have again failed adequately to consider the particularity of the historical context in which megaliths are found. It is the aim of this article, however, first to demonstrate that there is considerable evidence that many of the earthen and chambered tombs of western Europe referred symbolically to earlier and contemporary houses in central Europe and, to a lesser extent, in western Europe (Fig. 1). The tombs signified houses. To examine the significance of this symbolic association it will then be necessary to assess the symbolic and social context of long-houses in central Europe. It will be shown that there is evidence for elaboration of domestic space and that this elaboration of houses and domestic pottery increases and then decreases through time into the later Neolithic. It will be argued that the type of house and pottery symbolism identified in the central European early and middle Neolithic is appropriate in a social context where primary social strategies revolve around male–female relationships, which are themselves linked to competition between lineages for control of labour. It will be argued that long-barrow burial and long-houses are two ways of coping with and involving material culture in similar social strategies and that the existence of the long-mound tradition can only be partially explained in terms of adaptive behaviour. Rather, the way megaliths were involved actively in social strategies in western Europe depended on an existing historical context. The existence of the tombs, their form and function can only be adequately considered by assessing their value-laden meanings within European Neolithic society.

Tombs and houses

Many timber and stone chambered tombs in Atlantic
Europe are enclosed within a rectangular or trapezoidal mound
(Fig. 2). The apparent similarity between these shapes and the
plans of Linearbandkeramik (LBK), Stichbandkeramik (SBK),
Lengyel and Rössen houses in central and east-central Europe in
the 5th and 4th millennia BC (Fig. 3) has been noted by many
scholars, although significantly not by those explicitly espousing a
processual view (Renfrew 1976; Chapman 1981) or an ecological
approach (Jarman, Bailey and Jarman 1982). Daniel (1965, p. 86)
speculated that Oscar Montelius may not have been so wrong in
thinking that the European passage graves may have been lithic
funerary versions of wooden dwelling-houses. Childe (1949a),
Sprockhoff (1938) and Glob (1949) compared the long cairns
and barrows of northern and north-central Europe with long
houses. The use of LBK houses as a model for the long-mound
tradition has been suggested by Case (1969), Ashbee (1970),
Whittle (1977, p. 221), Kinnes (1981, p. 85), Powell *et al.* (1969)
and a detailed case has been made by Reed (1974) and Marshall
(1981). Grahame Clark (1980, p. 96) noted that the trapezoidal
burial mounds of Brittany and Kujavia recall domestic house
structures associated with the Lengyel culture of north-central
Europe and the trapezoidal houses of the Iron Gates on the lower
Danube.

The long-houses of central Europe cover the late 5th and
4th millennia BC. The earth and stone long-barrows on the other
hand cover the later part of the 4th millennium and continue in
use in different areas into the late 3rd and early 2nd millennia BC.
Reference to formal similarities between the houses and tombs
thus implies transformation from the houses to the tombs. In the
anti-diffusionist framework within which some archaeologists
have recently worked the stylistic similarities between houses and
tombs have either been disregarded, as we have seen, or various
alternative and more functional explanations of 'coincidental'

similarities have been sought (Fleming 1973). It is necessary,
therefore, to go beyond the numerous general statements of
affinity and to show that there are sufficient numbers of
similarities between houses and tombs to make the 'null
hypothesis' of no diffusion appear unreasonable. But it is of
interest to note at the outset that the similarities between long-
houses and long tombs are such that Barkaer, long thought to be
a site containing long-houses, has recently been convincingly
reinterpreted as a site with long burial-mounds (Glob 1975;
Madsen 1979).

Since long-houses and long burial-mounds overlap
chronologically in the second half of the 4th millennium BC, it is
in the cultures of that period in central and east-central Europe
that we should search for the closest parallels for the burial
monuments of Atlantic Europe. Both the Rössen and Lengyel
cultures of central and east-central Europe respectively continue
into this period and both have rectangular and trapezoidal long-
houses. It is the construction and shape of these houses that
provide the first two specific parallels for the Atlantic long burial-
mounds (see Figs. 2 and 3). First, timber long-barrows either
have continuous bedding trenches for the walls or lines of posts,
or some mixture of the two, and the same variety is found for the
houses. Second, Soudsky (1969) suggests that the distinctive
trapezoidal house form develops only after the early Neolithic in
central Europe, and it is clearly associated with the SBK, Rössen
and Lengyel contexts. However, some LBK houses at Elsloo,
Netherlands, already begin to show a trapezoidal form. For the
tombs, Fussell's Lodge long-barrow, dated to the second half of
the 4th millennium BC, has traces of vertical timbers in its
trapezoidal enclosure and must have looked from the outside
very similar to the trapezoidal timbered houses of central Europe.
Earthen long-barrows are generally trapezoidal in shape in
Britain and more triangular in Poland. Trapezoidal barrows are
also known from Denmark and north Germany but in these areas
rectangular barrows are more common (Madsen 1979, 318) and
can be compared with the rectangular long-houses which continue
in use alongside the trapezoidal forms. Trapezoidal cairns, limited
by a wall or by boulders, are found in Britain in the Severn-
Cotswold group, Clyde, Irish Court cairns and in the Orkney-
Cromarty long cairns. There are also examples to parallel the
rectangular earth barrows (Ashbee 1970, p. 90). Rectangular and
trapezoidal chambered cairns also occur in Brittany and the Paris
Basin.

While the rectangular and trapezoidal shapes of the houses
and barrows can be compared, it should be emphasised that the
formal similarities do not imply equivalence of size. Reed (1974,
p. 46) notes that while the lengths of a good many south English
long barrows fall comfortably within the range of LBK and
Rössen long houses, most long barrows are about twice the width
and length of most long houses. Marshall (1981) in a detailed
quantitative study has shown that the earthen long-barrows, the
gallery graves of the Severn-Cotswold group and of the Scottish-
Irish group are generally larger and wider than the trapezoidal
long houses but that the ratio between length and maximum
width is similar, especially when comparing the trapezoidal

Fig. 1. The distribution of Neolithic chambered tombs in Atlantic
Europe (horizontal shading) and the distribution of Bandkeramik
settlements and finds, with long houses (vertical shading).

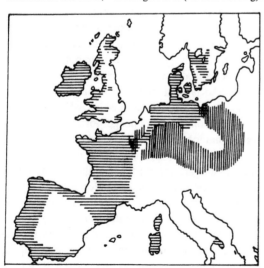

houses and the gallery graves. Thus the tombs studied are normally larger than the houses but they retain the same shape.

A further point of comparison between houses and tombs concerns orientation, since both generally have their long axis aligned E–W or NW–SE. However, it is first necessary to consider the position of the entrance of the houses and tombs. This is normally at the broader end of the trapezoidal houses, and the main burial chamber and entrance façade in the long barrows are also at the broader end although, in certain cases, other burial chambers in the barrow can be entered from the side. It is at the broad end of the trapezoidal houses that breaks occur in the wall foundations, and an entrance is clearly visible in this position at Postoloprty (Fig. 3). The highest concentrations of artifacts occur outside the presumed entrance at the wider end of the trapezoidal long houses at Brzesc Kujawski (Bogucki and Grygiel 1981). While it is possible that the tombs are broader and higher at one end in order to accommodate the stone or wooden chamber, rather than because of any formal similarity with trapezoidal long houses, such an argument ignores the orientation of the buildings: that the broader end of the trapezoidal tombs and houses is generally towards the east or southeast.

Madsen (1979, p. 318) notes that in Britain, Poland, north

Germany and Denmark the broader end of the trapezoidal earthen long barrows is to the east. In Britain Hoare noted in 1812 that the earthen long barrows had the broad end pointing to the east. In Brittany the entrances of the passage graves are generally to the south-east especially in the case of the long passaged dolmens (L'Helgouach 1965, pp. 76–9). The entrances of the gallery graves in the same area are to the east. The Cotswold-Severn tombs mainly face towards the east and in Shetland the entrances face east or southeast, as do the stalled Orkney cairns. Burl (1981) provides other examples of the overall tendency for the broader ends of trapezoidal mounds or the entrances of rectangular or circular passage grave mounds to face east. This is not to say that exceptions do not exist. The Clava passage graves and ring cairns of north-east Scotland generally face south-west and the chambered tombs on Arran show no preferred orientation. However, the overall tendency, particularly of long barrows, is for the entrance and the broader end to face east and south-east (Fig. 4). Soudsky (1969) has demonstrated that the broader end of trapezoidal long houses faces south-east, in the quadrant between 90 ° and 180° from north. The rectangular long-houses are, like the tombs and trapezoidal houses, orientated NW–SE (see Marshall 1981 for quantitative data). But the

Fig. 2. Long mound burial. (a) The structural sequence at Fussell's Lodge. (b) The structural sequence at Kilham. (Source: Kinnes 1981).

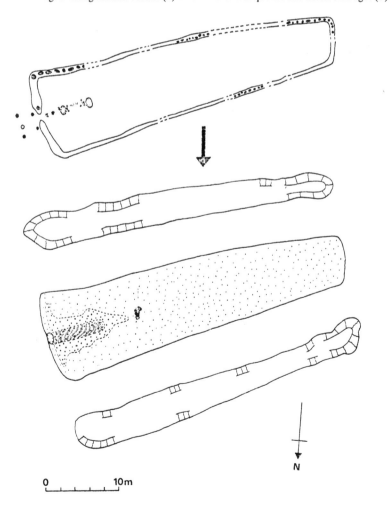

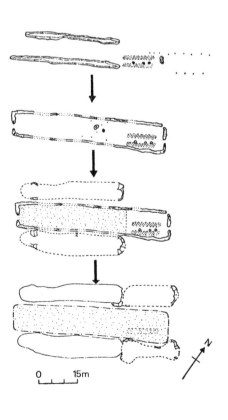

location of the entrance(s) in these houses has not been determined with any certainty. In view of the similarity with trapezoidal houses it would seem likely that the entrance is at the south-east end. Certainly, it is the north-western end which often has a continuous bedding trench, while the sides are often flanked by continuous ditches from which it is presumed that earth was taken to form the daub walls. Thus it seems likely that the south-eastern portion of the rectangular long-houses contained the entrance, and 4th millennium BC models of houses have the entrance at one shorter end (Piggott 1965, p. 46). However, a side entrance has at times been claimed for LBK long-houses with the 'Y' posts in the central section of the house being used to frame a door (Meyer-Christian 1976). Startin (1978) suggests that the 'Y' posts functioned as a brace against lateral winds and there is no evidence of an entrance in the central side area.

Thus, the third point of similarity between long-houses and long barrows is that the entrance in the trapezoidal forms is at the broader end, while the fourth similarity is that the entrances of the trapezoidal and rectangular forms generally face the east or south-east. The fifth point is that there is considerable elaboration of the entrance itself. The long barrows and passage graves frequently have large façades, with 'horns' pointing forwards from the entrance, forecourts and antechambers. There is often evidence for rituals and offerings in the forecourt area, leading to a distinction between the outer, entrance area with many artifacts, and the inner tomb frequently with few artifacts to accompany the skeletal remains. The entrance is often blocked by massive boulders, but may equally be a 'false' entrance, the real entrance being to the side of the mound. Many of these characteristics are found in both stone and earthen barrows. Wooden

Fig. 3. Ground plans of long houses from Neolithic Europe. 1. Postoloprty, Czechoslovakia. 2. Brzesc Kujawski, Poland. 3. Biskupin, Poland. 4. Aldenhoven, Germany. 5. Zwenkau, Germany. 6–7. Geleen, Netherlands. (Source: Marshall 1981)

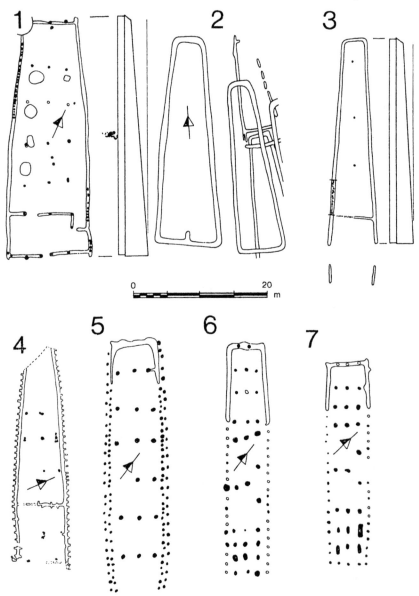

porches which have been effectively blocked by posts, as at Fussell's Lodge, recall the so-called 'false-portals' of the Severn-Cotswold laterally-chambered stone long barrows (Ashbee 1970, p. 92). There is a similar emphasis on façades and most of the Scandinavian earthen barrows have a substantial transverse bedding trench in the eastern end holding a timber façade. In Britain and Scandinavia the façade sometimes has projections at the sides forming 'horns' (e.g. Lindebjerg (Madsen 1979), East Heslerton, Skendleby and Willerby Wold (Ashbee 1977)). These various characteristics are also found in the long-houses of central Europe. Side projections or 'horns' at the broader, eastern end of trapezoidal long houses are found at, for example, Inden-Lamersdorf, Zwenkau and Brzesc Kujawski (Soudsky 1969) and a distinct entrance area has been identified at Postoloprty and Biskupin (*ibid.*). Occupation horizons have almost everywhere been removed by later land use but, as already noted, the late Lengyel sites of Brzesc Kujawski and Biskupin in the Polish lowlands have the highest concentrations of refuse pits near the entrance.

There is good evidence of a tripartite division of the long-houses which can to some extent be paralleled in the tombs. It has long been recognised that LBK houses are divided into three sections although the central section may occur on its own or with only one of the two end sections. In line with the fifth point made above, the clearest division of the trapezoidal long-houses is that which separates the room at the entrance or the entrance area from the inner portion of the house. For example, in the Rössen trapezoidal house at Deiringsen-Ruploh (Günther 1973) a clear division occurs one third of the way into the house. At Postoloprty the interior area with four hearths is partitioned off from the entrance room (Soudsky 1969). In his review of the trapezoidal long house Soudsky notes that many show no evidence of any internal divisions, but where there is one it is tripartite, with antechamber, central main room and store at the back. At Bochum-Hiltrop, for example, there is a partition separating off the back third of the house. The smaller Rössen and later houses which are divided into two rooms will be discussed below, but once again the division of space often occurs one third of the way into the house, near the entrance, in the classic 'megaron' plan. The earthen tombs frequently show a similar division, with the main burial chamber occurring in the third of the mound nearest the entrance in Britain and/or in the central portion in Scandinavia. At Bygholm Norremark, a house beneath the barrow has clear traces of a threefold division, while at Skibshoj and Troelstrup the eastern third is partitioned from the western two-thirds (Madsen 1979). A similar division in Britain can be seen at Kilham (Fig. 2). Multiple partitioning of long-barrows is a general characteristic in both Britain and Scandinavia, but it is the

Fig. 4. The orientation of tombs and long houses in Europe.
A. Armorican gallery graves (L'Helgouach 1965).   B. Armorican tombs with short and medium passages (L'Helgouach 1965).   C. Armorican tombs with long passages (L'Helgouach 1965).   D. Earthen long barrows from the southern northern regions of Britain (Ashbee 1970).
E. Rectangular and trapezoidal Neolithic long houses (Marshall 1981).   F. Megalithic tombs in Holland (Bakker 1979).

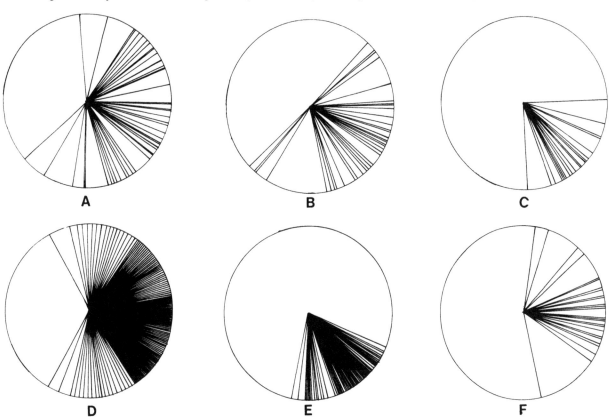

gallery graves of the Paris Basin that again show the specific principle at work. The 'allées couvertes' are divided one third of the way in (Fig. 5) and in Brittany the gallery graves normally have an antechamber and sometimes a back room. The rock-cut tombs (*hypogées*) of the Paris Basin are often divided into three distinct rooms, the inner room being the largest and containing the majority of the skeletal remains. It should be recognised that, in comparing long-houses and French gallery-graves parallels are being sought across at least a millennium, from the late 4th millennium to the late 3rd millennium BC. It is not the contention here that the houses acted as direct and immediate analogies for the late 3rd- and early 2nd-millennia gallery-graves, and there are intermediary forms in various parts of Atlantic Europe. A general and continuous underlying tradition is claimed, lasting millennia, finding surviving expression in different ways at different times in different places.

The seventh point of comparison between long tombs and long-houses concerns the use of decoration. The stone-built houses at Skara Brae, Orkney, contained stones incised with geometric decoration similar to that found in contemporary chambered tombs on Orkney, often in similar positions above and near entrances and within rooms (Hodder 1982c). The rich decoration of tombs in western Europe has long been of interest, the decoration occurring on the sides of galleries and transepts, on capstones, and in the Paris Basin for example, particularly in the entrance area (Fig. 5). The decoration of long-houses in central Europe may be less widely recognised because of the non-surviving timber-and-daub structures and removal of the occupation horizon. However, models of houses frequently have decoration similar to that on Danubian pottery. Decorated walls occur at Karanovo in southeast Europe and designs resembling pottery decoration are found on 4th-millennium BC houses in Hungary (Piggott 1965, p. 90). Neolithic huts at Grossgartach have wall plaster with red-and-white zig-zags on a yellow background. Specific links between decoration in tombs and the domestic context are also suggested by the frequent similarities between the designs used in the tombs and on domestic pottery. While it will be shown below that special funerary or ritual decorated pottery does exist (for example in Chassey and north European contexts), the decorated pottery of the earlier Breton

Fig. 5. Gallery graves (allées couvertes) and rock cut tombs (hypogées) from the SOM culture in the Paris Basin (Bailloud 1964).

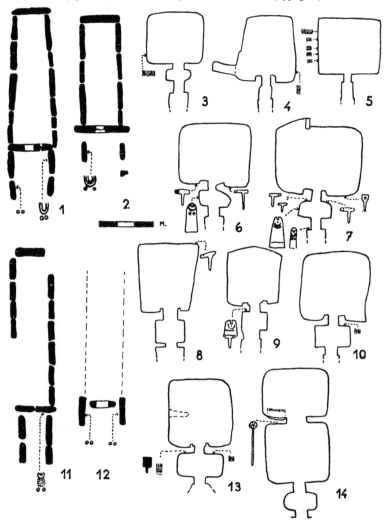

Neolithic, for example, has concentric arc designs recalling that found in the tombs in the same area. The use of features such as an eye motif on 'pots, bones and stones' in Spain and elsewhere in Atlantic Europe has been described by Crawford (1957, p. 60).

Eighth, both long houses and burial mounds are frequently associated with ditches flanking the long sides (see Figs. 2 and 6) although in some cases the tombs (for example Giants' Hill, Skendleby earthen long barrow) also have ditches at the rear and/or front. Quarry ditches along the narrows are a normal feature in Britain and Poland but are less common in Scandinavia and north Germany (Madsen 1979, p. 318). While it can of course be claimed that such ditches are simply functional consequences of the need to provide material for the house walls or barrow mounds, there is no necessary relationship: the material could have been obtained from elsewhere, or from differently shaped hollows. Whatever the reason for the construction of the side ditches, they do exhibit a close formal similarity between the houses and the mounds which suggests one type of monument evoked the other. In fact there are often precise similarities between the ditches in the two cases. Both are frequently irregular in outline (for example, see Willerby Wold – Ashbee 1970, p. 39) and are sometimes dug as a series of interconnecting pits. In view of the other similarities between the houses and tombs noted above, it is argued here that the similarity in the form and placing of the quarry ditches is significant.

Eight points of similarity between Neolithic houses in central Europe and long burial-mounds in Atlantic Europe have been identified, although each comparison involves a number of more detailed attributes. The main points can be summarised as follows.

1. Construction of houses and earthen long barrows includes use of continuous bedding trenches, lines of simple posts and some combination of the two techniques.
2. Trapezoidal and rectangular shapes with similar length/ maximum breadth ratios for trapezoidal forms.
3. The entrances of the trapezoidal mounds and houses are at the broader end.
4. The entrances of the rectangular and trapezoidal houses and barrows frequently face towards the south-east.

Fig. 6. An example of a LBK house with side ditches. Building 32 at Elsloo, Netherlands.

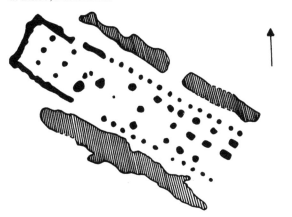

5. The entrances are elaborated, specifically with facades, antechambers, 'horns', or activity concentrations.
6. There is a tripartite division of the long house or mound, although frequently only one division is found one third of the way along the length from the entrance.
7. Tombs and houses frequently have internal decoration.
8. Ditches flank the long sides of houses and barrows.

This list of similarities concerns specifically the long barrows, gallery graves, rectangular and trapezoidal long-houses. But other traditions are known such as the circular house and the passage grave with circular or polygonal inner chamber. It has already been noted that some scholars have drawn parallels between houses and tombs for these types also (Daniel 1965, p. 86). Clark (1980, p. 96) has drawn specific attention to the domestic connotations of the stone-built ritual hearths in Hoedic and Teviec (see below) and in the trapezoidal tombs of Kujavia, and the burning found at the front of many tombs may recall the elaborate stone hearths in houses at Lepenski Vir on the lower Danube. In comparing the houses, tombs and ritual monuments in the Neolithic of the Orkney Islands, similarities were noted in the central position of a stone-lined hearth or area with burning and occupation debris, in the left/right symmetry, and in the use of the back area for storage. Similarities between the houses and tombs of Skara Brae and Quanterness were observed in the use of decoration, in the cellular plan, and in the long narrow entrances (Hodder 1982c). In addition, in the Orkney Islands, the protruding side-stones at intervals along the interior walls of the 'stalled cairns' are constructionally and formally similar to the divisions in the Knap of Howar houses (Fig. 7).

As in any analogical argument, any one point of comparison, on its own, could be seen as coincidental. But as the numbers of similarities increase it becomes unreasonable to argue for a lack of any significant relationship. It is claimed here that specific parallels exist in the 4th millennium BC between houses in central Europe and contemporary tombs in Atlantic Europe. But there is also a longer European tradition from the late 5th to the early 2nd millennia BC which can be followed at different times in different areas. For example, the early Neolithic LBK houses in the late 5th and early 4th millennia show most of the eight characteristics, while the gallery graves which continue in use into the early 2nd millennium in Brittany and the Paris Basin contain aspects of the same style. There is continuity in the tradition in Europe throughout the whole period although particular areas, such as the Paris Basin, may only have surviving evidence intermittently. In some local areas, such as the Orkneys, the idea of tombs representing houses (and vice versa) takes on a particular local form. In the Channel Islands a link between tombs and the domestic context is suggested by the finding of querns at La Hougue Mauger and La Hougue Bie.

Although local examples, as in the Orkneys, serve to give weight to the overall relationship between houses and tombs, it is the relationship between long houses and long tombs that is the primary concern in this study. It has been suggested that the long burial-mounds evoke symbolically the earlier and contemporary long-houses of central Europe. The complementarity in time and space of the long barrows and houses needs to be emphasised. Not only are the relevant types of houses earlier than and overlapping in time with the long barrows, but they also have a different spatial distribution (Fig. 1), being found in central and east-central Europe where they are mainly associated with single inhumation graves and inhumation cemeteries. There is clear spatial overlap between long-houses and long mounds in the Paris Basin, but here early Neolithic and Danubian houses with inhumation cemeteries are followed, after an interval, by late Neolithic chambered tombs, and some similar overlaps occur in north-western Europe. However, the tombs are largely confined to Atlantic Europe where houses are small and varied in appearance. Put crudely, the long-houses occur earlier in the centre of Europe, while the long burial-mounds in Atlantic Europe begin later, overlap in time, and continue later. It is a question, then, of the transmission and transformation of an idea, a way of doing things, from east to west, and from settlement to burial.

While certain aspects of the symbolic meaning of the

Fig. 7. Comparison of tombs (stalled cairns – A, B, C) and houses (D) in the Orkney Neolithic. A. Kierfea Hill. B. Knowe of Craie. C. Knowe of Yarso. D. Knap of Howar.

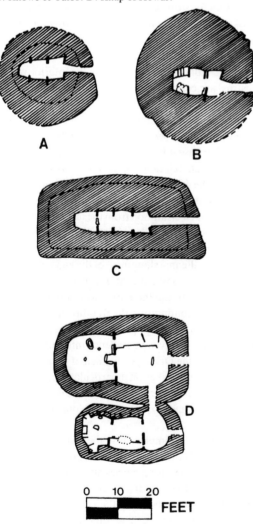

0 10 20
FEET

megalithic monuments of western Europe, have been suggested, essentially that they evoked houses, it is insufficient simply to catalogue formal similarities. However many points of comparison that can be found between tombs and houses, further support for the hypothesis can be provided if the forms being discussed can be placed within a social context. In other words, the hypothetical symbolic meaning carries greater conviction if it can be seen to play a part within a developing world of practice. It is necessary to consider why tombs were built like houses. If the symbolic evocation can be recognised to play an active part within the societies being considered, it becomes still more unreasonable to reject the formal similarities as coincidental. The close link between form and function, history and process is here apparent. Any restriction of the study to one side of the unity is inadequate.

The next task, then, is to examine the place of the long-houses within the early and middle Neolithic societies of central and east-central Europe. It will then be possible to return to the long burial-mounds, and consider what they might have evoked and how they might have functioned ideologically in their own social context.

Long-houses and central-European society

Because occupation and habitation horizons have rarely survived in central-European settlements it is difficult to assess the functions carried out in the different sections of the Neolithic long-houses. In the trapezoidal house at Postoloprty, Bohemia, four hearths have been identified in the inner room (Fig. 3 and Soudsky 1969), but there is little other direct and reliable evidence. Inference concerning the function of three- and two-roomed long-houses in central Europe has therefore been based on smaller houses of the 4th and 3rd millennia BC in central Europe and adjacent areas. For example, in the two-roomed houses at Aichbühl and Riedsachsen on the Federseemoor (Schmidt 1930–6) a clay oven generally occurred in the outer room in the inner right-hand corner with an open hearth immediately in front of it. In the inner room there was also an oven or an open hearth, generally against the partition to the right of the door. A hearth or oven occurs in both rooms at the Tripolye settlement at Ariuşd in Transylvania. At Niederwil in the Pfyn culture in Switzerland in the early 3rd millennium 30 one- or two-roomed houses have hearths inside one or both rooms (Waterbolk and van Zeist 1978). At Karanovo in Bulgaria, by the 3rd millennium BC a tripartite division of the houses occurs. Soudsky (1969) suggests that the antechamber has a religious function because of the occurrence of figurines, the large central room is for the main habitation, and the inner room has cooking functions as indicated by the finds of grinding-stones, storage-jars and hearths. As Childe was already able to remark in his 1949 review of house-types in temperate Europe, the timber buildings north of the Balkans have been compared to the megara of late Neolithic Thessally 'ad nauseum'. Soudsky (1969) has re-emphasised the similarities in the bipartite with small front room and tripartite plans, particularly in the presence of a 'forecourt' entrance area. Overall, Soudsky suggests that the LBK, SBK, Rössen and Lengyel rectangular and trapezoidal long houses had a front antechamber, a main central room, and a back store. In the very different settlement of Skara Brae on the Orkney Islands, the entrance leads into single roomed houses, with the main occupation area in the centre around the hearth, and the main storage area at the rear (Childe 1931; Hodder 1982c).

The functions to which particular rooms were put will have varied through time and space, but the main point to be emphasised here is that a linear organisation of space and of activities occurred, from the front to the back. The entrance of 4th and 3rd millennia houses in central Europe was, as far as we can observe, universally in one of the shorter sides. From there, a series of rooms and differences in activity led to the back enclosed end of the house. At Ariuşd the inner room is rather higher than the outer room (Childe 1949b). It is of interest that in the LBK houses it is often only the back end (the north-west end) that has a continuous bedding trench. Space is graded from front to back in that the back cannot be reached except by going through the front rooms or activity areas. The long rectangular and trapezoidal shapes reinforce the graded sequence. Elaboration of the entrance area noted in the houses, further emphasises the distinction between a front or public area and the inner recesses of the houses. The trapezoidal shape itself, with the entrance at the broader of the two short ends, brings the front into prominence in relation to the back.

A number of trapezoidal long-houses, for example at Postoloprty, Bylany and Bochum-Hiltrop, have an alcove on the right after entering, between the antechamber and central room. At Postoloprty the alcove occurs at the point where a ritual foundation-deposit was found. In the foundation trench were recovered a stone box made of grinding-stones containing pottery, a bone pin, and bones including a pig's skull. Soudsky (1969) has suggested that the small alcove thus had a ritual function and has drawn parallels with the ritual animal-deposits in the Tripolye culture.

Through time, the size and elaboration of houses increase and then gradually decrease. It has already been noted that by the end of the 4th millennium small rectangular houses, still with the tripartite or bipartite division and entrance at a short end occur in central Europe. In the late 4th and early 3rd millennia small two-roomed houses occur in the Michelsberg culture, but for much of the 3rd millennium, small unicellular houses are more common in Horgen and Baden contexts and in Britain and in the TRB culture in Atlantic Europe. The latter houses show little elaboration and complexity of the domestic context, and there is less of the earlier separation of activities.

Another aspect of the domestic context to which the archaeologist has ready access in the central European Neolithic is pottery. However produced, the majority of the pottery seems to have had a domestic use and it occurs richly in association with houses. Models of pots in use within houses are known from southeast Europe (Childe 1949b; Clark 1952), and the similarity between designs found on pots and on houses has already been described. Throughout Europe there is a clear trend for the gradual disappearance of elaborate decorated pottery in the period under consideration, in line with the gradual disappear-ance of large and complex house-structures. In the Danubian areas in the early Neolithic there is much fine decorated and, in the south-east, painted pottery. The complexity and richness of the LBK pottery at first increases through time (Hodder 1982b) and decorated pottery continues in, for example, the Rössen culture. But by the time of the Michelsberg culture in the late 4th and early 3rd millennia BC, decorated pottery is rare. A similar sequence has been noted in Hungary (Sherratt 1982). The early Körös phase has dispersed settlement and non-complex pottery, but the pottery of the following Tisza phase is elaborate, associated with long-houses and defended aggregated settlement. In the ensuing Tiszapolgar phase pottery is little decorated and houses are small and dispersed. In the Paris Basin, decorated pottery occurs in association with long-houses but is rare in the following Chassey and SOM phases when the substantial long-houses are no longer found. In Brittany pottery decoration is more elaborate in the early phases (L'Helgouach 1965). The increase and then gradual disappearance of decoration and formal complexity in the TRB sequence has been documented in detail for the Netherlands (Hodder 1982b). In Jutland, Denmark, Gebauer (1978) has noted that ritual vessel forms like clay ladles and pedestalled bowls are only present in the early part of the TRB Middle Neolithic and the amount of fine ornamented pottery gradually reduces. Conversely the storage vessels increased markedly through time. Going farther afield, the early Neolithic pottery in south France is largely restricted to fine, decorated wares. Similarly, in Calabria in south Italy, the early Stentinello pottery is fine and richly decorated, but through time the amount of coarse pottery gradually increases and by the Diana phase in the 3rd millennium, pottery is plain.

In general, then, the Neolithic of the late 5th and 4th millennia in central Europe, in contrast to the 3rd millennium, is characterised by gradually increasing elaboration of the domestic context through the organisation of space and activities, ritual and decoration. It is now possible to consider this domestic symbolic elaboration, and thus the significance of the long-houses, in the context of central European Neolithic society. It is widely accepted that social groups were at this time small-scale, largely acephalous, although with some degree of differentiation between lineages gradually emerging. Settlement pattern evidence shows the gradual increase in size of small, dispersed population-units. By the late 4th and 3rd millennia villages, often defended, occur but the degree of internal social differentiation in settlement and burial remains slight.

As a result of ethnoarchaeological studies on small scale, dispersed, acephalous lineage groups in east Africa, and as a result of more general comparative studies it has been possible to suggest the hypothesis that 'in small-scale lineage-based societies in which the major concern is to increase labour power, the control of women by men, and the negotiation of position by women will become the dominant feature of social relations and will often involve cultural elaboration of the domestic sphere' (Hodder 1983). This hypothesis involves two relationships which need to be explained. The first concerns the link between domestic symbolic complexity and male–female negotiation of social position, and the second concerns the link between male–female relationships and the control of reproduction.

In the Baringo district in Kenya, it was noted that containers were decorated, house compounds were large and the internal arrangement of houses was complex in areas and in societies in which lineage groups were trying to expand and to compete with other groups through increased reproduction. The restricting resource was labour rather than land, and women as reproducers could negotiate social position but men were concerned to control women and their reproduction. Put more generally, the maternal and paternal lines competed for the control of offspring and labour power. Women occupied a focal point in this tension, as the reproducers of labour, and it was in terms of the control of women and the domestic context and in terms of the negotiation of power by women that social conflict and much material patterning developed. The domestic context was the scene for the playing out of competition between lineages based on the control of women, and women used such strategies as the decoration of food containers in order to draw attention to and increase their focal role. A related argument, with direct relevance to the type of use of space identified in this study, is made by Donley (1982). The Swahili houses on the east African coast (and similar to Islamic houses in several parts of the world) are internally divided into a linear sequence of rooms. One enters at one of the shorter ends of the house and proceeds through the rooms to the back. The rooms are higher as one moves inwards, and they become more private and secluded. Decoration is used to protect areas of defilement. Donley demonstrates that the elaboration of the Swahili domestic context is concerned with control over women and of the purity of descent-groups. While the wider social and political context of the recent east African coast differs markedly from the central European Neolithic, a link between domestic symbolic elaboration and the position of women has been recognised in a wide range of societies from Braithwaite's (1982) study in south Sudan, to Okely's (1975) interpretation of Gypsy society, and to the South American groups examined by Hugh-Jones (1979).

Although it would be difficult to place much reliance on these ethnographic analogies without a careful consideration of the contexts involved, the widespread relationship between varying elaboration of the domestic context and the varying position of women is suggestive. This suggests that the type of organisation of space found in the long-houses of central Europe is likely to be linked to social strategies of control and seclusion. We are not dealing here with houses or rooms with multiple access, with courtyard plans or agglomerations of single rooms. Inner rooms can only be reached through outer rooms, in a linear sequence. The inner rooms are secluded and access is controlled. Also, house and pottery decoration draws attention to the domestic space and to food and drink which must at least partly have been prepared by women. The preparation and provision of food in the domestic context, for adults and offspring, has great symbolic potential in any society concerned with the reproduction and expansion of its labour power and with the control over its reproductive and productive potential.

The elaboration of the domestic world as part of male–female relationships occurs cross-culturally in a variety of different social contexts. But in the early Neolithic of central Europe a relevant context is immediately apparent. Settlement initially spread into relatively empty but rich and easily worked areas of loess soil. It is clear that labour, not land would have been the limiting resource. Competition between groups would have been in terms of control over reproduction. Productive success would have depended on women as reproducers, and descent groups would compete for the control of the labour power of offspring. In all this, women and the domestic world will have played a central role, the foci of social tensions. The elaboration of the material culture was part of the strategies of men and women, through maternal and paternal lines, to obtain access to labour.

As the social process of lineage competition built up through time, control of women in the house and settlement, and thus of descent and labour, would have assumed an increased importance, with women as the focal points of reproduction and exchange. Through time, houses become more substantial (Sherratt 1982), pottery more decorated, figurines more elaborate (Sherratt 1982). The agglomeration of settlements, a process seen in the 4th millennium in many parts of central Europe, both allowed greater control over women and descent, but also allowed cooperation between women leading to a greater need to seclude and control them through the organisation of house space. Through the late 5th and early 4th millennia all aspects of material culture from pottery and houses to figurines and settlement organisation demonstrate attempts to use materials to naturalise and mark out the position of women in the domestic context. In this way the central importance and power of women as reproducers and as the nodes of links to other lineages was emphasised but they were also secluded and controlled. The multivalent, ambiguous nature of material culture was played to the full.

By the late 4th and 3rd millennia, however, there is increased evidence for 'filling up' of the environment, further expansion of settlement onto less productive soils, the use of the plough and increased use of secondary animal products (Sherratt 1981). Gradually, through time, land became the major limiting resource, not labour. As Goody (1976) and Ingold (1980) have noted, in societies (such as hoe agriculturalists and milch pastoralists) where the amount of resources in the possession of a productive unit is a direct function of labour supply, there will be little attempt to restrict inheritance to particular descent lines and, as we have seen, competition between descent lines for the control over offspring will lead to multiple descent-claims and affiliations of individuals. But where (as amongst plough agriculturalists) there is a scarcity of productive resources rather than labour, there will be a pressure to restrict the number of dependants in a household and to confine the range of potential heirs to direct descendants. Thus as land became the critical resource as a result of the competition between descent groups, women would have less ability to negotiate their social position since they would no longer be at the focus of the competing claims between descent lines for the control of offspring. The domestic context would no longer be relevant as a forum for symbolic elaboration. Houses decrease in size and become simple in construction and content, pottery is plain, the role of women in the domestic context (but not necessarily in other spheres) is devalued. From another point of view, the decrease in house size and the removal of decoration from the domestic context can be seen as an active process. The 'closing' of lineage groups and the restriction of descent must involve strategies of legitimation in order to exclude certain individuals from inheritance and access to resources. The removal of elaboration from the domestic context devalues the woman as reproducer and the claims to inheritance made through women. The removal of complexity from domestic space and from pottery decoration helps to establish absolute control of descent lines by lineage heads. The woman is less able to use her position as reproducer to promote competing claims from other groups.

It would be of interest, in view of the above hypothesis, to examine changes in pottery production in the late 4th and 3rd millennia BC. For example, the uniformity of the plain Chassey, Michelsberg, Diana and other pottery may prove to indicate specialist and centralised production, and Peacock (1969) has demonstrated petrologically the centralised manufacture of plain Hembury ware in south-west England. Since such increases in the scale and organisation of production are often linked to shifts to male potters (Balfet 1966), it would be possible to see the changes in the 3rd millennium as involving removal of pottery and its associated symbolism from the domestic sphere of production in order to increase male dominance and control. However, much work remains to be done on the organisation of Neolithic pottery-production before such an hypothesis can be entertained.

It has been suggested that the long-houses of central Europe were large and elaborate and were internally organised so that they played a part in the competition between descent groups for the control over reproduction and labour. The major division in the houses between entrance and interior, between outside and inside is part of the strategy of seclusion by men of women and control of maternal ties. The trapezoidal form has been explained as part of the same contrasts, front against back. Soudsky (1969) suggests that the trapezoidal shape gives a better aerodynamic quality against increased winds. There is little evidence for changes in Neolithic wind-speed and such an hypothesis carries little conviction in relation to the trapezoidal shape of the long barrows.

Climatic arguments have also been suggested for the orientation of long-houses. Marshall (1981) shows that modern wind directions are considerably more varied than are the long-house orientations, but reconstructions of central- and eastern-European Neolithic wind-patterns have suggested a predominance of north-westerlies. However, even if wind direction is part of the explanation of the long-house orientations, the relationship between house, wind and orientation could have been invested with further significance. Certainly the equivalent orientation of many long mounds, the constructions of which are less likely to have been harmed by weather and wind, argues that the placing of the houses and mounds was significant. Relationships to the winds, sun, moon or stars could have provided a higher authority, a naturalisation of the social processes centred on the house itself.

Long mounds

It is now possible to return to Atlantic Europe and to consider the social context of the long burial-mounds. The spread of farming into western Europe from central Europe and the Mediterranean occurred mainly in the later 4th and 3rd millennia as part of the process of infill and intensification noted above (Whittle 1977). There is evidence of ploughing under barrows and it seems likely that a range of secondary animal products was in use, allowing occupation of a wider variety of environments. In line with the hypothesis already presented, houses are small and there is little elaboration of domestic space. A number of individual huts are known in Britain, and at Knardrup, Denmark, an early Neolithic TRB settlement consisted of three small single-celled houses (Larsen 1957). Initially, however, there is likely to have been a concern to increase reproduction and labour power. In the first stages of agricultural development aspects of the domestic context such as pottery may have been marked out and emphasised as part of the processes already outlined and the early appearance of decorated pottery in Scandinavia and Brittany has been mentioned. Generally, however, the Atlantic façade is characterised by poor and crudely decorated or undecorated pottery in relation to the wares of central and southeast Europe, and those areas with decorated pottery change to plainer pottery during the 3rd millennium.

According to the models used in this study, the Atlantic Neolithic should include societies in which the limiting resource is productive and in which attempts are made to restrict and control descent. It is in the same terms that the long mounds are described by Chapman. But it is now possible to reconsider these burial monuments in the light of the symbolic associations with central European long houses. The transference of the Neolithic house form to western European burial involved a large number of specific and complex symbolic meanings which must affect the way the functions of the tombs are interpreted.

The association between the house form and male–female relationships is strengthened by a consideration of the tombs. Here the surviving art, whether from stone monuments in Malta or France, shows clear depictions of women and female breasts. In the tombs of the Paris Basin shown in Fig. 5, these depictions are often set beside drawings of axes, although the male connotations of the latter cannot be demonstrated with any certainty. Other aspects of the tombs emphasise the principles already identified. In particular the elaboration of the entrance area, the façades and forecourts, the closing of the tombs and the difference in ritual and artifacts inside and outside the tomb all indicate the same concerns with an inner/outer dichotomy, with control and seclusion. No more eloquent testimony of the latter principles could be provided than the false portals. In nearly all types of chambered tomb the organisation of space is largely sequential and controlled, and several of the temples at Tarxien in Malta have the same structure as has been identified for central European houses – there is an overall trapezoidal form as one moves from the large front chambers to the small rear chambers.

But the long mounds are not houses, they are tombs. They bring the above signification to the context of the ancestors, death and the past. Also the context is not one of everyday experience. The long mounds form a separate ritual context. Links can be made, then, between the control of reproduction, ancestors and ritual. But there are other aspects of the tombs and the burial ritual which need to be included in any explanation. The first involves communality and participation. The labour involved in the construction of stone and earth tombs itself involves participation by the group and it is for this reason, and because of their monumentality, that they have been seen as social and territorial foci. Participation is also seen in other aspects of the tombs. In particular the partitioning of the mounds at South Street and Barkaer, for example, has suggested the division of the construction task between different work-groups. Similarly, the discontinuous nature of the long barrow ditches at Wor Barrow and elsewhere (Ashbee 1970, p. 47) recalls the discontinuous construction of causewayed enclosures in Britain and the suggestion made by Startin and Bradley (1981) that different task-groups were involved. As has long been recognised, the tombs are usually communal in nature and provide a special focus for the group as a whole. The rearrangement of skeletal remains and the 'mixing' of bones can again be seen as denying and resolving within-group differences. It can even be suggested, following Lévi-Strauss (1969), that the removal of flesh from bones may be associated with relationships between the maternal and paternal sides, with continuity and order (Rowlands 1980, p. 51).

A second aspect of the symbolism of the tombs concerns their orientation. As already described, many of the long tombs are aligned axially so that the entrances face to the southeast. The Clava passage graves are aligned to certain positions of the moon and sun (Burl 1981). There is no need to evoke Neolithic astronomer-priests and mathematicians for general relationships to, for example, the rising sun. The concern with time and with the movements of the sun and moon in relation to burial and the mundane world provide a higher authority for the social strategies symbolised and mediated in the tombs. The orientation to the sun and moon provided a naturalisation of the social order.

Having outlined various components of the symbolism of the long burial-mounds it is now possible to see how they may have been used in social strategies. It has been suggested that an initial concern of social units in Atlantic Europe in the late 4th and early 3rd millennia may have been to control women as reproducers. In the early stages of the Atlantic Neolithic, strategies similar to those outlined for central Europe may have been followed. But through time, again as in central Europe, extra-lineage ties established through women would have been restricted and controlled, and it has been shown that areas which do have decorated pottery in the early phases of the Neolithic (TRB in Scandinavia and Holland for example) gradually lose elaborate decoration. But in Atlantic Europe in both early and later phases, the position of women is emphasised in the context of communal ritual, outside the domestic sphere. Here women are depicted and the domestic 'house' context is elaborated. Women as reproducers, as the source and focus of the lineage are here celebrated. But only in the house of the ancestors does this

occur, in a context in which communal participation is stressed, and in which differences are denied. Domestic houses themselves, and in some areas pottery, are rarely elaborate. Women as reproducers and their position in the domestic context are, in the context of ritual, appropriated for the lineage as a whole. Their services are for the lineage alone and this control is legitimated by the ancestors and by higher authorities.

The above hypothesis is seen as plausible because it accounts for the richness and complexity of megalithic burial-ritual and for other aspects of the data from the Neolithic of Europe. There is a potential for the collection and consideration of further data to support or throw doubt on the hypothesis. In particular, more information is needed on economic subsistence strategies, on the organisation of craft production, on the internal organisation of houses, on pottery design, on the symbolism of axes and so on. I have not considered the evidence from the south-east of Europe, or the significance of figurines. But the steps so far taken indicate at least the potential of an approach which integrates the study of meaning and function. Other explanations are not so much wrong as limited. I have tried, in this section, to incorporate reference to existing theories concerning western Neolithic burial and society. It is possible to see now why and how collective monumental burials acted as territorial markers and legitimated access to restricted resources and such arguments have been developed and extended by the consideration of meaning and an active social context.

Other hypotheses which can be incorporated concern the development of social hierarchy in relation to megaliths in Atlantic Europe (Renfrew 1979; Shennan 1982). In reference to the Orkney Neolithic, it has been suggested that a centralised hierarchy developed through the control of rituals which were represented as being for the society as a whole (Hodder 1982c). By repeating in one ritual centre the patterns of activity found within dispersed groups, the major henges and those controlling the rituals in the henges could rise to dominance. It was through the appropriation of rituals for the larger society that individual lineages could come to dominate others (*cf.* Friedman 1975). Similarly, in western Europe generally, each burial mound formed the focus for members of a descent group. Because the burial house was the house of the whole descent group, those sections of a lineage most closely linked to the burial ritual could rise to dominance through the ideology of communal care. The elders or sub-groups most closely connected with the tombs could control the reproduction and continuation of the lineage itself and would be legitimated not only by the symbolism of reproduction, communality and denial of differences, but also by appeal to higher, 'natural' authorities. In the larger-scale competition between tomb-centred lineage groups, those groups which performed and acted more competently in relation to the symbolism and meaning of the tombs could also control and increase productive resources more successfully and would be able to rise to a superior position. As Shennan (1982) has noted, communal burial is in many areas associated with, but also masks, increasing social differentiation.

Atlantic and central Europe compared

As described in this article and in the work of, for example, Chapman (1981), Sherratt (1981) and Whittle (1977), similar social and economic developments occurred in west and central Europe during the Neolithic. In both areas competition for productive rather than reproductive resources became the major concern in the late 4th and 3rd millennia BC. There is widespread evidence for settlement infill, expansion of settlement into less productive areas, and intensification as seen in the use of the plough and secondary animal products. In both areas, as described by the model of Ingold (1980) and Goody (1976) and utilised in this study, attempts were made in conjunction with these developments to restrict inheritance and to 'close' lineage groups. Why then are long mounds part of these processes in Atlantic Europe, but not in central Europe?

One type of explanation for the occurrence of long mound-burial in Atlantic, but not central Europe concerns ecological conditions. The greater variety of subsistence resources available in the Atlantic zone (Clarke 1976) may have led to different adaptations and the megalithic monuments could be seen as part of a 'technocomplex' (Madsen 1979). It has been shown above that arguments for higher population-density in Atlantic Europe, leading to greater stress and competition and hence to megaliths have little sound basis. There is however, some ground for viewing monumental mound-burial as being linked to greater mobility of settlement in Atlantic Europe. Jarman, Bailey and Jarman (1982) have documented the frequent occurrence of communal burial mounds in areas of low arable potential, including the limestone plateaux of southern France and it has been suggested that the tombs in the Netherlands provided a focus for dispersed and relatively mobile groups. Within such an hypothesis, the tombs as houses would be appropriate symbols of continuity, stability and of the lineage itself.

On the other hand, there is little evidence that any significant difference existed between degrees of dispersal in central and western Europe by the third millennium BC. As already noted, by the late 4th and 3rd millennia BC, settlement had expanded, a more varied suite of environments was in use, and evidence for long-term stable occupation is infrequent. It is difficult to argue for any major difference in economic adaptation in central and Atlantic Europe at this time. Equally, monumental burial occurs in a great variety of ecological contexts in Atlantic Europe. For example, in southern Sweden Clark (1977) notes megalithic tombs on both high quality and on very poor soil associated with the use of coastal resources. Tombs connected with a largely fishing economy are known from the Scilly Isles (Clark 1980, p. 98) and from Carrowmore, Ireland (Burenhult 1980a, 1980b, 1981). Frequently, however, they occur in predominantly agricultural contexts. It is not possible to see megaliths as linked to any one subsistence strategy, in any one environment. Even if such a relationship were to be substantiated, it is not possible to derive a burial ritual directly from a type of subsistence. The types of adaptation that occurred in Atlantic Europe were enabled by the same framework of meaning that produced the tombs, and a two-way interaction between culture and ecology must be assumed.

Atlantic Europe is characterised by a series of burial and other traits which go to make up a tradition which needs to be explained in its own terms, in its own historical context. This is not to say that a static set of ideas determined the production of long barrows since we have seen how the symbolism of the tombs and of pottery was actively involved in social change, as a medium for action. It may be helpful to consider the historical tradition as a 'coping system' which enabled, but was also changed by, practical decisions and their effects.

It is possible to argue in Iberia, Brittany, England, Ireland and Scandinavia for some local contribution to the emergence of megalithic burial. The important evidence from Hoëdic and Teviec in Brittany for a Mesolithic origin for aspects of the megalithic and communal burial tradition is underlined by the uncalibrated C^{14} date of 4625 ± 300 bc from Hoëdic. At Teviec inhumations in graves with up to 6 individuals are found in clear mausolea with piles of stones on the bodies, while at Hoedic small slabs of stones were placed over the graves (Pequart 1954). There is evidence in both places for the addition of bodies and removing earlier bones into a pile with a skull on top, in the style of many Neolithic megalithic rituals. Although evidence for Mesolithic burial is limited, it would be possible to argue for an earlier tradition of various aspects of the megalithic burial-ritual in Atlantic Europe.

But the difference between Atlantic and central Europe does not only concern the use of megaliths. Monumental burial involves an emphasis on ritual outside the domestic context which is also seen in other spheres and in other times in Atlantic Europe. The precise nature of the ritual activities at English causewayed camps is yet to be determined but was frequently on an impressive scale (Mercer 1980). In Scandinavia, settlements are not known inside causewayed camps (Madsen 1977). The general tradition of major ritual monuments continues into the late 3rd millennium and the 2nd millennium in Britain where henges act as distinctive ritual centres with varying degrees of occupational activity. From Carnac to Stonehenge and to the 'temples' of Malta, Atlantic Europe is characterised by an investment in separate, non-domestic ritual which is wholly alien to the central European tradition. In the latter area and in southeast Europe, 'ritual' in the form of figurines, foundation-deposits, and shrines does occur, but within houses and settlements, closely linked to the domestic context. In Atlantic Europe the ritual is outside the domestic context, or at least it extends into a separate sphere on which most of the art and cultural elaboration often centre.

I have shown how these differences in the traditions of the two areas were related to generally similar social strategies. In other words, two rather different coping systems were described, and these involved similar successful adaptations in the two regions. There also seems to be evidence for continuity in the tradition from earlier into later times and a major concern must be to examine the longer-term historical continuities. Shennan (1982) has noted differences in the development of hierarchy and in the adoption of metallurgy in the two areas. In addition, I find it provocative and potentially exciting to note that in the Upper Palaeolithic in Europe painted caves are found in western Europe but not in central Europe despite careful research in the latter area, despite the existence of appropriate caves, and despite the occurrence of portable art in domestic contexts in central Europe. Upper Palaeolithic cave art is largely confined to Atlantic Europe and often occurs in clearly non-domestic contexts, in caves and parts of caves which are not used for habitation. Other similarities in the tradition which can be examined are that the Palaeolithic art uses methods which demonstrate participation (Marshak 1977) and the resolving of differences (Conkey 1982). Clearly the identification of these continuities requires further research and further papers, but the possibility exists of identifying long term cultural traditions which are actively implicated in social change.

Conclusion

In the above account the megaliths have been placed within a social context. This article thus continues in the directions taken by Renfrew, Chapman, Fleming and Reed. However, there are two differences from such work. First, I have not been concerned simply with the general appearance of societies – territorial behaviour and the use of restricted resources. All societies have such characteristics, but competition and access to resources vary structurally in different societies. In this article, following Goody and Ingold, I have used a model that, in the European Neolithic, competition was initially based on control of reproduction but later productive rather than reproductive resources became the limiting factor. It has been suggested that these organisational differences are associated in the Neolithic with changes in patterns of inheritance, in the relations between maternal and paternal claims on offspring and resources, and in the relations between men and women. The model allows the mundane and ubiquitous archaeological evidence of houses and pots to be incorporated directly in models of social change. These artifacts act ideologically in the sense that they are involved in objectifying and giving meaning to social strategies. In the first phase the domestic context is the central focus of competing claims to reproductive resources. Material culture is used to form a world in which women are to be emphasised, celebrated but controlled as reproducers of the lineage, and in which women and extra-lineage ties have a central importance. In the second phase the domestic context is withdrawn from its central focus by changes in material culture, and these changes are part of the developing social control of productive resources. Competing claims to the inheritance of those resources, whether land or livestock, are restricted by de-emphasising and devaluing the domestic context, the role of women as reproducers and the extra-lineage ties.

In reaching such a conclusion, and in relating the hypothesis to megalithic burial, it has been necessary, in contrast to published 'processual' studies, to consider the particular historical significance of houses, mound shapes, decoration and orientation, and this is the second difference from the 'processual' studies of megaliths. Individuals can only act socially within

ideologies which are historically contingent. The particular symbolism of artifacts can be examined by considering associations of form and use, and by showing that the symbolic significances inferred 'make sense' within active social strategies. It has been possible to see the diffusion of an idea, of a style of construction, as a socially active process. The house form which diffused from central Europe to Atlantic European burial had the significance of a domestic context in which reproductive potential and the control of that potential were marked out. In Atlantic Europe, however, this significance, further elaborated by the use of art depicting women, was transformed. In a ritual and ancestral burial context, female reproduction was appropriated by the lineage and competition between maternal and paternal claims to reproductive and productive resources was resolved in a non-domestic context. All aspects of burial and other rituals can be linked to the same concern with legitimating control of reproductive and productive resources through an ideology of communal work and participation for the lineage.

Ultimately the ideology, the way of coping, associated with the megaliths of western Europe cannot be explained only in terms of social strategies and adaptive potential. While ideas and practices diffuse from central to Atlantic Europe, the latter area transforms the meanings and uses the symbolism in rather different ways. While environmental differences between Atlantic and central Europe can be identified, the successful adaptations to those environments cannot be explained solely in terms of those adaptations. There is much scope for examining the varied appearances in different times and in different areas of the 'style' of the Neolithic of the Atlantic façade. While only brief reference has been made to possibilities of remarkable continuities in 'ways of doing things' in Atlantic Europe, it is now necessary to examine further the historical tradition which gives the appearance of monumental burial its specificity. The playing out of the historical tradition of Atlantic Europe must be understood partly in its own terms and the task is scarcely begun.

References

Ashbee, P. (1970) *The Earthen Long Barrow in Britain*, Dent, London
Bailloud, G. (1964) *Le Neolithique dans le Bassin Parisien*, supplement to *Gallia Prehistoire*, 2
Bakker, J.A. (1979) 'July 1878: Lukis and Dryden in Drente', *Antiquaries Journal* 59, pp. 9–18
Balfet, H. (1966) 'Ethnographic observations in North Africa and archaeological interpretation of the pottery of the Maghreb', in F.R. Matson Ed., *Ceramics and Man*. Viking Fund Publication in Anthropology 4
Bogucki, P. and Grygiel, R. (1981) 'The household cluster at Brzesc Kujawski 3: small-site methodology in the Polish lowlands', *World Archaeology* 13, pp. 59–72
Braithwaite, M. (1982) 'Decoration as ritual symbol: a theoretical proposal and an ethnographic study in southern Sudan', in I. Hodder Ed., *Symbolic and Structural Archaeology*, Cambridge University Press, Cambridge
Burenhult, G. (1980a) *The Archaeological Excavation at Carrowmore*, G. Burenhults Förlag, Stockholm
(1980b) *The Carrowmore Excavations: Excavation Season 1980*.

Stockholm Archaeological Reports 7, Institute of Archaeology, University of Stockholm

(1981) *The Carrowmore Excavations: Excavation Season 1981*, Stockholm Archaeological Reports 8, Institute of Archaeology, University of Stockholm

Burl, A. (1981) ' "By the light of the cinerary moon": chambered tombs and the astronomy of death', in C.L.N. Ruggles and A.W.R. Whittle Eds., *Astronomy and Society in Britain During the Period 4000–1500 BC*, BAR British Series 88

Case, H. (1969) 'Settlement patterns in the North Irish Neolithic', *Ulster Journal of Archaeology* 32, pp. 3–27

Chapman, R. (1981) 'The emergence of formal disposal areas and the "problem" of megalithic tombs in prehistoric Europe', in R. Chapman, I. Kinnes and K. Randsborg Eds., *The Archaeology of Death*, Cambridge University Press

Childe, V.G. (1925) *The Dawn of European Civilisation*, 1st edition. Kegan Paul, London

(1931) *Skara Brae*, Kegan Paul, London

(1949a) 'The origin of Neolithic culture in northern Europe', *Antiquity* 23, pp. 129–00

(1949b) 'Neolithic house-types in temperate Europe', *Proceedings of the Prehistoric Society* 15, pp. 77–85

(1957) *The Dawn of European Civilisation*, 6th edition. Routledge, London

Clark, J.G.D. (1952) *Prehistoric Europe: the Economic Basis*. Methuen, London

(1977) 'The economic context of dolmens and passage graves in Sweden' in V. Markotic Ed., *Ancient Europe and the Mediterranean*, Aris and Phillips, Warminster

(1980) *Mesolithic Prelude*, Edinburgh University Press, Edinburgh

Clarke, D.L. (1976) 'Mesolithic Europe: the economic basis', in G. Sieveking, I.H. Longworth and K. Wilson Eds., *Problems in Economic and Social Archaeology*, Duckworth, London

Conkey, M. (1982) 'Boundedness in art and society', in I. Hodder Ed., *Symbolic and Structural Archaeology*, Cambridge University Press

Crawford, O.G.S. (1957) *The Eye Goddess*, Phoenix House, London

Daniel, G.E. (1958) *The Megalith Builders of Western Europe*, London

(1965) 'Editorial', *Antiquity* 39

Donley, L. (1982) 'House power: Swahili space and symbolic markers', in I. Hodder Ed., *Symbolic and Structural Archaeology*. Cambridge University Press

Fleming, A. (1972) 'Vision and design: approaches to ceremonial monument typology', *Man* 7, pp. 57–72

(1973) 'Tombs for the living', *Man* 8, pp. 177–93

Friedman, J. (1975) 'Tribes, states and transformations', in M. Bloch Ed., *Marxist Analyses and Social Anthropology*, Malaby Press, London

Gebauer, A.B. (1978) 'The Middle Neolithic Funnel Beaker culture in south-west Jutland. An analysis of the pottery', *Kuml* 1978, pp. 117–57

Geupel, V. (1981) 'Zum Verhältnis Spätmesolithikum–Frühneolithikum in mettleren Elbe-Saale-Gebiet', *Mesolithikum in Europa. Veröffentlichungen des Museums für Ur- und Frühgeschichte Potsdam* 14/15, pp. 102–12

Gilman, A. (1976) 'Bronze Age dynamics in southeast Spain', *Dialectical Anthropology* 1, pp. 307–19

Glob, P.V. (1949) 'Barkaer, Danmarks aeldste landsby', *Fra Nationalmuseets Arbejdsmark 1949*, pp. 5–16

(1975) 'De dødes lange huse', *Skalk* 1975, 6

Goldstein, L.G. (1980) *Missippian Mortuary Practices: a Case Study of Two Cemeteries in the Lower Illinois Valley*, Northwestern University Archaeological Program, Scientific Papers, 4. Evanston, Illinois

Goody, J. (1976) *Production and Reproduction*, Cambridge University Press, Cambridge

Günther, K. (1973) 'Eine neue Variante des mittelneolithischen Trapezhauses', *Germania* 51, pp. 41-53

Hoare, R.C. (1812) *The Ancient History of South Wiltshire*, London

Hodder, I. (1982a) 'Theoretical archaeology: a reactionary view', in I. Hodder Ed., *Symbolic and Structural Archaeology*, Cambridge University Press

(1982b) 'Sequences of structural change in the Dutch Neolithic', in I. Hodder Ed., *Symbolic and Structural Archaeology*, Cambridge University Press

(1982c) *Symbols in Action*, Cambridge University Press

(1983) 'Boundaries as strategies: an ethnoarchaeological study', in S. Green and S. Perlman Eds., *Frontiers and Boundaries in Prehistory*, Academic Press, New York

Hugh-Jones, C. (1979) *From the Milk River*. Cambridge University Press

Ingold, T. (1980) *Hunters, Pastoralists and Ranchers*. Cambridge University Press

Jarman, M.R., Bailey, G.N. and Jarman, H.N. (1982) *Early European Agriculture*, Cambridge University Press

Kinnes, I. (1975) 'Monumental function in British Neolithic burial practices', *World Archaeology* 7, pp. 16–29

(1981) 'Dialogues with death', in R. Chapman, I. Kinnes and K. Randsborg Eds., *The Archaeology of Death*, Cambridge University Press

Kruk, J. (1980) *The Neolithic Settlement of Southern Poland*, BAR International Series 93

Larsen, K.A. (1957) 'Stenalderhuse på Knardrup Galgebakkez, *Kuml* 1957, pp. 24–43

Lévi-Strauss, C. (1969) *The Elementary Structures of Kinship*, 2nd edition. Beacon Press, Boston

L'Helgouach, J. (1965) *Les sepultures megalithiques en Armorique*, Rennes

Madsen, T. (1977) 'Toftum near Horsens. A causewayed camp from the transition between Early and Middle Neolithic', *Kuml* 1977, pp. 180–4

(1979) 'Earthen long narrows and timber structures: aspects of the early Neolithic mortuary practice in Denmark', *Proceedings of the Prehistoric Society* 45, pp. 301–20

Marshak, A. (1977) 'The meander as a system: the analysis and recognition of iconographic units in Upper Palaeolithic compositions', in P.J. Ucko Ed., *Form in Indigenous Art*, Duckworth, London

Marshall, A. (1981) 'Environmental adaptation and structural design in axially-pitched longhouses from Neolithic Europe', *World Archaeology* 13, pp. 101–21

Meier-Arendt, W. (1965) *Die bandkeramische Kultur im Untermaingebiet*, Bonn

Meillassoux, C. (1972) 'From reproduction to production', *Economy and Society* 1, pp. 93–105

Mercer, R.J. (1980) *Hambledon Hill: a Neolithic Landscape*, Edinburgh University Press, Edinburgh

Meyer-Christian, W. (1976) 'Die Y-Pfostenstellung in Häusen der älteren Linear-Bandkeramik', *Bonner Jahrbücher* 176, pp. 1–25

Montelius, O. (1899) *Der Orient und Europa*

Okely, J. (1975) 'Gypsy women: models in conflict', in S. Ardener Ed., *Perceiving Women*, Malaby Press, London

Peacock, D. (1969) 'Neolithic pottery production in Cornwall', *Antiquity* 43, pp. 145–9

Pequart, M. and S.-J. (1954) *Hoëdic*, De Sikkel, Anvers

Piggott, S. (1965) *Ancient Europe*, Edinburgh University Press, Edinburgh

Powell, T.G.E., Corcoran, J.X.W.P., Lynch, F. and Scott, J.G. (1969) *Megalithic Enquiries in the West of Britain*, Liverpool University Press, Liverpool

Reed, R.C. (1974) 'Earthen long barrows: a new perspective', *Archaeological Journal* 131, pp. 33–57

Renfrew, C. (1976) 'Megaliths, territories and populations', in S.J.

De Laet Ed., *Acculturation and Continuity in Atlantic Europe*, Dissertationes Archaeologicae Gandenses, De Tempel, Brugge

(1979) *Investigations in Orkney*, Society of Antiquaries, London

Rowlands, M.J. (1980) 'Kinship, alliance and exchange in the European Bronze Age', in J. Barrett and R. Bradley Eds., *Settlement and Society in the British Late Bronze Age*, BAR British Series 83

Saxe, A.A. (1970) *Social Dimensions of Mortuary Practices*, PhD Dissertation, University of Michigan

Schmidt, G. (1930–6) *Steinzeitliche Siedelungen in Federseemoor*, Augsburg and Stuttgart

Shanks, M. and Tilley, C. (1982) 'Ideology, symbolic power and ritual communication: a reinterpretation of Neolithic mortuary practices', in I. Hodder Ed., *Symbolic and Structural Archaeology*, Cambridge University Press

Shennan, S. (1982) 'Ideology, change and the European Early Bronze Age', in I. Hodder Ed., *Symbolic and Structural Archaeology*, Cambridge University Press

Sherratt, A. (1981) 'Plough and pastoralism: aspects of the secondary products revolution', in I. Hodder, G. Isaac and N. Hammond Eds., *Pattern of the Past*, Cambridge University Press

(1982) 'Mobile resources: settlement and exchange in early agricultural Europe', in C. Renfrew and S. Shennan Eds., *Ranking, Resource and Exchange*, Cambridge University Press

Sielman, B. (1972) 'Die frühneolithische Besiedlung Mitteleuropas', in J. Lüning Ed., *Die Anfänge des Neolithikums vom Orient bis Nordeuropa* 5a, Fundamenta, Köln

Soudsky, B. (1969) 'Etude de la maison neolithique', *Slovenská Archeologia* 17, pp. 5–96

Sprockhoff, E. (1938) *Die Nordische Megalithkultur*. Berlin and Leipzig

Srejovic, D. (1972) *Europe's First Monumental Sculpture: New Discoveries at Lepenski Vir*, Thames and Hudson, London

Startin, W. (1978) 'Linear pottery culture houses: reconstruction and manpower', *Proceedings of the Prehistoric Society* 44, pp. 143–59

Startin, W. and Bradley, R. (1981) 'Some notes on work organisation and society in prehistoric Wessex', in C.L.N. Ruggles and A.W.R. Whittle Eds., *Astronomy and Society in Britain During the Period 4000–1500 BC*, BAR British Series 88

Tilley, C. (1981) 'Conceptual frameworks for the explanation of socio-cultural change', in I. Hodder, G. Isaac and N. Hammond Eds., *Pattern of the Past*, Cambridge University Press

Waterbolk, H.T. and van Zeist, W. (1978) *Niederwil, eine Sidelung der Pfyner Kultur*. Berne and Stuttgart

Whittle, A.W.R. (1977) *The Earlier Neolithic of Southern England and its Continental Background*, BAR Supplementary Series 35

Woodburn, J. (1980) 'Hunters and gatherers today and reconstruction of the past', in E. Gellner Ed., *Soviet and Western Anthropology*, Duckworth, London

Chapter 6

Economic and ideological change: cyclical growth in the pre-state societies of Jutland
Michael Parker Pearson

A comparison of the ritual and profane aspects of Germanic society in Jutland, Denmark, from 500 BC to AD 600, as interpreted from funerary, votive and settlement contexts, highlights the accumulation of worldly power through the sacrifice of precious goods to the supernatural. The whole period was one of increasing wealth-destruction which halted abruptly in the seventh century AD. Agricultural production expanded until the fifth century when there occurred an economic crisis which continued into the sixth century. Within this long-term cycle of expansion and decline were three smaller cycles. In the first (500–50 BC) increasing quantities of prestigious items were sacrificed as votive offerings. At the end of the cycle they were placed in graves and no longer in votive contexts, possibly representing a transition in spiritual allegiance from deities of the bogs, lakes and other natural features, to ancestral powers. At the same time there were important changes in the privatization of agricultural property. In the second cycle (50 BC–AD 200) there was a cumulative increase in wealth-items as grave goods, accompanying a gradual elaboration and reworking of ritualized roles and categories. After a period of social unrest in the third century there was another increase in the removal of gold and silver from circulation (either in a single 'horizon' or gradually) between AD 400 and 600. Agricultural expansion and technological innovations within each cycle accompanied progressively unequal social relations.

While we know that past societies have gone through successive cycles of development and decline we have less idea why and how those changes occurred, especially in small scale, pre-state, agricultural societies. Of all the current theories of social change Marxist theory has perhaps received least attention from archaeologists, partly because of the political views of the researchers and partly because of the assumed poverty of the archaeological evidence. The integration of Marxist concepts with archaeological material has never proved simple but such an attempt is the aim of this paper. Some twenty-five years after the death of Childe, archaeologists in the West are once again developing Marxist ideas to study prehistoric societies (see contributions in Spriggs (Ed.) 1984). It is also to be noted, as Carr has remarked somewhat cynically, that theories of cyclical change recur at times of social and economic recession (1961, p. 43).

Although Childe considered that the pattern of the human past has been a series of troughs and crests (1942, p. 282) he never successfully developed a detailed analysis to distinguish cycles of cumulative growth and subsequent revolutionary change. His closest attempt, *Scotland Before the Scots*, was hampered by inadequate archaeological material and an over-emphasis on the materialist conception of the primary role of production (which lacked a sufficient appreciation of the relationship of production and consumption and an understanding of the role of ideology in directing economic activities). The detailed research that has been carried out on Iron-Age societies in Jutland provides material that can be used to examine the validity of a theory of short-term cycles forming a longer-term evolutionary trajectory. The implications of this enquiry for the broader spectrum of Marxist studies are interesting, since, through the long-term perspective provided, we may discern a certain blurring in the conventionally precise distinction between capitalism and non-capitalism.

Marx identified capital accumulation as central to

capitalism. In his view this was based on the capitalists' appropriation of surplus value, and a falling rate of profit was the inevitable outcome of such a process. Although Marx himself did not develop this argument fully, subsequent studies of both capitalist (Sweezy 1942; Mandel 1976; 1978; 1980) and non- or precapitalist societies (Friedman 1975; 1979; Ekholm 1980) have shown that variations on this process may result in discontinuous cyclical change. This cumulative expansion and crisis is clearly explained in Sweezy's book *The Theory of Capitalist Development*. Mandel has set out the evidence for long waves of economic expansion and stagnation (each cycle lasting about fifty years) in the nineteenth and twentieth centuries whilst also acknowledging that capitalist development in the long run might conform to a single large cycle (1980, p. 11). He states that cycles are asymmetric and conform to a pattern of boom followed by slump. Revolutionary changes are necessary to implement a period of expansion since the outcome of the depressive long wave is not predetermined by the logic of capitalist accumulation (1980, pp. 47–61).

Marxist analysts have frequently sought to demonstrate that the concept of surplus value exists only in capitalist societies. Surplus value is defined as the discrepancy between what workers produce and what they receive for their upkeep, since the wages and other financial outlays paid by the capitalist must always be less than the income for the commodities produced. Surplus value is the surplus product in money form (i.e. in the form of value) rather than in the form of luxury goods. For the capitalist this gives additional purchasing power not only for luxury goods but also for more machines, labour and raw materials. This permits reinvestment in the competition for accumulation of capital as surplus value is transformed into more capital (Mandel 1976, pp. 46–54). Sweezy states that in pre-capitalist societies simple commodity-exchange took place outside a framework of capital accumulation. Commodities might be produced for exchange into a primitive form of currency which could be transformed into an equivalent, and not greater, quantity of commodities. Without the process of capital accumulation crises would be unlikely (Sweezy 1942, pp. 134–6). Godelier's analysis of the production and exchange of 'salt money' amongst the Baruya (a 'Big Man' society in New Guinea) sought to demonstrate that their exchange of commodities was for the satisfaction of basic needs and not for the accumulation of this primitive currency in order to make a profit (1977, pp. 127–51). This would confirm Sweezy's proposition. Hindess and Hirst likewise characterize pre-capitalist societies as non-accumulative in that surplus labour can produce surplus but the social relations that permit accumulation and profit-making are absent (1975, pp. 267–70). While there has been a tendency to assume that non-capitalist societies are free of the profit mechanism the results of this study suggest that this is not the case.

There are certainly major qualitative differences which distinguish capitalism from earlier social forms; wage labour, with its contradiction between socialized labour and private appropriation, and the accumulation of capital are two of the main ones. However, it is still possible to recognize an inbuilt 'dynamic' in certain pre-capitalist societies in which capital can be accumulated so long as it is consumed. In other words capital is symbolic rather than economic. Its consumption can be understood as a kind of reinvestment if it is directed to win the support of supernatural forces such as deities and ancestors. Agricultural surplus can be transformed into luxury goods which may be sacrificed to gods. Exchanges between the living and the supernatural may then lead to accumulating debts among the living. An anthropological consideration of this phenomenon may be found in Friedman's study of Kachin tribal society in highland Burma (1975; 1979). He starts with the assumption that competing lineages are capable of producing a surplus which can be distributed to the community in the form of feasts and thereby converted into prestige. Only by producing a large surplus can lineages own items of wealth (cattle and imported prestige items). The need to consume increasing quantities of surplus and prestige items is fundamental for the maintenance or advancement of prestige and power. By giving gifts to gods, ancestors, marriage partners and feast-sharers, competitors can make debtors out of those who cannot return a similar or better gift or provide the same for their respective deities or ancestors. Those who cannot pay their debts pledge some of their labour to their creditors who can thus produce an even larger surplus and hence stand to increase their power even further. Friedman's analysis focussed on the generalized exchange of marriage partners – an asymmetrical model of wife-givers and wife-takers produces 'marriage chains' which eventually form circles (A–B–C– . . . n–A). In this way rich groups which inter-marry concentrate their wealth and consolidate their power. Leading lineages are then able to receive more wealth from their debtors by raising the brideprice paid for lineage daughters. This spiral consequently widens the gap between rich and poor.

The relationship between leading lineages and the rest of the community is further transformed by a change in the relationship between the living and the supernatural. Initially Kachin communicate with the spirit world through a village ancestor. As one lineage becomes increasingly wealthy the link with the ancestors becomes correspondingly closer (their prosperity being interpreted as the result of divine favour). The leading member of the lineage finally assumes the role of chief and mediator with the spirit world through his personal ancestor who replaces the village ancestors. Friedman has demonstrated that a kind of surplus value does exist in some pre- or non-capitalist societies, allowing the accumulation of wealth-items which are indirectly reinvested through enterprises like feasting and sacrifice. The debtors thus created repay their debts as gifts of surplus, labour or allegiance and increase the power of the chief even more. The final goal of increased power and prestige is the same in pre-capitalist and capitalist societies alike; however the mode of its accumulation is different.

Friedman outlines two contradictions between the forces and relations of production which develop until a crisis ensues. The first is the contradiction between the production of enough surplus for use and the production of an extra surplus for exchange. He equates this to the extraction of 'surplus value' though strictly speaking the term should be used only with capitalist societies. The second contradiction is manifested in the widening division between production and consumption – as consumption increases steadily (increasing competition and growing population) the surplus declines as production falls and returns diminish (soil exhaustion, movement onto less fertile land, intensified labour per unit area). Once past a certain point of diminished returns the working population is incapacitated by starvation and even lower productivity. Rebellions, coups and other kinds of active conflict often occur before this stage is reached. New cycles are then generated through major social and technological innovations (integration into nearby states, specialization in a wider exchange system, new rice-technologies).

It is not proposed that Friedman's interpretation of Kachin society applies directly to Denmark in the last millennia BC and the first millennia AD. They are very different historically, environmentally and socially, yet the cyclical process may apply, with certain modifications, to both societies. Indeed Friedman's structure may well be unsuitable for the societies in Highland Burma where he tried to apply it. Leach, who carried out the fieldwork on which Friedman based his study, claims that Friedman has totally misinterpreted the material though Leach does not support his allegations with factual evidence (Leach 1977, p. 163).

One archaeological application of this theory of debt-spirals creating class stratification and its consequent collapse is Frankenstein and Rowlands' analysis of the effects of Mediterranean contact on the peripheral societies of central Europe in the sixth to fifth centuries BC (1978). Frankenstein and Rowlands observe that the grave goods of a small section of that society gradually increased in wealth. They interpret the furnishing of lavish grave goods as a reflection of status and infer that the wealthy graves are those of different levels of chiefs and paramounts. They do not consider that the act of 'consuming' wealth by burying it with the dead may play an important role in creating the spiral of debts, with its concomitant centralization of power in the hands of a few. In contrast, this paper explores the theory that, in certain societies, supernatural ancestors become involved in the relationships of the living. The sacrifice of grave-gifts at burial becomes an economic institution of central importance, as wealth is taken out of circulation and consumed in acts of ritual supplication to the dead.

As most people know, facts do not speak for themselves but require interpretation through theoretical models. A few simple theoretical 'tools' are employed in this study to cross the divide between mute artefact and relevant social insight. Of particular interest is the ideological aspect of material culture, with artefacts embodying ideas and being used to represent or misrepresent social strategies and positions. A more detailed discussion of the relationship between ideology and power can be found elsewhere (Parker Pearson 1983). Some of the main points can be summarized as: 'categorization' (see Hodder 1979; Miller 1982), 'legitimation' (see Parker Pearson 1982) and 'competitive consumption for debt creation' (see Douglas and Isherwood 1978; Friedman 1979).

1. *Categorization*. Roles emphasizing gender distinctions, age grading and differing ethnicity may be employed to represent group identity. Antagonisms can be contained by strict role-playing since lifestyles and responsibilities are clearly demarcated and less open to dispute.

2. *Legitimation*. The status or social position of a group or individual can be reinforced by actions of competitive display designed to impress on others the power of that group or person. This can take many forms: constructing royal genealogies, building public monuments and memorials, holding lavish funerals or waging war on neighbouring territories.

3. *Competitive* consumption and indebtedness. If a gift is exchanged then a gift of similar or identical value should be returned. A spiral of increasingly expensive gift-exchange could then develop which would eventually ruin one partner and thus make them indebted to their competitor. Similarly those who can give most away to deities or deceased ancestors can increase their standing (equivalent to buying salvation, respectability and divine favour) as others become indebted to them through their inability to be so generous. Far from being ruined, the 'generous' competitors may then be able to collect tribute from their indebted 'inferiors'.

This paper is a summary of research being carried out on Iron-Age societies in southern Jutland (Denmark) to show how archaeological evidence from varying contexts (settlements, burials, votive deposits) can be used in an evolutionary theory of revolutionary change. This could only be done by taking a long term perspective from c. 500 BC to c. AD 600. This time range can be divided into three cycles of development:

1. Celtic or Pre-Roman Iron Age (PRIA) 500–50 BC.
2. Older Roman Iron Age (ORIA) 50 BC–AD 200.
3. Younger Roman Iron Age (YRIA) AD 200–400 and Older Germanic Iron Age (OGIA) AD 400–600.

Each phase is treated in three parts, corresponding to the three contexts of surviving archaeological material: graves, lake and bog depositions, settlements.

Graves represent one form of consumption directed by religious or spiritual values. They are also the context for the expression of central social values, as manifested in the treatment of the corpse and the selection and layout of its grave goods. The social identities given to different deceased individuals can be used to infer ritualized social orders. The degree to which they actually represent differences in day-to-day existence can be ascertained through comparison with aspects of settlement life. There are over two thousand excavated graves in southern Jutland for the Roman Iron Age alone and a recent study has concluded that a significant and representative sample of the original total has survived (Hedeager in press).

Prehistoric deposits in lakes or bogs are generally assumed to have had a ritual significance in Denmark. This is based partly on the Classical sources which note the sacred nature of natural features such as lakes and springs amongst the northern tribes. Many of these deposits would seem to have a ritual character since they are made in the same place at recurrent intervals and the artefacts are often 'killed' by being broken up. The size and quantity of items in a deposit make it unlikely that they were chance losses. The gold and silver hoards of the fifth and sixth centuries AD present more of a problem. Though many were found in bogs they might have been valuables buried at times of strife and not retrieved. If it is not possible to say that there was a ritual and spiritual motive behind certain of these depositions, we can still interpret the finds as a significant withdrawal of wealth from circulation.

Settlements of the iron age consist of farmsteads often grouped into villages or hamlets. The remains of animal byres and storage structures can be used to infer the productive capacity of different households (presumably family groups of some form or another). Changes in the production of agricultural commodities can then be compared with changes in the consumption of prestige items. Stylistic and production differences between farms can be studied in relation to differences between individual graves. In this way the changing expressions of class relationships may be examined.

One problem of looking at a wide range of material over a long time-span is the necessary geographical restriction of the research area. The Pre-Roman Iron Age material is taken from the whole of Jutland while my analyses of the Roman and Older Germanic periods are based on material from southern Jutland (the Amts or counties of Vejle, Ribe, Hadereslev, Tønder, Aabenraa and Sønderborg). This was a small part of the Germanic 'barbarian' societies on the northern periphery of the Mediterranean world. Changes within these societies must be understood in relation to the exchange networks which linked the northern tribes to southern Europe. This paper does not examine this question in detail since it has been dealt with elsewhere (Hedeager 1978; 1978a).

Cyclical change in Iron Age Jutland
The first cycle: the Pre-Roman Iron Age c. 500–50 BC

The beginning of the Early Iron Age in northern Europe and southern Scandinavia marked the collapse of a hierarchical society dependent on the control of imported bronze. Several writers have inferred 'chiefdom' forms of organization throughout the Bronze Age on the basis of gold and bronze goods in a few of the graves, and the large ceremonial bronze items (lurs, exotic helmets and large ornamented axes) (Randsborg 1974; Kristiansen 1981, pp. 244–5). Settlement excavations have also revealed differences in house form which might be interpreted as social inequalities (Becker 1980). Though there are aspects of continuity between the Late Bronze Age and earliest Iron Age the social changes may be interpreted as a revolutionary change from a hierarchical to an egalitarian society (L.C. Nielsen pers. comm.).

Settlement and production

The farmhouses in the earliest villages of the Iron Age show little variation in size. Since we can identify the stalling in the animal byres we can estimate how many large animals were kept by each household. In the village excavated at Grøntoft in western Jutland the earliest Iron Age phase (known as Period I and dating to c. 500–300 BC; Becker 1961) consisted of over thirty houses concentrated in two areas and oriented east–west (Fig. 1; Becker 1968; Becker 1971; Becker 1980, Fig. 6). A small cemetery was located some six hundred metres south-west of the centre of the village. The average number of large animals per household was 10, though ten farms had space for only 6–8 animals and five farms had space for as many as 14–16 animals (Fig. 2). Several structures, both longhouse-sized and small square-post buildings, had no remains or stalling or hearths. In some cases this was due to surface erosion but the rest presumably never had them. Their purpose is unknown but it would seem likely that they were barns, grain stores or workshops. They were grouped in five areas of the village and only one of them could possibly have had a definite association with a farmhouse (in terms of location, orientation and position of doorways) (Fig. 1). If these were storage or workshop facilities, they had a communal as opposed to privatized, location though we do not know if they were owned privately or were the communal property of the village.

Though field systems exist for the Early Iron Age in Jutland (Hatt 1931) our knowledge of land tenure and property ownership is poor and certainly for the moment there is little that field systems can tell us about ownership of agricultural production. For the purposes of this study however it is assumed that the animals stalled in each longhouse belonged to that household and that their numbers represent some measure of difference in the productive capacity of each household.

The next archaeologically definable phase of the Early Iron Age is known as Period II (Becker 1961) and is principally defined on ceramic changes. There are, however, certain problems regarding its chronological 'integrity'. Its relationship to the succeeding phase, Period IIIa, is not at all clear and there may be some degree of overlap.

A number of longhouses at Grøntoft with architectural features not found in Period I houses could be dated by stratigraphic and ceramic associations to Period II. They were built less than a hundred metres to the south and west of the original settlement; the exact location of the village had changed but there was still settlement continuity (a feature generally recognized for Jutland where continuity of location existed from as early as the Bronze Age up to the present day – settlements would be moved generally not more than half a kilometre at a time (L. Hvass 1980, p. 25)).

A new feature of the Period II settlement at Grøntoft was the fence which enclosed a group of farms (Fig. 3). It was not strong enough for defence but at least served to demarcate the farms inside it from the rest and might have helped to keep farm livestock under control. No differences have survived between the farms inside and those outside the fence – there were large and small farms in both areas. Beside architectural differences between farms of Period I and those of Period II, there were some new features which would have had social and economic consequences. The average living area (west half of longhouse) increased by four square metres and there was greater variation in

animal-stall space between longhouses (Fig. 2). The smallest
farms remained the same size as before (space for six to eight
animals) though the largest ones could now accommodate as
many as twenty animals. Even though we know very little about
land tenure, this change can be taken to indicate an increasing
difference in productivity between households, aiding the
development of a hierarchical society. Two kilometres away at
Grønbjerg a small isolated enclosure was excavated (Fig. 4) and
found to contain two longhouses and at least one outbuilding
(Becker 1980a). It is dated to Period II/IIIa (between 300 and 100
BC) and has several features typical of the later phase. The
outhouse, which is a smithy, is directly connected with the longhouse with stalling for fourteen animals (also some of the pottery

is a black-burnished ware similar to pottery found at Hodde,
which will be discussed later).

By the second century BC (end of Period II) dramatic
changes occurred in settlement organization which leave little
doubt that a small part of the population could produce substan-
tially more agricultural commodities than the rest. This greater
potential surplus is matched by the deposition of prestigious
imported commodities in grave and votive contexts.

An entire village of Period IIIa (c. 200–100 BC) has been
excavated at Hodde in central Jutland (Hvass 1973, 1975, 1975a
and b). At least five constructional phases have been recognized,
the final phase being destroyed by fire. In the first phase there was
only a single farm, surrounded by a palisade. It differed from

Fig. 1. Distribution of Iron Age settlement at Grøntoft (c. 500–200 BC) (after Becker 1980).

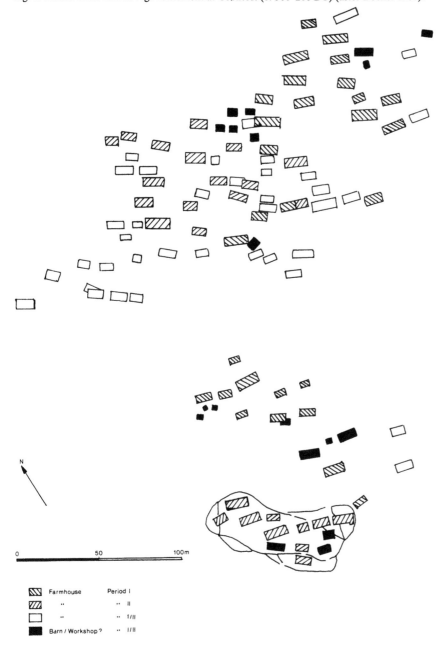

▨ Farmhouse	Period I	
▨ ″	″ II	
▢ ″	″ I/II	
■ Barn / Workshop ?	″ I/II	

Fig. 2. Changing living area and animal stalling in houses of the Pre-Roman Iron Age.

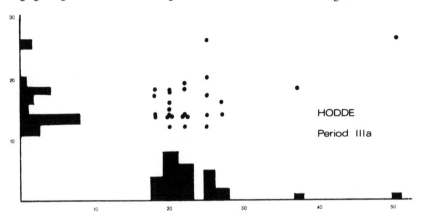

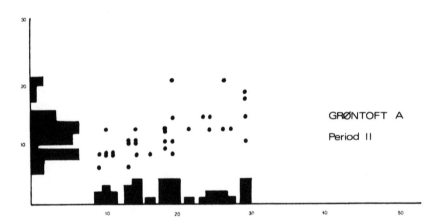

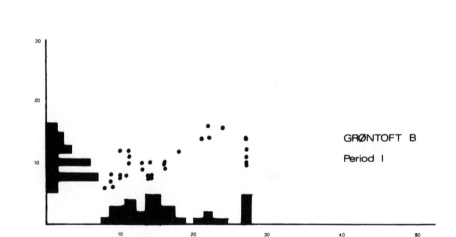

Size of living area in square metres

other farms by having twice the area of living space and stalling for 26–30 animals. Within its compound was a barn (within its own enclosure) and a four-post storehouse. The evidence from a similar structure at Overbygaard in northern Jutland suggests that the four-poster was probably a granary; this structure, partly below ground, had been burnt down and contained many storage pots filled with grain, as well as two swords and an axe head (Lund 1979). The farm at Hodde became the focus of a developing village which, in its heyday, numbered twenty-three farms within a palisade (Fig. 5). The buildings can be divided into farmhouses, barns, storehouses and smithies (Fig. 6) with each compound composed of a farmhouse with varying barn and storage facilities (Fig. 7). While the average living space and the number of animal stalls in each farm had increased since Period II (Fig. 2), the differences between farms were much more marked than ever before. Only one farm had as much stall space as the main farm and only six farm compounds contained more than one four-poster storehouse. At least fourteen farms had no storehouse while some longhouses had hearths but no stalls, possibly because they were farms with no animals of their own. In the final settlement phase a number of longhouses had become smaller (Hvass 1975, p. 155), a further indication of growing poverty and differentiation between the poor and the well-off. The differences in productive capacity between the initial main farm and the rest were complemented by stylistic differentiation. We may assume that the main farm was the most imposing building in the village since each structure in its compound was founded on deep wall-trenches and the compound enclosure itself was the most strongly defined boundary in the entire settlement. The distribution of differing ceramic types across the village also marks this farm apart from the rest; fine black-burnished pottery was strongly localized in the main farm area. The pottery was used as tableware and perhaps as small storage containers. Its appearance in contemporary and later graves as symbolic tableware-sets for the dead is an important feature which allows potentially direct

connection to be made between funerary and settlement contexts. While we must bear in mind that styles used in a domestic context by one social group may be used by a lesser social group for highly ritualized events such as funerals, it is equally possible that the events involving the preparation and eating of foods were also highly ritualized. As we shall see later, black-burnished tableware generally accompanies Period III burials which have unusual grave equipment.

Votive offerings

There appears to have been some continuity in the deposition of votive offerings from the Late Bronze Age into the Early Iron Age. Their quality and content was however diminished though their regular location in bogs and lakes was consistent with Bronze-Age tradition. The items deposited as votive offerings consisted of pottery vessels (sometimes containing food) (Becker 1971a), wooden ploughs (Glob 1945) and individual or collected metal dress-items. The dress fittings provide an interesting comparison between grave and votive deposits. Some occur regularly in both contexts, such as certain kinds of ring attachments (Becker 1961, Fig. 230) though the rest are found predominantly in one or the other context. Bracelets and armrings are not common features of cremation burials but are often found in large numbers in votive finds (Vebaek 1945). Heavy bronze neck rings, dating to the end of the Bronze Age and the early Pre-Roman Iron Age, show signs of extreme wear before disposal (Kristiansen 1981, p. 248) though a few of the very large ones had hardly been worn (Brøndsted 1960, p. 43). The majority of these neck rings were found in lakes or bogs, either singly or in pairs and separate from other bronze objects (Müller n.d., p. 30).

The bog deposits which have attracted most interest are the preserved human corpses (Dieck 1972; Glob 1977; Fischer 1979). Nine have been radiocarbon dated and they fall into two chronological groups; the earliest are Late Bronze Age and earliest Iron Age (650–425 BC) and the remaining five date to

Fig. 3. Two settlement phases at Grøntoft A (300–200 BC) (Becker 1965).

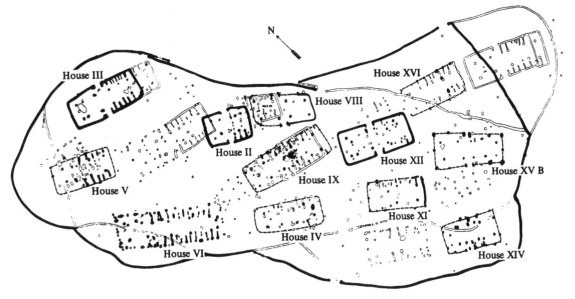

200 BC–AD 50. These two groups coincide with the two periods of revolutionary change at the beginning and the end of the Pre-Roman Iron Age but the standard deviation of the radio-carbon dates prevents us from establishing whether the bodies were buried at around the same time or over several hundred years. These spectacular finds are extremely enigmatic for a number of reasons. If they can be classed as a variant of funerary rites, they represent a ritual form which is diametrically opposed to the norm. They were placed naked in peatbogs and always singly; there was no evidence of grave markers and the majority of well-preserved ones showed signs of violent death – hanged, throat slit or clubbed to death. A second interesting feature among the well-preserved corpses is the delicate physique and fineness of skin which indicates that they did no manual agricul-tural labour (Glob 1977, p. 163). It would seem that they were members of a group separate from the longhouse farmers who inhabited villages such as Grøntoft. Since they were not involved in the direct production of agricultural goods these people must have lived on the surplus of others and in one sense qualify as members of an elite. They may have been ritual specialists or members of an aristocracy, toppled by revolutions or coups. Classical sources mention that the Germans put people to death in this manner for crimes such as cowardice and adultery (Tacitus 1970, p. 111) though the exact reasons may be more complex than the classical authors realized.

Few votive offerings can be securely dated to Period II. A

number of them would seem to belong to either Period II or Period IIIa. One is a large shallow boat, nineteen metres long, from a small bog at Hjortspring (Rosenberg 1937). Associated with the boat were bones of horse, pig, sheep, cow and dog and a large amount of weaponry; eight swords and three blade-fragments, 138 iron spears (with thirty-one tipped with wood or

Fig. 4. The small enclosure at Grønbjerg c. 200 BC (Becker 1980a).

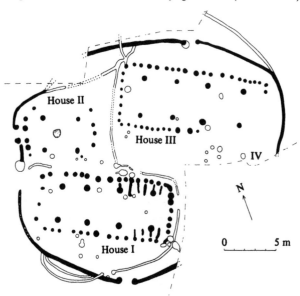

Fig. 5. The main settlement phase at Hodde 200–100 BC (Hvass 1975).

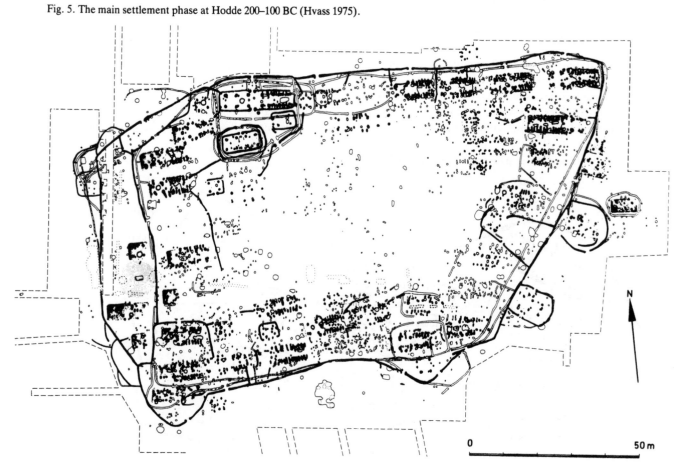

bone) and about 150 wooden shields. A slightly later weapon deposit is also known from Krogsbølle on the neighbouring island of Funen (Becker 1948). These kinds of deposits have been interpreted as the remains of battles. Whether or not this is the case, they demonstrate that enough surplus was being produced to allow the destruction of valuable items (notably the boat and the imported iron swords; Klindt-Jensen 1953, p. 84). Another item buried around this period was a very large cauldron of bronze, broken up and placed with an axehead in a pit on a low

hill at Braa, though not associated with any human bones (Klindt-Jensen 1953). The cauldron is dated by Megaw (1970) to La Tène Id (in Becker's Period II) though the iron axe associated with it is similar to one found in the Period IIIa settlement at Hodde (Hvass pers. comm.). Cast bronze fittings, presumably from a cauldron, were found at Store Vildmose and are stylistically similar to the Braa fittings. While the pottery and fibulae from graves and votive deposits of the late pre-Roman Iron Age can be divided into Periods IIIa and IIIb, many of the exotic items are

Fig. 6. Hodde – arrangement of house types (after Hvass 1975).

Farmhouse

House without Stalls

Storage Hut / Workshop ?

Smithy

0   50 m

Fig. 7. Hodde – arrangement of different compounds (after Hvass 1975).

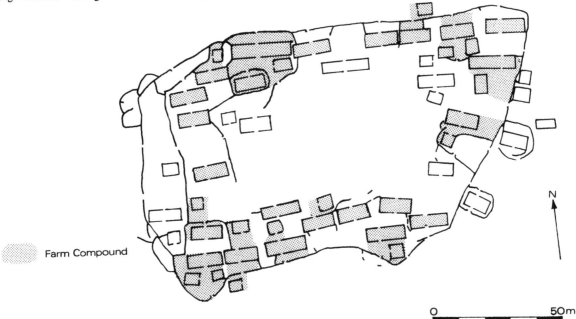

Farm Compound

0   50m

not so securely dated, and for this reason the whole group will be considered together. During this period votive offerings reach their most impressive form in the course of the Pre-Roman Iron Age and then, with the exception of offerings of pottery, and possibly textiles and ploughs, cease all together until the Younger Roman Iron Age (c. AD 200–500). These votive offerings include two elaborate bronze-inland wooden wagons from Dejbjerg, a gold torc from Dronninglund and a gold-inlaid silver cauldron from Gundestrup. The cauldron's date of deposition is very difficult to ascertain but has been assigned by Brøndsted to Period III (1960, pp. 82–3).

Burial practices. The funerary practices of Period I were relatively simple and uniform. The body was cremated in full dress and the surviving ashes and metal dress fittings were collected up and placed in a storage pot which was then buried under a small, shallow mound. While the mounds were relatively the same size, they were constructed in many different ways, often surrounded by ditches or stake-circles. The grave goods were restricted to iron or bronze dress-items such as thick-headed pins, belt fittings and single ornaments (Becker 1961; Jørgensen 1971; 1972; 1975). The graves are located in large cemeteries of up to 1500 cremations under mounds and carefully respect each other despite being placed close together. The horizontal stratigraphy (Becker 1961, p. 180; Jørgensen 1975, Fig. 1) would suggest that spatial segregation on the lines of age, sex or family lineage division was subsumed under a community ideology for the dead. The only prominent divisions between graves are the segregation of urns in cemeteries and urns buried in secondary graves in earlier prehistoric mounds, and the different sizes of the mounds (though even the largest would have required only a small amount of effort to build, unlike many of the Bronze-Age mounds).

The graves assigned to Period II are too few for detailed analysis and their scarcity adds to the doubt surrounding the chronological distinction between Periods II and IIIa. Some burials of this period stand out, however, with grave equipment which includes large iron belts (Klindt-Jensen 1953, pp. 87–9). In Period III a few graves in Denmark mark a break in continuity (located away from earlier cemeteries and containing large quantities of prestige items and sacrificed animals). Cremations at Langaa on Funen and Kraghede in northern Jutland contained the burnt remains of wagons, cauldrons, weaponry and other items.[1] Another change in burial practices at this time was the inclusion of weapons on the funeral pyre and their burial with the ashes. There are some fifty-three weapon graves of Period III in Jutland (Nielsen 1975) some of which are very well equipped.[2] In Period IIIb silver first appears in two Jutland graves at Farre (Thorvildsen 1951) and Vorbasse (Hvass pers. comm.). Black-burnished pottery occurs in nine Period IIIb cremation burials in southern Jutland (five of them are weapon graves and the rest are female graves equipped with knives, fibulae and needles) and in the Period IIIa graves at Kraghede.

There are some very profound changes during this Pre-Roman Iron Age. From a stage which might be regarded as one of 'primitive communism' Iron-Age society is gradually transformed as competition between farms increases with the more successful getting larger. Accompanying the growing rift between those who can increase their surplus and those who remain with the same productive capacity is the cumulative deposition of imported valuables as votive gifts, presumably to placate or enlist the support of supernatural forces. This gradual process culminates in a sudden and revolutionary series of changes (Fig. 8). The gap between the rich and the poor is formalized into a clearly marked class relationship defined ideologically in several ways. While animals had always been kept privately it is only in the second century BC that storage structures were placed in the privacy of a well defined compound. Such changes could be well explained as the manifestations of new rights of private property (Stummann Hansen 1981). There may also be a link between the growing differences in surplus production and the increase in gifts to gods. A gift is thought to oblige the recipient (in this case the deity) to reciprocate, by bestowing divine favour on those making the gift. This fund of divine favour has the effect of increasing the respect and indebtedness of others towards those producers who have 'bought' their closeness by making such gifts (see Parker Pearson 1983).

In this situation the wealthy become wealthier and the poor become indebted to the wealthy (Friedman 1975; 1979). The emergent elite class consolidates its position of power by transferring 'gifts to gods' to 'gifts to ancestors'. The important thing to note here is that to destroy valuable commodities with the dead, instead of 'giving' them to lakes and other natural features, implies that certain of the dead are invested with powers previously attributed to external supernatural forces. The successor to the deceased thus has ideological legitimation for a political

Key to Fig. 8.

Silver ornament
Gold ornament
Gold ring
Silver cup
Glass cup
Silver neckring
Gold horn
Swords
Bronze ladle
Bronze cauldron
Wagon
Boat

Fig. 8. Chronological distribution of consumed wealth and productive potential from 500 bc to the birth of Christ.

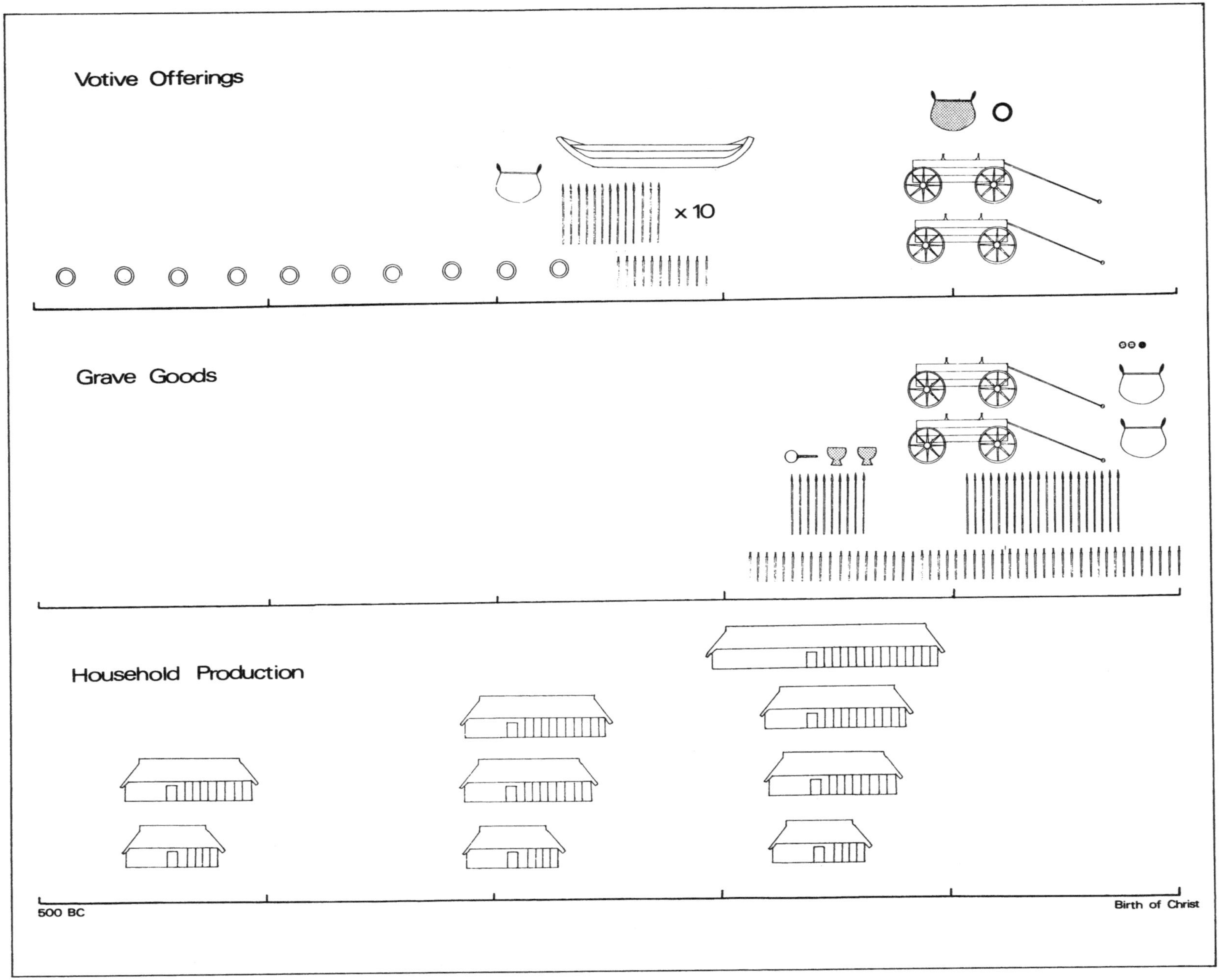

Votive Offerings

Grave Goods

Household Production

500 BC

Birth of Christ

position by being directly related to a deity. This 'privatization' of the supernatural fits well with the concurrent changes in private property and the stylistic distinctions (in architecture and ceramics) which categorize the newly emergent classes.

The second cycle: the Older Roman Iron Age 50 BC to c. AD 200

The Older Roman Iron Age has been conventionally known as the period when the first Roman imports appears in Denmark. It is the least well documented period of the early Iron Age since burial is the only context which has been extensively researched. No settlements of this period have been excavated in their entirety and votive deposits had virtually ceased at the end of the Pre-Roman Iron Age. The chronology of grave assemblages has been worked out on fibulae and Roman imports (Albrectsen 1956) and as many as five phases have been recognized (Liversage 1980). An accurate chronology based on ceramics and fibulae also exists for southern Jutland (Jarl Hansen 1982). The distinction between Roman and pre-Roman, although stylistic, need not be chronological and it is likely that the two periods overlap (Bech 1976). The earliest graves of the Older Roman Iron Age may well be contemporary with the latest ones of Period IIIb.

Burial practices
Early phase of the Older Roman Iron Age

Throughout Denmark and other areas of north-west Europe there are a number of burials dated to the early first century AD which stand out with their Roman equipment, normally drinking sets. One of these was a cremation inside a black-burnished pot from Tombølgaard in southern Jutland. It was covered by a bronze Roman dish and contained a bronze Roman saucepan, gold jewellery, a silver fibula and two drinking-horns (Norling-Christensen 1960). The view that wealthy 'Celtic' graves were replaced by wealthy 'Roman' ones over a passage of time is complicated by the concurrence of Celtic and Roman Iron-Age styles (of weaponry, dress ornament and ceramics) in the same grave assemblage from burials such as Dons 1 and Sønder Vilstrup. The conventional archaeological interpretation of such assemblages might be that they represent a transitional chronological phase, though it may be nearer the truth to interpret the difference between Celtic and Roman in terms of a broader European ideological and political conflict as the Roman frontier advanced to the Rhine and the Danube. The 'transitional' assemblages would represent a slightly later reworking of conflicting ideologies.

Another change that occurs around about the time of the birth of Christ is the introduction of inhumation burial. This rite is closely related to the use of imported Roman commodities as grave equipment in contrast to the association of cremation with Celtic equipment; with a few exceptions, notably Tombølgaard (see above) and Avnevig, an inhumation with a Celtic-influenced Hannoveran brooch (Anon. 1957). Approximately one in ten of every burial recovered from this phase is an inhumation. The relationship between this rite and black-burnished tableware as

grave goods is quite strong; thirty-eight out of a total of around forty-five inhumations of probable first-century date are equipped with black-burnished pottery, in contrast to eighteen cremations, four of which contained Roman imports.

With the exception of the few lavishly equipped 'Fürstengraber' inhumations (Gebühr 1974), the inhumations of the first century (and probably most of the second century) were poorly equipped. Unlike contemporary 2nd–1st century AD cremations, some inhumations were buried under mounds (e.g. Hvejsel; Lund-Hansen 1974) and a few possessed gold rings but otherwise their assemblages were little different in quantity of metalwork from the average cremation burial. The most usual equipment was a bronze or iron fibula, a knife and perhaps a pair of shears or a razor, along with a few black-burnished pots. An analysis of textile impressions on the metalwork in some of these graves demonstrates that the clothing of the deceased was of mediocre quality (Bender Jørgensen 1979, pp. 38–9). Black-burnished pottery was still in use on the largest farms such as the Older Roman Iron Age longhouse at Dankirke (Finn Ole Nielsen pers. comm., Thorvildsen 1972), suggesting that its distribution was still restricted to a dominant social group (the same impression can be formed from its rare appearance in certain grave assemblages as noted above). However, more extensive excavations in ORIA settlements must be carried out before we can be sure that smaller farms did not have access to this commodity. There are certain important 'stylistic' features which separate the two funerary groups; the provision of shears, spurs, gold rings and black-burnished pottery is closely correlated with inhumation and, where it survives, mound construction; while in only two cases was weaponry placed in inhumations since it is otherwise found only in cremations (until the late 2nd/early 3rd centuries).

Unlike the 2nd–1st centuries BC and the earliest 1st century AD, characterized by rising destruction of imported commodities in graves, the 1st/early 2nd centuries AD are characterized by symbolic categorization between classes in death without consuming large amounts of gold, silver or bronze. The distinction between social groups is both subtle and heavily ritualized to provide a framework in which individuals 'know their place'. A further ritualized division develops among groups that cremate their dead in Period IIIb and the early phase of the ORIA. Males and females, with the exception of young children, are buried in separate areas within the same cemetery and even in different cemeteries (this seems to be the case in northern Germany too; Capelle 1971). The phenomenon is true for the distinction between inhumations and cremations, though amongst inhumations there is little evidence for sexual differentiation, either in terms of grave-location or grave-equipment (osteological analysis reveals that male cremations are equipped with swords, shields, spears, razors and long knives and females with paired or multiple sets of fibulae, small curved knives, sewing needles and bone pins; Dehn unpub., Hvass pers. comm.).

It is important to understand why there might be so few valuables placed with the dead at this time, in comparison with the earlier period of deposition. It would be easy to explain this change in purely external terms, that the intensity of exchange with the Roman world (and the Celtic world, now occupied by Roman forces) fluctuated and had markedly declined by this time. The absence of precious metals and imported valuables in buried contexts may be the result of their disappearance from circulation. A corollary of this is that large quantities of surplus could no longer be produced for conversion into valuables. The settlement evidence sheds some light on this problem. From stratified layers of a farmhouse at Fredbjerg dating to the first century AD, came the remains of a wagon similar to those of the first century BC (Jensen 1980). Its presence in a rubbish context indicates that it was thrown away instead of being used as a grave good or recycled as scrap. At Ginderup in north-western Jutland a Roman coin-hoard of twenty-four silver coins and one gold coin was found under the floor of a small building. The coins date between 124–103 BC and AD 74 and the hoard is estimated to have been deposited not later than the beginning of the second century AD (Hatt 1935, pp. 47–50). For whatever reason the coin hoard was concealed, it does indicate that silver was in circulation in the early second century AD though it was not commonly used as grave equipment. At Dankirke in southern Jutland fragments of imported bronze cauldron were found in ORIA rubbish-layers but we must wait until the pottery in these deposits has been dated more closely (Jarl Hansen, pers. comm.).

Longhouses excavated at Dankirk (Thorvildsen 1972), Fredbjerg (Jensen 1980) and Myrthue (Thomsen 1964) are of the same size, if not larger than the main farm at Hodde, indicating that some houses were capable of producing a surplus. The large-area excavation of part of an ORIA settlement at Rugsted Lund in central Jutland has uncovered twenty-one houses which are, on average, larger than the farms at Hodde(Adamsen unpub.). However there is still not enough settlement evidence for this period to be able to compare social structure as represented in settlements and in graves. It would seem likely that farms of this period were capable of surplus production though the wealth found in graves is not a reflection of the capacity to produce a surplus at any one time nor does it directly reflect fluctuations in the circulation of valuable commodities. We must find another explanation for the withdrawal of commodities from circulation for placing in graves, such as the suggestion above that cumulative class-differentiation and indebtedness increasingly threaten the established elite who respond by enlisting the help of the ancestors. However, ancestral aid does not solve the dilemma until there are changes of a revolutionary nature (rebellions, tribal wars, new technology) which will temporarily end growing contradictions.

The later phase of the Older Roman Iron Age

Though the quantity of imported valuables in graves of the later first and early second centuries is small, nevertheless it marks the beginning of a cumulative process of grave-good deposition. The number of bronze fibulae in burials remains constant throughout the ORIA (Fig. 9). The rate of deposition of bronze, then, remains steady throughout the ORIA, but we should note that the deposition of gold and silver, and indeed of finished *Roman* bronzes increases steadily amongst a small

section of the population (Fig. 10). Until we have a full settlement sequence for the ORIA we can only conjecture on the development of increasing inequalities in surplus production.

By the late second century AD nearly all the gold, silver, glass and Roman bronzes (over 90%) come from eighteen graves in southern Jutland. The double inhumation at Dollerup (Fig. 11) is the richest, with two Roman bronze buckets, two Roman silver cups, two drinking-horns, silver and silver inlaid fibulae, three gold rings, nineteen silver fittings and very high quality fabrics (Voss and Ørsnes-Christensen 1948; Bender Jørgensen 1979, p. 44). While this is the only grave in the area to have been categorized as part of the 'Fürstengraber' phenomenon across north-west Europe, it is stylistically related to the other wealthy graves of southern Jutland and must be considered in the context of those other graves. Some of the wealthy graves are cremations which are buried in mounds and contain a startling variety of bronze and iron drinking and fighting equipment along with the gold, silver and bronze dress-fittings. Confirmation of the wealth gap comes from an analysis of the textiles, which are of fine quality in these wealthy graves and ordinary quality in the rest (Bender Jørgensen 1979, pp. 44–5).

The pattern of destruction of weapons on funeral pyres also changed gradually during the first and second centuries AD. Swords were increasingly uncommon grave goods and none are found in second-century graves though spears and shields were often destroyed. By the late second and early third centuries AD swords were beginning to appear again but this time predominantly in the particularly wealthy inhumations and cremations. The rare occurrence of swords in ordinary weapon-graves might be explained in terms of class differences with lower social groups, who did not possess swords, emulating ruling-class ancestor rituals.

Another case of stylistic emulation can be made for the procurement of black-burnished pottery which, by the second century was increasingly a feature of cremations with few or no grave goods. Conversely it was seldom a component of the

Fig. 9. Chronological distribution of ORIA fibulae placed in burials.

OLDER ROMAN IRON AGE FIBULAE

	Late 1st BC Early 1st AD	Late 1st AD Early 2nd AD	2nd AD	Late 2nd AD Early 3rd AD
Gold & Silver			1	1
Gold & Bronze				1
Silver	3	8	8	3
Silver & Bronze		1	1	2
Bronze	44	61	52	33
Iron	26	6	3	7

wealthy graves of the late second and early third centuries. Other ceramic stylistic changes included the diversification of decorative motifs on ordinary pottery (Jarl Hansen 1982). The simple horizontal-groove decoration of the first century AD was augmented or replaced by more diverse styles while numbers of different pot forms increased. The pottery of the wealthy graves at the end of the ORIA is generally of a different form and decoration from earlier styles; in some cases it is imported from northern Germany and in others the underside is painted with white spots (though not all the painted pottery is associated with wealthy burials). The segregation between cremation and inhumation, as mentioned above, also gradually broke down as an indicator of class. Likewise male and female distinctions became less meaningful. Spatial segregation of male and female graves was less common and a number of graves contained objects which had male associations together with those that had female associations. Virtually all ritual conventions which had served to keep people apart at the beginning of the ORIA had collapsed, presumably through a continuous process of emulation of ruling-class values. The increasing deposition of valuables in graves would be the only clear way of demonstrating worldly power, that is, by 'buying' ancestral legitimation.

The resulting crisis involved most of Scandinavia and north-western Europe which entered a period of tribal conflict in the third century AD. The lack of settlement evidence for this period means that we have to rely primarily on the burial evidence to document this crisis (increased consumption of wealth creating debt and poverty amongst the majority of the population). Evidence for warfare and territorial aggression comes from within southern Jutland as well as north-west Europe as a whole. A ditched and banked wooden palisade which has been traced for twelve kilometres was constructed to keep out groups to the north and to block the overland trade-route between Jutland and Schleswig. Its three phases of construction were dated by eight radiocarbon samples to AD 123, AD 140 and AD 201 (Neumann 1977).

In the latter part of the third century AD large quantities of weaponry were broken up and thrown into lakes in Jutland. They may well have been deposited after battles and could signify a period of conflict (their significance will be discussed below). Haderslev fiord on the east coast of Jutland was blockaded with underwater defences which have been dated to 260 ± 100, 240 ± 100 and 290 ± 100 radiocarbon years AD (Crumlin-Pedersen 1975). Roman documents indicate that the empire faced its greatest threat in over two centuries. In the second half of the third century the northern frontier was breached from Britain to the Black Sea by barbarian incursions, including Saxon sea raids on Britain and France, and Alamannic and Frankish attacks on the Rhine and Danube frontier (Luttwak 1976, pp. 146–50). While there is no doubt that this resulted partly from weaknesses within the Empire it should now be recognized that tensions within the barbarian world probably provided some impetus for these attacks.

The third cycle: third to fifth/sixth centuries AD (Younger Roman Iron Age–Older Germanic Iron Age)

The chronology of the YRIA and OGIA in southern Jutland is not entirely satisfactorily worked out. Earlier studies (Mackeprang 1943) have been improved upon by the analysis of chronological sequences throughout Denmark and parts of north-western Europe (Lund-Hansen 1976; Jensen 1976; Jensen 1979a) to allow dress-items, and to a lesser extent, pottery, to be adequately dated. In southern Jutland the large number of settlements and cemeteries recently excavated, as well as the impressive weapon deposits in lakes (excavated in the nineteenth century as well as recently) provide an extraordinary range of material culture from different social contexts. When placed in chronological sequence, the material provides the clearest evidence for the processes of social change which characterize the Iron Age in Jutland.

Settlement evidence

There is now a considerable body of excavated settlement evidence for the YRIA and OGIA in southern Jutland (Jensen 1980a; Vorting 1973; Haderslev Museum 1979; 1980; Hatt 1958; Hvass 1976; 1977; 1978; 1979; 1979a; Thorvildsen 1972; Andersen 1978; Egeberg Hansen 1980). The settlement at Vorbasse has been the most extensively excavated and has been divided into three main chronological phases which roughly correspond to the third, fourth, and fifth centuries AD (Hvass 1979). The settlement provides a palimpsest of village and farmstead development during the third cycle of Iron Age social evolution (Fig. 12). The

Key to Fig. 10.

⊗	Silver ornament
●	Gold ornament
⊙	Gold ring
	Silver cup
	Glass cup
○	Silver neckring
	Gold horn
‖‖‖	Swords
	Bronze ladle
	Bronze cauldron
	Wagon
	Boat

Fig. 10. Chronological distribution of consumed wealth from the birth of Christ to the sixth century.

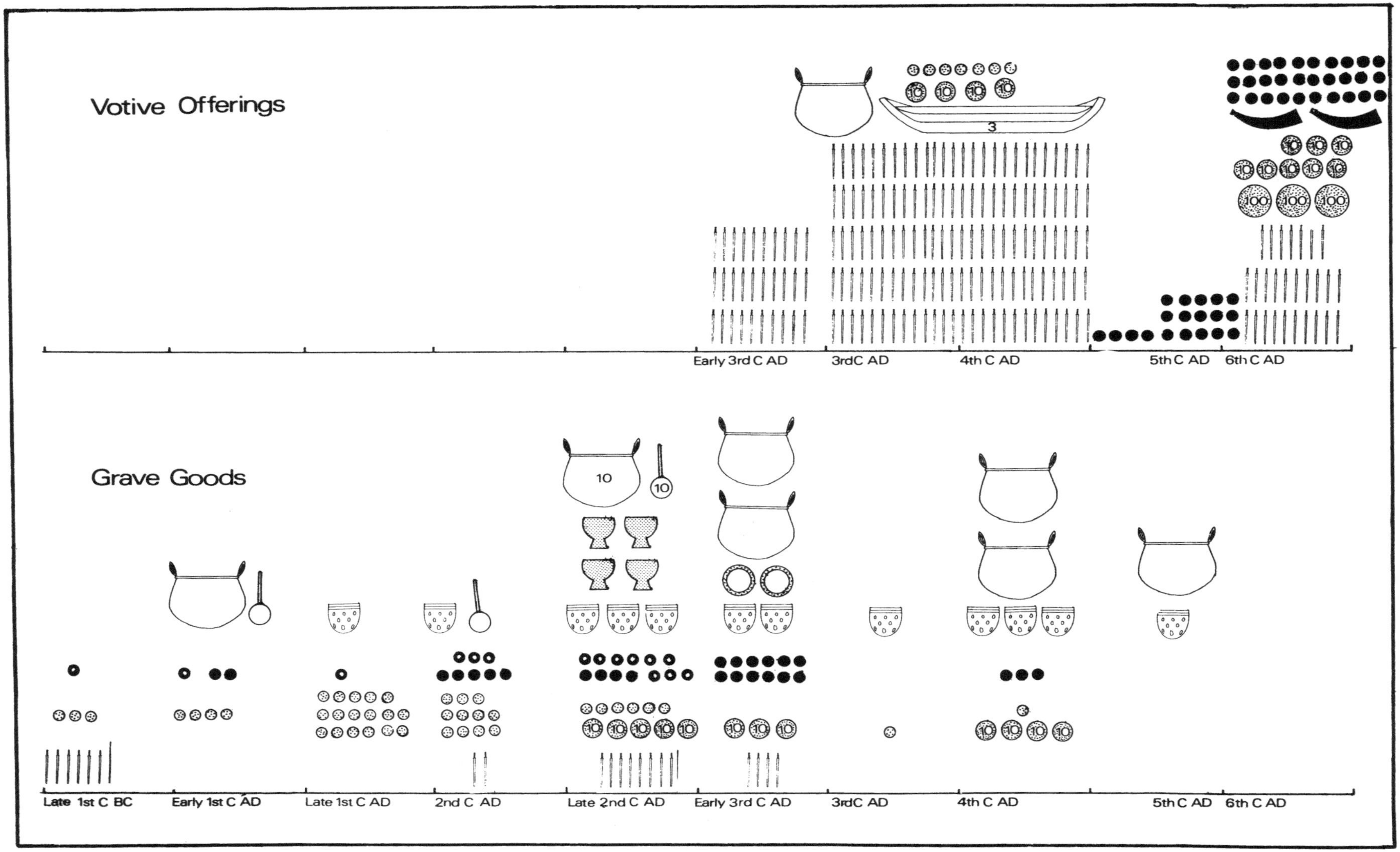

settlement plan is not published in the same detail as plans of earlier settlements like Hodde and Grøntoft, and stall-remains in the farmhouses are poorly preserved, making detailed analyses of living-space, animal numbers and storage-space more difficult.

At Vorbasse there are a number of new architectural and productive features which are common to all YRIA settlements excavated so far. The village is composed of up to twenty farms arranged in rows, indicating some form of planned layout. The farms were no longer arranged within a village enclosure but each was separated from the other by adjoining rectangular compounds. The double row of posts which formed the compound

palisade was a clearer demarcation of property than any previous boundary structures within settlements. The farm unit now consisted of the farmhouse and one or two outbuildings (including lean-to structures against the palisade). The farmhouse had more living space at the west end than before and an estimated average of twenty-four large animal stalls. An extra storage and working area was added on to the eastern end of the longhouse. It was often open-ended and only very rarely contained a hearth, making it unlikely that this was a living-area. One outbuilding had been an animal byre and one or two had hearths which suggests that they were the habitations of impoverished groups, presum-

Fig. 11. The Fürstengrab double burial at Dollerup (Voss and Ørsnes-Christensen 1948).

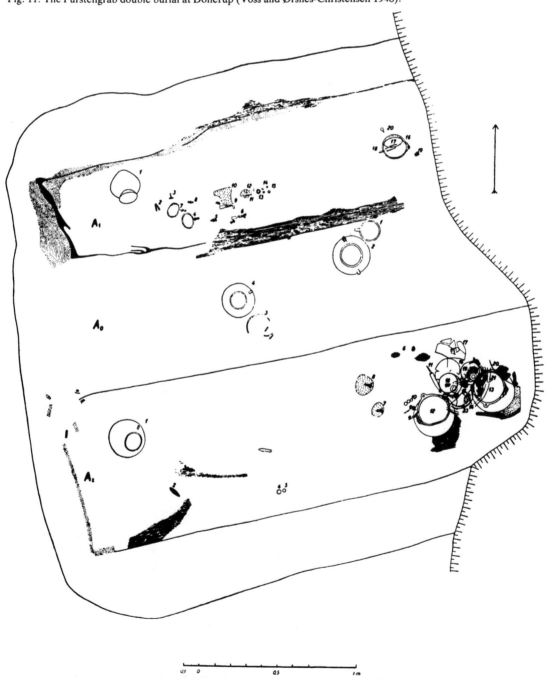

Fig. 12. Changing settlement layout at Vorbasse in the third, fourth and fifth centuries AD (Hvass 1979).

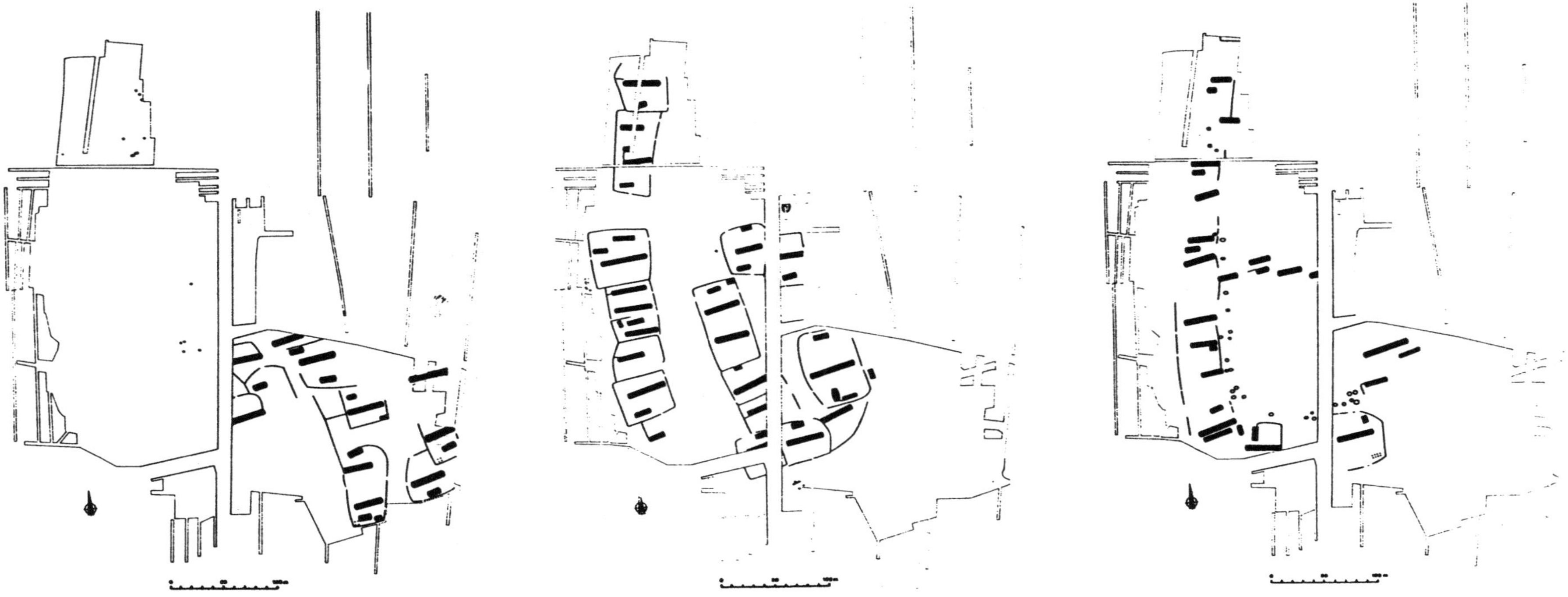

ably involved in some sort of relationship of dependence to the main household. Unfortunately it is not clear whether they belong to an earlier or later phase.

The area of third-century occupation at Vorbasse has not been fully excavated though ten farms can be reconstructed (Hvass 1979, Fig. 3). There seems to be little difference between farm units though a main farm may have existed to the east outside the excavated area (at least three inhumation cemeteries of this period have been found in different parts of the site and would appear to correspond to individual farm-units; one in the eastern area had graves far more lavishly equipped than the others and would fit the theory that a dominant household existed in the village). The fourth-century layout (Fig. 12) included a farm which was distinct from the others in several ways with its large farmhouse and compound and four outbuildings (none of the others have more than two). By the fifth century the productive capacity of the settlement as a whole had markedly declined, with each farm smaller than before and none possessing more than one outbuilding (at this time sunken-floored huts were constructed outside the farm compounds but their small size limited the amount of storage-space). The main farm still retained its dominant position but was limited to one, or possibly two, outhouses. This reduction in production is most satisfactorily explained as an economic crisis, and after this phase the settlement was temporarily deserted, a phenomenon known for contemporary settlements in northern Europe (Hvass 1978, p. 106; 1979, p. 35). Corroborative evidence comes from the late YRIA settlement excavated at Mølleparken (Haderslev Museum 1979, pp. 7-8). Four small farmhouses were located to the north of a larger one which possessed three outbuildings. This large farmhouse had a second hearth at its eastern end and conceivably housed two groups of people.

Settlement evidence for the OGIA has been found at Nørre Snede in central Jutland where a large section of the village has been excavated (Egeberg Hansen 1980). As many as three or four phases of rebuilding have been identified within each compound. The average size of the longhouses is less than at fifth-century Vorbasse and there are not more than one or two barns or four-post structures within the compound (1980, Fig. 2). The economic depression recognized at Vorbasse in the fifth century would seem to worsen in the sixth century.

Funerary evidence

The number of burials known from the YRIA of southern Jutland is less than the number of ORIA graves. It is likely that this is due to retrieval differences – the vast majority of YRIA graves are inhumations dug deep into sandhills and less likely to be recognized by agricultural and other activities than the shallow cremation graves and stone-lined inhumations of the ORIA. A number of YRIA cemeteries have, however, been extensively excavated and provide important spatial as well as chronological information (e.g. Broholm 1953).

The earliest funerary structures of the period are stylistically, though not necessarily chronologically, separate from the lavish grave assemblages that characterize the end of the ORIA.

Rectangular post structures supporting funeral pyres have been found at Farre and Enderupskov, the former with an unknown quantity of glass vessels, glass-bead necklaces, and vessels and fittings of bronze and silver (Thorvildsen 1951) and the latter with imported Terra Sigillata (manufactured c. 150 AD), a gaming set, glass beads and bronze items (Neumann 1970). Inhumation graves of the third century of TRIA style contained pottery and full dress-sets. Imported Roman drinking equipment was now rare in southern Jutland graves (but frequently found in graves on the Danish islands) (Neumann 1953). Metal dress-fittings, especially fibulae, were often of silver, and were widely distributed throughout the population. This contrasts with the latest ORIA graves when the distribution of silver was limited to the graves of a few individuals. The break in stylistic continuity, like that of the PRIA/ORIA division included changes of settlement location and cemetery location. As mentioned above, it is quite likely that stylistically distinct assemblages overlapped chronologically, but were kept rigidly apart as categorical opposites. We could express this in another way as the challenge of an 'alternative' culture to the existing order at a time of crisis. It is certainly to be noticed that each period of crisis is marked by the appearance of an innovatory repertoire of styles which are kept separate from the conventional assemblages.

There are few graves which may be dated with certainty to the fourth century AD. This is probably due to the absence of typologically distinct metal dress-fitting styles in the graves. Items of silver or gold are particular rare in those graves which have been identified. An inhumation cemetery at Hjemsted contained over seventy burials dating principally to the fourth and fifth centuries AD. Only a few of the graves produced finds of valuable commodities – these were fifth-century females wearing necklaces with silver pendants (Andersen 1978). A wooden chamber-grave of the late fourth century from Enderupskov contained a glass vessel, a spear, a knife and buckle and a bronze fibula (Rieck 1980) but otherwise there are few impressive burials of late YRIA and OGIA date. While the accumulation of valuables in graves did not follow the same process of incremental growth as before in ORIA the quality of dress worn by the deceased declined for the majority of the population. By the fifth century items of silver and glass were restricted to very few graves, and in those contexts were relatively plentiful.

Votive offerings

During this period burials were replaced by votive deposits as the central context for the destruction of wealth. These deposits are some of the most impressive archaeological remains from the Iron Age and include huge quantities of weapons (Engelhardt 1969; 1970) and numerous gold hoards (the latter are not easily definable as 'votive' offerings). The depositions of military equipment were made in lakes on either side of the sea dividing Jutland from Funen, an area which had become deserted in the YRIA (Fig. 13).

Recent excavations have demonstrated that this equipment was broken up and thrown into the lake in a single instance with later offerings of equipment being made in exactly the same place up to two hundred years later (this continuity would support the idea that these lakes had a sacred character; Ilkaer and Lønstrup pers. comm.). The interpretation of the deposits as collective sacrifices of war spoils was partly based on references from classical sources (Ørsnes 1963, pp. 232–3) and the composition of the assemblages can be broken down into a pyramidal structure. The third-to-fourth century deposit at Ejsbøl comprised nine horse-bits and harnesses, nine saddle-fittings, eight or nine pairs of spurs, sixty swords, sixty belt-buckles, sixty-two knives, over 175 shields, over 191 spears and over 203 throwing lances (Orsnes 1968, Fig. 4). These could have equipped three types of warrior – mounted swordsmen, swordsmen on foot and warriors on foot equipped only with shields and spears. The ratio of mounted to foot soldiers (1:20) was equivalent to the division between main farm and other farms at Vorbasse at the same date and might well have represented a hierarchical division within a war band. No trace of the warriors has ever been found, though the bones of their horses, severely mutilated, were thrown in with their weapons (Engelhardt 1866). Remains of three boats from the deposit at Nydam suggest that war bands came from the eastern islands and Baltic Sea, but some of the fibulae are of a localized Jutish style (Jensen 1979, Fig. 2), suggesting that at least one of the weapon offerings was made with local equipment. The fibulae from the Thorsbjerg deposit further south in Schleswig indicate that the army to which they belonged came from the area between the Elbe and the Rhine (Ilkjaer and Lønstrup 1982, pp. 98–9). Since the swords were all Roman imports and the other weapons not distinguishable into regional styles little more can be said about the geographical origin of the warriors. While our knowledge about battles which may have preceded these offerings is uncertain, there is no doubt that the decision was taken to dump valuable items, rather than keep them in circulation. The production and procurement of these weapons, especially the imported swords, must have made considerable demands on the production of agricultural surplus or other 'commodities' for which they might be exchanged, which might, for instance, include slaves, or time spent in military service as a Roman mercenary. In southern incremental growth. There were three depositions at Nydam (Ilkaer and Lønstrup 1977); a small one in the third century sixth centuries with about one hundred silver sword-and-dress-fittings but no weapons (Kjaer n.d.). There were at least two depositions at Ejsbøl; the main one in the late third or fourth century (C2/3) and a smaller one with bronze weapon-fittings and three ornate swords with silver dress-fittings in the OGIA (Ørsnes 1963).

Many gold hoards in Denmark and north-west Europe have been dated to the OGIA on the basis of the gold bracteates which they contain though there is still some uncertainty about their assignment to the fourth to sixth centuries (Munksgaard 1978, p. 341). They were imitations of Roman gold medallions

Fig. 13a. Distribution of settlement areas (shaded) in the ORIA.

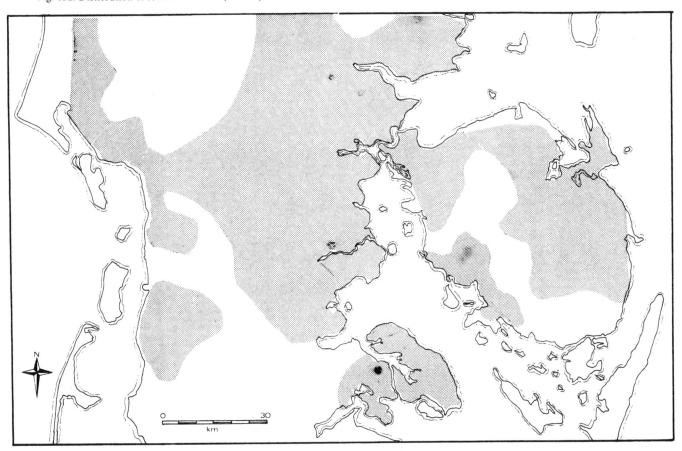

and were worn around the neck as lucky charms (some have runic inscriptions indicating this). In general they have been found in hoards of personal jewellery, with gold or silver fibulae, glass beads, gold pendants, gold arm- and finger-rings, gold sword-fittings and gold or electrum bars. In Jutland they have never been found in burials and were most commonly found while ploughing or peat cutting. It is uncertain how many came from bogs (and were thus more likely to have been offerings in sacred places) because many were found in the nineteenth century when their exact context was not accurately recorded. Bracteates have been divided into three chronological groups on the basis of style and association (Mackeprang 1952). This scheme demonstrates an accelerating increase in the deposition of gold hoards containing bracteates from the fourth to the sixth century (Fig. 10).[3] The most impressive gold hoard from southern Jutland is reckoned to date from the sixth century and consisted of two solid gold horns (now lost) weighing about 7.5 kg from Gallehus (Hartner 1969), equivalent to 1,650 Roman gold coins (Hvass 1980, p. 55).

Three large hoards of 'scrapped' silver (Roman plate, Roman coins, dress-fittings, rings, rods and wire, and ingots) have been found in Denmark and dated to between 500 and 600 AD (Voss 1954; Munksgaard 1955). One was found in southern Jutland at Simmersted and weighed 983 g (Munksgaard 1955).

Summary

The more equal distribution of wealth on which YRIA society was initially based (in contrast to the late ORIA social structure) gradually developed into a widening gap between rich and poor. After a thousand years of Iron-Age social development, the conspicuous consumption of weaponry, gold and silver had reached its peak. The economic crisis which accompanied this might well have been the worst so far. Productive capacity declined as consumption of valuables increased. Funerary ritual was replaced by 'offerings' (partly in lakes and bogs, and partly on dry land) as the main context for the destruction and disposal of objects of high value (all of which had come in some form or another from within the Roman Empire and at great expense, whether by exchange for barbarian commodities, by raiding and plunder, or in return for services to the Romans). This may well represent the transition from an ancestor cult to the worship of the Germanic pantheon of deities which is recorded in the Viking sagas. Certainly the ideological underpinning for the destruction of wealth had changed, even though the mechanism remained the same, as the situation escalated into a severe crisis.

The fifth and sixth centuries AD are known from documentary sources as a period of migration when groups from Jutland and the North Sea coastline left their homelands to colonize

Fig. 13b. Distribution of weapon deposits (black circles) in relation to settlement areas (shaded) in the YRIA.

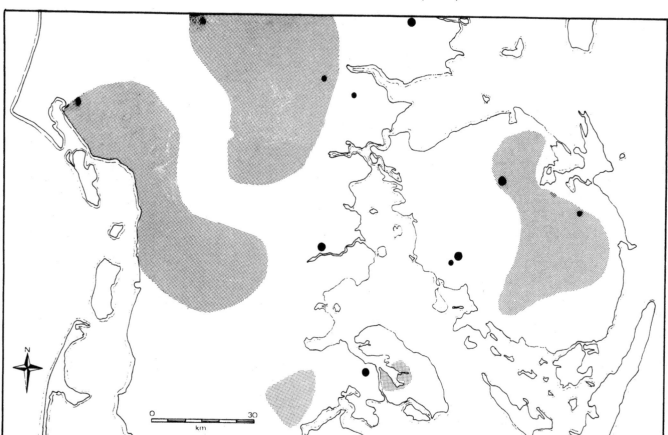

Britain. The economic and social conditions which lay behind the migrations should now be fairly clear. While it might be possible to understand the development of successive waves of expansion and crisis the exact historical outcomes of each crisis (emigration, tribal war, revolution) could never be determined from what went before. It should be apparent to even the most traditional archaeologist that the Anglo-Saxon migrations, which for so long influenced prehistorians' social interpretations, were the result of longer-term social processes of change.

Conclusion

One outcome of this study is to suggest further work that might be done to provide a more detailed and balanced approach to the Iron Age in southern Jutland. A detailed record of ORIA house forms and village morphology still remains to be collected in order to examine changes in production between the birth of Christ and c. AD 250. Systematic area surveys of settlement patterns must be carried out to find out more about settlement density, settlement movement and change, and its relationship to land availability and potential fertility. For example, it would be useful to determine whether poorer land is colonized towards the end of a cycle, and to study the chronological and social context of soil exhaustion (Nielsen 1980), the dating and extent of reafforestation (Andersen 1954) and the population dynamics within each cycle and throughout the Iron Age. Further chronological studies of artefact types are also needed to fix dates as closely and absolutely as possible.

The Danish archaeological evidence tells us very little about anthropological areas of interest such as marriage-exchange and feasting but nevertheless the three main contexts of settlement, funeral ritual and sacrificial ritual show many of the cumulative processes similar to those inferred or extrapolated by Friedman. The increase in productive capacity, the cumulative difference between 'rich' and 'poor', the increased quantity and quality of wealth-items deposited in ritual contexts and the final economic recession with its social conflict and revolutionary changes are all features of the developmental cycle. They can be linked together by an inferred process of growing consumption in which increasingly unequal exchanges (between the living and spirits as well as among the living) build up debts between a consolidating aristocracy and a dependent population. The competitive spiral makes greater demands on the production of a surplus until productive output can no longer match consumption. At the same time material categorization of roles breaks down as conspicuous display becomes the only way of demonstrating and acquiring power.

The material remains from which archaeologists can infer changing productive output and disposal for consumption are in fact much better than the bits and pieces that anthropologists such as Friedman have used. Relations between the living and the supernatural can likewise be measured over long time-spans. Comparison between the different archaeological contexts shows no contradictions between the changing ritual representation of power and its practical application. The basis for a process of accumulation, which allows consumption to rise and inequalities

to develop would seem to have originated at least as long ago as the Iron Age in north-west Europe. However it is important to point out that prestige could only be accumulated by acquiring symbolic capital (by giving away or destroying commodities) since the institutions for economic capital accumulation had not yet emerged. The ideological sanction for consumption came not from the fetishized nature of money in determining value (as is the case in capitalism) but from the ritual gift-giving and sacrifice by the living to the supernatural forces of the ancestors and deities. The reified categories of economy and religion that we have imposed on the world did not exist at that time when each worked through the other. Archaeology has a major contribution to make in this field, which has hitherto been neglected, of understanding the short-term cycles of production and consumption which form an evolutionary development linking earliest human societies with modern capitalism.

While a series of consumption cycles can be defined throughout the period studied, it should be noted that the level of consumption is greater within each successive cycle. The observable cycle of expansion and stagnation in agricultural production covers the whole period from its initial growth in the earlier pre-Roman Iron Age until the economic recession of the fifth and sixth centuries. It would appear that short-term changes in the consumption of wealth occurred within a longer-term cycle in which rising consumption and the growth and decline of production combined in a crisis of major proportions (Fig. 14). The seventh and eighth centuries are severely underrepresented archaeologically (Andersen 1979). Though some settlements have been found (Becker et al. 1979), even with silver and gold coins (Bendixen 1972), there are no well-equipped graves or large treasure hoards. However this crisis was not severe enough to prevent the economic expansion and state formation which had occurred by the mid-tenth century (Randsborg 1980).

Notes

1. A cremation-grave at Langaa on Funen consisted of a large bronze cauldron containing the burnt remains of a wagon, a sword, three daggers, two shields, a gold ring and an old Etruscan bronze pitcher (this jug must have been in circulation for over two hundred years; Klindt-Jensen 1957). At Kradhede in northern Jutland one grave contained the burnt remains of a wagon, three spears, a dagger, iron shears, bronze tweezers, a La Tène fibula and the whole carcasses of at least two horses, two pigs and a sheep as well as bones of ox and sheep. A slightly later cremation burial from Kraghede was placed inside a bronze cauldron and accompanied by a sword, a dagger, a spear, a La Tène fibula and a gold ring (Klindt-Jensen 1949, pp. 203–6). At Husby, just across the German border from southern Jutland, the remains of a wagon and a cauldron also accompanied a cremation burial (Raddatz 1967).

2. A burial from Sønder Vilstrup had two swords, a shield, a spear, a razor, two knives, and a fibula (Jørgensen 1968).

3. It is equally possible that the gold hoards were deposited at a single 'horizon'. Mackeprang's chronological divisions of bracteates on stylistic grounds suggests that they were produced at different dates but the dates of deposition are much less certain. The regular occurrence of early styles of bracteates in hoards containing later types does throw some doubt on the reconstruction of a cumulative process of deposition.

Acknowledgements
The material for this research was collected in Denmark in 1981 and 1982, principally with the help of colleagues at Aarhus University, Copenhagen University, Danish Ancient Monuments Commission, Danish National Museum, Haderslev Museum, Esbjerg Museum, Vejle Museum, Kolding Museum, Sønderborg Museum, Ribe Museum and Schleswig Museum. I am particularly indebted to the following for their help: Steen Andersen, C.J. Becker, Jørn Christoffersen, Torben Dehn, Michael Gebühr, Lotte Hedeager, Steen Hvass, Gitte Høy, Jørgen Ilkaer, Henrik Jarl Hansen, Stig Jensen, Erik Jørgensen, Kirsten Jørgensen, Kristian Kristiansen, Holger Larsen, Michael Lavenborg, David Liversage, Jørn Lønstrup, Ulla Lund Hansen, Finn Ole Nielsen, Leif Christian Nielsen, Berit Pouly Hansen, Klavs Randsborg, Fleming Rieck, Steffan Stummann Hansen, Marie-Louise Sørensen, Margrethe Watt and Mogens Ørsnes. I would also like to thank the following for information in advance of publication: Christian Adamsen, Jens-Henrik Bech, Torben Dehn, Lotte Hedeager, Steen Hvass, Jørgen Ilkaer, Henrik Jarl Hansen, Jørn Lønstrup, Leif Christian Nielsen and Margrethe Watt. Permission to publish excavation plans was kindly given by Prof. C.J. Becker, Steen Hvass, Olfert Voss and Mogens Ørsnes. My special thanks go to Marie-Louise Sørensen and Finn Ole Nielsen for their kindness and hospitality during my stay in Denmark. I am also grateful to my colleagues in Cambridge, especially Andreas Drobny, Jane Grenville, Roger Thomas and Todd Whitelaw, where a shortened version of this paper was presented at a seminar. Helpful criticisms were also received at the Iron Age Death conference in Durham in November 1982.

References
Adamsen, C. (unpublished) 'Rugsted Lund. Foreløbig beretning'

Albrectsen, E. (1956) *Fynske Jernaldergrave*, vol. 2, *Aeldre romersk jernalder*, Copenhagen
Andersen, A. (1954) 'Two standard pollen diagrams from South Jutland', in J. Iversen Ed., *Studies in Vegetational History*, C.A. Reitzels Forlag, Copenhagen, pp. 188–209
Andersen, S.W. (1978) 'Jernaldergravpladser paa Hjemsted Banke ved Skaerbaek', *Antikvariske Studier* 2, pp. 217–19
    (1979) 'Mellem Kongeaa og graense i den sene jernalder', *Nordslesvig Museer* 6, pp. 42–52
Anon. (1957) 'Langdyssen ved Avnevig', *Haderslev Amt Museum* 6, pp. 12–20
Bech, J.-H. (1976) 'Paa baggrund af en gennemgang af Danske gravfund ønskes en redegørelse for kulturudviklingen paa overgangen mellem førromersk og romersk jernalder i Danmark i relation til udviklingen i Norge/Sverige og paa kontinentet', Speciale, University of Aarhus
Becker, C.J. (1948) 'Der zeitliche stellung des Hjortspring-Fundes innerhalb der vorrömischen Eisenzeit in Dänemark', *Acta Archaeologica* 19, pp. 145–88
    (1961) *Førromersk Jernalder i Syd- og Midjylland*, Nationalmuseet, Copenhagen
    (1965) 'Ein früheisenzeitliches Dorf bei Grøntoft, Westjütland. Vorbericht uber die ausgrabungen 1961–3', *Acta Archaeologica* 36, pp. 209–22
    (1968) 'Das zweite früheisenzeitliche Dorf bei Grøntoft, Westjütland', *Acta Archaeologica* 39, pp. 235–54.
    (1971) 'Früheisenzeitliche Dörfer bei Grøntoft, Westjütland. 3. Vorbericht: Die Ausgrabungen 1967–68', *Acta Archaeologica* 42, pp. 79–110
    (1971a) ' "Mosepotter" fra Danmarks jernalder: problemer omkring

Fig. 14. Approximate chronological distribution of wealth consumption and productive capacity 500 BC–600 AD. A long cycle of production consumption is composed of three consumption cycles.

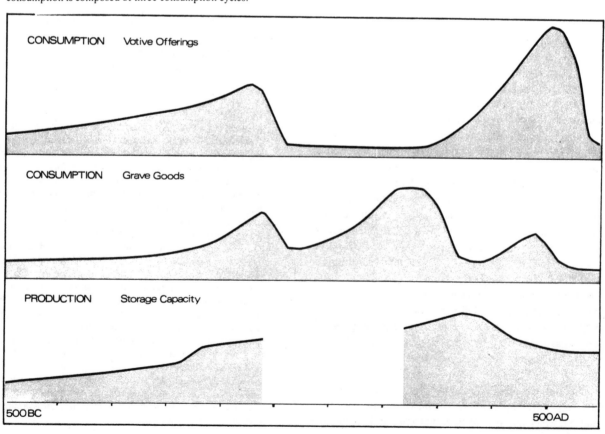

mosefundne lerkar og deres tolkning', *Aarbøger for Nordisk Oldkundighed og Historie*, pp. 5–60

(1980) 'Bebyggelsesformer i Danmarks yngre bronzealder', in H. Thrane Ed., *Broncealderbebyggelse i Norden*, Odense University, Odense, pp. 127–41

(1980a) 'Ein Einzelhof aus der jüngeren vorrömischen Eisenzeit in Westjütland', *Offa* 37, pp. 59–62

Becker, C.J., Bender Jørgensen, L., Hvass, S., Nielsen, L.C. and Stoumann, I. (1979) 'Viking-age settlements in West and Central Jutland. Recent excavations', *Acta Archaeologica* 50, pp. 89–208

Bender Jørgensen, L. (1979) 'Cloth of the Roman Iron Age in Denmark', *Acta Archaeologica* 50, pp. 1–60

Bendixen, K. (1972) 'Mønterne fra Dankirke'. *Nationalmuseets Arbejtsmark*, pp. 61–6

Broholm, H.C. (1953) 'To jydske gravpladser fra Yngre Romersk Jernalder', *Aarbøger for nordiske Oldkundlighed og Historie*, pp. 63–116

Brøndsted, J. (1960) *Danmarks Oldtid III: Jernalderen*, Gyldendalske Boghandel, Nordiske Forlag, Copenhagen

Capelle, T. (1971) *Studien über elbegermanischen Graberfelder in der ausgehender Latenezeit und der älteren römischen Kaizerzeit*, Karl Wachholtz Verlag, Neumünster

Carr, E.H. (1961) *What is History?*, Penguin, Harmondsworth

Childe, V.G. (1942) *What happened in History*, Penguin, Harmondsworth

(1946) *Scotland before the Scots*, Methuen, London

Crumlin-Pedersen, O. (1975) ' "Ae Lei" og "Margrethes bro" ', *Nordslesvig Museer* 2, pp. 9–25

Dehn, T. (unpublished) 'Karensdal'.

Dieck, A. (1972) 'Stand und Aufgaben der Moorleichenforschung', *Archaeologische Korrespondenzblatt* 2, pp. 365–68

Douglas, M. and Isherwood, B. (1978) *The World of Goods: Towards an Anthropology of Consumption*, Allen Lane, London

Egeberg Hansen, T. (1980) 'En aeldre germanertidslandsby i Nr. Snede', *Antikvariske Studier* 4, pp. 309–10

Eggers, H.J. (1951) *Der Römische Import im Freien Germanien*, Hamburg Museum für Völkerkunde und Vorgeschichte, Hamburg

Ekholm, K. (1980) 'On the limits of civilization: the structure and dynamics of global systems', *Dialectical Anthropology* 5, pp. 155–66

Engelhardt, C. (1866) *Denmark in the Early Iron Age; Illustrated by Recent Discoveries in the Peat Mosses of Slesvig (Thorsbjerg and Nydam)*, London

(1969) *Thorsbjerg Mosefund. Sønderjyske og Fynske Mosefund*, Bind I, Forlaget Zac, Copenhagen

(1970) *Nydam Mosefund. Sønderjyske og Fynske Mosefund*, Bind II, Forlaget Zac, Copenhagen

Fischer, C. (1979) 'Moseligene fra Bjaeldskovdal', *Kuml*, pp. 7–44

Frankenstein, S. and Rowlands, M. (1978) 'The internal structure and regional context of Early Iron Age society in south-western Germany', *Bulletin of the University of London Institute of Archaeology* 15, pp. 73–112

Friedman, J. (1975) 'Tribes, States and Transformations', in M. Bloch Ed., *Marxist Analyses and Social Anthropology*, Malaby Press, London, pp. 161–202

(1979) *System, Structure and Contradiction: the Evolution of 'Asiatic' Social Formations*, National Museum, Copenhagen

Glob, P.V. (1945) 'Ploughs of the Døstrup type found in Denmark', *Acta Archaeologica* 16, pp. 93–111

(1977) *The Bog People*, Faber, London

Godelier, M. (1977) *Perspectives in Marxist Anthropology*, Cambridge University Press

Gebühr, M. (1974) 'Zur Definition älterkaizerzeitlicher Fürstengräber vom Lübsow-Typ', *Praehistorische Zeitschrift* 49, pp. 82–128

Haderslev Museum (1979) *Haderslev Museum Aarsberetning*

(1980) *Haderslev Museum Aarsberetning*

Hartner, W. (1969) *Die Goldhörner von Gallehus*, Franz Steiner Verlag, Wiesbaden

Hatt, G. (1931) 'Prehistoric fields in Jylland', *Acta Archaeologica* 2, pp. 117–58

(1935) 'Jernaldersbopladsen ved Ginderup i Thy', *Nationalmuseets Arbejtsmark*, pp. 37–51

(1958) 'A dwelling site of Early Migration period at Oxbøl, southwest Jutland', *Acta Archaeologica* 29, pp. 142–54

Hedeager, L. (1978) 'A quantitative analysis of Roman imports north of the Limes (0–400 AD) < and the question of Roman-Germanic exchange', in K. Kristiansen and C. Paludan-Müller Eds., *New Directions in Scandinavian Archaeology*, National Museum, Copenhagen

(1978a) 'Processes towards State Formation in Early Iron Age Denmark', in K. Kristiansen and C. Paludan-Müller Eds., *New Directions in Scandinavian Archaeology*, National Museum, Copenhagen

(in press) 'Grave finds from the Roman Iron Age', in K. Kristiansen Ed., *The Representativity of Archaeological Remains from Danish Prehistory*

Hindess, B. and Hirst, P.Q. (1975) *Pre-capitalist Modes of Production*, Routledge and Kegan Paul, London

Hingst, H. (1974) *Jevenstedt. Ein urnenfriedhof der alteren vorromischen eisenzeit im Kreise Rendsburg-Eckernforde, Holstein*, Karl Wachholz Verlag, Neumunster

Hodder, I. (1979) 'Economic and Social Stress and Material Culture Patterning', *American Antiquity* 44, pp. 446–54

Hvass, L. (1980) *Danmarkshistorien Oldtid: Jernalderen 1 – Landsbyen og samfundet*, Sesam, Copenhagen

(1980a) *Danmarkshistorien Oldtid: Jernalderen 2 – Bønder, Købmaend og Krigskarle*, Sesam, Copenhagen

Hvass, S. (1973) 'Hodde – en vestjysk jernalderlandsby med social deling', *Mark og Montre*, pp. 10–21

(1975) 'Das eisenzeitliche Dorf bei Hodde, Westjütland', *Acta Archaeologica* 46, pp. 142–58

(1975a) 'Jernalderlandsbyen i Hodde', *Mark og Montre*, pp. 28–36

(1975b) 'Hodde – et 2000-aarigt landsbysamfund i Vestjylland', *Nationalmuseets Arbejtsmark*, pp. 75–85

(1976) 'Udgravingerne i Vorbasse: en landsby fra 4.–5. aarh. og fra vikingtid, samt en brandtomt fra yngre stenalder og to kvinde-gravpladser fra ca. aar 0', *Mark og Montre*, pp. 38–52

(1977) 'Udgravningerne i Vorbasse', *Fra Ribe Amt*, pp. 345–85

(1978) 'Die volkerwanderungszeitliche siedlung Vorbasse, Mittel-jutland', *Acta Archaeologica* 49, pp. 61–111

(1979) 'Fem aars udgravninger i Vorbasse', *Mark og Montre*, pp. 27–39

(1979a) 'Jernalderlandsbyerne ved Vorbasse', *Nationalmuseets Arbejtsmark*, pp. 105–12

(1982) 'Huse fra romersk og germansk jerlander i Danmark', in B. Myhre, B. Stoklund and P. Gjaerder Eds., *Vestnordisk byggeskikk gjennom to tusen aar: tradisjon og forandring fra romertid til det 19 aarhundre – Arkeologiske Museum i Stavanger* 7, pp. 130–45

Ilkaer, J. and Lønstrup, J. (1977) 'Der ønskes en behandling af typologiske og kronologiske problemer i Danske yngre romersk jernalderes vaabenfund fra moser', Speciale, University of Aarhus

(1982) 'Interpretation of the Great Votive Deposits of Iron Age Weapons', *Journal of Danish Archaeology*, 1, pp. 95–103

Jakobsen, J.L. (1975) 'Kastrup: Offer eller gravplads?', *Nordslesvigske Museer* 2, pp. 30–7

Jarl Hansen, H. (1982) 'Drengsted: en aeldre Romersk Urnegravplads fra Sønderjylland (Del 1). En behandling af den aeldre Romerske Gravkeramik i syd- or sønderjylland med henblik paa en opstilling og datering af keramiktyper ved hjaelp af EDB (Del 2)', Speciale, University of Copenhagen

Jensen, S. (1976) 'Fynsk keramik. I gravfund fra sen romersk jernalder', *Kuml*, pp. 151–90

(1979) 'En undersøgelse af den sociale og den geografiske udbredelse af udvalgte genstande fra Yngre Romersk jernalder', in M.-L. Sørensen and K. Levinsen Eds., *Archaeology as a Social Science*, *Kontaktstencil* 16, pp. 80–90

(1979a) 'En nordjyske grav fra romerske jernalder. Sen romersk jernalderes kronologie i Nordvesteuropa', *Kuml*, pp. 167–98

(1980) 'Fredbjerg fundet: en bronzebeslaaet pragtvogn paa en Vesthimmerlandsk jernalderboplads', *Kuml*, pp. 169–216

(1980a) 'To sydvestjyske bopladser fra aeldre germansk jernalder', *Mark og Montre*, pp. 23–36

Jensen, J.A. (1970) 'Da er der glade dag', *Skalk* 1970, 5, pp. 3–9

Jørgensen, E. (1968) 'Sønder Vilstrup-fundet. En gravplads fra den aeldre jernalder', *Aarbøger for Nordiske Oldkundighed og Historie*, pp. 32–90

(1971) 'Tuegravpladsen ved Aarupgaard', *Haderslev Amts Museum* 13.2, pp. 72–7

(1972) 'Tuegravpladsen ved Aarupgaard II', *Haderslev Amts Museum* 13.3, pp. 105–9

(1975) 'Tuernes Mysterier', *Skalk* 1975, 1, pp. 3–10

Kjaer, H. (n.d.) 'Et nyt fund fra Nydam Mose', *Nordiske Fortidsminder* I, pp. 181–96

Klindt-Jensen, O. (1949) 'Foreign influences in Denmark's Early Iron Age', *Acta Archaeologica*, 20, pp. 1–230

(1953) *Bronzekedelen fra Braa: Tidlige Keltiske Indflydelser i Danmark*, Universitetsforlaget i Aarhus, Aarhus

(1957) 'To importfund fra yngre romertid. Nogle synspunkter om absolut datering', *Aarbøger for Nordiske Oldkundighed og Historie*, pp. 105–28

Kristiansen, K. (1981) 'Economic models for Bronze Age Scandinavia – towards an integrated approach', in A. Sheridan and G. Bailey Eds., *Economic Archaeology: towards an integration of ecological and social approaches*, British Archaeological Reports, International Series 96, pp. 239–303

Leach, E. (1977) 'A view from the bridge', in M. Spriggs Ed., *Archaeology and Anthropology – Areas of Mutual Interest*, British Archaeological Reports, Supplementary Series 19, Oxford, pp. 161–76

Liversage, D. (1980) *Material and Interpretation. The archaeology of Sjaelland in the Early Roman Iron Age*, National Museum, Copenhagen

Lund, J. (1979) 'Tre Førromerske kaeldre fra Overbygaard', *Kuml*, pp. 109–40

Lund Hansen, U. (1974) 'Hvejsel-gravpladsen', *Nationalmuseets Arbejtsmark*, pp. 157–8

(1976) 'Das Gräberfeld bei Harpelev, Seeland: studien zur jüngeren römischen kaizerzeit in der seelandischen inselgruppe', *Acta Archaeologica* 47, pp. 91–160

Luttwak, E.N. (1976) *The Grand Strategy of the Roman Empire: From the First Century AD to the Third*, Johns Hopkins University Press, Baltimore

Mackeprang, M. (1943) *Kulturbeziehungen im nordischen Raum dees 3.–5. Jahrhunderts. Keramische Studien* (Hamburger Schriften zur Vorgeschichte und germanischen Frügeschichte 3), Leipzig

(1952) *De Nordiske Guldbrakteater*, Universitetsforlaget i Aarhus, Aarhus

Mandel, E. (1976) 'Introduction' to K. Marx, *Capital: a Critique of Political Economy*, Volume I, Penguin, Harmondsworth, pp. 11–86

(1978) 'Introduction' to K. Marx, *Capital: a Critique of Political Economy*, Volume II, Penguin, Harmondsworth, pp. 11–79

(1980) *Long Waves of Capitalist Development – the Marxist interpretation*, Cambridge University Press

Megaw, J.V.S. (1970) *Art of the European Iron Age*, Adams and Dart, Bath

Miller, D. (1982) 'Structures and strategies: an aspect of the relationship between social hierarchy and cultural change', in I. Hodder Ed., *Symbolic and Structural Archaeology*, Cambridge University Press, pp. 89–98

Müller, S. (n.d.) 'Nogle Halsringe fra Slutningen af Bronzealderen og fra den aeldeste Jernalder', *Nordiske Fortidsminder* I, Copenhagen, pp. 1–18

Munksgaard, E. (1955) 'Late Antique scrap silver found in Denmark. The Hardenberg, Hostentorp and Simmersted hoards', *Acta Archaeologica* 26, pp. 31–68

(1978) 'Brakteaten', in J. Hoops Ed., *Reallexikon der Germanischen Altertumskunde*, Volume 3, Walter de Gruyter, Berlin, pp. 338–41

Neumann, H. (1953) 'Et løveglas fra Rinlandet', *Kuml*, pp. 137–54

(1970) 'Et dødehus fra Enderupskov', *Kuml*, pp. 157–70

(1977) 'Die Befestigungsanlage Olgerdige und der jütische Heerweg', in H.-J. Hässler Ed., *Studien zur Sachsenforschung*, Verlag August Lax, Hildesheim

Nielsen, J.L. (1975) 'Aspekter af det førromerske vabengravmiljø i Jylland', *Hikuin* 2, pp. 89–96

Nielsen, S. (1980) 'Det forhistoriske landbrug. Nogle bemaerkninger om agerjordens beskaffenhed', *Antikvariske Studier* 4, pp. 103–34

Norling-Christensen, H. (1960) 'Romerske industriprodukter i Sønderjylland', in Nistorisk Samfund for Als og Sundeved *Jens Raben: et mindeskrift*, Museet paa Sønderborg Slot, Sønderborg, pp. 129–48

Parker Pearson, M. (1982) 'Mortuary practices, society and ideology: an ethnoarchaeological study', in I. Hodder Ed., *Symbolic and Structural Archaeology*, Cambridge University Press, pp. 99–113

(1984) 'Social change, ideology and the archaeological record', in M. Spriggs Ed., *Marxist Perspectives in Archaeology*, Cambridge University Press

Raddat, K. (1967) *Das wagengrab der jüngeren vorrömischen eisenzeit von Husby, Kreis Flensburg*, Karl Wachholtz Verlag, Neumünster

Randsborg, K. (1974) 'Social stratification in Early Bronze Age Denmark: a study in the regulation of cultural systems', *Praehistorische Zeitschrift* 49, pp. 38–61

(1980) *The Viking age in Denmark: the Formation of a State*, Duckworth, London

Rieck, F.R. (1980) 'Yngre romertids kammergrav i Enderupskov', *Nordslesvigske Museer* 7, pp. 27–36

Rosenberg, G. (1937) 'Hjortspringfundet', *Nordiske Fortidsminder* III.1, Copenhagen, pp. 9–111

Spriggs, M. Ed. (1984) *Marxist Perspectives in Archaeology*, Cambridge University Press, Cambridge

Stummann Hansen, S. (1981) 'The rights of property in the early iron age in Denmark', *Second International Archaeological Student Conference (Szeged 1980)*, Elte University Press, Budapest, pp. 31–50

Sweezy, P.M. (1942) *The Theory of Capitalist Development: Principles of Marxian Political Economy*, Modern Reader Paperbacks, New York

Tacitus (1970) *The Agricola and the Germania*, Penguin, Harmondsworth

Thomsen, N. (1964) 'Myrthue, et gaardanlaeg fra jernalder', *Kuml*, pp. 15–30

Thorvildsen, E. (1972) 'Dankirke', *Nationalmuseets Arbejtsmark*, pp. 47–60

Thorvildsen, K. (1951) 'En gravplads med dødehus ved Farre', *Kuml*, pp. 75–90

Vebaek, C.L. (1945) 'An Early Iron Age sacrificial bog in East Jutland', *Acta Archaeologica* 16, pp. 195–210

Vorting, H.C. (1973) 'Endnu er bopladsforekomst fra germansk jerlander i Esbjerg', *Mark og Montre*, pp. 22–7

Voss, O. (1954) 'The Hostentorp silver hoard and its period. A study of a Danish find of scrap silver from about 500 A.D.', *Acta Archaeologica* 25, pp. 171–220

Voss, O. and Ørsnes-Christensen, M. (1948) 'Der Dollerup-fund. Ein doppelgrab aus der römischen Eisenzeit', *Acta Archaeologica* 19, pp. 209–72

Ørsnes, M. (1963) 'The weapon find in Ejsbøl Mose at Haderslev', *Acta Archaeologica* 34, pp. 232–47

(1970) 'Der Moorfund von Ejsbøl bei Hadersleben und die Deutungsprobleme der grossen nordgermanischen Waffenopferfunde', in H. Jankuhn Ed., *Vorgeschichtliche Heiligtümer und Opferplätze in Mittel- und Nordeuropa*, Vandenhoeck & Ruprecht, Göttingen

Chapter 7

**Ritual and prestige
in the prehistory of
Wessex *c*. 2200–1400 BC:
a new dimension to
the archaeological evidence**
Mary Braithwaite

Certain problematic aspects of the notion of ideology as commonly constructed, and as applied to material culture and historical processes are discussed. The notions of discourse and prestige are introduced as means towards the resolution of these problems. It is argued that certain aspects of the archaeology of Wessex *c*. 2200–1400 bc are best interpreted by means of a notion of competing and dynamic prestige systems. Many aspects of the radical alterations in the content and patterning of the archaeological record noted by prehistorians may be understood by positing a decisive and radical alteration in the systems of prestige and ritual practiced in Wessex. Although some criticisms are made of other interpretations of the Wessex material, the intention of this chapter is rather to supplement these by highlighting aspects of the record neglected in other accounts but of crucial importance in understanding much of the archaeological record.

Theoretical introduction

As archaeologists we are necessarily concerned with the symbolic dimension of social practices. The significance of ceramic design, burial practices, or refuse deposition, for example, lies in their symbolic and semantic character within a particular social and historical formation. Symbols and systems of symbols, as major elements in social action, may be seen as functioning in various ways. Bourdieu (1979), for instance, argues that a symbolic system can be seen as having three functions: as a means of communication, as an instrument for the knowledge and construction of the objective world, and as instrument of domination by establishing and legitimating, through its ideological effect, the dominant culture and concealing that

culture's methods of division. Ideology, understood as the modes through which exploitation and domination in social relations are legitimised, operates as much through the forms of social life as through a system of shared beliefs and values. In fact, the two are inextricably linked through social action. Such a position as this is currently being argued by several archaeologists (see, for example, Hodder 1982 and other papers in this volume), and I would also subscribe to the general emphases of the arguments. However, two major issues are raised by such a position and I shall focus on these in this brief theoretical introduction. One issue concerns the role of material forms in action in any social formation, and the other concerns the notion of ideology.

The specific roles that material forms play in social practices have not been sufficiently theorised in many recent discussions of archaeological theory. I would argue that the significance of material symbols in social practices, particularly those of political importance, cannot be assumed *a priori* and is a problem for investigation in any given social and historical context. Bauman (1971) has considered the relationship between signs and social structure. He argued for an analytical distinction between signs which are primary in relation to position in the social structure and signs which are secondary or derivative in relation to social position. By extension he then argued for a distinction of sociocultural systems between those in which rights to signs are derivative from social position and those in which social position is derivative from possession of signs. The significance of material symbols in terms of political strategies by individuals or groups within these hypothetical schemes is clearly different. Examples in real life might be the difference, perceived in fairly crude terms, between Western capitalist society and Hindu society. In fact what are being contrasted are two quite different systems of prestige. The position and status of individuals or groups in each society are constructed by means of very different criteria, values and beliefs. Material symbols have a correspondingly different significance in terms of political strategies in the two systems.

Moore (1981) notes that archaeologists have made little effort to understand the role of belief in social action, despite the fact that belief systems are principle generative factors responsible for the cultural processes which form the archaeological record. The doctrine of *karma* and notions of purity and impurity are crucial to understanding the production, use and deposition of material items in Hindu society (Dumont 1972; Miller 1982). In Azande society in Sudan, wealth gained through the production and sale of goods is regarded with suspicion and distrust, and production of material items is curtailed by the belief system. The Zande belief-system, involving notions of witchcraft, serves to control the political and material ambitions of the people. This, together with the related system of prestige which differs for different categories of people, determines how material symbols can be used in political practices (Braithwaite forthcoming). The exact content of belief systems may be irretrievable from the archaeological record, but their operation is not. Through awareness of the significance of prestige in social and material practices it is possible to take account of just such a notion as belief.

In taking prestige as one focus of analysis, material culture and social action are not regarded as analytically separate problems, and many difficulties of interpretation (highlighted by the concern with 'middle-range theory') can be circumvented. It also allows sensitivity to the socially and historically specific relationship between a particular prestige system and the conditions of its reproduction – for instance, the associated economic dimensions. Feminist anthropology in particular has drawn attention to the need for social theories that do not specify in advance of investigation specific relationships between a prestige system and other dimensions of social activity. Of course, recognition of the relative autonomy of different dimensions of social practices in any given social formation and of the historical specificity of many features of social formations has been of some concern in Marxist anthropology (Friedman 1974; Godelier 1977), but these problems have not been adequately dealt with at a theoretical level. Ortner and Whitehead (1981) argue that the social organisation of prestige – 'society's rules and mechanisms governing status differentiation' (p. 12) – is the link between the structure of social relations and the culturally-specific practices, values and beliefs of individuals and groups in a society.

Prestige systems are systems of beliefs, values and representations. Different groups of people or individuals within any society have different prestige positions allocated to them or acquired by them. The strategies used by individuals, and the positions attained through these, depend on the content of the prestige-system. Although the discussion by Ortner and

Whitehead (1981) is focussed primarily on the cultural construction of gender and sexuality, it is an important contribution to the establishment of general approaches for the study of social relations and cultural practices. They note the position of Weber (1958) that prestige-systems are structurally significant and historically dynamic, and also the important contributions of other social scientists (e.g. Dumont 1972; Goldman 1970; Bloch 1977) on the nature and working of prestige-systems. They also argue for the importance of determining for each social instance how prestige is culturally articulated and justified – 'One must ask what ideas are invoked to transform "raw" social power into "cooked" esteem, and to establish the rules . . . that govern how this esteem may be enhanced, diminished, adulterated, parlayed, or cashed in' (p. 15) – and also 'how various sets of prestige structures . . . arise from and in turn play back upon deeper . . . social arrangements such as the organization of production' (p. 15). As archaeologists we also need to investigate the specific roles played by material symbols in different prestige systems.

The other major issue that is highlighted by the theoretical position set out in the initial paragraph lies with the notion of ideology. On several grounds this particular conception of ideology appears to raise certain problems for archaeologists. In several recent accounts of prehistory this concept of ideology has been linked with the notion of ritual in interpretations that attempt to understand certain past material practices as ideological devices, designed to maintain and legitimise the political status quo. 'Ritual is one form, albeit a particularly powerful form, of legitimising social hierarchies' (Shanks and Tilley 1982, p. 133). 'The past, especially through ritual communication (including the context of death), is often used to "naturalise" and legitimate hierarchies of power and inequality which would otherwise be unstable' (Parker Pearson 1982, p. 101). While these positions importantly stress that cultural practices and forms are specific constructions of 'reality' rather than mere reflection, they have certain problems as well.

In these formulations symbolic and ritual practices are identified as ideological in function. No theoretical space is given to the potential of symbolism and ritual to be politically subversive and the problem of representation or 'discourse' (in the sense of a system of meaning and representation) as a whole is left unexplored and problematic. In addition, the relationship of symbolic and ritual practice to social and ideological change is also left unexamined. Clearly many ritual and symbolic practices are ideological in intent and function, but ritual practices, and readings of those practices, that do not legitimise social hierarchies or social inequalities also exist, and symbols can convey multiple and contradictory meanings. Turner (1967) has, in particular, been concerned with the plurality of meaning and behaviour associated with symbols, and has noted the existence of discrepancies between the meanings attributed to certain ritual symbols by informants and behaviour exhibited by them in situations dominated by these symbols. Similarly, ritual practices that attempt to subvert the dominant political system also exist. One example is the case of the Zande secret societies which were outlawed by the dominant political hierarchy, but which not only involved elaborate rituals in which many of the subordinate people in the Zande political system took part, but which also acted as a powerful means of mediating social change by, and for, those subordinate groups (Evans-Pritchard 1937; Braithwaite forthcoming). Of course, discourse that attempts to establish or represent alternative sets of political relations may be 'muted' (Ardener 1975), but it nevertheless exists, both potentially and actually, and can be a means of change in terms of the social and the ideological systems.

Asad (1979) is concerned with the problem of the relationship between structures of meaning (i.e. discourse) and the processes and forms of history, and he notes difficulties with present uses of the concept of ideology. He notes the absence in anthropology 'of an adequate understanding of authoritative discourse – i.e. of materially founded discourse which seeks continually to preempt the space of radically opposed utterances and so to prevent them from being uttered. For authoritative discourse . . . authorises neither "Reality" nor "Experience" but other discourse – texts, speech, visual images, etc., which are being structured in terms of given (imposed) concepts, and reproduced in terms of essential meanings. Even when action is authorised, it is as discourse that such action establishes its authority. The action is read as being authorised, but the reading and the action are not identical – that is why it is always logically possible to have an alternative reading' (Asad 1979, p. 621). Bloch (1977) also deals with the problems of formulating theories of social change and argues that neither traditional concepts of social structure as an integrated totality of social classifications and meanings nor the Marxist theory of determining infrastructure and determined superstructure can cope with the problem of the creation of new concepts. However, as Asad (1979) points out, Bloch's solution – of alternative discourses being drawn from culture's contact with nature – is not acceptable either. If it were acceptable 'it would not explain how people, who are presumably all in direct contact with the same nature, come to have very different concepts within the same society, and how they are able to engage in ideological arguments about the basic transformation of social conditions in which they all live' (Asad 1979, p. 612).

We need, therefore, a fuller conception than exists at present within archaeology of the relationships between ritual, representation and ideology in order to understand social and ideological change. It must be acknowledged that alternative discourses and meanings inhere in ritual and symbolic practices, both intentionally, as in the case of the Zande secret societies, or unintentionally, through the contradictions and ambiguities of symbolic discourse and practice. Factors of social change may be many and complex, but we must attempt to acknowledge this at a theoretical and analytical level.

The study

This paper consists of an interpretation of aspects of the archaeology of, in conventional terms, the Late Neolithic and Early Bronze Ages of Wessex. The main focus of attention is on the period c. 2200–1400 bc, although some reference will be made to periods preceding and succeeding this span. Burgess

(1980) has outlined the difficulties of working within the conventional Age-system for this period of prehistory, and it is clear that these traditional divisions are inappropriate for dealing with and understanding the archaeology of the third and second millennia bc. In this paper I shall use Whittle's scheme of division for the period c. 2200–1400 bc (1981, p. 298). Whittle divides the period into an early Beaker phase, which dates from 2200/2100 to 1800/1700 bc, and a late Beaker/Urn phase, which dates from 1800/1700 bc to after 1500 bc. The period following this latter phase will be called the Later Bronze Age, from 1500/1400 to 1100/1000 bc, Whittle's scheme of division has proved to be most appropriate for making chronological divisions in the archaeological data and although it may appear rather crude is in fact the most detailed scheme of division that the chronological evidence will support. Petersen (1977) also argued for such a three-fold division, and even when satisfactory sampling in relation to radiocarbon dates is undertaken it is clear that a fine chronology cannot be produced with any certainty (Kinnes 1981).

The study in this paper is based largely on published material.[1] This does, of course, entail certain problems, but the study is intended to be as much an exploration and application of certain theoretical ideas as a new interpretation of Wessex's prehistory. It is hoped that it will complement some recent attempts to reconstruct the prehistory of Wessex (e.g. papers in Barrett and Bradley 1980) and, perhaps, challenge other interpretations (Renfrew 1973, 1974b; Burgess 1980).

Wessex c. 2200 to 1400 BC

The archaeology of this period in the prehistory of Wessex is well known (Piggott 1938; Renfrew 1973, 1974a; Fleming 1971; Burgess 1980; Megaw and Simpson 1979). Fig. 1 shows the major sites of the period c. 2200 to 1400 bc and the distribution of barrows in the region. The archaeology is dominated by sepulchral and other apparently ritual sites. Settlement evidence is notoriously scanty until the Later Bronze Age, when the character of the evidence changes. From the earlier emphasis on ritual sites and practices the evidence consists in the later Bronze Age of settlements with related cemeteries and field systems. Part of the change in settlement evidence is no doubt due to the apparent absence of enclosures to settlement sites prior to the Later Bronze Age, thus making their recognition more difficult. Nevertheless, the relationship of settlement to ceremonial and sepulchral sites of the early Beaker and late Beaker/Urn periods is unclear.

The burials and other ritual sites of the early Beaker and late Beaker/Urn periods cluster in four main areas of the Wessex downland. Fleming (1971) has noted the distribution of barrows in Wessex and has argued that there exist four special areas of barrow concentrations in the area. These four areas of barrow concentrations focus on what may be seen as complexes of ritual sites. Although there are substantial variations in the nature and arrangement of the ritual sites between each area, each ritual complex is apparently made up of several henge sites, of varying proportions and character and of varying dates of construction, and other ritual sites. There may be a cursus, as in the Salisbury Plain and Cranborne Chase areas, or an avenue of stones closely associated with some of the henges, as in the case of Salisbury Plain and the Marlborough Downs, and the collections of pits containing similar assemblages to material from the henge sites (Barrett, Bradley, Green and Lewis 1981; Wainwright and Longworth 1971b) indicate other ritual sites and activities.

Thus, it is possible to see Wessex during the period *c.* 2200–1400 bc containing four main foci or complexes of ritual sites. However, contrary to Renfrew (1973), it does not seem possible to suggest the existence of boundaries between different regions in Wessex. The use of Thiessen polygons is highly abstract

and is quite inappropriate for hypothesising the existence of boundaries between regions in prehistory. Fried (1975) has argued that the notion of highly discrete political units and of closely bounded populations in a territorial sense in a pre-state society is ill-founded, and there is, in any case, an absence of evidence for boundaries between regions in the archaeological evidence of Wessex at this period.

Burl (1969) has demonstrated the absence of any patterns of regional similarity in the architecture and associated material assemblages of henge monuments in Britain, and 'similarities in

Fig. 1. Map to show major sites of Wessex *c.* 2200–1400 bc.

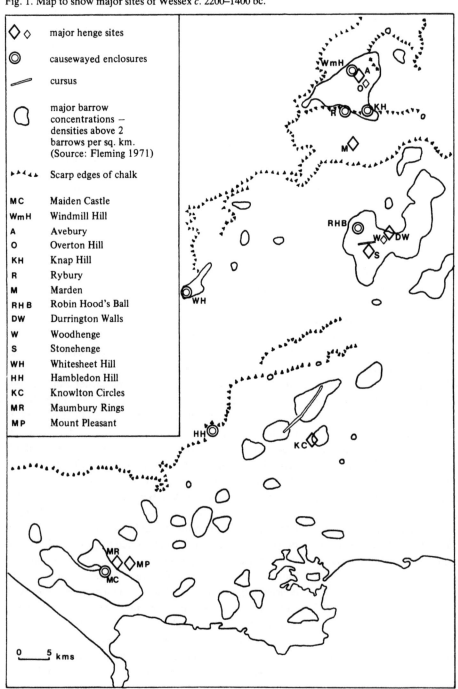

◇◇	major henge sites
◎	causewayed enclosures
/	cursus
⌒	major barrow concentrations — densities above 2 barrows per sq. km. (Source: Fleming 1971)
▸▴◂▴	Scarp edges of chalk
M C	Maiden Castle
WmH	Windmill Hill
A	Avebury
O	Overton Hill
KH	Knap Hill
R	Rybury
M	Marden
RHB	Robin Hood's Ball
DW	Durrington Walls
W	Woodhenge
S	Stonehenge
WH	Whitesheet Hill
HH	Hambledon Hill
KC	Knowlton Circles
MR	Maumbury Rings
MP	Mount Pleasant

0 — 5 kms

architecture . . . of many stone circles' also suggests a 'unity across Britain' (Burl 1976, p. 18). A similar lack of regional variation in ceramic styles has also been noted. Although widespread variations in certain aspects of Peterborough and Beaker ceramic styles have been recognised (Smith 1956, 1974; Clarke 1970; Lanting and van der Waals 1972), no clear-cut boundaries exist between style areas. Lanting and van der Waals' study of Beaker styles did recognise regional traditions, but there 'apparently . . . existed a complicated pattern of cross-influencing, which tended to blur the lines of division' (1972, p. 28). The stylistic groupings identified in Grooved-ware ceramics (Smith 1956; Wainwright and Longworth 1971b) would now appear to have little validity (Clarke 1983) and there is considerable need for a complete reassessment of this and other groupings of Late Neolithic pottery. Ceramic analysis by Friedrich (1970) challenges decisively the value of traditional methods of ceramic classification by archaeologists, particularly in relation to the identification of regional and social group variation in design. Nevertheless, clear-cut spatial boundaries in the archaeological evidence appear to be absent within Wessex during the early Beaker and late Beaker/Urn periods.

Contradiction in the ritual practices

One of the problems of functionalist accounts of Wessex prehistory, seen particularly in Renfrew's influential interpretations (1973, 1974b, 1976), is reconciling certain aspects of the archaeological evidence with the view of society as an integrated and harmonious system of inter-related parts. Although the accepted view of Wessex at this period – that many of the large, non-sepulchral ritual sites are communal monuments and that the burial practices represent the individualistic and hierarchical nature of contemporary society – involves an implicit reference to contradiction between certain ritual practices of the period, the possibility of contemporary, but contradictory ritual practices has not been seriously examined. In this paper I shall demonstrate that, in fact, such an observation is crucial to understanding this

period of Wessex's prehistory. Let us first look at aspects of the relationship between these 'communal' ritual sites and the burials of the early Beaker and late Beaker/Urn periods.

Chronological relationship between henges and burials

The development of individual burial under round barrow and of the major monuments of Wessex, in particular henges, apparently occurred in tandem from *c.* 2200 bc onwards (Fig. 2; Kinnes 1979; Burgess and Shennan 1976; Whittle 1981). However, as Figs. 2 and 3 demonstrate, while the majority of burials date to the late Beaker/Urn period, the main period of construction of the henge sites was the period *c.* 2200 to 1800 bc, in other words the early Beaker period. Petersen (1977) records that the bulk of non-Deverel Rimbury associated burials in Wessex concentrate in the period *c.* 1500 to 1200 bc, and, as Fig. 3 shows, very few burials in Wessex can be certainly dated to the early Beaker period. Although the absence of datable associated artefacts and/or radiocarbon dates means that the number of excavated burials actually belonging to this early period cannot be assessed, there does seem to be a real scarcity of formal burials in Wessex prior to *c.* 1800 bc compared to the two later periods.

In contrast to this overall pattern, construction dates for the henges of Wessex cluster in the period *c.* 2200 to 1800 bc. Contrary to Wainwright (1971, 1979), who argues for a common foundation date of *c.* 2000 bc, the dates from primary contexts alone at the excavated henges of Wessex span a period of roughly five hundred and fifty radiocarbon years. It is clear, nonetheless, that by the main period of burial practices many of the communal monuments in Wessex were either no longer in use, as at Woodhenge (Cunnington 1929; Wainwright 1979) and the Sanctuary (Cunnington 1931), or had radically altered in form and use.

Burgess (1980) argues that *c.* 1700 bc saw dramatic changes in the use of the major ceremonial monuments, and this does appear true for Wessex. At Stonehenge there was a radical change of plan, with dates associated with this falling within the

Fig. 2. Chronological relationship between non-sepulchral ritual sites (mainly henges) and burials in Wessex – dates calibrated using Clark (1975) and at two-sigma confidence limits.

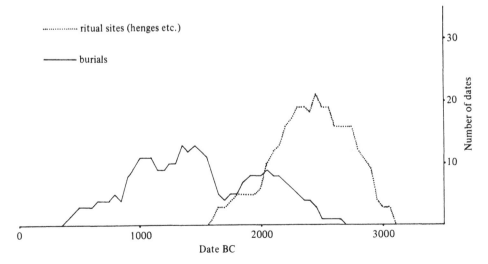

period *c.* 1870–1510 bc (Atkinson 1960). At Durrington Walls, close to Stonehenge, the timber structures were no longer standing and the ditches were half filled in by *c.* 1800 bc. The bulk of the debris recovered in the excavations came from secondary deposits, post-dating *c.* 1800 bc, particularly from the holes left by the vast posts of the timber circles within the site. The ditch deposits show a contrast between primary and secondary deposits, with hearths, substantial quantities of debris from various productive activities, and a change in ceramic assemblage deposited at the site suggesting changed facets of the site's use. The formerly exclusive use of Grooved-ware ceramics, perhaps brought to the site from widely dispersed areas and serving a specialised function, was altered by the introduction of Beaker pottery onto the site. Mount Pleasant henge, in Dorset, experienced similar changes in the character of its use and in aspects of its appearance (Wainwright 1979). Here too the occurrence of Beaker pottery is dated to a secondary phase, post-dating *c.* 1800 bc, and it is this date that also witnesses major structural changes at the site. The small site of Woodhenge was not constructed until *c.* 1900/1800 bc and had a relatively short life (Cunnington 1929; Wainwright 1979). Radiocarbon dates are unfortunately absent from the Marlborough Downs sites, although ceramic evidence suggests that both Avebury and the Sanctuary were not in use after *c.* 1800/1700 bc (Smith 1965a; Cunnington 1931).

Thus, in overall terms the henge sites and individual burial practices were contemporary, but the main periods of construction and use for each were not. As the henge and related sites changed and declined in use, the main period of barrow construction and of burials began.

Spatial relationships

Whittle (1981) is the only prehistorian to previously and explicitly note the possibility of a contradiction between certain facets of the archaeological evidence of this period. He has noted the spatial relationship of some Beaker burials to major henges in the Stonehenge area. Here, early 'non-basic' Beaker associated burials – those datable on grounds of associated items to the early Beaker period – are found at some distance from the ritual complex itself, and only later, with the richer Beaker burial assemblages of the late Beaker/Urn period, do burials cluster closer to the complex. 'It is possible therefore to argue that at an early phase richer Beaker burials and major henges were in some sense in competition, or that the users of each were involved in activities contradictory to each other' (Whittle 1981, p. 329). As will be shown later Whittle's suggestion is very pertinent.

Unfortunately, the paucity of burials datable to the early Beaker phase in other areas of Wessex makes it impossible to assess the relevance of Whittle's observation to other ritual foci of Wessex. In spite of this, the change is reminiscent of other changes in the relationship of burials to henge sites between the early Beaker and late Beaker/Urn period. I shall look at these changes later.

The individual and the collective – aspects of the burial and henge evidence

A contrast between individual burial practices and collective rituals at henge sites has been a part of interpretations of Wessex prehistory for some time, but these have generally been seen as part of an evolution through time of ritual practices reflecting an evolution of social structure (e.g. Renfrew 1973 and 1974b). While my study challenges this view, there does appear to be a clear contrast in the representations and emphases of the ritual practices of the henges and the burials. In the former collective action would appear to have played an important part, and in the latter the individual, or certain groupings of individuals, were stressed. Let us look first at the burial record and then at the evidence of the henge sites.

Burial record *c.* 2200–1400 bc

A much more detailed and reliable assessment than can be presented here must await the results of Cogbill's study of Bronze Age mortuary remains from the southern counties of England (forthcoming). However, a brief assessment of the available evidence will be attempted here. The variety of burial practices that can be dated to the period *c.* 2200–1400 bc is immense, from single unaccompanied cremation to multiple burials, both inhumed and cremated, from flat, unmarked grave to large barrow – and including burials from sites not regarded as primarily sepulchral monuments, such as Woodhenge (Cunnington 1929), the Sanctuary (Cunnington 1931) and, most notably of course, Stonehenge. At Stonehenge excavations have produced twenty-six groups of inhumed and sixty-six groups of cremated human bone (Berridge pers. comm.). I shall initially concern myself with those burial practices not associated with the major ceremonial sites.

I shall argue that the traditional notion of individual burial is correct, in that the individuality of each burial was asserted through a variety of means. Even where several bodies were buried apparently contemporaneously in one barrow, as at Stockbridge Down (Stone and Gray Hill 1940) and at Earl's Farm

Fig. 3. Numbers and relative percentages of burials in Wessex datable to one or other of the three periods (published sites only).

	Total number of burials	Relative percentage
early Beaker period	30	2.9
late Beaker/ Urn period	217	20.9
Later Bronze Age	793	76.2
	——	——
	1040	100.0

Down (Christie 1967), each burial was separated spatially and physically from other burials. The use of pots as containers for the ashes or the construction of graves separates each burial both in spatial and physical ways, and the use of a different rite may also be seen as functioning in a similar way. In many cases a combination of methods had been used to separate and distinguish each burial.

Amesbury G71, the Earl's Farm Down barrow, also demonstrates the general frequency of single to multiple burial deposits in Wessex. Quantified assessment of the burial data was not possible, but the proportion of multiple burial-deposits to those with only one individual was very small in all three phases of the second millennium bc (Fig. 4). Most multiple burial-deposits were only two individuals, and the majority of these involved an adult and child. Both female and male adults were included, although the female/child combination was more common than the male with a child. As Petersen (1977) records, and as Pierpoint (1981) also notes in the Yorkshire Bronze Age data, there is an imbalance in favour of males in burials from the early Beaker period in Wessex. The number of sexed burials datable to this period is so small, however, that the imbalance has no statistical significance and may be unreal.

Overall, single burial predominated in the period *c.* 2200–1400 bc, with the individual being asserted strongly through the use of space and physical boundaries in the burial practices.

Collective rituals – the henge sites of Wessex

Startin and Bradley (1981) have demonstrated the very massive labour-investment involved in the construction of the henges of Wessex, and it does seem clear that large groups of people must have been involved in their construction, if not also in their use. Startin and Bradley (1981) also argue that the technique of construction of the massive boundary ditches to the sites may be significant in terms of the 'character of the labour force'. They demonstrate that although some of the earlier henge monuments in Wessex, such as Stonehenge and Maumbury Rings, employ, like the Early Neolithic causewayed enclosures, a pit-digging technique for construction of the enclosure ditches, the larger and later henges employ a trench-digging technique.[2] Startin and Bradley argue that the 'form of the monument no

longer emphasised the diverse character of the labour force' and that the layout of the later henges 'can be described as "unitary" rather than "segmentary"' (1981, p. 293). Given that archaeological form and style also carry images and representations, Startin and Bradley's ideas may have some significance.

These massive, penannular boundaries may have been intended to express an image of the collectivity, symbolising unity between the different peoples using the sites. They may also have functioned to mark off, in a very clear and dramatic way, those activities undertaken inside them from the external world. A common aspect of important ceremonies and rituals is the way in which boundaries (of time or space, or physical and conceptual boundaries) are often used to protect the discourse from evaluation against other discourse and practices. The dramatic boundaries of the henge sites of Wessex may have been more than just physical markers. As Atkinson suggested for Stonehenge, the 'symbolic as well as the physical function of the earthwork is surely that of a barrier, a boundary between the sacred and the secular, or the initiated and the profane' (1960, p. 170). What I am suggesting is that rather than separating groups of people from one another, the boundaries of the henges may have separated off the discourse of those rituals enacted within them from evaluation against other forms of discourse. As we shall see later, during the main period of use of many of the henges an alternative system of ritual and prestige was being established in Wessex. This system was to effectively challenge the legitimacy of the older discourse associated with the henge sites, and in this we might see the reason for protecting and marking out this latter discourse in such a dramatic way.

Another reason for suggesting that the rituals of the henge sites, and perhaps of other sites connected with the henges, involved groups of people from a wide area is the evidence of the material debris deposited at many of these sites. Some of the henge sites, such as Stonehenge and Avebury, are relatively clean of debris in their ditches and interiors, but others, such as Mount Pleasant and Durrington Walls, are rich in debris. However, the stone types recovered from excavations at these sites are interesting for their diversity and for the distance of some of the sources from the sites. There are, of course, the well known, imported stones used to construct some of the circles at Stonehenge, and also the occurrence of complete, and fragmentary stone axes at and around the ceremonial sites (Roe 1966; 1979; Sheridan 1979). Many of these stone axes or axe fragments were made from rock sources from Cornwall or the Lake District, or from other places at considerable distances from the ritual foci of Wessex. As well as this well known evidence, fragments of other imported stones have been recovered from many of the sites in Wessex. Fragments of sarsen from the Marlborough Downs were recovered during the excavations at Durrington Walls (Wainwright and Longworth 1971a, p. 183), and Late Neolithic levels at Windmill Hill causewayed enclosure produced stone from various sources within a radius of around thirty miles of the site (Smith 1965a, pp. 116–21). A similar range of stone flakes of various types of stone were also recovered from excavations at the 'occupation site' on West Kennet Avenue (Smith 1965a, p. 234).

Fig. 4.

	early Beaker period	late Beaker/ Urn period	Later Bronze Age
% of burials in each period with more than one individual*	8%	15%	5%
% of individuals* buried in multiple burials in each period	15%	32%	9%

* aged and/or sexed individuals only

The food debris recovered from excavations at some of the early Beaker period ritual sites also features a wide variety of sources. Both domestic and wild animals are represented, and also foodstuffs from distant coastal areas. Marine shells, particularly oysters, scallops and mussels, were recovered from the sites of Durrington Walls and Woodhenge, and from the pits at Ratfyn and Woodlands (Wainwright and Longworth 1971b, p. 265). Late Neolithic levels at Windmill Hill (Smith 1965a, p. 135) and pits containing Grooved and Peterborough wares at Down Farm, Dorset (Green pers. comm.), have also produced marine shells. Their presence at these sites points to an emphasis on contacts with various and often distant areas.

It is possible, therefore, to concur with the generally accepted view of the henge, and related, sites of the early Beaker period in Wessex as being communal ceremonial sites, constructed and used by large groups of people from surrounding areas. In this they appear to contrast notably with the burial practices of the early Beaker and late Beaker/Urn periods in which the individual is emphasised. Other contrasts between the types of ritual activity have been noted earlier. Such contrasts can also be seen in the material associations of the two 'complexes' of ritual activity and I shall consider these below. I shall concentrate first on the early Beaker period, and then on the late Beaker/Urn period. It was at the period 1800/1700 bc that the well known features of the Early Bronze Age in Wessex occurred – the introduction of Collared Urns and Food Vessels; a change in the distribution of barrows; dramatic changes in the fate of the major ceremonial monuments. As we shall see, this point in the prehistory of Wessex is of major importance not only in terms of the material record.

Contrasts in some of the items associated with the two ritual complexes in the early Beaker period

One of the reasons for the longevity of the thesis that the Beaker 'package' represented a migration of new people into Britain is that this 'package' of associated items was not only very different from indigenous and other contemporary assemblages, but was also a complex of practices and objects that in the early Beaker period did not occur within indigenous assemblages or sites. Megaw and Simpson (1979) still make such a division in the archaeology of the early Beaker period, although, as we have seen, this division cannot be supported on chronological grounds. Such aspects of the archaeology of the early Beaker period as have been defined as the Mace-head Complex (Roe 1968) and the Beaker package (Burgess and Shennan 1976) apparently represent contemporary practices that are not only different in kind but that also do not occur in association, at least until the late Beaker/Urn period.

I have already noted the changing ceramic associations at the two henge sites of Durrington Walls and Mount Pleasant, with Beaker pottery being a late addition to the ceramic assemblage. Similar changes occurred at Stonehenge. Here, Beaker pottery did not occur until Phase II, which has dates of 1728 ± 68 bc (BM-1164), 1770 ± 100 bc (HAR-2013) and 1620 ± 110 bc (I-2384). As at Durrington Walls and Mount Pleasant, the addition of Beaker pottery to the assemblage occurred after 1800/1700 bc. Dates are not available for the Sanctuary or for Avebury in the Marlborough Downs although a similar pattern to the Stonehenge ceramics can be traced at these two sites (Cunnington 1931; Smith 1965a). At the major ceremonial sites in Wessex the use and deposition of Beaker pottery occurred not only at a secondary phase in their use, but also after the use of Beaker ceramics in burials in similar areas of Wessex.

Other aspects of the evidence demonstrate that prior to 1800/1700 bc the two complexes of ritual activity in Wessex maintained distinctively different 'packages' of material associations. Prior to 1800/1700 bc metal items were apparently only being deposited in graves, and do not appear to have been deposited in any context at the major ceremonial sites, or indeed with any material type used at these sites. Other items that have been considered prestige objects, such as the fine stone artefacts, were being deposited at the henge and related sites, so the absence of that other prestige material of the early Beaker period, bronze, would appear to be significant. Only after 1800/1700 BC were the Arreton axes and daggers carved at Stonehenge (Atkinson 1960, pp. 43–7 and 91–3) and the mint-condition, flanged bronze axe deposited in the main enclosure ditch at Mount Pleasant (Wainwright 1979).

I shall later discuss other changes that occur in the archaeological evidence from the two complexes of ritual activity in Wessex between the early Beaker and the late Beaker/Urn period. Before doing this I wish to look at what the existence of these two complexes may imply, and at the kinds of discourse that they may each have been representing.

Ritual discourse in the early Beaker period

Bradley and Hodder (1979, p. 97) have suggested that 'the separate assemblages in late Neolithic Britain might symbolise different rights of access to status and resources', and Clarke (1976) had earlier argued that the Beaker assemblage symbolised access to prestigious exchange networks. The well-known continental associations of the Beaker assemblage need no demonstration, while the Grooved-ware/henge complex has associations which indicate contacts with the west and north-west of Britain and with Ireland. There are similarities between decoration on Grooved-ware ceramics in Wessex and the art of the Boyne valley tombs in Ireland, and links with the Prescelly Mountains of Wales in the stones at Stonehenge. The sources of stone for the fine stone axes and mace-heads of the Grooved-ware complex also indicate western and north-western contacts. If the separate assemblages of the early Beaker period in Wessex symbolise differential access to status and resources, and also differential access to exchange networks, then why were these separate assemblages focussed on, and used in, such different kinds of ritual activities?

Why was the Beaker assemblage focussed on sepulchral activities in the early Beaker period and the Grooved ware/Peterborough ware assemblages focussed on communal rituals – of feasting and ceremonial as at Durrington Walls and Mount Pleasant, of time and death at Stonehenge (Thorpe 1983), and involving massive and complex constructions at Avebury and other sites? Bloch (1977) has demonstrated the importance of ritual in the process of leadership in small-scale societies and has argued that the institutionalisation of power in ritual can be an effective means of protecting and legitimating that power. Major ceremonial rituals in small-scale societies are frequently concerned with the establishment and reiteration of particular relationships between people, and between people, objects and images. Such rituals may also be concerned with the reiteration and construction of particular kinds of prestige, and through this may be constructed particular kinds of relationships of status and power. I am suggesting here that the ritual practices observable in the archaeological record of Wessex in the early Beaker period were concerned in part with the construction of particular kinds of prestige.

I have already indicated the emphasis in the archaeology of the major early Beaker-period monuments on links between dispersed areas and on cooperation between diverse groups. There also appear to have been references made, in the ritual activities, to practices of some antiquity. One notable feature is the same differential selection and use of human skeletal material as occurred in Early Neolithic practices at mortuary sites and causewayed enclosures in Wessex (Smith 1965a; Mercer 1980). assemblages from Early Neolithic tombs is the special treatment given to skull and long bones (Ashbee 1970; Shanks and Tilley 1982) and selection of these same bones has been noted at many causewayed enclosures in Wessex (Smith 1965; Mercer 1980). Human skeletal material has been recovered during excavations at the henge sites in Wessex. At Durrington Walls skull fragments and a complete tibia were recovered (Wainwright and Longworth 1971a, p. 191), and at Mount Pleasant skull fragments and part of a long bone were found (Wainwright 1979). The same pattern of selection of long bones and skull fragments occurred at Maumbury Rings (Bradley 1975), Avebury (Smith 1965a), Woodhenge (Cunnington 1929) and the Sanctuary (Cunnington 1931).

Other similarities in the archaeological evidence from Early Neolithic causewayed enclosures, most of which in Wessex were still used in the early Beaker period, and early Beaker-period henges and Grooved-ware sites can be noted. There is, for example, the occurrence of whole and fragments of fine stone axes in ditch and other deposits at causewayed enclosures and henges and from other contexts associated with 'Late Neolithic' material. Similarities in the debris deposited at causewayed enclosures and early Beaker-period sites, such as complete, often articulated animal bones, ritual deposits of human and animal skeletons in enclosure ditches, the deposition of still-usable antler tools and often large amounts of food debris, also exist. And there is the re-use of sites that had been constructed in the Early Neolithic – the causewayed enclosures of Windmill Hill (Smith 1965a) and Hambledon Hill (Mercer 1980), and the small causewayed enclosure of Stonehenge (Berridge pers. comm.).[2] The continuing significance and use of items and sites from the Early Neolithic into the early Beaker period suggests that part of the ritual discourse associated with the henge and related sites involved reference to past traditions and associations. Giddens

(1981, pp. 93–4) argues the importance of tradition in the legitimation of power and prestige in pre-capitalist, and capitalist, societies. In the communal monuments of the early Beaker period we can perhaps see the use of traditional items and practices to legitimate and reinforce the discourse of the ceremonies and rituals enacted at these sites. The dramatic use of ritual devices – of decoration on the ceramics (Braithwaite 1982a), of time (Thorpe 1983) and of massive boundaries and impressive structures – implies a concern with protecting the discourse of the rituals from evaluation against other ritual discourses in society. Since it was the sepulchral practices associated with the Beaker complex that flourished as the henge traditions declined and altered it may be that it was the discourse of the Beaker complex that posed a threat to the legitimacy of that traditional discourse of the henges and associated sites.

Competing ritual discourses – a framework for the evidence

Rowlands, in a paper primarily concerned with the Later Bronze Age in southern England, suggests that the Wessex Early Bronze Age might be understood as a 'temporary and possibly "last ditch" fusion of Neolithic and EBA political practice before a complete transformation took place by the end of the period' (1980, p. 35). He suggests that a Crow–Omaha type kinship system developed in the Late Bronze Age in southern England and that this system grew out of a society that 'had formerly been relatively closed (i.e. where rank had been ordered and directed by kinship and alliance)' and in which 'status depended on genealogical distance or ideological claims to founding ancestors' (p. 20). One interesting feature of Early Neolithic activity is the relative paucity of items that might be considered prestige objects. Sheridan (1979), in a study of the Neolithic stone-axe trade from south-west Britain, argued that for the period c. 3300–2600 bc 'the absence of concentrations of material at great distances from source, or of hierarchical settlement systems, militates against the idea of redistribution centres and/or unequal access to goods at this stage. Moreover . . . the relatively small output from Cornish sources over this 700 year period – when compared to that of Gps. I and III in the Late Neolithic – does not suggest mass, or specialist, production of axes' (p. 25).

Similarly, the overall homogeneity of the material culture of the Early Neolithic in Britain (Smith 1974) suggests that goods were not being used to symbolise status inequalities. Bradley (1982a) also notes that it is only with the development of Peterborough and Grooved wares, and their associated artefacts, that much assemblage variation is apparent. This may not, however, imply that there were no marked social inequalities in the Early Neolithic, but rather that material items were not being used in practices designed to symbolise or accrue prestige and status. One of the notable features of the debris deposited at the causewayed enclosures of Wessex is the evidence of food consumption (Smith 1971). MacCormack (1981, p. 162) notes that where 'there are spheres of conveyance, food is always found in the category characterised by altruistic generalised reciprocity. Food is life-giving, urgent, domestic. It is readily available and necessarily shared'. As Sahlins has commented, it 'has far too much social value – ultimately because it has too much use value – to have exchange value' (1974, p. 215). While such generosity is in practice not necessarily altruistic (Bourdieu 1977, pp. 171–4) and does incur social debts and can be used to accrue prestige, it is frequently not a means of acquiring prestige through its direct conversion into other goods in pre-capitalist societies. The consumption of food and other goods, such as fine stone axes, at Early Neolithic causewayed enclosures, combined with the other evidence noted above, suggests that status and prestige depended primarily on non-material criteria in the Early Neolithic of Wessex.

Shanks and Tilley (1982) argue that political authority in the Early Neolithic may have been based, at least partly, on the projection of authority into the past through the ancestors. While long barrows and tombs may not have been primarily sepulchral monuments (Ashbee 1982; Barrett pers. comm.), it is clear that the dead were being used in the activities connected with these monuments – perhaps as a form of legitimation. It may, thus, be that in the Early Neolithic status depended on ascribed criteria such as genealogy, rather than on the ownership and display of prestige goods. Bauman (1971) notes that culturally 'stagnant' social systems are those in which rights to signs are derivative from social position, and we can in this instance note the relatively unchanging character of the material assemblages of the Early Neolithic. We may conclude, therefore, that Rowlands' suggestion that Neolithic 'political practice' was transformed only by the advent of Early Bronze Age political practice is correct. In the Early Neolithic and into the early Beaker period status 'depended on genealogical distance or ideological claims to founding ancestors' (Rowlands 1980, p. 20).

If the ritual discourse of the henge, and related, sites of the early Beaker period was concerned with emphasising a unity between groups and the unchanging nature, through reference to past traditions, of the system of prestige (and related relations of power), why was the discourse surrounded and marked out by such a panoply of ritual devices? Ritual devices, such as decoration, time, dance, and other dramatic gestures, attempt to protect and legitimate the discourse of the rituals. I suggest that the Beaker complex of artefacts and activities represents an attempt to establish an alternative discourse. This alternative

discourse was concerned with establishing a system of prestige radically different from the traditional system. I shall argue below that prior to 1800/1700 bc this new discourse, associated with the Beaker complex, was couched in terms drawn from the traditional discourse in order to establish the legitimacy of the new system of prestige. After 1800/1700 bc the new prestige system increasingly established its own discourse, which was based more centrally on the use of material symbols and on new contacts and trade links. By 1500/1400 bc the change to this new system had finally been accomplished, and those elements we term Later Bronze Age represent the establishment of a new system of prestige, and of new relations of power. Let us look first at the way in which the new prestige system was being established prior to 1800/1700 bc.

Establishment of new system of prestige – early Beaker period

The Beaker 'package' in Britain is well known (Clarke 1970; Lanting and van der Waals 1972; Burgess and Shennan 1976; Whittle 1981). In many interpretations emphasis has been placed on notions such as prestige and competition for status to explain the significance of the burial-goods. The deposition, however, of goods, with burials suggests that status and prestige were obtained through the dead and not directly through the living. Not until after 1500/1400 bc do metal items occur in domestic contexts, and as I have already noted, prior to 1800/1700 bc metal items were deposited in burial contexts only. There appears to have been a progressive change in the contexts in which metal items were deposited through the early Beaker, late Beaker/Urn and Later Bronze Age periods. I have summarised these changes in Fig. 5.

I am suggesting that prior to 1800/1700 bc those material items that occurred in burial contexts could only be used to signify or accrue prestige indirectly through the dead, and thus perhaps through the ancestors. In order to establish the legitimacy and efficacy of the material symbols of the Beaker complex it was initially necessary to draw on those sources of prestige connected with the traditional system of prestige. The dead, and therefore perhaps genealogy, were used to legitimate the new prestige symbols connected with the Beaker package. Prior to 1800/1700 bc the process was tentative, with burials few in number and generally overshadowed by the rituals associated with the henge sites. Borrowing of traditions of decoration and of material associations from the traditional, communal ritual practices was very slight. After 1800/1700 bc, however, there was increasing borrowing of styles of artefacts and decoration and of artefacts themselves from the communal ritual complex to the burial complex. And also at this time came the decline in use of some of the early Beaker communal ritual sites and dramatic changes in use and appearance of others. Let us look at some of these changes.

Burial assemblages after 1800/1700 bc

It has been noted by many prehistorians that although certain 'basic' artefact associations are common to all Beaker style groups or phases, other associations change through the

Fig. 5. Summary of changing contexts of deposition of metal items in Wessex *c.* 2200–1100 bc.

early Beaker period	late Beaker/ Urn period	Later Bronze Age
burials	burials	
	some henges	
	hoards	
		hoards
		river deposits
		settlements

sequence (Clarke 1970; Lanting and van der Waals 1972; Case 1977). Whittle (1981, p. 331) has summarised these changes in Beaker artefact associations as a change from 'more developed metalwork with imitative flint daggers, to battleaxes, rings and buttons' by the late Beaker/Urn phase. Some of the changes in stone artefacts between the early Beaker and late Beaker/Urn phase are particularly interesting.

Where the context of deposition is known, all battle-axes in Wessex have come from burials or barrows, and these can be dated on the basis of associations to the late Beaker/Urn period (Roe 1966, 1979; Sheridan 1979). Other fine stone objects, such as polished axes and hammer-stones, also appear in late Beaker/Urn and 'Wessex Culture' graves, but there are no similar occurrences in early Beaker period graves. In the early Beaker period instead fine stone axes occur at the communal ritual sites and at other contexts associated with the Grooved-ware complex. Roe has argued that stone mace-heads were the precursors of battle-axes (1968, 1979). However, mace heads, like the polished stone axes, have associations which date them to the early Beaker period and relate them to the Grooved-ware complex. Battle-axes and axe-hammers, in contrast, not only come from burials dated to the following period, the late Beaker/Urn period, but were also made from different rock sources to the mace heads. Fig. 6a and b summarise these changes. What we can see is a contrast between sepulchral and communal ritual associations. There was a change in the form of fine stone items and also in the contexts of their deposition between the early Beaker and late Beaker/Urn periods. In the early Beaker period fine stone artefacts had occurred in the communal, ritual contexts, but by the late Beaker/Urn period burials also contained such artefacts.

A similar pattern of change can be noted in the ceramic evidence. Prior to 1800/1700 bc Beaker material occurred in burials, but not in the communal ritual contexts in Wessex. By *c.*

1700 bc new ceramic types were being used in burials that, unlike Beakers, drew on ceramic styles connected with the communal ritual complexes. The new ceramic types, primarily Collared Urns, drew on Peterborough ceramics for many of the stylistic and formal characteristics (Longworth 1961). Peterborough ceramic styles had been a major part of the ceramic assemblages in the Marlborough Downs ritual sites (Smith 1965a) and also at some of the Cranborne Chase sites (Barrett, Bradley, Green and Lewis 1981), but were relatively scarce at the Salisbury Plain and South Dorset sites. And later, with the development of Biconical Urns and some of the Deverel Rimbury ceramics there was conspicuous borrowing of stylistic and formal traits from Grooved-ware ceramics to sepulchral pottery (Smith 1956; Ellison 1975). Prior to 1800/1700 bc, therefore, the sepulchral ceramics were entirely new and contrasted with contemporary assemblages at the communal ritual sites. After 1800/1700 bc there was increasingly significant borrowing of stylistic and formal traits from Peterborough and Grooved wares by sepulchral ceramic types. This borrowing after 1800/1700 bc suggests that by the late Beaker/Urn period it had become possible for the new ritual discourse to copy and use symbols that in the early Beaker period had been associated only with the traditional system of prestige and ritual practices.

From 1800/1700 bc to 1500/1400 bc there appears to have been a progressive move towards the establishment of those principles and practices that Rowlands (1980) argues were in existence by the Later Bronze Age in southern England. Nevertheless, the late Beaker/Urn period was still characterised by a political compromise between new and old practices and principles. What were these new practices and principles, and how was this new discourse established? By looking now at the Later Bronze Age in southern England we may be able to begin answering these questions.

The new discourse and the Later Bronze-Age political system

I have already referred briefly to Rowlands' paper (1980), but I wish to quote at greater length from this paper. It will be remembered that Rowlands suggests the existence of a Crow–Omaha kinship system in the Later Bronze Age of southern England. Such systems

> are often highly unstable structures that have been historically incorporated into extensive trading networks that

Fig. 6a. Change in rock sources used for stone artefacts (source: Sheridan 1979).

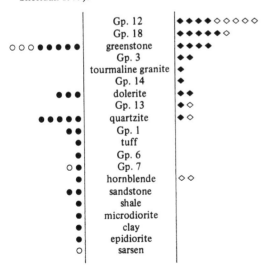

Fig. 6b. Change in context of deposition of stone artefacts in Wessex.

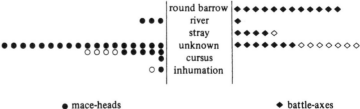

allow forms of wealth to be accumulated and that generate different kinds of demand from those which had existed previously. It is as if a society that had formerly been relatively closed (i.e. where rank had been ordered and directed by kinship and alliance) was 'burst open' and new relations of dominance came to develop, based directly on the ability to accumulate wealth and to use it to succeed in the wider arena of competitive status rivalry . . . The transformation from elementary to transitional structure implies, therefore, the dissolution of one form of hierarchy for another to take its place, but where the same cultural elements may be in existence and their possession is now a matter essentially of overt wealth distinctions, rather than genealogical distance or ideological claims to founding ancestors. (Rowlands 1980, p. 20)

Rowlands suggests that this transformation of system by the Later Bronze Age probably started well back in the Early Bronze Age and Late Neolithic. 'In this respect, the Wessex EBA could probably be understood as a temporary and possibly "last ditch" fusion of Neolithic and EBA political practice before a complete transformation took place by the end of this period' (Rowlands 1980, p. 35).

It is not necessary to accept Rowlands' more specific arguments for an Omaha kinship system in the Later Bronze Age to realise that aspects of his model capture well some of the changes that occur in the archaeological evidence in Wessex during the second millennium bc. I have already noted this in connection with certain facets of the archaeological evidence. However, the lack of attention paid in Rowlands' account to the ideological changes that must necessarily have accompanied the possible changes in kinship relations means that many of the changes that can be recognised in the evidence are left unexplained. This problem also applies to other accounts of the Later Bronze Age and its evolution from the Early Bronze Age (Barrett 1980; Bradley 1980; Barrett and Bradley 1980), although these stress other important dimensions of the changes that appear to have occurred during these periods in southern England. One of the changes that occurs through the three periods dealt with in this study is in the context of deposition of metalwork. Some aspects of this change have already been noted, but there are other aspects that are of some interest in relation to the developments towards the Later Bronze-Age system of political and kinship practices.

Deposition of metalwork – aspects of the changing contexts

Bradley (1982b) has suggested that aspects of the archaeology of the Later Bronze Age in southern England suggest political practices designed to accrue prestige and 'symbolic capital' through the 'conspicuous consumption' of metalwork and other items. He notes in particular the deposition of wealth in hoards and rivers. Ellison (1981) also noted that the 'variety of grave goods found in association with Early Bronze Age inhumation and cremation burials which includes weapons, tools, ornaments, many ceramic types and the whole panoply of 'Wessex Culture" prestige items cannot be matched in the succeeding period. A

probable change in religious or other attitudes led to the exclusion of metal items from graves' (p. 422).

The context of deposition of goods is, in fact, of some significance in understanding what political functions and ideological practices such deposition represented. And the change from deposition in graves to deposition in rivers or bogs is more significant than Ellison appears to imply. I have already argued that the early Beaker and late Beaker/Urn burial practices represent a compromise between two different sources and symbols of prestige, and I have noted that until the Later Bronze Age metalwork was deposited only in ritual contexts. With the establishment of Later Bronze-Age practices metal objects appeared for the first time in contexts associated with everyday activities. There are, for example, finds of metalwork from the settlement site of South Lodge Camp (Pitt-Rivers 1898) and from the sites on Thorny Down (Stone 1941) and Burderop Down (Gingell 1980) in Wessex. It was also only at this later stage, after *c.* 1500 BC, that metal production appears to have 'taken-off', and became organised for anticipated and large-scale demand (Rowlands 1976). Prior to 1500/1400 bc the restriction on the ways in which metal items could be used to accrue and symbolise prestige effectively constrained the demand and production of such goods.

Changing role of burial practices

Alongside this change in the way in which metalwork and other goods were used to accrue prestige occurred changes in the role that burial practices played in relation to the prestige system. Two interesting features of the burial evidence through the three periods are the gradual change from inhumation to cremation and the parallel change from grave goods accompanying the body to no grave goods at all. Detailed chronological evidence is unavailable to map these changes precisely, and the changes were complex and not unilinear through time, but these were two facets of the overall pattern of changes in burial practices from the early Beaker period to the Later Bronze Age.

No satisfactory explanation has been put forward for the change from inhumation to cremation in the Bronze Age of Wessex, although Rowlands (1980, p. 51) suggests that 'inhumation : survival of bones : continuity as a prerogative of high rank may be contrasted with cremation : burning and destruction of flesh and bones : destruction of individual identity : low rank' for the Bronze Age of Europe as a whole. Although the equation of burial rite with rank would not appear to explain the changes through time in the southern English evidence, the suggestion that cremation was equivalent to the destruction of the individual identity and that inhumation was equivalent to continuity does appear to fit with other aspects of the changing burial practices.

We can note a crude contrast between earlier and later burial traditions in this period of Wessex's prehistory. In the earlier traditions the individual was asserted and the identity of the individual was seen as continuing into death. The laying out of the complete body, perhaps clothed, and accompanied by food and tools and other items would indicate this interpretation is correct. At the other end of the spectrum were the Later Bronze-

Age traditions, where all evidence of the individual's identity was destroyed at death and the continuity between life and death was ritually broken. The highly efficient cremation and crushing of skeletal remains, the placing of these or a token deposit of bones in an urn or pit, and the lack of clear social differentiation in burial rite (Petersen 1977; Ellison 1981), would all seem to function to obfuscate the identity of the individual. The dead body appears to have been converted into a material substance, rather than treated like a living being as in the earlier traditions. Fig. 7 depicts the changes at those barrows where evidence is available. The sequence is by no means simple or unilinear, and I have described the overall trends.

One of the interesting aspects of this would appear to be that, if Rowlands (1980) is correct in his suggestion of the kind of kinship system in existence during the Later Bronze Age, then the relations of power that he proposes were being denied in the mortuary remains. In the earlier part of the period *c.* 2200–1100 bc, however, the burial practices would suggest that genealogy was important as a source of prestige, and that the representations at death were concerned not only with, as Shennan (1982) suggests, the 'naturalisation' of social differences, but also with the drawing on of traditional sources of prestige to sanction a new discourse of political and prestige activities.

One other piece of evidence that also supports the suggestion that genealogy, or at least kin-based status, was important as a source of prestige is that of the relationship between burial rite, grave goods and the dimensions of age and gender. Petersen (1977) could fine no definite correlations between age and gender and any other variable, such as sequential position or position on plan, or presence/absence of any type of grave good. There were no one-to-one correlations between age and gender and any variable. Age and gender were not primary points of differentiation in terms of grave goods deposited in the early Beaker and late Beaker/Urn period. Nevertheless, age and gender do appear to have been of secondary significance in relation to grave goods. For example, almost all the items that accompany female burials also accompany male burials, but some items that occur in male burials do not occur in female burials. If grave goods represent status, this *may* imply that although in burial practices the male gender was given a higher status than the female, the status of gender as a whole was subordinate to some other principle of differentiation.[3]

The evidence of the individual, inhumation burials, in which the individual's identity was emphasised and the continuity between life and death marked out, suggests that Shennan's argument (1982), that these early burials represent a 'naturalisation' of relationships in life, may be correct. If this is the case, then the evidence presented above may suggest that birth within a particular social group was a significant principle of social differentiation. From this, we may be able to suggest that there

Fig. 7. Chronological changes in burial rite at selected sites in Wessex (chronological positions of burials within each period not exact).

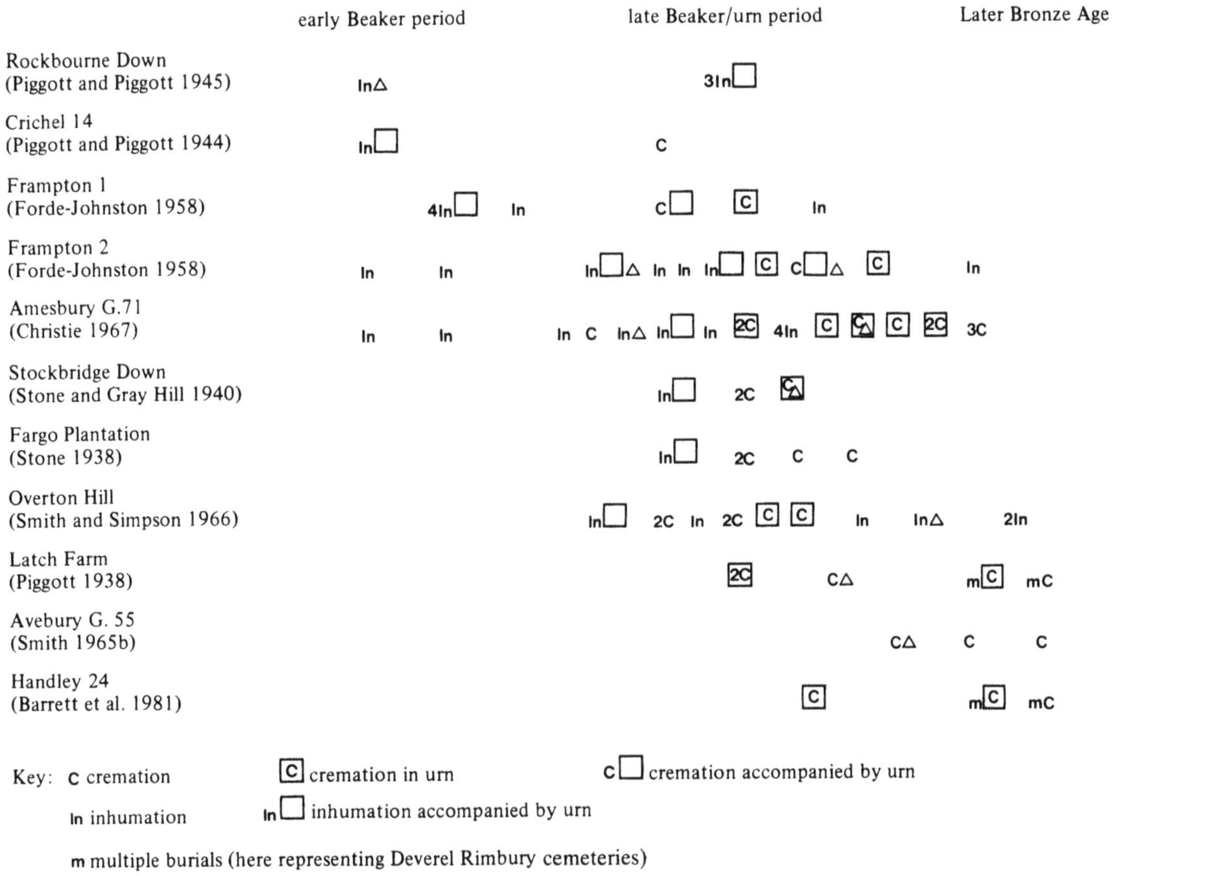

existed in the early Beaker and late Beaker/Urn periods in Wessex some kind of hierarchical social system. Ortner (1981) demonstrates that in hierarchical societies the status of any individual is primarily based on birth within a particular social unit, and only secondarily on other characteristics, such as age or gender, achievement or occupation. Thus, if the representations at death were more or less direct representations of social patterns in life, then it may be that in the early Beaker and late Beaker/Urn periods in Wessex there was, as has previously been suggested, some kind of hierarchical system. The more specific nature of this system cannot at present be determined, primarily because the archaeological evidence is inadequate and partial. Hierarchical social systems take a wide variety of forms, and as Kinnes has recently noted, 'Hierarchical systems do not demand an "elite" . . . any more than they require a chieftain, a figure whose *archaeological* definition seems currently to rest on accounts of one atypical and ephemeral Polynesian example of the institution' (1982, p. 146).[4]

In summary of these previous points, I am arguing that through the three periods of Wessex's prehistory examined here there was a gradual move away from the genealogical basis of the earlier system of prestige and towards a system in which material symbols, such as metal artefacts, were used more directly to signify status and accrue prestige. I have so far traced the ways in which the new system of prestige and ritual initially set its discourse in the language of the old, with an emphasis on burial practices which represented the significance of kin-based status and perhaps genealogy and which legitimated the use of new material symbols, and those practices and trade contacts associated with these symbols. Gradually and effectively the new discourse based on burial ritual took over symbols from the old system of prestige and established its own discourse. This ultimately resulted in the dramatic changes in Wessex's prehistory that are characterised by Later Bronze Age developments in southern England – changes in possible kinship system (Rowlands 1980), in metal production (Rowlands 1976), and in economic and land use practices (Barrett 1980; Bradley 1980; Barrett and Bradley 1980). However, it is important to stress that the social, economic and geographical changes that have been the focus of these studies had origins much further back in prehistory than these authors imply. Similarly, the changes also have ideological dimensions that have rarely been taken into account in previous models of Wessex's prehistory, and yet as has been shown here such dimensions are crucial for understanding many facets of the archaeological evidence.

The fate of the traditional system of prestige

It has been argued that major changes took place in the distribution of power in the Later Bronze Age in southern England (Rowlands 1980; Barrett 1980; Bradley 1980), and I have so far demonstrated the changes that occurred in the ritual discourse and systems of prestige prior to this period. What happened to the old 'core' areas on the chalklands of Wessex and to the old system of ritual and prestige? Barrett (1976) has argued,

as Smith (1956) had earlier done, that the Deverel Rimbury ceramic tradition originated earlier than 1400 bc, and demonstrated that dates as early as 1500 bc meant that considerable overlap occurred between the end of the Early Bronze-Age traditions and those of the Late Bronze Age. This observation was later taken up in interpretations of the possible relationship between the chalkland areas, where the Early Bronze-Age traditions were coming to an end, and the coastal and river valley areas, where the Deverel Rimbury phenomena were beginning (Barrett 1980; Bradley 1980, 1981; Barrett and Bradley 1980).

Barrett (1980) suggests that the growing isolation of the chalkland 'core' areas can be seen in the later Wessex graves in the absence of objects from the newly developing metal traditions of the 'buffer' zones of the coast and valley lands, and also in the deposition of worn and outdated styles of metalwork in the same graves. He argues that the Acton Park metalworking traditions began during the life of the later Wessex graves, but that its products did not enter the burials, which had instead the older Camerton-Snowshill daggers deposited long after they had been replaced elsewhere by other styles.

What do the rich graves of the chalkland areas, traditionally termed 'Wessex Culture' graves, represent? One aspect of the evidence is that the Wessex Culture phenomenon – rich graves with new ceramic types, elaborate and finely worked bronze and gold objects, imported faience and amber beads and other exotic objects – occurred at the same time as the widespread adoption and spread of late Beaker/Urn period burial practices, particularly the cremation burials with Collared Urns. The Wessex I graves in particular, with their inhumation burials and fine gold objects (Apsimon 1954; Annable and Simpson 1964), were in notable contrast to the majority of contemporary burials. Burgess (1980, pp. 98–111) has summarised the various debates concerning the significance of the 'Wessex Culture' and many of these are well known. What I wish to argue here is that these rich burials represent not the 'flowering' of an aristocratic and dominant culture, but rather an attempt to maintain prestige and power by the older system of ritual and status, in the face of increasingly successful attempts to transfer power and prestige elsewhere.

I have previously argued that by the late Beaker/Urn period the older system of prestige, based on the communal ritual sites, had failed to maintain the distinctiveness of its material associations and activities and was forced increasingly to respond to practices and styles established by the new system of ritual discourse. The traditional discourse could no longer prevent its symbols and practices from being copied by the new discourse, which was doing exactly this. I suggest that one of the responses was the carving of the Arreton axes and daggers at Stonehenge, and another was the development of the rich 'Wessex Culture' burials. While elsewhere cremation burial became the dominant burial rite, in the core ritual-areas of Wessex the rich burials of Wessex I, which date roughly to the latter part of the late Beaker/Urn period, still maintained inhumation as the dominant rite. In this we can see an attempt to maintain the significance of genealogy as a source of prestige, while elsewhere such a source of prestige was being abandoned. It was also an attempt to employ the newly established discourse in a way which would regain prestige for the old 'core' areas of Wessex.

The material objects included in the 'Wessex Culture' graves were extremely elaborate and finely made. They need no demonstration here for they are a well known aspect of the archaeological record of Wessex. I suggest that such fine objects were used in the burials because they could not readily be copied or acquired by other groups in contemporary society. Such copying of symbols had, as I have shown, occurred in relation to other facets of the material culture of the trditional system of discourse. And by the latter part of the late Beaker/Urn period the new discourse had successfully established itself as the dominant discourse in Wessex. If the old 'core' areas of Wessex were to regain their former influence and status, then they would have to couch their ritual discourse in the terms of the now dominant discourse. Wessex I represents just such an attempt. That this attempt was ultimately unsuccessful can perhaps be demonstrated by the character of the Wessex II burials.

By Wessex II, which was roughly contemporary with the early part of the Later Bronze Age, cremation had been introduced and grave goods were becoming less elaborate. Gold objects were rarely deposited in Wessex II graves and some of the bronze objects, as I have already noted, were worn and out-dated. Although the 'core' ritual areas of the Wessex chalkland were still ritual centres – with activity at Stonehenge (Atkinson 1960) and Mount Pleasant (Wainwright 1979) – they appear to respond to changes established elsewhere, rather than establish changes themselves. Eventually, after the tradition had been established in areas surrounding the chalklands, Deverel Rimbury assemblages and practices were adopted in the Wessex downland regions (Barrett, Bradley, Green and Lewis 1981; Gingell 1980; Berridge pers. comm.). The chalkland areas were not to regain their former preeminence, and in the time-lag between the adoption of plain ware styles of pottery in the latter part of the Later Bronze Age in lowland areas and the adoption of these styles in the chalk downland (Kinnes 1981) we can perhaps see the general failure of the chalklands to effect and control changes in political and cultural affairs in Wessex.

Conclusion

This study has been concerned with demonstrating the significance of the concepts of prestige and ritual discourse in relation to the archaeology of Wessex c. 2200–1400 bc. It has been argued that in all accounts of the relationship between material culture and social practices it is necessary to be aware of the political and representational dimensions of material practices. This has been shown to be particularly so when attempting to understand the patterns and changes represented in the archaeology of Wessex during the period c. 2200–1400 bc.

What has been argued is that the period c. 2200–1400 bc in Wessex – the early Beaker and late Beaker/Urn periods – witnessed a radical change in the systems by which prestige was acquired and maintained within Wessex society. This change involved a decisive alteration in the role of material culture in the ritual and prestige practices, and also alterations in the role of

burial ritual in the Wessex chalkland region. In the course of the period, the traditional system of prestige, with its discourse focussed on past time and traditions and on communal ceremonies and dramatic ritual sites, was gradually but effectively challenged by a new system of prestige, which placed more significance on the role of material artefacts as sources and symbols of status and prestige. Prior to 1800/1700 bc in Wessex the burial practices associated with the new system of prestige were established slowly and tentatively, with the traditional system responding to the challenge posed by this alternative discourse by using a whole panoply of ritual devices to protect and legitimate its own discourse.

During the late Beaker/Urn period, c. 1800–1500 bc, the new discourse appears to have been increasingly able to borrow symbols and representations from the traditional prestige system, in order, it has been suggested, to legitimate the symbols and practices associated with it. In this we can see the failure of the traditional system of prestige not only to protect its own discourse and its symbols from use within other discourses, but also the general failure of the traditional system of prestige to maintain its former position of authority. By 1500/1400 bc the new system of prestige was firmly established, and the concomitant changes in metalwork production, in land use, in settlement patterns, and in burial practices witness the success of the discourse associated with the new system of prestige, and also, perhaps, of a radically different system of political and kinship relations to that in the previous period. In the rich burials of the 'Wessex Culture' can be seen a final and unsuccessful attempt by the older system of prestige, still focussed in the old 'core' areas of the chalk downland, to re-establish its status and former position of authority. Eventually, these areas were forced to respond to changes established elsewhere and were unable to take any initiative in cultural changes in the south of England.

It has not been my intention in this paper to focus on wider aspects of the prehistory of Wessex c. 2200–1400 bc, but rather to establish a framework for understanding the changing significance of material culture in the ritual and prestige practices during this period. This I regard as a necessary and primary step in the construction of other dimensions of the changes and patterns represented in the archaeological record. The construction of these other dimensions – in particular the social and political formations of the period and the organisation of production necessary for the reproduction of the system – will be dependent on further investigation of the archaeological record and on the development and refinement of adequate theoretical concepts and models.

Notes

1. This paper is based on work undertaken as part of my PhD thesis, a third part of which is a study and interpretation of aspects of the archaeology of Wessex in the third and second millennia bc.
2. Recent radiocarbon dates from Stonehenge place the first phase of the site in the Early Neolithic period, contemporary with the later long barrows and with phases of use of some of the causewayed enclosures of Wessex. It is interesting, therefore, that the first

cutting of the ditch at Stonehenge was done using the pit-digging technique characteristic of the causewayed enclosures (Startin and Bradley 1981). In view of the continued use of Early Neolithic sites into the early Beaker period and of the evidence of earlier activity at many of the early Beaker period ceremonial sites it should not be surprising that Stonehenge itself started out in life as an Early Neolithic enclosure.

3. I have elsewhere (Braithwaite 1982b) argued that the *problem* of the status of gender in relation to social differentiation has not been taken into account in many discussions of gender and social structure in prehistory. Ortner and Whitehead (1981) also demonstrate the necessity of considering gender as a problem for analysis in any given social situation and of investigating the specifically cultural constructions of gender. This has major implications for the construction of adequate models of social relations for pre-capitalist societies since most, if not all, such models (e.g. those of Meillassoux and other Marxist anthropologists, and those presented in texts on prehistory) in current use are flawed by serious errors of ethnocentrism and androcentrism. This is a vast and important topic in itself and I have quite consciously avoided the debate in this study. As a result this paper says nothing about the social actors involved in the practices discussed in the study and makes no attempt to deal with the possible social formations of this period in the prehistory of Wessex. We have yet to investigate such problems as the significance of reproduction (Harris and Young 1981), the kinds of decision-making structures (Leacock 1975) and the form and importance of gender relations (Ortner and Whitehead 1981) in pre-capitalist societies, although these are of some relevance to prehistoric studies. The impact of world capitalism on ostensibly non-capitalist societies is of major importance to archaeologists wishing to draw on the ethnographic record and on anthropology in order to construct aspects of past societies – not only in relation to patterns of social relations (including the status of gender and of different genders), but also the relative autonomy and determinacy of different dimensions of social systems.

4. A similar point to note 3 is relevant here. Kinnes (1982) is quite correct to be so scathing about the use of such a model for prehistoric societies, although its acceptance appears to be based more on its appeal to particular contemporary ideologies than to the 'goodness of fit' between the model and archaeological data. The construction of adequate models will depend, however, not only on better archaeological evidence than exists at present for Wessex in the period *c*. 2200–1400 bc, but also, as I have noted above, on a clearer understanding of the ethnographic record in relation to archaeological problems.

Acknowledgements

Firstly, I wish to thank a series of people who very generously read and criticised the first, and very inadequate, draft of this paper – Danny Miller, Chris Tilley and Alasdair Whittle – and also John Barrett and Ian Hodder for their comments and time spent on the thesis chapters that this study draws on. It is not due to their extremely helpful, although sometimes contradictory, advice that this study is somewhat limited in scope. I also wish to thank Alan Lane for his constant help, encouragement and affection generally. I owe a debt to several friends, in particular Henrietta Moore, for support in arguing that the adequacy of theoretical and analytical concepts in relation to prehistory rests on the further development of critical and feminist work. It is not easy to reject currently available, but biased models, when in so doing one cannot produce what prehistorians wish to hear.

References

Annable, F.K. and Simpson, D.D.A. (1964) *Guide Catalogue of the Neolithic and Bronze Age Collections in Devizes Museum*, Devizes Museum

Apsimon, A.M. (1954) 'Dagger graves in the Wessex bronze age', *10th Annual Report of the University of London Institute of Archaeology*, pp. 37–62

Ardener, S. (1975) 'Introduction', in S. Ardener Ed., *Perceiving Women*, London, Dent

Asad, T. (1979) 'Anthropology and the analysis of ideology', *Man* 14 (4), pp. 607–27

Ashbee, P. (1970) *The Earthen Long Barrow in Britain*, Dent, London
    (1982) 'A reconstruction of the British Neolithic', *Antiquity* Vol. LVI No. 217, pp. 134–8

Atkinson, R.J.C. (1960) *Stonehenge*, Harmondsworth, Penguin

Barrett, J.C. (1976) 'Deverel-Rimbury: problems of chronology and interpretation', in C.B. Burgess and R. Miket Eds., *Settlement and Economy in the Third and Second Millennia B.C.*, BAR 33, pp. 289–307, Oxford

Barrett, J. (1980) 'The evolution of later Bronze Age settlement', in J. Barrett and R. Bradley Eds., *Settlement and Society in the British Later Bronze Age*, BAR British Series 83(i), Oxford

Barrett, J. and Bradley, R. (1980) 'The later Bronze Age in the Thames Valley', in J. Barrett and R. Bradley Eds., *Settlement and Society in the British Later Bronze Age*, BAR 83(i), Oxford
    Eds. (1980) *Settlement and Society in the British Later Bronze Age*, Oxford, BAR British Series 83(i) and (ii)

Barrett, J., Bradley, R., Green, M. and Lewis, R. (1981) 'The earlier prehistoric settlement of Cranborne Chase – the first results of current fieldwork', *The Antiquaries Journal* 61 (2), pp. 203–37

Bauman, Z. (1971) 'Semiotics and the function of culture', in J. Kristeva Ed., *Essays in Semiotics*, The Hague–Paris, Mouton

Bloch, M. (1977) 'The past and the present in the past', *Man* 12, pp. 278–92

Bourdieu, P. (1977) *Outline of a Theory of Practice* (Cambridge Studies in Social Anthropology), Cambridge University Press
    (1979) 'Symbolic power', *Critique of Anthropology* 13 and 14, pp. 77–87

Bradley, R. (1975) 'Maumbury Rings, Dorchester: the excavations of 1908–1913', *Archaeologia* 105, pp. 1–98
    (1980) 'Subsistence, exchange and technology – a social framework for the Bronze Age in Southern England *c*. 1400–700 b.c.', in J. Barrett and R. Bradley Eds., *Settlement and Society in the British Later Bronze Age*, BAR British Series 83(i)
    (1981) ' "Various styles of urn": cemeteries and settlement in Southern England *c*. 1400–1000 b.c.', in R. Chapman, I. Kinnes and K. Randsborg Eds., *The Archaeology of Death*, Cambridge University Press
    (1982a) 'Position and possession: assemblage variation in the British neolithic', *Oxford Journal of Archaeology* 1 (1), pp. 27–38
    (1982b) 'The destruction of wealth in later prehistory', *Man* 17 (1), pp. 108–22

Bradley, R. and Hodder, I. (1979) 'British prehistory: an integrated view', *Man* NS 14, pp. 93–104

Braithwaite, M. (1982a) 'Decoration as ritual symbol: a theoretical proposal and an ethnographic study in southern Sudan', in I. Hodder Ed., *Symbolic and Structural Archaeology* (New Directions in Archaeology), Cambridge University Press
    (1982b) 'Feminist perspectives on British prehistory', paper presented to the Fourth Annual Conference of the Theoretical Archaeology Group, University of Durham
    (1983) *Aspects of the relationship between material culture and social action: ethnographic and archaeological investigations*, PhD thesis, University of Cambridge

Burgess, C. (1980) *The Age of Stonehenge*, London, Dent

Burgess, C.B. and Shennan, S. (1976) 'The Beaker phenomenon: some suggestions', in C.B. Burgess and R. Miket Eds., *Settlement and Economy in the third and second millennia B.C.*, BAR 33

Burl, H.A.W. (1969) 'Henges: internal features and regional groups', *Archaeological Journal* 126, pp. 1–28

(1976) *The Stone Circles of the British Isles*. Yale University Press

Case, H. (1977) 'The Beaker culture in Britain and Ireland', in R. Mercer Ed., *Beakers in Britain and Europe: Four Studies*, BAR S26, Oxford

Christie, P.M. (1967) 'A barrow-cemetery of the second millennium b.c. in Wiltshire, England', *Proceedings of the Prehistoric Society* 33, pp. 336–66

Clark, R.M. (1975) 'A calibration curve for radiocarbon dates', *Antiquity* 49, pp. 251–66

Clarke, D.L. (1970) *Beaker Pottery of Great Britain and Ireland* (Gulbenkian Archaeological Series), Cambridge University Press

(1976) 'The Beaker network – social and economic models', in J.N. Lanting and J.D. van der Waals Eds., *Glockenbecher symposium Oberried 1974*, Bussum (Netherlands), Fibula–Van Dishoek

Clarke, D.V. (1983) 'Grooved Ware', Paper presented at the Scottish Archaeological Forum, University of Glasgow

Cunnington, M.E. (1929) *Woodhenge*, Devizes, Simpson and Co.

(1931) 'The "Sanctuary" on Overton Hill, near Avebury', *Wiltshire Archaeological Magazine* 45, pp. 300–35

Dumont, L. (1972) *Homo Hierarchicus*, London, Paladin

Ellison, A. (1975) *Pottery and Settlements of the Later Bronze Age in Southern England*, PhD thesis, University of Cambridge

(1981) 'Towards a socioeconomic model for the Middle Bronze Age in southern England', in I. Hodder, G. Isaac and N. Hammond Eds., *Pattern of the Past: Studies in Honour of David Clarke*, Cambridge University Press

Evans-Pritchard, E.E. (1937) *Witchcraft, Oracles and Magic among the Azande*, Oxford, Clarendon Press

Fleming, A. (1971) 'Territorial patterns in bronze-age Wessex', *Proceedings of the Prehistoric Society* 37, pp. 138–66

Forde-Johnston, J. (1958) 'The excavation of two barrows at Frampton in Dorset', *Proceedings of the Dorset Natural History and Archaeological Society* 80, pp. 111–32

Fried, M.H. (1975) *The Notion of Tribe*, Menlo Park, California, Cummings

Friedman, J. (1974) 'Marxism, structuralism and vulgar materialism', *Man* 9, pp. 444–69

Friedrich, M.H. (1970) 'Design structure and social interaction: archaeological implications of an ethnographic analysis', *American Antiquity* 35 (3), pp. 332–43

Giddens, A. (1981) *A Contemporary Critique of Historical Materialism* (Contemporary Social Theory), London, Macmillan

Gingell, C. (1980) 'The Marlborough Downs in the Bronze Age: the first results of current research', in J. Barrett and R. Bradley Eds., *Settlement and Society in the British Later Bronze Age*, BAR British Series 83(i)

Godelier, M. (1977) *Perspectives in Marxist Anthropology*, Cambridge University Press

Goldman, I. (1970) *Ancient Polynesian Society*, University of Chicago Press

Harris, O. and Young, K. (1981) 'Engendered Structures: some problems in the analysis of reproduction', in J.S. Kahn and J.R. Llobera Eds., *The Anthropology of Pre-Capitalist Societies*, London, Macmillan

Hodder, I. Ed. (1982) *Symbolic and Structural Archaeology* (New Directions in Archaeology), Cambridge University Press

Kinnes, I. (1979) *Round Barrows and Ring-Ditches in the British Neolithic* (British Museum Occasional Paper No. 7), London

(1981) 'British Museum radiocarbon measurements XII', *Radiocarbon* 23 (1), pp. 14–15

(1982) 'Letter', *Scottish Archaeological Review* 1 (2), pp. 146–7

Lanting, J.N. and van der Walls, J.D. (1972) 'British beakers as seen from the Continent', *Helinium* 12, pp. 20–46

Leacock, E. (1975) 'Class, commodity and the status of women', in R. Rohrlich-Leavitt Ed., *Women Cross-Culturally: Change and Challenge*, The Hague–Paris, Mouton

Longworth, I.H. (1961) 'The origins and development of the primary series of collared urns in England and Wales', *Proceedings of the Prehistoric Society* 27, pp. 263–306

MacCormack, C. (1981) 'Exchange and hierarchy', in A. Sheridan and G. Bailey Eds., *Economic Archaeology: Towards an Integration of Ecological and Social Approaches*, BAR International Series 96

Megaw, J.V.S. and Simpson, D.D.A. (1979) *Introduction to British Prehistory*, Leicester University Press

Mercer, R. (1980) *Hambledon Hill: a Neolithic Landscape*, Edinburgh University Press

Miller, D. (1982) 'Structures and strategies: an aspect of the relationship between social hierarchy and cultural change', in I. Hodder Ed., *Symbolic and Structural Archaeology* (New Directions in Archaeology), Cambridge University Press

Moore, H. (1981) 'Bone refuse – possibilities for the future', in A. Sheridan and G. Bailey Eds., *Economic Archaeology: Towards an Integration of Ecological and Social Approaches*, Oxford, British Archaeological Reports International Series 96

Ortner, S.B. (1981) 'Gender and sexuality in hierarchical societies: the case of Polynesia and some comparative implications', in S.B. Ortner and H. Whitehead Eds., *Sexual Meanings: the Cultural Construction of Gender and Sexuality*, Cambridge University Press

Ortner, S.B. and Whitehead, H. Eds. (1981) *Sexual Meanings: the Cultural Construction of Gender and Sexuality*, Cambridge University Press

Parker Pearson, M. (1982) 'Mortuary practices, society and ideology: an ethnoarchaeological study', in I. Hodder Ed., *Symbolic and Structural Archaeology* (New Directions in Archaeology), Cambridge University Press

Petersen, F.F. (1977) *Bronze Age Funerary Monuments in England and Wales*, PhD thesis, University of Edinburgh

Pierpoint, S. (1981) *Social Patterns in Yorkshire Prehistory 3500–750 BC*, BAR 74

Piggott, C.M. (1938) 'A Middle Bronze Age Barrow and Deverel-Rimbury urnfield at Latch Farm, Christchurch, Hampshire', *Proceedings of the Prehistoric Society* 4, pp. 169–87

Piggott, S. (1938) 'The early bronze age in Wessex', *Proceedings of the Prehistoric Society* 4, pp. 52–106

Piggott, S. and Piggott, C.M. (1944) 'Excavation of barrows on Crichel and Launceston Downs, Dorset', *Archaeologia* 90, pp. 47–80

(1945) 'The excavation of a barrow on Rockbourne Down', *Proceedings of the Hampshire Field Club* 16 (2). pp. 156–62

Pitt-Rivers, A.H.L.-F. (1898) *Excavations in Cranborne Chase, nr. Rushmore*, vol. IV

Renfrew, A.C. (1973) 'Social organisation in neolithic Wessex', in A.C. Renfrew Ed., *The Explanation of Culture Change: Models in Prehistory*, London, Duckworth

Ed. (1974a) *British Prehistory: a New Outline*, London, Duckworth

(1974b) 'Beyond a subsistence economy: the evolution of social organisation in prehistoric Europe', in C.B. Moore Ed., *Reconstructing Complex Societies*. Supplement to the *Bulletin of the American Schools of Oriental Research* No. 20

(1976) 'Megaliths, territories and populations', in J. de Laet Ed., *Acculturation and Continuity in Atlantic Europe*, Brugge, De Tempel

Roe, F.E.S. (1966) 'The battle-axe series in Britain', *Proceedings of the Prehistoric Society* 32, pp. 199–245

(1968) 'Stone mace-heads and the latest neolithic cultures of the British Isles', in J.M. Coles and D.D.A. Simpson Eds., *Studies in Ancient Europe: Essays Presented to Stuart Piggott*, Leicester University Press

(1979) 'Typology of stone implements with shaftholes', in T.H.McK. Clough and W.A. Cummins Eds., *Stone Axe Studies*, London, CBA Research Report 23

Rowlands, M.J. (1976) *The Organisation of Middle Bronze Age Metal-working*, Oxford, BAR 31

(1980) 'Kinship, alliance and exchange in the European Bronze Age', in J. Barrett and R. Bradley Eds., *Settlement and Society in the British Later Bronze Age*, BAR British Series 83(i)

Sahlins, M.D. (1974) *Stone Age Economics*, London, Tavistock

Shanks, M. and Tilley, C. (1982) 'Ideology, symbolic power and ritual communication: a reinterpretation of Neolithic mortuary practices', in I. Hodder Ed., *Symbolic and Structural Archaeology* (New Directions in Archaeology), Cambridge University Press

Shennan, S. (1982) 'Ideology, change and the European Early Bronze Age', in I. Hodder Ed., *Symbolic and Structural Archaeology* (New Directions in Archaeology), Cambridge University Press

Sheridan, J.A. (1979) *The Study of Neolithic Stone Axe 'Trade' in South-West Britain*, B.A. Thesis, University of Cambridge

Smith, I.F. (1956) *The Decorative Art of Neolithic Ceramics in South-Eastern England and its Relations*, Unpublished PhD thesis, University of London

(1965a) *Windmill Hill and Avebury: Excavations by Alexander Keiller*, Oxford, Clarendon Press

(1965b) 'Excavation of a bell barrow, Avebury G.55', *Wiltshire Archaeological Magazine* 60, pp. 24–46

(1971) 'Causewayed enclosures', in D.D.A. Simpson Ed., *Economy and Settlement in Neolithic and Early Bronze Age Britain and Europe*, Leicester University Press

(1974) 'The neolithic', in C. Renfrew Ed., *British Prehistory: a New Outline*, London, Duckworth

Smith, I.F. and Simpson, D.D.A (1966) 'Excavation of a round barrow on Overton Hill, North Wiltshire, England', *Proceedings of the Prehistoric Society* 32, pp. 122–55

Startin, B. and Bradley, R. (1981) 'Some notes on work organisation and society in prehistoric Wessex', in C.L.N. Ruggles and A.W.R. Whittle Eds., *Astronomy and Society in Britain During the Period 4000–1500 B.C.*, BAR 88

Stone, J.F.S. (1938) 'An Early Bronze Age grave in Fargo Plantation near Stonehenge', *Wiltshire Archaeological Magazine* 48, pp. 357–70

(1941) 'The Deverel-Rimbury settlement on Thorny Down, Winterbourne Gunner, south Wiltshire', *Proceedings of the Prehistoric Society* 7, pp. 114–33

Stone, J.F.S. and Gray Hill, N. (1940) 'A round barrow on Stockbridge Down, Hampshire', *Antiquaries Journal* 20, pp. 39–51

Thorpe, I.J. (1983) 'Prehistoric British Astronomy – towards a social context', *Scottish Archaeological Review* 2 (1), pp. 2–10

Turner, V. (1967) *The Forest of Symbols: Aspects of Ndembu Ritual*, Cornell University Press, Ithaca, N.Y.

Wainwright, G.J. (1971) 'The excavation of a Late Neolithic enclosure at Marden, Wiltshire', *Antiquaries Journal* 51, pp. 177–239

(1979) *Mount Pleasant, Dorset: excavations 1970–1971*, Report of the Research Committee of the Society of Antiquaries of London No. XXXVII

Wainwright, G.J. and Longworth, I.H. (1971a) *Durrington Walls: Excavations 1966–68*, Report of the Research Committee of the Society of Antiquaries of London XXIX

(1971b) 'The Rinyo-Clacton Culture Re-considered', in G.J. Wainwright and I.H. Longworth, *Durrington Walls: Excavations 1966–1968*, Report of the Research Committee of the Society of Antiquaries of London No. XXIX

Weber, M. (1958) 'Class, status, party', in H.H. Gerth and C. Wright Mills Eds., *From Max Weber*, Oxford University Press

Whittle, A. (1981) 'Later neolithic society in Britain: a realignment', in C.L.N. Ruggles and A.W.R. Whittle Eds., *Astronomy and Society in Britain During the Period 4000–1500 B.C.* Oxford, BAR 88

Men make their own history, but they do not make it just as they please; they do not make it under circumstances chosen by themselves, but under circumstances directly encountered, given and transmitted from the past. The tradition of all the dead generations weighs like a nightmare on the brain of the living.

Marx, *Eighteenth Brumaire*

Chapter 8

Ideology and the legitimation of power in the middle neolithic of southern Sweden
Christopher Tilley

The focus of this paper is on diachronic analysis and it attempts to operationalise the theoretical perspective outlined in Chapter 1 to a substantive body of prehistoric data to provide an explanation for the change from the Funnel Neck Beaker to the Battle-Axe/Corded-Ware tradition in southern Sweden. Firstly a general theoretical position is put forward for the understanding of power strategies and modes of legitimising asymmetrical power relations in small-scale, lineage-based societies. A series of detailed archaeological analyses are discussed dealing with economic and environmental evidence, orientation relationships between sites, mortuary practices, contexts of artifact deposition, and aspects of ceramic design structure. A number of homologies are shown to link disparate aspects of the archaeological evidence and interpreted as attempts to legitimise authority in relation to both between-group and within-group power differentials. It is argued that the failure of ideological practices, involving the manipulation of material culture, to legitimate social domination and conceal social contradictions led, ultimately, to a legitimation crisis and the collapse of the social order manifested in the change from the Funnel Beaker to Battle-Axe tradition.

Introduction

This paper is in three parts. In part one a social model is erected concerned with generalised features of asymmetrical power relationships in lineage-based societies and modes of ideological legitimation of the social order. In part two a substantive body of archaeological data is analysed in which aspects of the change from the Funnel Neck Beaker (TRB) to the Battle-Axe/Corded-Ware tradition (BAC) are considered. In part three this evidence is drawn together and a number of homologies are demonstrated to underlie disparate aspects of the material-culture patterning. The results of the archaeological analyses are then interpreted in the light of the perspective outlined in part one. It is suggested that an explanation for the change from the TRB to the BAC can be found in the development of increasing contradictions between the structuring principles orientating the form and nature of social relations in the TRB and the eventual failure of types of ideological legitimation to sustain the misrepresentation of power relationships. Most of the paper will be concerned with developments taking place in the TRB sequence and the archaeological evidence for these changes will be contrasted with the initial phase of the BAC or with the entire BAC sequence, where appropriate.

I: Social model

This model is partly based on a reading of the work of French Marxist anthropologists concerned with lineage-based systems (Meillassoux 1972; 1981; Rey 1979; Terray 1975; 1979), but also takes into account feminist positions and other approaches. Firstly social relations of production are discussed. Secondly the relevance of the concepts of exploitation, domination and power to a conceptualisation of these social relations is considered and related to social contradictions and the possibility of social transformations. Forms of legitimising power relations in such a social context are outlined, and the role of material culture as playing a part in ideological legitimation indicated.

Social relations of production

In small-scale segmentary societies units of production are built up on the basis of real or fictive kinship. Households form the minimal units of production and consumption, and a number of such households may be linked by a common ancestor or ancestors forming a lineage group or the basic unit within which the appropriation of surplus labour takes place. The local community typically consists of one or more lineages or lineage branches with an elder or elders at the head. Technical activities in the production process are organised socially and the division of labour may be largely based upon sex and age, although a systematic division of labour is possible involving co-operative work teams organised in relation to various aspects of agricultural production such as hunting, fishing, guarding crops etc. Relatively under-productive necessary labour absorbs a large proportion of the total labour expended and production is geared primarily to use-value or the satisfaction of existing wants, which remain relatively limited (Sahlins 1972). Of primary importance is the personal non-economic link between producers founded on kin ties as opposed to the impersonal primary economic link established in the capitalist production process.

At a very general level the relations of production involve the social appropriation of the natural environment through socially organised labour and the redistribution of the product of labour within groups and the establishment and maintenance of relationships between groups. Kinship links provide the means for the reticulated redistribution of the labour-product through a network of individuals which goes far beyond those participating in any particular labour process. This redistribution of the labour-product ensures both the reproduction of the individual labourers and the economy as a whole. Typically this takes the form of prestations of the labour-product from junior members of the lineage group to the elders who both supervise and co-ordinate redistribution to unproductive members of the community (the aged and children), the producers themselves, and to other lineage groups by such means as feasting thus maintaining inter-lineage links. Redistribution thus provides the economic conditions of existence for a wide network of intra- and inter-lineage social relationships. It depends on a system of pre-given kin relations in which individuals receive their portion of the labour-product on the basis of their position within a specific group, rather than according to temporary personal relationships which may be established with others. In particular no social basis exists for assessing and rewarding relative contributions to the total

labour-product. Kinship relations serve as a double mechanism involving the extraction of surplus labour on the one hand and the co-ordination of communal labour on the other hand. As a result of the intrinsic delays involved in agricultural production the relationships between producers tend to be long lasting or permanent. In diachronic perspective the agricultural cycle consists of 'an endlessly repeated series of advances and returns of the product between the productive groups which operate from one season to the next' (Meillassoux 1981, p. 43). This may result in an evaluating hierarchy dividing those who come first from those who come after (*ibid.*, p. 42). Such a situation serves to support a hierarchical structure of social relations predicated on anteriority or age in which the elders provide the socially necessary, but nevertheless non-productive task, of co-ordinating social labour and managing the redistribution of the labour product.

Exploitation, domination and power

A substantial amount of the work of Marxist anthropologists has centered around the relevance of the concepts of exploitation and social domination to the study of pre-capitalist social formations, or to be more accurate, the 'primitive communist mode of production'. The major questions to arise are (a) whether exploitation takes place at all or is this purely a product of class societies? (b) if exploitation does take place, who are the exploited and by what means does this exploitation take place? No attempt is made here to enter into the details and historical development of the debate (Kahn 1981 provides a brief review). It will suffice to say that some authors such as Hindess and Hirst (1975) consider that social relations are essentially egalitarian, suggesting that a distinction should be held between the appropriation of surplus on the one hand and exploitation on the other, with no necessary connection existing between the two. By contrast Meillassoux (1964; 1972; 1981), Rey (1975; 1979) and Terray in his later work (Terray 1975; 1979) all argue that definite forms of exploitation exist. The difference between the positions taken by these authors can be related to which categories of agents can be considered to be exploited, and how this exploitation can be conceptualised in terms of Marxist theory. To Rey and Terray this entails the imputation of classes whereas Meillassoux denies that classes exist. This argument depends essentially on exactly how a class is to be defined. Here the term 'class' will be reserved for capitalist social formations and it is suggested that no necessary connection exists between the emergence of classes and the development of exploitative social relations, which can exist in all social formations. Exploitation will be defined as a situation in which an individual or a group of non-producers appropriates the surplus product created by the labour of direct producers which is then harnessed to further the sectional interests of these non-producers. Exploitation is, therefore, to be connected with forms of social domination. It involves a definite asymmetry of social power in which relations of autonomy and dependence are both produced, and through the passage of time reproduced, differentiating between those social actors who exercise control and those who are controlled.

Social control and the exercise of exploitative power in

small-scale societies can only involve the control of people and their labour-product. The means of material production (technologies etc.) are so simple that they are accessible to all and do not provide any possible foundation for domination. The *possible* sources of control, therefore, relate to (i) control over the circulation of the surplus labour-product and the organisation of subsistence activities (ii) control over the reproductive capacities of individuals within the social group i.e. biological reproduction (iii) socially defined statuses/positions/life-chances (iv) control over knowledge or non-material resources deemed to be essential to the well-being of the group (v) control of the means of social signification related to social standing e.g. prestige items.

Meillassoux (1972; 1981) has argued that a fundamental feature of lineage systems or 'domestic communities' is the control of elders over the biological means of group reproduction. An essential mechanism by means of which elders maintain their authority is by establishing control over procreative women who are used to establish marriage alliances with other groups. The effect of such a system is to reduce women, in part, to objects of exchange so that they become counters in a system of power in which their sexual capacity for human reproduction is exploited. By means of the control of women the elders can also control the possibilities for marriage of junior men. In order to bolster up this form of control marriage within the local lineage or domestic group must be prohibited hence 'endogamy becomes incest, and sexual prohibition a taboo' (Meillassoux 1981, p. 45). The reproduction of the local community is thus seen by Meillassoux in terms of the reproduction of human labour-power and this is identified with control over human reproduction and the 'means' of that reproduction, women. The analysis suggests that control over women is isomorphic with control over the differential allocation of labour between individual societal units. However as Edholm, Harris and Young (1977) and Harris and Young (1981, p. 120) have pointed out there is no necessary relationship between the two, nor is the control of procreative women the only means of achieving the differential allocation of labour-power between domestic units, and thus the primary source of social power.

The sexual division of labour in many small-scale societies may result in a situation in which not only the elders (usually male) but also men as a whole can be regarded as exploiting women through the extraction of their labour-product which passes into the hands of their husbands and ultimately enters into the managerial sphere of the elders. Despite, or perhaps as a result of the dominant place women occupy as producers and in the sphere of 'domestic' labour they may not acquire any definite status within the social relations of production. Mackintosh writes, in her feminist critique of Meillassoux: 'it is not the "domestic community" which has existed from pre-history, but female subordination. Control of women's fertility and sexuality, labour and progeny, has always been sought by dominant groups and classes as *one* means of control of reproduction of the social system. And this control has always had to be fought for, and maintained by political, economic and ideological means' (Mackintosh 1977, p. 126, my emphasis). The essential point of

Mackintosh's critique is that Meillassoux analyses the subordination of women, as a *given* rather than as a fundamental contradiction, source of struggle and clash of interests within domestic communities (*ibid.*, p. 122). The sexual division of labour may be complementary, that is in instances in which there is a recognition of exchange between the sexes with each producer controlling his/her labour-product. However in lineage systems in which the product is appropriated at various managerial levels (household/elder) this complementarity often ceases to exist. It may result in a 'quite systematic "non-valorisation" of women's labour, which derives from the nature of social relations between the sexes' (Edholm, Harris and Young 1977, p. 123). Molyneux (1977) amongst others, has argued that the sexual division of labour is neither to be viewed as merely a technical division nor as a 'natural' development predicated on the fact that women, not men, give birth to children etc. but that it correlates with a sexual hierarchy acting to distribute men and women to, respectively, superior and inferior positions. Female agents play a considerable, if not a primary role in the production process. The sexual division of labour, characteristic of all small-scale societies, does not arise in some spontaneous, natural way but is actively maintained by determinate social practices, in kin relations, in mythology and in ritual. It is the site of an important inequality both in terms of labour effort expended and in the differential social evaluation of forms of production; women typically confined to the 'domestic sphere' of cooking, child rearing etc., manual labour on the fields and excluded from political decision making while men engage in, albeit the production of primary staples, but also in prestigious hunting activities (normally contributing very little to calorific output), in managing the labour product, and in highly visible, public juridical and ideological practices: 'women's exclusion from certain forms of representation is yet another means by which they are controlled, by which their invisibility is created . . . their disappearance is socially created and constantly reaffirmed' (Edholm, Harris and Young 1977, 126). Like virtually all other facets of social life the subordination of women and their exploitative domination by men is not cross-culturally valid. For example Iroquois women seem to have been in a position of considerable power controlling the economic organisation of their social system (Brown 1975). Although such examples appear to be the exception rather than the rule (mother's brothers are usually in important positions of power in matrilineal and matrilocal societies) it need *not* concern us to be gender *specific* in a prehistoric context i.e. to suggest that men control and exploit women or vice versa unless, of course, this can be unequivocally demonstrated from the substantive data. The important point to be made is that sexual differences in small-scale societies are in the vast majority of known cases transcribed into relations of inequality, domination and exploitation. Gender differences are the site of considerable tension and negotiation for position and social standing. Differential power relations along sexual lines, and the need to bolster up these differences, to naturalise and legitimise them are commonplace.

So far we have discussed the possibility of the exploitation of individuals in relation to gender differences and, concomitantly, the differential distribution of life-chances translated along these gender differences. Elders are also able to reinforce their authority by reserving for their own use a disproportionate amount of social surplus which rather than being redistributed to the direct producers is used to acquire and gain control over prestige goods, serving to enhance their social standing in relation to others both within the local community and in relation to other social groups. The need to acquire such prestige goods on the part of junior members of the lineage in order to engage in exchange relationships increases their degree of dependency on the elders and the need to make continual prestations of goods and services.

Another medium of social control is differential access to knowledge, usually ritual knowledge, thought to be essential to the well-being of the group. Economic activity in a large number of small-scale societies is very much related to a presumed conjunction between the producers and the supernatural. The powers of the spirits, mediated through the ancestors to the elders are seen as directly influencing prosperity. Production becomes presented as the benevolent intervention of the spirits in the world of the living which, in turn, serves to legitimate a structure of social relations depending on a principle of anteriority in the production process. Offerings must regularly be made in order to maintain the benevolence of the spirit world in the form of prescribed ritual acts, knowledge of the significance and content of which is confined to elders and/or age-sets. The continued reproduction of the social group is thus conceived as being dependent upon a relationship with the supernatural which can only be maintained by those in positions of authority.

Contradictions and transformations

A major structural contradiction can be posited as being present in small-scale lineage societies, a contradiction between a supposed symmetry of kin relations within the local group requiring disinterested reciprocity and the asymmetry of power relations between individuals and groups involving exploitative social relations. Kin relations, in the process, become transformed into political relations. Friedman (1975) and Friedman and Rowlands (1977) have demonstrated how generalised exchange between a number of lineage groups may lead to the development of hierarchies between them. These unstable hierarchies may be transformed into positions of relative rank through such means as the manipulation of surpluses, communal feasting etc. Lineages which are able to produce feasts large enough to feed the entire local community are deemed to be able to do so because of the influence of the spirit world. As influence is regarded in terms of genealogical proximity, lineages with large, socially displayed and consumed surpluses are able to claim positions of anteriority in relation to the spirit world which confers rank. This obviously results in a transformation of the social relationships existing between individual lineage-groups. In the patrilineal, patrilocal groups which Friedman uses as the basis for the model differences between local groups may be reinforced by the valorisation of bridewealth from being merely a counter in a system of identical exchange (a bride for a bride) to having differential exchange value, a direct form of wealth. Such pro-

cesses of competition and hierarchisation between local lineage groups directly contradict the fact that each individual group has no independent structural existence but forms part and parcel of a wider social network. The successful demographic expansion of one such local unit or a significant degree of increase in productive output can directly undermine the conditions of existence for its continued growth by increasing internal social contradictions.

Although transformations may take place in the nature of between-group relations leading to asymmetries of prestige and power, differential power relations predicated on unequal access to social resources are already present within the local group and are likely to be reproduced in a fairly stable form. We have seen that exploitative social relations exist between social agents, primarily on the basis of sex (men/women) and age (elders/ juniors). These differences may frequently be reinforced by such means as age-sets and a great deal of emphasis marking changes in the social position of individuals in relation to others e.g. initiation rites. Individuals pass through different social statuses during their lives in which different forms of behaviour are expected. This has clear implications for the degree of solidarity attainable by those who are dominated. As a result of the division of social labour in terms of sex and age and the nature of life-cycle rituals it is relatively easy to present differential access to resources, and therefore power as part of the natural order of things. For example as a result of the double exploitation of women by men and younger men and women by elders in certain lineage groups the contradictions involved in the latter form of exploitation can be displaced in terms of the general opposition men/women.

Legitimation of power

It has been argued in the discussion above that definite forms of social inequality involving the differential exercise of power and social control are *characteristic* features of small-scale societies. The nature of such power differentials and the constitution of the exploited group(s) is unlikely to be known through a consideration of the archaeological record in most cases and must be posited in theory. Furthermore small-scale societies, in common with capitalist social formations, are inherently *contradictory* social totalities (Tilley 1982b, p. 36). Definite forms of contradiction exist between the structuring principles on which they are based. Now whether or not the social order is reproduced or transformed depends, quite crucially, on the manner in which the exercise of power by individuals/groups over others is legitimated. The exercise of social control to maintain the hegemony of specific interest-groups must always appear to be purely arbitrary unless it can be neutralised, presented as immutable and self-evident, or part of the natural order of things. The reproduction of the social order entailing the reproduction of relations of inequality cannot be conceived as being an automatic repetitive process as it simultaneously involves the reproduction of contradictions between the structural principles orientating the actions of individuals and groups. These contradictions can never be dissipated but only temporally displaced. This entails that relations of social dominance can only be sustained through the considerable social cost of strategies which must be continuously repeated, because in pre-capitalist social formations there are no social conditions present which permit a lasting appropriation of social labour. Social dominance, in its various forms, must be continually disguised and misrepresented by means of the ideological legitimation of the social order. What is contingent and arbitrary must be made to appear to be natural.

It has been suggested in some detail elsewhere (Shanks and Tilley 1982) that mortuary ritual, in common with other life-cycle rituals, may serve to act as a particularly powerful plausibility structure serving to legitimate sectional interests hence the ubiquity of such practices in small-scale societies. Now such a proposition immediately leads us into terminological difficulties and claims that rituals do much more than merely legitimate asymmetrical power-relations; they simply cannot be 'written-off' in this manner. A commonly accepted tenet in anthropology is that the term 'ritual' should refer to all forms of symbolic behaviour. Ritual actions are not just associated with forms of institutionalised religion (e.g. contributions in La Fontaine 1972). In such an approach the domains of the symbolic and the ritual become fused, and a common assumption made is that human action in this realm, as opposed to more mundane aspects of life, refers to cultural values about the world, social relations and the place of people in the cosmos. Such a position assumes, implicitly or explicitly, the existence of a normative consensus without which social life would be impossible. Viewing social formations as contradictory totalities leads to the rejection of any thesis that social integration must be *ipso facto* dependent on consensual unity. Rituals do indeed express values and meanings but these should not be confused as being generally accepted by all individuals and groups in society in that these values and meanings are in their interests. Asad puts the point this way: 'is the system which is supposed to be necessary for thinking and speaking (whether speculatively, or with authoritative force) about social life to be identified with what is necessary for living in it?' (Asad 1979, p. 613).

Accepting the view that ritual is inextricably bound up with symbolism and hence a component of all social practices we will distinguish between public institutional and non-institutional ritual practices. It is the former that play a crucial role in the legitimation of the social order. Of course there may be rituals that effectively serve to challenge hierarchies (Bourdillon 1978) but these are usually unstable because of the lack of institutionalisation and what is essentially being manifested in both forms is *power*, either attempts to maintain existing power bases or to subvert them.

Power relations are simultaneously affirmed and misrepresented through ritual activities. Two recurrent types of institutionalised ritual activities may be distinguished: (i) rites of passage in which individuals are transferred from one social status to another, and (ii) calendrical rites associated with fertility and the passage of the seasons. The former are always rituals of status-elevation while the latter may involve status-reversal (Turner 1969, p. 161). Rituals are so strongly embedded in social life because they provide an anchoring point for the affirmation of

power on the part of specific individuals or groups and the legitimation of the social order.

The general form in which Van Gennep (1909) described rites of passage as involving rituals of separation, marginal rites and rites of aggregation has been verified over and over again (e.g. Turner 1967; Leach 1976; La Fontaine 1977). Rites of passage are serial in form characterised by a tripartite structure. The purposes of such rites are to transfer individuals from one social status to another. Individuals can only achieve this change of status by going through these rites. Status is socially mediated and hence becomes invested with power because such rituals, while transferring people from one status to another, also serve to demarcate status in terms of an evaluative hierarchy thus maintaining discrete social divisions. Intimately associated with such rites is the relationship between power and knowledge. The process of initiation into a higher status involves the acquisition of knowledge in the marginal state. It does not matter what this knowledge actually is but what is important is that this knowledge exists and demarcates those who possess it and those who do not. Knowledge is power and power is knowledge. This knowledge cannot be acquired by the individual but must be imparted by those in positions of power and serves to legitimate social divisions. The fewer people who possess this knowledge the greater its value, and the value of this information is greatest when it ceases to be useful: when one person has it and does not transmit it, hence the knowledge assumed to be held by the dead is the most powerful knowledge of all and the authority of the elders is by virtue of their closeness to the ancestors who possess this ultimate knowledge (Barth 1975, p. 217; La Fontaine 1977). Authority, ultimately vested in knowledge and, mediated through ritual, becomes projected into the past and naturalised. Furthermore this power/knowledge relationship is intimately associated with the passage of time. The elders possess most knowledge by virtue of being old, by their ancestral proximity.

Rituals of status-reversal, often associated with calendrical rites, in which the high become low and the low become high reaffirm the position of those in power by this very inversion of the hierarchical principle. Reversal is only possible precisely because it is a temporary liminal state. The liminality of the reversed state symbolises its irregularity and hence asserts the impossibility of the social order to be other than it is. Turner comments that 'it is appropriate that rituals of status-reversal are often located either at fixed points in the annual cycle or in relation to movable feasts that vary within a limited period of time, for structural regularity is here reflected in temporal order' (Turner 1969, pp. 165–6). Again there is an intimate association between the passage of time and the legitimation of power.

In the account so far we have outlined an intimate connection between ritual, power/knowledge, and the passage of time. Power is established through ritual by access to knowledge and linked to time. Power becomes articulated onto time which serves to naturalise social control. Authority is projected into the past and onto a mystical plane associated with the possession of knowledge in a manner in which the principles underlying social relationships appear to be handed down from the dead to the living and thereby are unquestionable. Another important characteristic of institutionalised rituals is their formality, reserve and apartness from daily activities. This permits the elaboration of symbolic forms which allude to social reality not by presenting it, or expressing it, but by presenting it as other than it really is by characterising society as a unitary, harmonious whole involving song, dance and material symbols. Ritual communication is protected against direct evaluation, against empirical reality by its formalised premises (Bloch 1977). Thus ritual creates a legitimate form of inequality in an imaginary world dislocated from ordinary experience. In calendrical rituals associated with fertility and social renewal it is in the sphere of gifts to gods that social relationships between people are played out, misrepresented and thus reproduced.

As we have seen in Chapter 1 above, ideology is to be understood as a practice or set of practices operating to secure the reproduction of relations of dominance between individuals and groups. It may serve to conceal contradictions between the structuring principles orientating social actions and social practices, misrepresenting an arbitrary social order as an immutable social order. Ritual is thus ideological activity. Rituals, through stressing the importance of certain principles of social order such as the power/knowledge relationship, simultaneously do so only by blocking the expression of other principles which may be contradictory. Representation is thus partial and distorted and forms of representation effected through material culture may be actively utilized to displace or 'resolve' contradictions which have their basis in social practices. Material culture thus may be a particularly effective medium through which to legitimate the social order precisely because of its materiality which gives it a relative permanence and efficacy to 'act back' and serve to restructure social practices. The immediate ideological effect of material culture may be to dissolve oppositional elements present in society forming instead an inseparable unity as a form of signifying practice. It can be manipulated in specific contexts to create on an imaginary plane a universe whose content and form differs entirely from social reality, but whose components are akin, recognisable and therefore acceptable. This role of material culture as playing part and parcel of the legitimation of power relationships is now considered below in a specific case study.

II: Case study

The existence of communal burial in megalithic tombs during the TRB suggests their use by distinctive corporate groups or lineages as Renfrew (1973a; 1973b, pp. 146–56; 1976; 1981) has argued at length. Whilst we should be aware of the theoretical indeterminacy of the term 'lineage', and rejecting any conception of a distinctive 'lineage mode of production' as favoured by Rey (1979), amongst others, the term lineage will be used here as a shorthand expression for those social groups Douglas has described as possessing 'strong group and weak grid' i.e. societies with a strong sense of identity to outsiders with a weakly developed degree of social differentiation (Douglas 1970; 1978). The archaeological evidence does not suggest any form of centralised political hierarchy during the TRB but the repetition of

equivalent acephalous units across space. The evidence thus suggests that we are dealing with the kinds of social groups discussed above.

The study region

The study region, Scania, forms the most southerly province of Sweden. It forms a more or less natural region for study, approximately square in shape, and bounded by the sea on three sides. The region has a total area of 11,284 km² of which 376 km² comprises surface water. Although making up barely 3% of the total land area of Sweden it has now, and in the historical and prehistoric past, the densest concentration of rural settlement, and accounts for 17% of the total arable land in the country. Scania is essentially a lowland region with the land nowhere exceeding 212 m above sea level. The majority of the landscape consists of a flat or undulating plain with gentle slopes and small differences in relative relief; 45% of the region is under 100 m above sea level and 29% under 33 m. Horst ridges, topographically well defined, aligned in a roughly northwest–southeast direction break up the lowland (Fig. 1). The vegetation period varies between 250 and 270 days, slightly longer in coastal districts, mean annual temperature is *c.* 7°C and mean annual precipitation varies between 600 and 700 mm. The bedrock is extremely heterogeneous as the area lies within what has been termed the Fennoscandian boundary, transitional between ancient rocks of Pre-Cambrian age to the north and younger rocks formed in the central European sedimentary basin to the south. The soils are brown earths and podsols and are largely

Fig. 1. The study region: location, topography and main drainage.

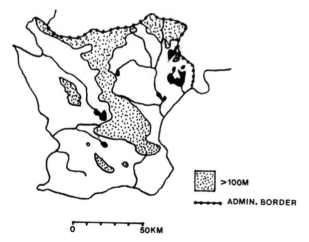

>100M

ADMIN. BORDER

0   50KM

derived from post-glacial moraine deposits, although as most of the material was transported relatively short distances an obvious relationship exists between surface soils and the underlying rocks.

Chronology and periodisation of the TRB and BAC

Both the relative and absolute chronology of the Scanian middle neolithic are dependent on a consideration of the Danish material, an unsatisfactory state of affairs, explicable in terms of the historical development of middle neolithic (MN) studies in Sweden, and the paucity of radiocarbon determinations available. On the basis of a large number of Danish MN dates and the few determinations from Scania, which do show good concordance with those from Denmark, the entire period under consideration can be dated to between *c.* 2600 bc and *c.* 1900 bc (3370 BC–2385 BC) (Bakker 1979, pp. 142–5; Davidsen 1974; 1978, pp. 170–1; Larsson 1982, p. 87; Malmros and Tauber 1975; Nielsen 1977; Tauber 1972). The final phase of the TRB has been dated to between *c.* 2280 bc–2140 bc while the entire duration of the BAC is between *c.* 2200 bc and 1900 bc. There appears to be little chronological overlap between the two traditions, and a more or less unilineal line of development is indicated by the C14 dates.

A four-phase division of the Scanian TRB willbe adopted following the work of Bagge and Kaelas (1950; 1952; Kaelas 1953a) and a three-phase division of the BAC (Tilley 1982a) based, primarily, on ceramic typology. The relative chronology proposed by Bagge and Kaelas is identical to the standard Danish TRB chronology established by Becker (1954) except that he defined a fifth and final phase for the Danish ceramics. This final phase has not been thought to exist in Scania (Davidsen 1978, p. 165; Ebbesen 1975, p. 142) but two recent excavations have questioned this assumption (Larsson 1982; Roth 1967). If a fifth and final TRB phase does exist in Scania it appears to be confined to settlement ceramics. On the basis of the radiocarbon dates available it is almost impossible to assess accurately the relative duration of the TRB and BAC phases since the standard deviations of the dates, considered together, are frequently longer than the average time-distances between the periods dated. As Bakker (1979, p. 141) notes there is no standard procedure which can be used to construct the boundary lines between the periods which, in practice, is done haphazardly.

The majority of the monumental megalithic tombs of the TRB tradition, the dolmens and passage graves, were constructed during a relatively brief period (*c.* 2700 bc–2500 bc) (Kaelas 1967; Kjaerum 1967) corresponding to the end of the early Neolithic, during which the first dolmens were constructed, and the initial phase of the middle Neolithic. Construction had all but ended by phase II of the MN TRB.

The change from the TRB to the BAC – general characteristics

The major features of the change from the TRB to the BAC manifested in the archaeological record can be summarised as follows:

(1)   A change from an extremely clustered site distribution to a less clustered distribution, possibly associated with the exploitation of a broader range of environmental zones.

(2)   A change from collective burial in monumental megalithic tombs to single flat-grave inhumation.

(3)   A change from a diversified pattern of site orientations to a more uniform arrangement.

(4)   A technological discontinuity in vessel-manufacturing techniques (Hulthén 1977, p. 144) and the appearance of new artifact types such as the battle-axe.

(5)   A change from a plethora of vessel forms to simple bowl forms.

(6)   An alteration and simplification of ceramic design structure.

Some aspects of these changes will be examined in detail below.

Site location, economic and environmental evidence

This study is heavily dependent on the distribution of TRB and BAC mortuary sites since few MN TRB settlement sites are known from the study region and the vast majority of the non-grave finds attributable to the BAC cannot be interpreted as representing occupation sites. It is assumed that a fairly close connection must have existed between the distribution of the burial sites and contemporary domestic settlements. For the TRB we have some evidence to support this contention, while for the BAC it remains largely supposition. Most of the TRB settlement sites discovered in Scania are the result of rescue excavations. In only one area, the Hagestad district of south-east Scania, has systematic survey work been carried out. This has resulted in the discovery of a series of MN TRB sites in close proximity to the tombs at distances varying from a few hundred metres to two or three kilometres (Strömberg 1971a, p. 371; 1977, pp. 14–15; 1980; Hulthén 1977, p. 86, Fig. 59). Isolated MN TRB settlement sites in other areas are in all cases in close proximity to the tombs. Recent rescue excavations associated with the industrial expansion of Malmö in the south-west of the region have resulted in the discovery of some twenty domestic sites within a few kilometres of the Hindby Mosse dolmen (Fig. 9, nr. 22) (Svensson, pers. comm.). This may suggest in this area at least a dispersed pattern of individual homesteads associated with a tomb as the quantity of artifact materials and the areal extent of the culture layers is usually very restricted. A similar connection between BAC settlement sites and graves appears to occur in the Hagestad area in the south-east of the region (Strömberg 1982, p. 57) but no unequivocal evidence is available for other areas of the study region.

In Scania some 107 megalithic tombs are known (Fig. 2).This distribution map has been compiled from a survey of the published literature and Riksantikvarieämbetet (national monuments records) reports. A few erroneous sites may have been included, but determination of megalithic tombs, because of the nature of the monuments, is normally likely to be reliable. Of these, forty-eight are dolmens, forty-nine passage graves and ten sites are either unclassifiable or probably remains of megalithic tombs. As a whole the tombs can be grouped into five fairly nucleated clusters on a visual basis (Fig. 2: 1–5). Other sites are rather more isolated, often grouped in pairs or strung out along the coast. As is apparent from Fig. 2, the overall distribution is strongly coastal and riverine. Many tombs must have been destroyed, but the overall distribution is unlikely to be merely the result of differential destruction. In all 124 BAC grave sites have been discovered. These occur either singly or are grouped in gravefields of two, three or four and in one exceptional case thirteen graves. The distribution (Fig. 3) is similar to that for the TRB tombs except that larger numbers of graves are found in inland areas (Table 1).

Straight-line distances between all the megalithic tombs were computed using topographic maps at a scale of 1:50,000. This was repeated separately for the dolmens and the passage graves and also carried out for BAC grave sites. In the rare cases where TRB tombs were closer than 100 m these were treated as

Table 1 *Distances of grave-types from the nearest coastline. Figures in brackets indicate percentages.* + *Treating contiguous sites (< 100 m.) or graves in the same gravefield as one site.*

	0–5 km	5.1–10 km	10.1–15 km	Over 15 km	Total
All TRB sites	54 (54.0)	21 (21.0)	13 (13.0)	13 (13.0)	100+
All BAC sites	36 (41.3)	21 (24.1)	9 (10.3)	21 (24.1)	87+
Dolmens	22 (47.8)	8 (17.4)	9 (19.6)	7 (15.2)	46
Passage graves	25 (55.5)	11 (29.4)	4 (8.8)	5 (11.1)	45

Fig. 2. The distribution of megalithic tombs in the study region. The main sub-regional clusters are indicated.

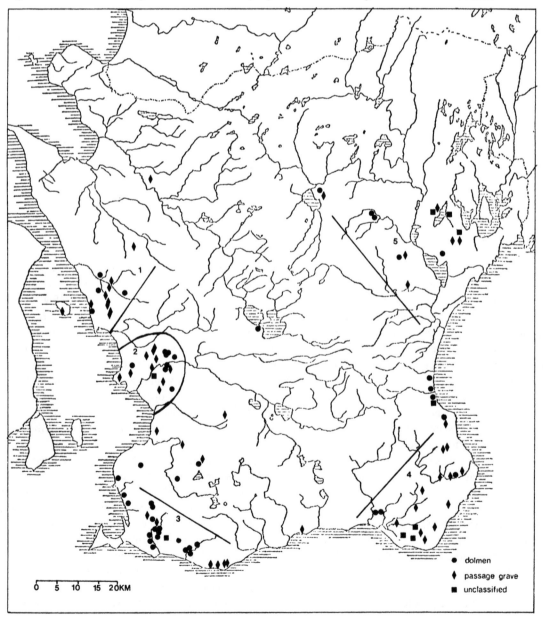

equivalent and the distance measured to the next nearest neighbour. All BAC graves in gravefields were treated as one site. The distribution of the graves was investigated by nearest-neighbour analysis (Hodder and Orton 1976, pp. 38–51) excluding sites closer to the coast than to their first nearest neighbour in order to avoid boundary effects (*ibid.*, pp. 41–3; Donnelly 1978). The results are shown in Fig. 4.[1] The trend towards a less clustered distribution seems to be essentially linear through time, the majority of the dolmens being constructed before the passage graves (Kaelas 1981).

A large number of grain impressions in MN TRB pottery have been extensively studied by Hjelmqvist (1955; 1962; 1964; 1979; 1982) from both grave and settlement contexts. A consistent picture emerges from all the TRB sites with the two primitive wheats, emmer (*T. dicoccum*) and einkorn (*T. monococcum*) dominating, together making up *c.* 76% of all determined seed impressions. Einkorn is quantitatively better represented at almost all the sites although emmer may have increased in importance during the TRB (Hjelmqvist 1982, p. 113). Naked and hulled barley are present at most sites, but in low absolute and relative frequencies. Pulses appear to have been quite unimport-

ant, only two pea impressions being certainly identified. For the BAC only six cereal impressions have been identified, all of barley. That this figure is so low is almost certainly due to the fact that BAC pottery, in comparison with many TRB ceramics, is very thin walled. In Denmark there is evidence for an increase in barley cultivation in the final phase of the TRB (Davidsen 1978, p. 140; Rowley-Conwy 1978) and it also dominates both in Scania and Denmark in the late neolithic and Bronze Age. However, there is too little evidence to support any hypothesis of a change to predominantly barley cultivation in the BAC.

Animal remains are usually poorly preserved, few in number and no quantitative studies have been carried out. At the Hindby Mosse settlement site bone remains of cattle, sheep/goat, pig and red deer were reported along with large numbers of fish hooks (Salomonsson 1971, p. 74). Cattle, pig, sheep/goat and red deer are also recorded at a few other sites in varying combinations (Gejvall 1973; Persson 1982; Strömberg 1968, p. 128; 1978, p. 83). In Denmark there is evidence for an increase in importance of cattle during the TRB, with pig dominating in the early phases (Higham 1969; Madsen n.d.). Hunting and gathering appears to have played an additive role throughout the TRB. For

Fig. 3. The distribution of Battle-Axe/Corded-Ware grave sites in the study region (source: Tilley 1982a).

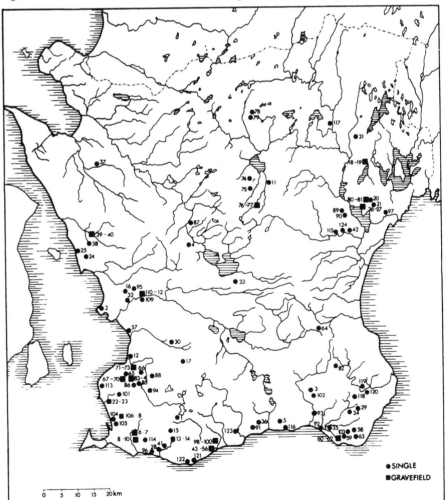

the BAC the only economic evidence comes from animal bones (mostly artifacts) in the graves (Møhl 1962; Malmer 1962, p. 800, Table 99). Of these over 50% represent wild animals, roe and red deer predominating. The domestic species represented are pig and sheep/goat. As Malmer points out (*ibid.*, p. 800) the reliability of this evidence, as economic indicators, is extremely dubious.

Clark (1977) has noted a strong regional correlation between the distribution of the megalithic graves and lime-rich, tractable soils. This feature is also true for the majority of the BAC grave sites. Only the lighter, better drained, sandy soils would have been readily accessible with a neolithic technology. It is questionable whether ard marks found under some Danish megalithic tombs really do imply animal traction as Sherratt has suggested (Sherratt 1981). Higham, in a detailed analysis of the bone remains from a number of TRB sites, found nothing to suggest either the use of animals for traction or keeping large numbers of sheep for wool (Higham 1969, p. 206). If a 'secondary products revolution', associated with the use of the plough did occur in Scandinavia it would seem to be later than the MN.

In order to investigate the relationship between sites and land-use patterns more closely a series of site catchment analyses were carried out (Higgs and Vita Finzi 1970; Jarman 1972). Two potential land-use categories were defined: (i) high potential arable land, i.e. light, easily worked, sandy soils with a low clay and boulder content (ii) permanent all year round grazing areas likely to be available along river courses and in marsh areas. Both of these potential land-use categories could be assessed accurately using soil maps (Sveriges Geologiska Undersökning series Aa, scale 1:50,000) dating from the late nineteenth and early twentieth centuries. It was not really possible to draw any finer distinctions in terms of potential land-use categories because recent soil maps were only available for a small part of the region. In addition these recent maps, because of extensive drainage during the last one hundred years, tended to give a distorted picture of the extent of waterlogged deposits. Site catchments were analysed using,

alternatively, 500 m and 1 km radius catchments for twenty TRB settlement sites, representing virtually all those mentioned in the published literature, and 1 km and 2 km radius catchments for a sample of twenty TRB tombs and twenty BAC grave sites drawn using a table of random numbers. The results of these studies were then compared with a random sample of twenty control catchments (Fig. 5). An obvious difference exists between the control catchments and those of the settlement and TRB and BAC grave sites in that the former contain negligible quantities of high potential arable land and permanent grazing areas. Secondly a considerable difference (significant at $p = >0.001$ using a chi-square test for independence on the sums of the hectare figures) exists between the 1 km radius catchments for TRB settlement sites and the TRB tombs. The majority of the former contain significantly larger areas of arable and permanent grazing potential. This may suggest that the tombs were located on the edges of some site territories rather than at their centres, an assumption often made. No significant differences seem to exist between the catchments of the TRB tombs and those of BAC grave sites. Finally the 0.5 km radius catchments for the TRB settlement sites indicates, primarily, selection for high class arable land with a variable permanent grazing potential. A few of the catchments with low arable potential are indicative of temporary hunting and gathering locations. However, it should be borne in mind that the arable area actually required for small-scale agrarian populations will have been small (Flannery 1976).

The period under consideration broadly corresponds to the later half of the early sub-boreal (SB1) pollen zone as dated by Nilsson (1961; 1964) for southern and central Scania and Digerfeldt (1974; 1975) for north-eastern and western Scania. The main feature of the development of the forest vegetation, which had attained stable climax conditions with a maximum extension during the preceding late Atlantic period, during the SB1 is a retrogression of the broad-leaved climax forests primarily associated with human influence following the introduction of

Fig. 4. The trend in R values for (A) all TRB and BAC grave sites and (B) dolmens (D), passage graves (PG) and all BAC grave sites for first, second and third nearest neighbours (1, 2, 3).

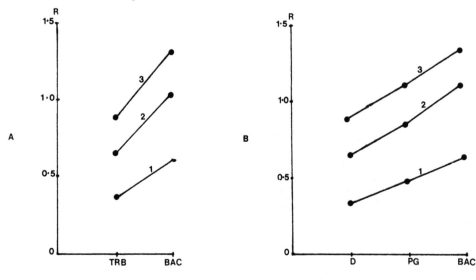

agriculture. The general increase in non-arboreal pollen (NAP) levels is considerably more marked in the pollen diagrams from the south and west of Scania than in the north-east[2] (Digerfeldt 1974) or in Blekinge (Berglund 1966), the county immediately to the north-east of Scania. In these areas no megalithic tombs are known, and few BAC sites. The overall extent of the forest clearance is rather difficult to establish from the pollen diagrams. The increase in NAP at the beginning of the 'land occupation phase' in the early neolithic is only of moderate proportions (*c.* 6–15%) and never amounts to anything like the high values associated with late glacial layers, taken to indicate sparse tree cover (Nilsson 1948, pp. 43–4). Cleared areas were probably small and the majority of the region must still have remained densely forested. More extensively settled areas may have been gradually converted into unstable regeneration woodlands with considerable shrub cover (Berglund 1969, p. 22; Bartholin et al.

Fig. 5. Potential land-use categories for the sites. Catchment size radius is shown. Key: A – arable land; G – permanent grazing; O – other. The points of the triangles represent 100% of each category. 1 and 2: TRB settlement sites; 3 and 4: megalithic tombs; 5 and 6: BAC grave sites; 7: random control catchments.

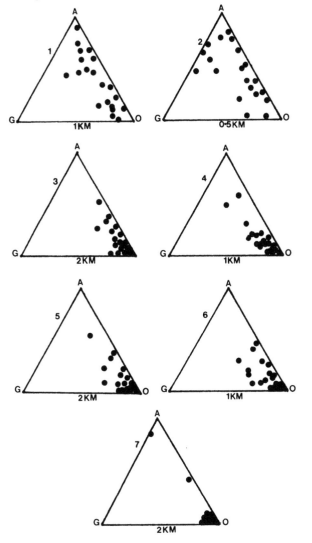

1981, pp. 45–6). The trend in the pollen diagrams does not seem to be linear. They show an increase in AP (arboreal pollen) during the middle of SB1 (*c.* 2600 BC) i.e. at the beginning of the MN, followed by an increase in NAP levels towards the end of SB1 (*c.* 2200 BC) which Berglund (1969) suggests represents an expansion stage. To what extent these fluctuations of AP and NAP during SB1 actually do relate to significant expansions and decreases of the area of cleared land is unclear. Taking the pollen curves at face value they suggest an initial land-clearance phase during the early neolithic followed by a static period in the early MN (megalithic TRB) followed by an increased extent of clearance during the final TRB and BAC. This might be correlated with the spread of BAC sites into more inland areas (Fig. 3, Table 1).

Both the TRB and BAC appear to have been characterised by cereal-based economies, supplemented by hunting, fishing, gathering and livestock. In view of the predominantly forested environment a cattle-based economy as proposed in *Early European Agriculture* to be associated with megalithic tombs (Jarman, Bailey and Jarman Eds., Ch. 7) is extremely unlikely in this case (see also calculations in Halstead 1981, p. 314). It is significant that the pig, well suited to forest foraging, is the quantitatively best represented species on a large number of Danish sites, with cattle increasing proportionally during the TRB sequence (Higham 1969; Madsen n.d.).

No drastic environmental changes took place during the period under consideration and, based on the numbers of grave sites in the lack of other reliable evidence, there is no evidence for any significant increase in population levels. The data, such as it is, does not indicate much if any change in economic practices. The catchment analyses suggest that both TRB and BAC sites were largely restricted to a limited range of high quality, tractable, arable soils. There is nothing which suggests the need to compete for scarce or critical resources. The sites are quite densely clustered in areas of high agricultural potential but, equally, there are large empty spaces with equally good soils in which no tombs or settlement sites are known. This is unlikely to be solely the result of differential site-destruction. If we are to explain the change from the TRB to the BAC, therefore, we must look to social factors.

Space, time and place

The outstanding feature of the MN TRB is the construction and repeated use of monumental megalithic tombs. The monumentality of these tombs has not gone unnoticed by archaeologists but attempts to explain this monumentality have tried to relate it to the need to control resources such as land in the face of population pressure (Renfrew 1976; Chapman 1981). Leaving aside the absence of any evidence for population pressure these explanations have failed to account for the form and historical significance of these monuments (see Hodder, Ch. 5 above). In this section we will consider them in relation to space-time referents and a sense of *place* (Tuan 1974).

Space and time should not be conceived as neutral backdrops to action but as being actively involved in it. People define space and time and, in turn, space and time mediate and structure social relationships. Space and time are inextricably bound up together. For example we say it takes so many hours to go from A to B. Social life is given shape and form through space and, therefore, societies generate social principles for marking boundaries on the ground and mapping social relationships. These relationships may not be so much projected onto a symbolic plane but transformed through it. In this sense space does not merely reflect social organisation but once space has been bounded and shaped it is no longer a neutral datum; it exerts influence. Objects and architecture are affected by their place in the space of others. Presence, position and absence or 'negative presence' are of crucial importance (S. Ardener 1981). Places stand out and are vested with meanings and significance. They are far more than merely locational nodes in a spatial lattice. Places exist through time and in space, and sacred places, such as the megaliths, command awe and respect and this is an obvious reason for their monumentality. They have survived to the present day whereas contemporary domestic settlements have long since become invisible. The permanence of these sacred places thus contrasts with the mundane world of the living. The megaliths deny time, they assert permanence, continuity and stability and as such serve to project the present into the future and into the past existing independently from the flux and change of the world of the living. They are material symbols of power through which time is denied and space mediated.

There can be little doube as to the importance of the megaliths as public symbols. In an essentially flat or undulating region, such as the study area, they must have been impressive landmarks, at least at short distances, with a high imageability. They are designed to impinge upon the eye. As Fleming (1973) puts it they are tombs for the living as much as for the dead. They also may have acted as instruments for the creation and maintenance of political and social space. This proposition is examined below.

The orientation of the architectural components of archaeological sites is one of the most frequently recorded classes of information yet rarely are any detailed analyses undertaken. If any investigation of orientation is taken at all this normally takes the form of summary statistics of how many sites are orientated in such and such a direction rather than another. At this point the analysis normally concludes, or rather fails to conclude, what the significance of orientating a particular site or series of sites in one direction rather than another might be. Insufficient attention has been paid to the relationships between sites.

A number of questions can be raised concerning the relationships between the orientation of the megaliths: Do any principles seem to underlie the overall pattern? For instance, does the orientation of one tomb appear to have any effect upon that of another or is it a purely random relationship? If there are principles underlying the orientation of the sites do these hold good for the entire distribution in the study area or vary between sub-regional groups? Do natural boundaries in the landscape, such as river-valleys, have any effect upon the orientation of the tombs?

Initially it is suggested that if tombs are aligned in the same direction this may symbolise social relations of identity between the social groups who erected them. Conversely, if orientated in opposing directions (e.g. N–S/W–E) this may symbolise the opposition or relations of non-identity between social groups, metaphorically represented through spatial alignments. However, such relationships may be opposed in other areas, and so in the same material form relations of both identity and non-identity may be expressed in terms of directional symbolism. An essential assumption of this work is that the tombs, as a whole, and regardless of their particular time of construction, all acted together as symbolic and social markers being vested with social significance.

All information which it was possible to obtain with regard to the orientation of the megalithic tombs was collected from publications and Riksantikvarieämbetet reports. This information is almost always expressed in terms of different cardinal points of the compass but is detailed enough for our purposes. For dolmens there is information for the orientation of the chamber, and for those with long, as opposed to round mounds, for the orientation of the mound and/or stone setting. For passage graves there are data for the orientation of the chamber, passage and the direction in which the passage entrance faces. As most passage graves were built with a circular surrounding mound no information is available for this feature except in the few cases in which an elongated axis was present.

In order to obtain an objective measure of the degree of similarity or difference between the orientation of an architectural component, such as the chamber, of one site and another a simple orientation index was devised. If we take, for example, the orientation of the chamber of a dolmen or a passage grave there are eight major axes along which it can lie: N–S / W–E / NE–SW / NW–SE / ENE–WSW / ESE–WNW / NNW–SSE / NNE–SSW. If we compare the orientation of the chamber of two sites there are thirty-six possible different combinations. Taking the axes along which the chambers are orientated there are four possible cases of rotation through 90 ° (e.g. N–S/W–E), eight possible cases of rotation through 67°, 45°, 23° and eight cases where the chamber can be orientated in the same direction. A simple matrix can be used to summarise these relationships. Five categories can be distinguished to summarise the degree of similarity in the orientation of two sites:

Class 1 rotation on an axis through 90°
Class 2 rotation on an axis through 67°
Class 3 rotation on an axis through 45°
Class 4 rotation on an axis through 23°
Class 5 orientation along the same axis

Class 1 relationships are relationships of total opposition on an axis while class 5 relationships are identical. Sites may fall between these two extremes (classes 2–4) to a varying degree. Considering the relationship between the direction in which the passage entrance of passage graves face nine possible orientation classes through 180° are derivable from a situation in which passage entrances face each other, but in fact are opposed, being rotated through 180° on the same axis, to that in which passage

Table 2 *The frequency of classes of orientation relationships between first nearest neighbours. A: chamber of dolmens and passage graves; B: chamber of passage graves; C: chamber of dolmens; D: passage-axis of passage graves; E: mound/stone setting of long dolmens; F: passage-entrance of passage graves. Class 1: rotation through 90° (A–E), 180° (F). Class 5 (A–E), 9 (F) orientation in the same direction.*

Class	A	B	C	D	E	F
1	5	5	3	0	0	0
2	11	6	1	3	4	5
3	10	6	3	5	4	2
4	6	9	2	10	3	2
5	5	5	1	3	4	0
6						0
7						2
8						5
9						4

entrances face in the same direction, being orientated on the same axis.

Orientation relationships: nearest neighbours

The first analysis was concerned to determine the degree of similarity between the orientation of nearest neighbours. Are neighbouring tombs always orientated in the same direction and, if not, what degree of variability is there? The only possible basis for comparison between dolmens and passage graves is between the orientation of the chamber. For sites with two chambers in the same mound the orientation of both these chambers as compared with that of the first nearest neighbour. In cases where two sites were the nearest neighbour of each other the relationship was only counted once to avoid distortion. Table 2 presents the results of a series of analyses.

One point to emerge from this table is the overall lack of similarity between the orientation of first nearest neighbours along all dimensions. Secondly the majority of the tombs are neither orientated in the same or completely opposite directions but fall midway between these two extremes. In no cases are the passage axes of passage graves, the mound/stone settings of dolmens and the entrances of passage graves orientated in completely opposing directions. This type of correlation, based on first nearest neighbours, is rather unsatisfactory for a number of reasons; because of the lack of information for some sites and that many first nearest neighbours were pairs of tombs rather than different sites. The analysis also assumes that the relationship between the orientation of first nearest neighbours was particularly important which may or may not be the case. Rather than extend the analysis to *n* nearest neighbours it was decided to analyse the orientation relationships between sub-regional clusters of tombs where sufficient evidence permitted. Quite obviously, when we are searching for some underlying structure as regards the directional placement of the tombs it is essential that

relevant information is available for all or the majority of sites in any sub-regional group.

Tombs in the Håslöv/Skegrie area

This area is in the south-west of the study region and thirteen megalithic graves are closely clustered along a roughly north-south river axis (Fig. 6). Of these sites ten are dolmens, two are passage graves and one unclassified site possesses two adjoining chambers. All the dolmens, with the exception of site 15 which has a round mound, are long dolmens. One of these dolmens (site no. 29) has two chambers, both orientated in the same direction. Five of the sites are to the east of the river axis and eight are to the west. This natural boundary or axis in the landscape appears to provide a clear division between the sites to the east or west of it in terms of directional placement. All the grave *mounds* of the megaliths lying to the west of the river axis are orientated

Fig. 6. The distribution of megalithic tombs in the Håslöv/Skegrie area of the study region. 1: dolmen; 2: passage grave; 3: unclassified.

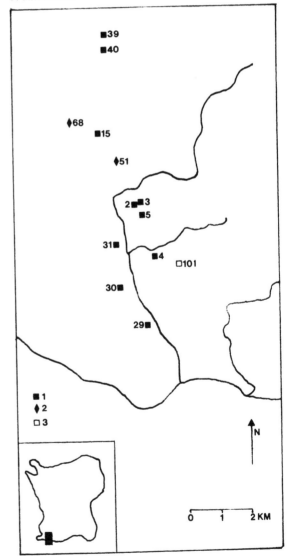

in a different direction from each other. As grave 15 is circular, admittedly, there is no information as regards its orientation but this feature in itself makes it distinctive from all the other grave mounds. By contrast every grave *mound* of the sites to the east of the river axis is orientated in the same direction: NW–SE. There appears to be quite a clear contrast between the directional placement of the grave mounds of the site according to which side of a north–south river-axis they lie. Taking the group as a whole only one site (no. 29) to the west of the river, possesses a grave mound orientated in the same direction as those to the east of the river.

The *chamber* of every tomb to the west of the river is orientated in a different direction. There is a complete lack of uniformity. Unfortunately information for chamber orientation was only available for site 101 to the east of the river axis. If we compare the orientation of the chamber of every tomb to the west of the river with that of every other tomb on the western side, there are twenty-eight different possible relationships. There appears to be an underlying structure to the orientation of the chambers of these tombs in relation to each other. Firstly every tomb has a class 1, 2, 3 and 4 relationship to another tomb. Even though every site is orientated in a different direction the degree of distinction in terms of directional placement varies between them. Class 1 relationships (rotation through 90°) occur between sites 39/68; 15/51; 31/29; 30/40. Only one of these relationships occurs between sites adjacent to each other in the sequence (nos. 15/51). The pattern to emerge, at first glance, is a seemingly chaotic set of relationships with a complete lack of any regularity. However, looking a little more closely we can see that the two sites at either end of the distribution (nos. 29/39) possess a class 4 relation, the next two sites from either end of the distribution have a class 1 relation and for the next four sites this sequence is repeated (Fig. 7).

Superficially the orientation relationships between these sites display an almost anarchic dissimilarity yet underneath this apparent lack of coherence runs a definite structure characterised by similarity and opposition. Class 4 orientation relations only require slight rotation through 23°. So the sites at either end of the distribution are different from each other, but not too dissimilar. The next two sites from either end of the distribution directly oppose each other, yet are not too dissimilar from the sites at either end, and so on.

It might be argued that the underlying structure found in relation to the orientation classes existing between the tombs west of the river axis could be the result of a random process in which the orientation of one site is not actually related to that of others, as postulated here. In order to investigate this possibility a computer simulation of random permutations of orientations between the eight sites was run and the resulting orientation relationships assessed. For this study a group of random permutations of eight positive integers was generated. Each of these integers were then converted into site orientations. Orientation relationships were then assessed, using the five classes discussed above, between those sites at either end of the distribution, the next two sites from either end of the distribution and so on. 700

separate simulations were performed. A class 4 orientation relationship occurred between the sites at either end of the distribution 163 times. In only eight simulations was the next orientation relationship between the second site from either end of the distribution a class 1 relationship, with a class 4 relationship also existing between the sites at either end. In four simulations out of the 700 a 4141 pattern, as exists between the sites, did occur. It is therefore concluded that it is extremely unlikely that such a set of orientation relationships between the sites could occur solely as a result of chance or random processes.

Turning once more to the orientation relationships between the grave *mounds* on either side of the river none of these are in direct opposition (class 1 relationship) so despite the overall differences between the orientation of the grave mounds on either side of the river axis these do not take the form of categorical oppositions. The two chambers of site 29 west of the river are 'balanced' by the two chambers of site 101 east of the river and the passage entrances of site 51 and one of the passages at site 101 face each other, displaying reflective symmetry.

From analyses of other sub-regional groups of tombs in the study region one particularly interesting feature arose: groups of tombs were only clearly opposed in the sense that a number of tombs either did or did not share the same orientation in relation to other groups when placed along N–S river axes. This did not occur for tombs along W–E river axes or for groups of tombs not related to a river axis. In these cases the sets of orientation relationships were extremely ramified and no coherent differences occurred between the tombs situated on either side of the

Fig. 7. Classes of chamber-orientation relationships for the megalithic tombs west of the river in the Håslöv/Skegrie area of the study region.

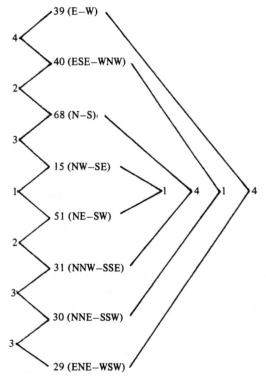

river axis. This may suggest a special symbolic significance accorded to a N–S axis, contrasting with W–E.

By contrast to the complicated sets of orientation relationships existing between the TRB tombs the BAC flat graves exhibit considerable unity. In the earliest phase all the graves are orientated either N–S or NNE–SSW. The BAC graves are not highly visible landmarks and complex sets of similarities and oppositions in their directional placement are no longer evident. The overall unity in BAC burial practices (see below) is matched by a lack of variability in grave placement.

Mortuary practices

Human burial at the megalithic tombs involved an elaborate sequence of associated activities including the deposition of large quantities of elaborately decorated ceramics, caches of broken and unbroken axes and flint fragments (mostly unretouched), amber beads, in many cases, and the sprinkling of red ochre in some tombs (Strömberg 1971a; 1971b). Different types of flooring were put in the same tombs, which were used successively for long time-periods.

In Scania the human bone-remains have only been described in sufficient detail to permit a quantitative analysis at two sites, Ramshög and Carlshögen (Strömberg 1971a). These analyses have been discussed in detail in a previous publication (Shanks and Tilley 1982) and here only a few points will be made. Collective burial was practised and the osteological remains were completely disarticulated. There is clear evidence for the deliberate selection and ordering of body-parts which were differentially grouped in a number of piles in and at the tombs. Differences in the frequency of various skeletel parts such as the skull, ribs, upper and lower limb-bones, were too great to be accounted for solely in terms of differential preservation. Regrouping of the disarticulated remains was carried out incorporating basic body symmetries such as upper and lower halves of the body, trunk/limbs and right/left body-parts. Contrasts also exist in the treatment of juvenile and adult remains, but no clear male/female distinctions are evident. At one of the sites, Carlshögen, the disarticulated bone remains were segregated by laterally placed stone slabs dividing the chamber of the tomb into sections.

Reliable and detailed qualitative comparisons with the human osteological material at other tombs are difficult to make since most of the excavations are old, bone material is usually not well preserved, and insufficient attention was paid to stratigraphic relationships. Site publications are brief and mainly concerned with the description of artifacts. Chamber division does appear to be a common feature in passage graves (Strömberg 1971a, pp. 251–66). The only other comparison that can be made is that disarticulation always occurs (Almgren 1910, p. 72; Hansen 1923, pp. 283–8; 1924, p. 5; 1930, pp. 77–8; 1938, p. 25; Strömberg 1971b, p. 12).

A series of radiocarbon dates are available for Ramshög and Carlshögen (Strömberg 1971a, pp. 200–4). These indicate that the majority of the osteological remains at Ramshög were deposited during phase Ib of the TRB (*c.* 2600 bc) while for Carlshögen the dates indicate deposition during the final phases

of the TRB (*c.* 2270 bc). In the light of these temporal differences it is interesting to note (i) that evidence for the selection and arrangement of bones and the symbolic exploitation of bodily boundaries is more marked at the later tomb; (ii) virtually all the human bones recovered from Carlshögen were confined to bounded, demarcated sections of the chamber while at Ramshög the human remains were found in the chamber, the passage and in earth graves immediately outside the tomb.

Although inhumation is the dominant burial practice connected with the megaliths finds of burnt or scorched bones are known from five dolmens and eight passage graves (Burenhult 1973; Strömberg 1968, pp. 197–200 and refs.; 1971a, p. 100). The finds are usually small and amount to no more than a few bone fragments. These have been made in the chamber, passage, immediately outside the passage entrance, and in the close vicinity of the tombs. In one case at the Hindby Mosse dolmen (Burenhult 1973) there were seventy-one discrete concentrations of burnt bone. Most of these were placed directly under the slabs of the cairn in a confined area on the eastern side of the tomb and are clearly associated with its construction (*ibid.*, p. 43). Of these bone fragments 94% consisted of human skull remains from some ten individuals. It is in precisely the area where these burnt bone fragments were buried that pottery was successively deposited during the TRB. At the Trollasten dolmen eleven concentrations of burnt bone were discovered in a low cairn outside the tomb. Two further concentrations were situated in the chamber and the passage. These bone concentrations, consisting of skull-remains, vertebrae, ribs and long bones in varying associations were deposited with flint artifacts and axes, the latter dateable to phase III or IV of the TRB (Strömberg 1968, pp. 119–36). It is on, in and under the low stone cairn that a large pottery concentration occurs. At the Gillhög passage grave burnt bone deposits, stratigraphically related to a primary phase of use, were found immediately outside the entrance to the tomb again associated with a large concentration of ceramics (Rydbeck 1932, pp. 38–9).

These burnt bone-remains have been discussed in relation to sacrifice or cannibalism, but in the light of the evidence for deliberate selection and arrangement of bone materials during the TRB other interpretations may be more plausible. It was noted (Shanks and Tilley 1982) that specific classes of bones such as the skull, upper and lower limbs, were consistently under or over-represented at Ramshög and Carlshögen so that selection of skeletal parts must have taken place at some stage either before or after interment. Destruction of these bones by burning is a possible explanation for what happened to at least some of them in the light of the evidence discussed above. Furthermore, just as the selection, arrangement and disarticulation of skeletal remains destroys individuality, another means of achieving this is by burning.

In the BAC there is a substantial change in the nature of mortuary practices. Individuality is emphasised for the first time and single crouched inhumations in flat graves become the norm, but continued use of megalithic tombs is documented in thirteen cases (Malmer 1962, pp. 246–53; Strömberg 1968, p. 225; 1971a, p. 52). Reliable evidence is available from thirty graves as regards the positioning of the interment. In twenty-one cases the skeleton was on the left hand side and on the right hand side in six cases. The dead were invariably placed with the head facing east (Malmer 1975, p. 40). Three 'mass' burials are known, each containing more than two skeletons. There is one recorded case of an extended skeleton and one of a double grave. All these unusual burials are confined to the two largest gravefields, Kastanjegården, Malmö (Winge 1976) and Lilla Bedinge (Malmer 1962, pp. 152–80) and can be dated to phases II and III of the BAC. Of the 124 burials known, 116 possessed grave goods and there is no evidence for any significant hierarchical distinctions between them or consistent relationships between artifact associations and other features of the mortuary practices such as the positioning of the body or physical characteristics of the grave itself (Tilley 1982a, pp. 12–22). Grave goods such as battle-axes, ceramics, flint axes and chisels were placed in the graves in a delimited range of positions with battle-axes by the head, ceramics either by the feet or the head and axes behind the back (Malmer 1962, pp. 209–19; 1975, pp. 42–4). Grave goods may have been differentiated on the basis of sex or age but the number of anatomically sexed graves is too few to firmly establish this. Overall there is considerable uniformity in mortuary practices.

Ceramics

Megalkitkeramiken är intensiv, nästan explosiv, kortvarig och intern.[3] (Folke Hansen 1938, p. 27)

In this graphic statement Hansen, who excavated so many of the Scanian passage graves in the first three decades of the twentieth century, summed up his belief that there was something important and quite dramatic connected with the production and deposition of vast quantities of ceramics at the tombs, and the first feature to strike anyone is the sheer variety and magnitude of the material. Despite the relatively brief period of time during which the dolmens and passage graves were constructed they continued to be centres of activity throughout the TRB. The Scanian megalithic tombs are unique in the entire western European distribution in that massive quantities of sherd materials have been recovered, principally around and immediately outside the entrances to the tombs. These frequently number tens of thousands of sherds, representing up to a thousand or more vessels. The rate of the deposition of the vessels was not uniform throughout the TRB. Bagge and Kaelas (1950; 1952) in a pioneering study analysed the sherd materials from five sites in detail and grouped them according to temporal phases. Material from the earliest phase only amounted to between 1 and 5% of the material, phase II 50–65%, phase III up to 30% and phase IV between 1 and 5%. These figures are also generalisable to the material from other megalithic graves in Scania in which the amount of material attributable to phases I and IV is slight or negligible. If a fifth and final phase of the TRB can be distinguished in Scania it only appears to occur in settlement ceramics, as noted above. Few ceramics can, therefore, be associated with the initial period of construction of the tombs and at some stage in phase IV ceramic materials ceased to be deposited at the tombs.

Quantities of ceramic materials differ considerably between the tombs. Fig. 8 shows the quantities of sherd materials recovered from the more reliably and extensively excavated sites. These have been grouped into broad classes because, undoubtedly, some differences in the frequency of sherd materials recovered are partially a result of the extent of the excavated area and varying refinement in excavation techniques from the beginning of the twentieth century to the present day.[4] However, there is reason to believe that early excavations were fairly reliable. For example the Hög passage grave has been excavated twice (Hansen 1923; Petré and Salomonsson 1967). The later investigation only recovered a small additional quantity of sherd materials. In addition the extensive and meticulous excavations in the Hagestad area of south-east Scania conducted by Strömberg confirm that differences existing between the tombs are not to be attributed to either the extent or the sophistication of the excavations.

Returning to Fig. 8 it is evident from an inspection of the overall distribution of the megalithic tombs (cf. Figs. 8 and 2) that the more isolated sites, nos. 6, 65 and 97 (see Fig. 9), all possess small quantities of sherd material, while it is those sites forming part of quite densely packed sub-regional clusters in which the largest quantities of sherd materials occur. A clear hierarchy of sites appears to exist in which, within local groups of tombs, one or two sites stand out from the others in terms of the quantities of ceramics deposited. Spearman's coefficient of rank-correlation was used to test whether any relationship might exist between the size of the tomb and the quantity of ceramics deposited. Grave size was estimated on the basis of a variety of criteria: chamber area, passage length and/or mound size for different groups of tombs. These tests were all negative. No consistent relationship exists between the size of the tombs and the amount of ceramic materials deposited.

Early theories attempted to account for the distribution of sherd materials outside the tombs by suggesting that they were the remains of vessels periodically cleared out of the chamber and dumped outside the passage entrance. Thick layers 20 cm or more deep are quite usual, and the majority of the sherds are restricted to an area of c. 10–15 m^2. These occur in many cases in, under and over low stone cairns, stone settings or pavements. At some sites layers of sherds are separated by comparatively barren stone layers and no investigators have ever found remains of the same vessel both inside the chamber and outside the tomb. Hansen's early investigations (Hansen 1918a; 1918b; 1923; 1930; 1938) were instrumental in seriously questioning the validity of the cleaning hypothesis and it is now generally accepted that the vast majority of the pots were never taken inside the tombs but were deposited outside. In all documented cases the numbers of complete vessels discovered inside the chamber, as represented by sherds, amount to no more than ten or twenty, in many cases less, a striking contrast to the hundreds of vessels represented outside the tombs. Remains of more or less complete vessels have been found in situ in the chambers of the tombs in cases where there was little post-depositional disturbance, notably Storegården (Hansen 1930, p. 71, Fig. 39) and a symmetrical distribution of vessels in relation to the passage opening may be indicated. At sites where the spatial distribution of the sherds has been recorded outside the passage entrance an asymmetrical distribution is characteristic. The majority of the sherds are found immediately outside and to the right of the passage entrance (10 cases) with a roughly symmetrical distribution present in another three.

At none of the tombs have any complete crushed vessels been found in the area outside the passage entrance in situ. It can be established that this is not entirely the result of post-depositional disturbance as many of the finds were beneath the plough layer. It is rare to find all the sherds of a single vessel and Hansen even suggested that parts of vessels may have been taken away after deposition (Hansen 1938, p. 24). Be that as it may, all the material is extremely fragmentary. Careful studies of the distri-

bution of sherds from the same vessel (Burenhult 1973, Figs. 25–44; Strömberg 1968, pp. 184–9; 1971a, pp. 351–2) suggest deliberate vessel-crushing. Computer seriation studies of sherds from the same vessels may indicate that some vessels were originally arranged in roughly semi-circular arcs outside the tombs (Saers, pers. comm.).

Studies of ceramic design

This section will consider firstly between-site relationships in the TRB based on an analysis of sherd materials, controlling for chronological variation. Secondly temporal changes in characteristics of ceramic design will be outlined for the TRB sequence at the tombs and compared and contrasted with the earliest phase of the BAC using restored or restorable vessels which can be

Fig. 8. Quantities of sherd materials at the major excavated sites. 1: <1,000; 2: 1–5,000; 3: 5–10,000; 4: 10–15,000; 5: >15,000.

accurately dated. Other general contrasts such as that between settlement and tomb will also be noted in the course of the discussion.

Relationships between TRB sites

This study is based on an analysis of the decorated sherds from twenty-three TRB sites. Two of these are dolmens, sixteen are passage graves, one is an unclassified megalithic tomb and four are settlement sites (Table 3). Ceramic materials were analysed from all excavated sites in the Lödde/Kävlinge sub-regional group of tombs (Fig. 2: 2), where inter-site distances do not exceed 15 km and in the case of first, second and third nearest neighbours are considerably less. TRB sites were selected for study so that they embraced all other areas of the study region, including isolated sites and those forming parts of other sub-regional clusters (Figs. 2 and 9). The design attribute, rather than the sherd or individual vessels, provides the basic unit of analysis. Sample size varies considerably from site to site, dependent on the size of the collections[5] (Table 4). In all a total of 11,983 design attributes at the least inclusive level of the classification system were recorded from 8,033 individual sherds.

The classification system utilised in the study of designs on the sherd material is hierarchical in form, involving the partitioning of the total data-set from more to less inclusive levels. It emphasises alternative attribute states at each level so that no single design can be assigned to two different classes at the same level. The list of attributes to be recorded was defined in terms of formal variation in geometric possibilities which could be reliably recorded from the fragmentary sherd material following suggestions of Friedrich (1970), Redman (1977; 1978) and S. Plog (1980,

Fig. 9. The distribution of the sites from which sherd material was studied. 1: megalithic tomb; 2: settlement site. Inset refers to Figs. 13–15.

Table 3 *List of the sites from which sherd materials were studied and primary references. D: dolmen; PG: passage grave; S: settlement site ATA: unpublished excavation report in Antikvarisk-Topografiska Arkivet, Stockholm; LUHM: Lunds Universitets Historiska Museum; STHM: Statens Historiska Museum, Stockholm; MHM: Malmö Museum, Malmö.*

Site Name	No.	Class	Mus. Cat. No.	References
Trollakistan	6	D	LUHM., uncatalogued	Larsson 1979
Hindby Mosse	22	D	MHM.2800	Burenhult 1973
Gillhög	49	PG	LUHM.28200	Forssander 1930 (ATA), Rydbeck 1932
Storegården	50	PG	LUHM.26760	Hansen 1930
Laxmas Åkarp	56	PG	LUHM.21059	Hansen 1924 (ATA)
Glumslövs Backar 1	62	PG	STHM.24760	Kaelas 1953b (ATA)
Bjärsgård 2	65	PG	LUHM.28879	Stjernquist 1949
Hög	70	PG	LUHM.20156	Hansen 1923 Petré and Salomonsson 1967
Örum 5	71	PG	STHM.16917	Bagge and Kaelas 1952
Gantofta	74	PG	STHM.13521	Almgren 1910
Åsahögen	77	PG	STHM.2549	Bruzelius 1822
Lackalänga 10	80	PG	LUHM.20979	Hansen 1923a (ATA)
Erkedösen	82	PG	LUHM.19669	Hansen 1918a
Ramshög	84	PG	STHM.19753	Bagge and Kaelas 1952 Strömberg 1971a
Sarslöv 4	91	PG	LUHM.20155	Hansen 1923
Västra Hoby 13	92	PG	LUHM.28208	Forssander 1936
Kungsdösen	96	PG	LUHM.19670	Hansen 1918a
Ö. Vram 1	97	PG	LUHM.28919	Bagge and Kaelas 1952
Albertshög	102	D/PG	LUHM., uncatalogued	Strömberg 1971a
Hindby Mosse	S1	S	MHM.1505	Salomonsson 1971 Tinz and Wahlund Franck 1980
Hagestad 8	S2	S	LUHM., uncatalogued	Strömberg 1961
Böste Fiskläge	S3	S	LUHM.19668	Hansen 1918a
Löddeköpinge 26:1	S4	S	LUHM., uncatalogued	Wihlborg 1976

pp. 44–53). At the most inclusive level two alternative attribute states were recorded, whether individual design attributes were bounded or unbounded. The basic distinction that is being made here is in terms of the closure or non-closure of any particular design. It is suggested that this is a fundamental distinction dependent on the formal properties by means of which space is divided up. The undecorated vessel surface is considered to be an empty carrier-space consisting of continuous or vacant parts through which, by analogy, movement is unrestricted. Once decorated in some manner this carrier-space becomes partitioned in two forms: (1) the space can be partitioned by lines or boundaries so that movement through that space becomes restricted or channelled but is still possible through all or part of it so that no area of that carrier-space is entirely enclosed by any single division or combination of divisions; (2) the space may be divided so that segments of it are completely enclosed and bounded off from other segments so that movement is not possible into some areas of the carrier-space except by means of transgressing boundaries. A bounded design is thus defined as one having lines or boundaries on all sides with or without internal decoration or infill within these boundaries. An unbounded design, by contrast,

serves to break up the continuous space of the vessel surface without entirely enclosing any area of it.

At level 2 of the classification system for TRB ceramics twelve primary bounded or unbounded forms were distinguished (Fig. 10). These form the main elements utilised to create the overall design-structure of the pottery and may be combined, infilled or have secondary appended forms. Each of these primary forms were subsequently divided according to alternative attributable states at less inclusive levels of the classification system. Beyond level 2 of the classification system many of the subdivisions made of the primary units were non-equivalent since the geometric form of the primary unit puts limitations upon the nature of further subdivisions. For example some of the subdivisions made for the bounded forms (Fig. 10: 11–15) are clearly non-equivalent such as whether a triangle has its base orientated to the top or bottom of the pot which may not be compared with whether lozenges are orientated in a horizontal or a vertical field. However, types of infill categories (dots, merging lines etc.) are directly comparable between the primary motif forms (*cf.* Figs. 11 and 12).

It should be noted that the classification system, as it is

Table 4 *The frequency of investigated sherds and design attributes distinguished from the sites studied.*

Site No.	Investigated Sherds	Design Attributes
6	29	39
22	674	1161
49	918	1490
50	284	472
56	43	55
62	1148	1663
65	30	33
70	195	309
71	159	254
74	27	44
77	8	25
80	177	291
82	24	28
84	585	960
91	103	178
92	1348	2137
96	345	503
97	55	78
102	34	51
S1	1666	2019
S2	22	30
S3	97	101
S4	62	62
Total:	8033	11983

restricted to geometric possibilities for dividing up space, does not consider the technique by means of which this was achieved, e.g. impression of a line by means of a comb, cord or shell, which forms another level of analysis not considered here. Hårdh (1982) is currently investigating microvariations in ornamentation techniques between tombs in the Lödde/Kävlinge group which may complement the analyses discussed here.

All distinguished design attributes were coded numerically according to the alternative attribute states defined for the primary forms at each level of the classification system. The numerical codes for each individual design were typed into the Cambridge IBM 370/165 computer and frequency-counts made for individual sites using SAS (SAS Institution 1979), which were then used, as appropriate and possible, for subsequent multivariate analyses. Only a few results of this detailed analysis can be presented here.

Differentiation between settlement and funerary ceramics

The settlement ceramics are predominantly unbounded (70–95% of the total sample analysed from each site). By contrast at only three of the tombs are there higher percentages of unbounded than bounded designs, but these sites all possessed low absolute frequencies of sherds so that little reliability can be placed on this result. Apart from these cases ten tombs possess c.

15% more bounded than unbounded designs and six approximately equal frequencies. A chi-square test confirmed that significant differences do exist between the settlement and grave material ($p = 0.0001$). At level 2 of the classification system (Fig. 10) the contrast is replicated. At the settlement sites between 38 and 43% of the designs utilised consist of simple pitted ornamentation, whereas at the tombs this motif form was either absent or accounted for up to a maximum of 7% on the designs. Other general contrasts between settlement and tomb may also be noted. The quantity of the sherd material at the settlement sites is usually small, ranging from a few hundred fragments to no more than two or three thousand, with only one major exception, the Hindby Mosse settlement site (Fig. 9: S1) which may have had a special ceremonial importance. Thick-walled cooking and storage vessels are largely confined to settlement contexts as are circular clay discs (baking plates?). Angular vessel forms such as pedestalled bowls and various types of brimmed and hanging beakers occur mainly in grave contexts and the frequency of decorated sherd material is considerably higher at the tombs (c. 40–60%) than in settlement contexts (c. 15–20%). Detailed statistics for some sites are given by Hulthén (Hulthén 1977, pp. 85–121). Designs impressed by means of comb-stamps are very frequent at the tombs whereas a large proportion of the settlement ceramics are decorated by means of pitted impressions or with simple 'stab and drag' techniques. The deposition of red ochre and amber beads is confined to grave contexts. Finally the monumental architecture of the tombs contrasts to the almost complete lack of any structural evidence from settlement contexts, as discussed above.

Variation between TRB sites

Similarities and differences in the nature of ceramic design between the TRB sites will be discussed here in relation to the frequency of infill categories for the following primary bounded design forms distinguished at level 2 of the classification system: lozenges, triangles, bands and zig-zag bands (Fig. 10: 11–14). The following infill classes were defined: 1 cross hatching, 2 merging lines, 3 perpendicular lines, 4 dotted/dashed infill, 5 parallel lines, 6 oblique lines sloping left to right, top to bottom, 7 oblique lines sloping right to left, top to bottom. For bands an additional infill category was recorded which does not occur as infill for the other primary forms: interlocking lines or dashes.[6] Figs. 11 and 12 show these infill categories for triangles and bands in relation to other levels of the classification system, defined individually, for these primary forms. No particular chronological significance can be granted to these infill categories as they all occur on a variety of vessel types throughout all or most of the duration of the Scanian TRB. It is assumed, therefore, that any variation existing between the sites represents valid spatial patterning, largely uninfluenced by chronological factors. In order to further maintain chronological control, analyses were undertaken separately for each of the primary forms so that any possible temporal differences in the frequency of occurrence of the primary forms in relation to each other would not distort the results.

Figs. 13, 14 and 15 show, respectively, the percentages of

each of the infill categories for triangles, bands in a horizontal field (Fig. 12: 131) and bands in a vertical field without appended forms (Fig. 12: 1321), for the tombs in the Lödde/Kävlinge sub-regional group (Fig. 2: 2; Fig. 9). It is apparent that considerable differences exist between the sites in terms of the proportional representation of the infill categories, even at a localised level. Chi-square tests, where sufficient observations/category allowed were undertaken between all the twenty three sites investigated and for sub-regional groups and pairs of sites in order to test the null hypothesis of no significant differences in the representation of the infill classes from site to site. These tests were performed separately for each of the primary motif types mentioned above and except between a few individual pairs of tombs were all significant (p = >0.01) confirming that substantial differences do exist. Fig. 16 gives the results of a series of principal components analyses (Doran and Hodson 1975), using standardised frequencies of the infill categories as input-data for each site and excluding dotted/dashed infill (except for triangles) because of its very low absolute frequency at most sites. Merging infill was also excluded for bands in a horizontal field for the same reason. The numbers of sites included in each individual analysis varies according to permissible sample size for a meaningful statistical analysis. It is clear from the plots of the sites against the first two principal components that no consistent relationship exists between intersite similarity and between-site distance. There is no indication of a marked fall-off of similarity with distance between sites. For example sites in the Lödde/Kävlinge sub-regional group are sometimes clustered close to each other on the plots but also, in other cases, with sites located at distances 70 km or more away. Differences between first nearest neighbours are frequently as great or greater than between distant sites.

The results of these analyses were confirmed by multi-dimensional scaling analyses (Doran and Hodson 1975; Zvulun 1978). The Gower coefficient (Gower 1971) was used to compute a similarity matrix between the sites using percentages of infill categories as input for each site. The analysis was then run using the Minissan programme originated by E.E. Roskam in the MDS(X) series. Fig. 17A and B show the results, respectively for bands in a horizontal and a vertical field. The Gower coefficient

was also used to compute a similarity matrix for the presence/absence of the six classes of appended forms for bands in a vertical field (see Fig. 12) in relation to infill categories and a multi-dimensional scaling analysis run (Fig. 17C). Again variation between nearby sites is as great or greater than between distant sites and no clear pattern of coherent sub-regional differences emerges. The overall picture is one of a complex cross-cutting of similarities and differences, varying for each of the primary forms.

The frequency of the representation of the infill categories varies not only between individual sites according to individual bounded forms, but also between the bounded forms themselves (Fig. 18). Chi-square tests (p = 0.001) confirmed that a statistically significant relationship does exist between the choice of infill categories according to the bounded forms. The only consistent *relationship* to exist between *all* the bounded forms is that oblique infill, right to left is always more frequent than oblique infill, left to right, apart from dotted/dashed infill which is in all cases the least frequently represented infill category.

Temporal changes in the organisation of ceramic design

Aspects of temporal change in ceramic design organisation will be discussed here in relation to analyses of 180 restored or restorable TRB vessels which could be securely dated according to a four-phase periodisation and thirteen partial or complete BAC vessels which could all be dated to phase I of the BAC. It should be noted that the latter represents a complete sampling of the available material. Of the TRB vessels thirty-four could be assigned to phase I, seventy to phase II, sixty to phase III and sixteen to phase IV.

Fig. 19A shows the percentages of bounded designs on vessels according to this periodisation. These increase during phases II and III of the TRB and decline sharly in phase IV until in the earliest phase of the BAC no bounded designs are utilised in the design structure of the vessels. The use of bounded designs reaches a peak in phase III of the TRB in which almost 60% of all designs are bounded. Fig. 19B shows the percentage of vessels possessing cross-referencing between bounded or unbounded designs, in either a horizontal or a vertical field. By cross-referencing is meant whether a design is repeated on different

Fig. 10. Levels 1 and 2 of the classification system for TRB ceramic design. At level 1 the attributes of boundedness/non-boundedness are differentiated. Level 2 represents the primary motif forms from which TRB ceramic design structures are built up: 11–15 primary bounded forms, 21–7 primary unbounded forms. For discussion see text.

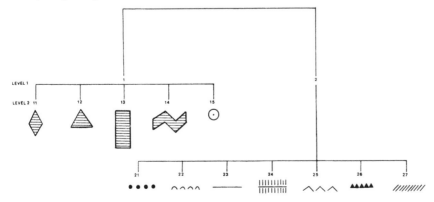

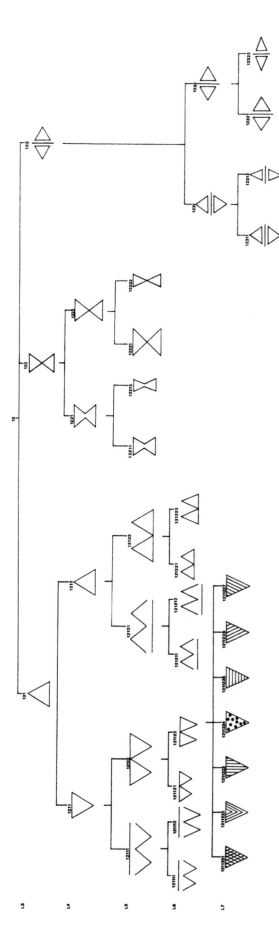

Fig. 11. Levels of the classification system for triangles. At level 3 triangles were subdivided according to whether they occurred singly or in rows one below the other (121), rather than being paired or opposed with the points meeting (122, 123). The latter forms are not considered in the text. Level 4: base orientation in relation to vessel rim (1211: base to top, 1212: base to bottom). Level 5: further subdivision according to whether the triangles are merging or non-merging. Level 6: merging and non-merging forms subdivided again according to whether they are isosceles or scalene in form. Level 7: final subdivision in relation to infill categories.

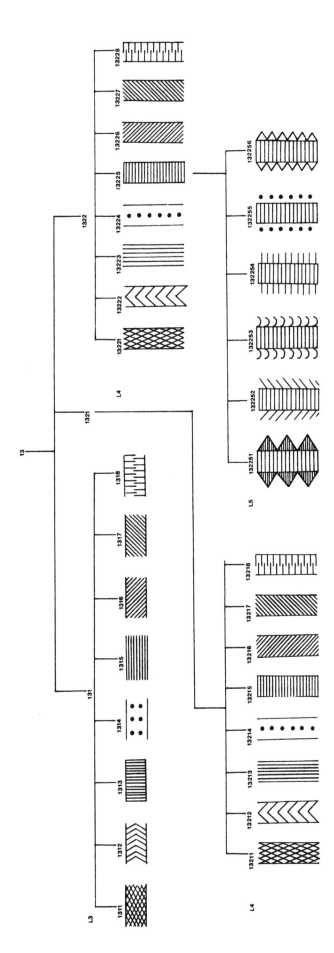

Fig. 12. Levels of the classification system for bands. Level 3: subdivision according to field and possession/non-possession of appended forms. 131: horizontal bands. These never possess appended forms. 1321: vertical bands without appended forms. 1322: vertical bands with appended forms. Level 4: further subdivision according to infill categories. Level 5: vertical bands with appended forms subdivided on this basis.

areas of the vessel surface with intermediate designs present in between. Cross-referencing between unbounded designs reaches a peak in phase II of the TRB declining slightly during phases III and IV. Cross-referencing between bounded designs is most frequent in phase III. In the earliest phase of the BAC cross-referencing is absent. Fig. 19C shows the percentages of vessels possessing a division between neck and belly areas on the vessel profile in which two contrasted units of decorative features are demarcated by a straight line(s) or by short, incised, vertical lines, in most cases corresponding to a break in the vessel profile. Very few vessels possess this feature in phases I or IV of the TRB while between 55 and 60% have this characteristic in phases II and III. No vessels attributable to the earliest phase of the BAC possess a neck/belly division. Fig. 19D shows percentages of vessels with four or more primary design forms at level 2 of the TRB classification system.[7] Again the picture to result is similar to the others with the most complex vessels occurring in phases II and III of the TRB with comparatively few in phases I and IV and none in the earliest BAC phase. Finally Fig. 19C shows percentages of vessels possessing mirror symmetry in either a horizontal or a vertical field. The highest proportion of vessels possessing this feature occurs in phase III of the TRB and mirror symmetry is wholly absent in the earliest phase of the BAC.

These trends in the organisation of ceramic design are paralleled by changes in vessel shape from simple rounded and pedestalled bowls and funnel beakers in the initial TRB phases to the production of more angular brimmed beaker forms and shouldered bowls during the TRB. All vessels belonging to the earliest phase of the BAC are simple rounded wide-mouthed bowl forms with no significant breaks in the vessel profile.

Design sequences

The sequence of designs in zones down the pots from the rim to the base was recorded at level 2 of the TRB classification system except for banded designs (Fig. 12) and lines (unbounded design form 23, Fig. 10) which were differentiated at level 3 in order to take account of basic horizontal/vertical distinctions in the organisation of ceramic design. For vertical bands no distinction was made as to whether or not they possessed appended forms for this analysis. The design occurring in the top zone of the vessel, on or immediately below the rim on the outside was coded as A, the following design was also coded as A if it was the same as the first design or as B if it was different. A series of alternating zones on any particular vessel can thus be described in terms of alphabetical sequences e.g. ABCABBD (see Hodder 1982a for similar work on Dutch TRB pottery). Table 5 gives the frequency of TRB vessels with particular design sequences according to the four-phase periodisation. The initial impression gained from such

Fig. 13. Percentages of infill categories for all triangles for sites in the Lödde/Kävlinge sub-regional group of megalithic tombs (see Fig. 9). Key identifies categories and refers to Level 7 of Fig. 11. 1: cross hatching; 2: merging; 3: perpendicular; 4: dotted/dashed; 5: parallel; 6: oblique, left to right; 7: oblique, right to left.

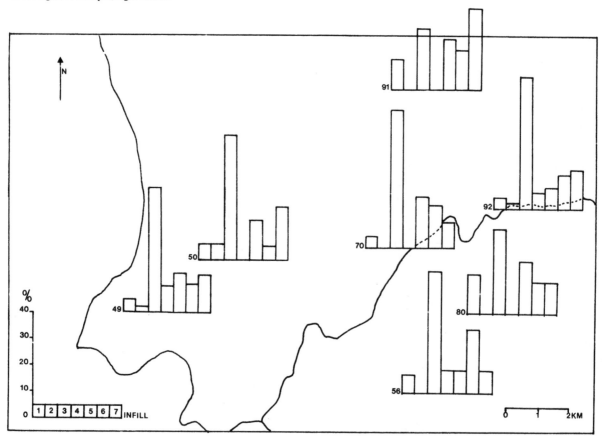

an analysis is one of considerable complexity as regards design combinations. The overall length of the sequence, as represented by this type of analysis, is considerably longer and more complex on a larger proportion of vessels from phases II and III as opposed to phases I and IV. A chi-square test ($p = 0.01$) dismissed the null hypothesis of no significant differences between the phases as regards the length of design sequences (an arbitrary division being made between those vessels with a design sequence of four or less characters and those with more than four). The frequency of vessels characterised by simple repetition of designs or ABAB sequences, irrespective of the length of any particular sequence, is highest in phases I and IV while more complicated sequences are characteristic of phases II and III. The relative frequency of additive sequences is also significantly higher in the middle phases of the TRB. All BAC vessels belonging to the earliest phase have simple A or AB sequences separated by undecorated areas of the vessel surface.

The sequence of bounded and unbounded designs was also coded for the vessels from the rim to the base. Table 6 gives the frequencies of those design sequences which occurred on three or more TRB vessels. Numbers of vessels with solely bounded designs are low for all phases of the TRB while vessels with an entirely unbounded design-structure are most frequent during the earliest and the latest phase. The proportion of vessels possessing simple repetition of bounded/unbounded designs changes significantly during the TRB phases. Either entirely unbounded designs or simple alternative of bounded/unbounded designs is sufficient to account for the overall design structure of most vessels from the earliest and latest TRB phases but only between 35 and 43% of the vessels from the second and third phases of the TRB can be captured by such a simple formula. These vessels exhibit a complex interplay of fields of variable length made up by bounded or unbounded designs. All BAC vessels belonging to the earliest phase, as noted above, possess an entirely unbounded design structure.

III: Homologies and transformations in the Scanian TRB

The evidence which has been discussed above will now be

Fig. 14. Percentages of infill categories for bands in a horizontal field for sites in the Lödde/Kävlinge sub-regional group of megalithic tombs (see Fig. 9). Key identifies categories and refers to level 4 of Fig. 12, nos. 1311–1318. 1: cross hatching; 2: merging; 3: perpendicular; 4: dotted/dashed; 5: parallel; 6: oblique, left to right; 7: oblique, right to left; 8: interlocking.

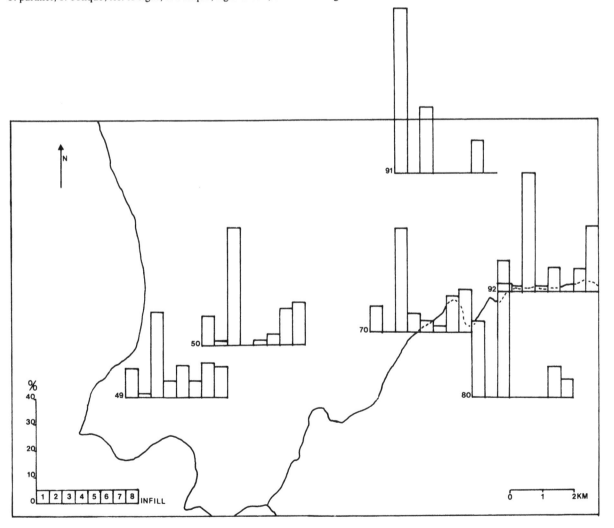

Table 5 *The frequency of vessels possessing various alphabetically coded design sequences, according to the periodisation of the TRB.*

	Period				
Sequence	Ib	II	III	IV	Total
A	2	–	–	1	3
AB	11	1	4	3	19
AAB	1	1	–	–	2
ABA	4	1	1	2	8
ABB	–	1	1	–	2
ABC	4	6	10	1	21
AABA	1	–	–	–	1
ABAA	–	–	1	1	2
ABAB	1	–	–	1	2
ABAC	2	7	4	2	15
ABBC	–	1	–	–	1
ABCA	1	2	3	–	6
ABCB	–	2	2	–	4
ABCC	–	–	1	–	1
ABCD	1	12	6	1	20
AAABC	–	1	–	–	1
ABAAC	–	1	–	–	1
ABACA	–	2	1	–	3
ABACD	–	1	–	–	1
ABBCC	–	1	–	–	1
ABBCD	–	1	–	–	1
ABCAC	–	1	–	–	1
ABCAD	–	5	2	–	7
ABCBC	1	–	–	–	1
ABCBD	–	2	2	1	5
ABCDA	2	–	–	–	2
ABCDB	1	–	1	1	3
ABCDC	–	2	–	–	2
ABCDE	–	8	4	–	12
ABAACA	–	1	–	–	1
ABABAB	–	–	–	1	1
ABACAC	–	–	1	–	1
ABACAD	–	–	4	–	4
ABACDA	–	1	–	–	1
ABBBBC	–	–	1	–	1
ABBCAB	–	–	1	–	1
ABCBCB	–	–	–	1	1
ABCBDB	1	–	–	–	1
ABCBDE	–	–	1	–	1
ABCDBA	1	–	–	–	1
ABCDEB	–	1	–	–	1
ABCDED	–	–	1	–	1
ABCDEF	–	–	1	–	1
Longer	–	8	7	–	15
Total	34	70	60	16	180

Table 6 *Frequency of vessels with different sequences of bounded/unbounded designs according to the periodisation of the TRB.*

	Period				
Sequence	Ib	II	III	IV	Total
B	4	8	7	–	19
U	17	5	–	9	31
BU	1	1	1	–	3
UB	1	4	1	–	7
BUBU	2	1	1	2	6
UBUB	6	3	11	1	21
BBU	–	4	–	–	4
UUB	–	4	–	–	4
Total	31	30	21	12	94
% of vessels	91	43	35	75	52

B: bounded design; U: unbounded design

drawn together. The first feature to note is the clear differentiation that exists between settlement and tomb. This may be conceptualised in terms of what Goffman (1959) has referred to as 'back' and 'front' space regions, between the private and the public spheres. Quite obviously this is a matter of degree in the case being considered rather than an either/or situation. Control of the setting would seem to be fundamental to the public play of social relations between actors. The tombs may be conceived as 'front' space regions in which public display and ritual took place, key settings for 'staged' social performances serving to legitimate reproduced relations of autonomy and dependence between and within local groups. The distinction between settlement and tomb is clearly drawn in:

1. Distinctive artifact-types marking out the domestic and funerary spheres.
2. The monumentality and permanence of tombs in contrast to the settlements.
3. Probable location of the tombs on the peripheries of cultivated areas.
4. Between the contexts of the production and conspicuous consumption of wealth e.g. pottery.
5. The stress on boundedness at the tombs in the treatment of the human remains and the ceramic designs.
6. The conceptual boundary between the contexts of life and the living and death and the ancestors.

A number of features of the analysis of the TRB material culture patterning suggests the presence of a series of structural homologies between the principles used to structure the material world and thus relate to the social world:

1. A stress on boundedness at the tombs. This is manifested in the exploitation of bodily boundaries (upper/lower body parts, posterior/anterior) and the grouping of the bones into clearly demarcated sections of the tomb-chamber in some cases. This is replicated in the predominant use of bounded forms for funerary ceramics.
2. Left/right distinctions apparent in the selection and treat-

ment of the human remains also occur in the infill characteristics of the ceramic designs and the distribution of the ceramics in relation to the passage entrances of the tombs.

3. The unity of the natural and cultural order are systematically broken down. Skeletal parts are completely disarticulated and rearranged in groups bearing little or no resemblance to the natural ordering of the skeleton. Similarly pottery is broken or crushed, its individuality or wholeness of form is destroyed.

4. The complex sets of cross-cutting orientation relationships between the tombs are replicated in the considerable differences and similarities between ceramic design attributes between neighbouring and distant sites.

These homologies in the material culture patterning suggest a concordance between different forms of symbolic expression, each acts to reinforce the others and serves to enhance their meaning. Repetition creates familiarity and familiarity lends itself to the naturalisation of arbitrary social categories. Consonance can be seen to exist between different spheres of experience and action. Adopting the conception of ritual as a form of ideological activity these homologies can be interpreted as an attempt to create and maintain a particular set of principles serving to structure social reality and the nature of the social world.

What principles are involved and being stressed through the medium of material culture? How do they relate to the kinds

of social strategies between individuals and groups that we sketched in the first part of this paper? Firstly it can be suggested that the expression of boundedness at the tombs serves to create an us/them distinction and opposition between different social groups using individual tombs. This simultaneously reaffirms solidarity of the members of the local group in relation to outsiders. Within-group antagonisms and differential power relations can be displaced by reference to competition between groups manifested in terms of status, rank and prestige. Concomitantly within-group coherence is achieved by reference to outsiders, social groups are symbolically marked out and social boundaries asserted between them.

The study of the orientation-relationships suggests considerable tension and ambiguity in relation to between-group relations. Fritz (1978, p. 41) has indicated that through the incorporation of directional symbolism relations of identity and non-identity, openness and closedness, sequence and rank, balance and equilibrium are given concrete geometric expression. Architecture, as with other types of material culture patterning, is both a product of organised action and a constraint on future action. Once a structure has been raised people must move through, toward or away from it, and experience changing morphologies and relationships. In a spatial order the social order may be experienced and visibly reinforced. Space becomes socially structured and given 'weight' (Kus 1982). The plethora of

Fig. 15. Percentages of infill categories for bands in a vertical field for sites in the Lödde/Kävlinge sub-regional group of megalithic tombs (see Fig. 9). Key identifies categories and refers to level 4 of Fig. 12, nos. 13211–13218. 1: cross hatching; 2: merging; 3: perpendicular; 4: dotted/dashed; 5: parallel; 6: oblique, left to right; 7: oblique, right to left; 8: interlocking.

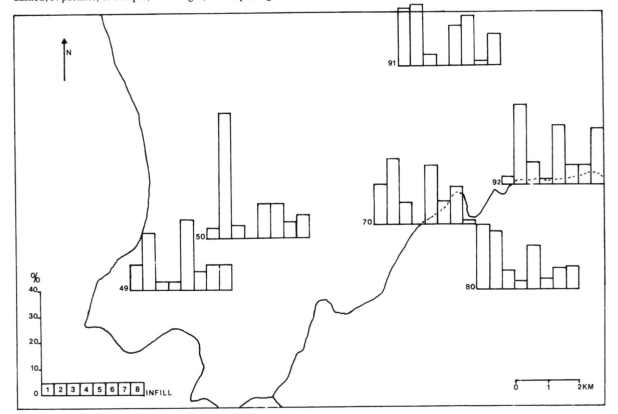

Fig. 16. Sites plotted against principal component 1 (horizontal axis) and component 2 (vertical axis), in relation to infill categories for primary bounded forms. A: lozenges; B: triangles; C: bands in a horizontal field; D: bands in a vertical field with or without appended forms; E: zig-zag bands (see Fig. 10, Level 2, Fig. 11, Level 7, Fig. 12, Level 4 and text). Site numbers refer to Fig. 9. Symbols indicate sites < 15 km apart.

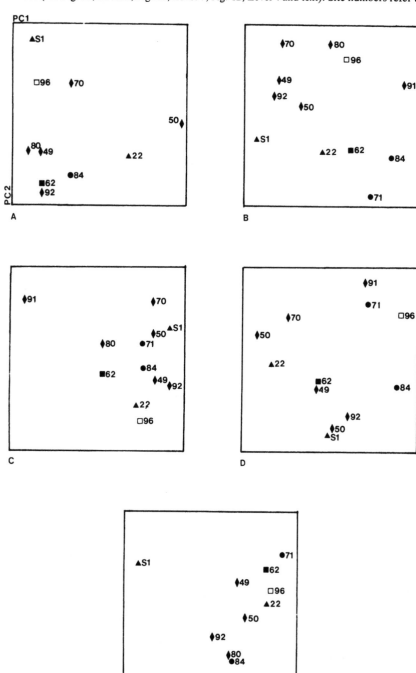

different orientation-relationships characteristic of the megalithic tombs suggests that directional symbolism was used to mark out and distinguish between groups. In relation to N–S river-axes oppositions between different groups of tombs are evident and they are being naturalised in relation to natural boundaries in the landscape. From a study of the orientation-relationships between the tombs it is evident that these oppositions are rarely categorical between first nearest neighbours or groups of nearby sites. A structure can be seen to underlie the sets of orientation-relationships in that they are unified despite divisions. These features may indicate the essentially contradictory nature of between-group social strategies involving interdependence in a whole series of exchanges of subsistence goods in times of shortage, and other materials, yet at the same time behaving as independent political units engaging in status competition. There is thus a need to simultaneously affirm the unity of the group in relation to others yet in a situation of interdependency this cannot be given the form of a categorical opposition.

The left/right distinction may indicate an emphasis on symmetry rather than asymmetry and thus a denial of asymmetrical relationships in life. For example social oppositions can be translated into the conceptual opposition left/right (Faron 1962, p. 1158). Antithetical social oppositions can thus be subsumed, by means of a partial and relative expression of the ordering of reality, into an abstract complementary dualism.

The disarticulation and rearrangement of the human bones and the evidence for vessel-crushing activities at the tombs may be an attempt to achieve a semblance of resonance and unity between individuals and the material products of the production-process and so, simultaneously, serve as a denial of asymmetrical social relationships in life and the social appropriation of the labour-product. Differences become translated into self-sameness. Just as it is impossible to discern the discrete individual in the patterning of the human remains (and we all know that discrete individuals do in fact exist in society) ceramic form is broken down and complete vessels become indistinguishable in the mass of sherd materials. It is the ceremonial *act* of vessel-smashing that is, of course, of interest here not the resultant mass of sherd materials.

In the multivariate analyses of some aspects of ceramic design-attributes presented above no clear fall-off of similarity with distance was evident. The picture to arise was one of a complex cross-cutting of similarities and differences both between nearby sites and distant sites. It is very unlikely that the observed patterning could arise solely as a result of ceramic exchange, because the contrasts between the sites are both too consistent and too great. If the contrasts were entirely due to ceramic exchange we might expect a random permutation of infill classes both within and between the tombs and such an expectation conflicts with the observed patterning. Furthermore spatial autocorrelation studies of vessel shape attributes showed no evidence of any spatial structure to the distribution of any but two of 14 definable vessel classes whether using raw measurements (e.g. vessel height), ratios of vessel shape attributes or principal

Fig. 17. Sites plotted against the first (vertical axis) and the second (horizontal axis) dimensions of a multidimensional scaling analysis. A: infill categories for bands in a horizontal field (stress: .097). B: infill categories for bands in a vertical field with or without appended forms (stress: .140). C: presence/absence data for vertical bands with appended forms (stress: .100). Numbers refer to Fig. 9. Symbols indicate sites < 15 km apart.

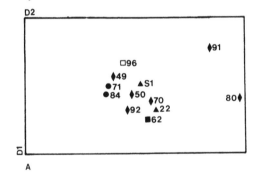

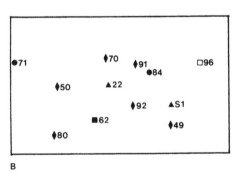

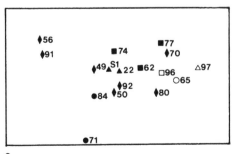

component scores as input data. Detailed thin-section analyses of pottery have only been carried out in a small area of south-east Scania (Hulthén 1977) but because the entire study region is heavily glaciated it is impossible to tie down possible clay sources with any degree of accuracy. Hulthén (1977, p. 120) suggested that the majority of the ceramics from Ramshög were produced on one neighbouring settlement site and it seems reasonable to conclude that the majority of the ceramics at individual tombs were produced on one or a number of settlement sites in the immediate vicinity. It is therefore hypothesised that aspects of ceramic design were actively used to mark out differences between competing local groups and stress social divisions. However, as with the orientation-relationships these differences were simultaneously denied in the same medium. No simplistic unitary explanation is tenable. From a purely formal analysis of ceramic design-attributes it is possible to delimit exactly which attributes exhibit variability between sites and those features which are invariant and common to all sites. For example in

relation to the various levels of the classification system for individual triangles (Fig. 11) at all sites where this design form was quantitatively well represented the majority of the triangles were characterised by (a) the possession of bases orientated to the top rather than the bottom of the vessel, (b) being non-merging rather than merging, and (c) scalene and not isosceles. The major axis of variability between the sites was represented in terms of infill characteristics. Formal studies of this nature can be related to specific sets of design rules which may be referred to a common conceptual scheme (see Hodder 1982b, pp. 170–81). A detailed analysis of this sort is beyond the scope of this paper but represents a further avenue of research.

The successive use of the megalithic tombs is indicative of a continuous presencing of the past in the present in which ceremonial acts take place at regular intervals, in an analogous way to the cyclical repetition of the seasons. Their monumentality suggests that the authority of dominant groups of individuals is being projected into the past and thus legitimated by the strength

Fig. 18. Histograms showing the percentages of infill categories in relation to bands subdivided at level 3 of the classification system (see Fig. 12) and for all lozenges, triangles and zig-zag bands. 131: bands in a horizontal field; 1321 bands in a vertical field; 1322 bands in a vertical field with appended forms; 11 lozenges; 12 triangles; 14 zig-zag bands. Infill categories: 1 cross-hatching; 2 merging; 3 perpendicular; 4 dotted/dashed; 5 parallel; 6 oblique, left to right; 7 oblique, right to left; 8 interlocking.

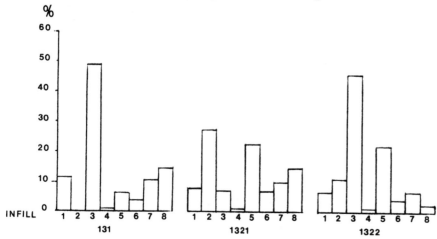

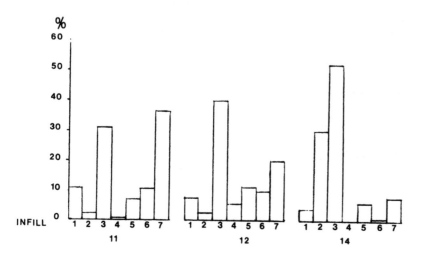

of tradition, the social order being identified with the sacred order and thus made to appear to be natural and immutable – hence the relevance of the quotation from Marx at the beginning of this paper. Tradition and repetitiveness serve to assert that the contingent, the could-be-otherwise, becomes naturalised as an inevitable ongoing order inscribed in the social world and the spiritual cosmos.

It would seem to be reasonable to interpret the deposition of ceramics, and other materials at the tombs as 'gifts to the gods' or the spirit world. Through these gifts the naturalisation of social divisions was achieved. The tombs were the sites of the conspicuous consumption of social wealth. Virtually all the pottery is highly decorated and complex in shape so that it may be regarded as a major vehicle of prestige and competitive status-display, and the tombs were the sites of its deliberate destruction. In some small-scale societies it is the destruction of social wealth, rather than its accumulation, or valorisation through the media of social exchange mechanisms, that forms the basis on which prestige and social power are built. For example destruction of blankets and other commodities amongst the Kwakitul indicated the complete disregard of the property destroyed, thus conferring prestige and reinforcing political power (Boas 1966). It may also indicate a model of destruction as being necessary for the regeneration of wealth, or be presented as such. In this connection it is interesting to note the comparatively high frequencies of cereal impressions from the pottery deposited at the tombs. Some of the pots very possibly contained grain and other products, so there appears to be a direct association between human bones, death, the ances-

Fig. 19. Aspects of temporal change in ceramic design according to a four-phase division of the TRB and including the earliest phase of the BAC. A: percentages of bounded designs on vessels. B: (1) percentages of vessels possessing cross-referencing between unbounded designs; (2) percentages of vessels possessing cross-referencing between bounded designs. C: (1) percentages of vessels with a neck/belly division; (2) percentages of vessels possessing mirror symmetry. D: percentages of vessels with four or more primary forms at level 2 of the classification system.

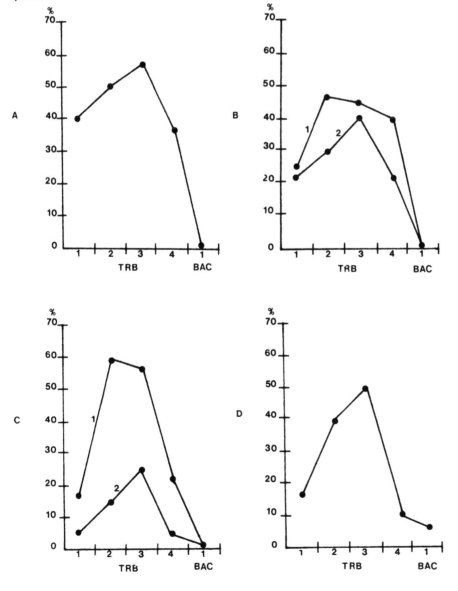

tors and pottery, life, grain and fertility. Death and destruction are thus linked here with fertility, life and the continuance of the social order.

The considerable differences that have been demonstrated between the tombs in terms of the quantities of ceramic materials deposited is indicative of an uneven distribution of social power developing during the TRB between local groups involved in competitive status-displays leading to the hierarchisation of some groups in relation to others. Differences in political power would then be reinforced in the form of feasting and social displays in which the elders consumed socially appropriated wealth, such as the highly decorated ceramics, converting it into individual prestige and power. The arena of successful status-display between groups would then further establish the position and power of the elders within the local group. Some support to this thesis may be granted from the observation that it is only in cases where the megalithic tombs are tightly grouped together, in clusters or pairs, that extremely large quantities of ceramics occur.[8] They are few on the more isolated sites in central Scania.

Through time we have seen that there is an increase in the nature and the tempo of the activities taking place at the tombs. Increasing quantities of ceramics are deposited during phases II and III of the TRB. It is in precisely these phases that the vessels possess the most complicated shapes and the most elaborate decorations. Overall there is an increased emphasis on boundedness, but the design sequences no longer involve simple repetition of bounded/unbounded designs. The overall form of the design sequences becomes more complicated and involuted. Cross referencing between bounded and unbounded designs and the use of mirror symmetry becomes more frequent. Corresponding to these changes in ceramic design there is an increased complexity in the mortuary practices connected with the disposal of the human body, an increased emphasis on the exploitation of bodily boundaries and the grouping of bones in demarcated areas of the tombs. The need to legitimate authority is increasing.

One striking feature of TRB ceramic art, in common with much of the art of small-scale societies, either past or present, is that it is entirely abstract and geometrical in form. It does not represent anything in the way, for example, that palaeolithic cave art clearly represents animals and people. Gombrich (1979, p. 151) notes a conflict or tension between what he takes to be the two major functions of perception; the perception of things and the perception of order: 'as soon as shape is identified as a thing or a creature it becomes transformed. No wonder non-figurative artists fight the tendency of looking for representational elements in their shapes and colours, for such projections can have the most disruptive effects on the dynamics of form. Meaning can subvert order, just as order can subvert meaning' (*ibid.*, p. 158). Forge has written of Abelam flat painting: 'elements, in this case graphic elements modified by colour, carry the meaning. The meaning is not that a painting or carving is a picture or representation *of* anything in the natural or spirit world, rather it is *about* the relationship between things' (Forge 1973, p. 189 emphasis in original).

We will suggest then that the art of TRB ceramics is fundamentally to do with principles of social order. Whether individual designs such as triangles represent mountains or houses need not concern us. What is of importance, along one dimension, is the relationship between particular types of designs, their sequence and form. Lévi-Strauss has commented that the graphic art of the Caduveo Indians 'is to be interpreted, and its mysterious appeal and seemingly gratuitous complexity to be explained, as the phantasm of a society ardently and insatiably seeking a means of expressing symbolically the institutions it might have, if its interests and superstitions did not stand in the way' (Lévi-Strauss 1973, p. 256). In other words the art embraces an ideal, the way things might be rather than the way they are. It misrepresents social practices.

Now if we are right in our assumption that an emphasis on boundedness serves to express an us/them, insider/outsider dichotomy between different groups then this has interesting implications for the increasing ramifications of the ceramic design structure. Given that two opposing principles are being stressed: boundedness at the tombs and unboundedness at the settlements the deliberate cross-referencing which occurs between bounded/unbounded designs as part of the design structure of the funerary ceramics could be seen as an attempt to resolve these differences. Oppositional elements become transformed into a spontaneous whole. The ceramic style is thus used to resolve contradictions which have their basis in social practices. The structured formal sequences of bounded/unbounded designs create an inseparable unity as a signifying practice in which oppositions between structural principles are resolved or denied. The ceramic designs, juxtaposed in relationship to each other, are not therefore *reflections* of reality, but are actively used to create an ideal of reality in which a formal order is expressed linking opposing principles.

In phase IV of the TRB all aspects of ceramic design become simplified and at some stage the tombs ceased to be centres of ritual activity and the change to the BAC occurred. The individual is asserted for the first time in burial practices and there is little evidence of elaborate ritual surrounding the funerary activities. A small range of grave goods accompany the dead, but no hierarchical distinctions are apparent. Vessel shapes are simple and all designs in the earliest phase are unbounded (rising to *c.* 14% in later phases). The graves and, possibly, associated settlements are more uniformly spread out across the landscape. No complex, structured, orientation relationships are apparent and there is little evidence of conspicuous consumption of wealth. Ceramic designs are similar throughout the study region (Tilley 1982a) and no complex cross-cutting similarities and differences are apparent between the ceramic designs utilised. There is little emphasis on elaborate collective rituals, as in the TRB, and the material-culture patterning does not suggest the presence of competing local groups or any great asymmetries in the allocation and appropriation of resources. There is an emphasis on connectedness and widespread social links.

A possible explanation for the change from the TRB to the BAC can be found in the increasingly antagonistic development of contradictions between the structuring principles orientating the actions of individuals and groups in the TRB. It is hypothesised that the change from the TRB to the BAC resulted from a legitimation crisis in which the ideological justification for, and misrepresentation of, asymmetries in social power and social control could no longer be sustained through cultural manipulation in the sphere of ritual activities. The misrepresentation of the social order through means of material culture obviously played one part in a whole host of other activities which have left no trace in the archaeological record. Ultimately the failure to validate social divisions within the between groups led to the breakdown of lineage-based social control, leading to a more egalitarian set of social relationships in the BAC.

The general concept of a legitimation crisis is drawn from the work of Habermas (Habermas 1975). One of the most important features of Habermas' analysis of possible crisis tendencies in late capitalism is that it is a deliberate attempt to ground a conception of change in a manner in which economic reductionism is entirely circumvented and the ideological sphere is elevated so that it takes on an important explanatory role rather than being something which merely reflects the contingencies of the economic base. Ideological elements of social totalities are no longer regarded as ethereal monsters wandering around in the superstructure merely reflecting changes in other regions. This is not the place to discuss Habermas' position in any detail (see also Held 1982; Habermas 1982, pp. 278–81) and only a few points will be made. According to Habermas system-crises (economic and rationality) can be *potentially* displaced in the capitalist mode of production. However, this is only at the cost of increasing pressures on the state to legitimate the social order in more and more comprehensive ways. This, in the end, may undermine their ultimate effectiveness. He proposes that:

> crisis occurrences owe their objectivity to the fact that they issue from unresolved steering problems. Identity crises are connected with steering problems. Although the subjects are not generally conscious of them, these steering problems create secondary problems that do affect consciousness in a specific way – precisely in such a way as to endanger social integration. (Habermas 1975, p. 4)

In particular, as implied by this statement, and outlined explicitly elsewhere in *Legitimation Crisis*, the notion of a legitimation crisis is predicated on a further conception, that of a motivation crisis arising from the systematic undermining of meanings motivating social actions, the ultimate outcome of which may be the collapse of mass loyalty to the state. Unfortunately Habermas tends to conflate legitimation crises and motivation crises in an unsatisfactory way in which they are either indistinguishable, or the latter is in some sense dependent on the former, that until legitimation problems occur the mass of social actors are unable to penetrate the ideological fog misrepresenting their social conditions of existence which is largely internalised and, therefore, remains unquestioned.

However it can be argued that it is precisely because social actors have *some* degree of discursive penetration of their social conditions of existence that forms of ideological legitimation of the social order can never be completely all-embracing. As a result social reproduction must always be contingent rather than

assured, and legitimation crises can occur. Nevertheless the stability of any social order in which there are basic inequalities must be largely dependent on the continued effectiveness of legitimations which *are* capable of withstanding a substantial degree of discursive evaluation.

The comments made by Bott in her discussion of the Tongan *kava* ceremony are instructive in this regard even though the Tonga are *not* representative of the kind of social organisation we have been considering:

> One thing all these social situations [ceremonial ritual] have in common is a confrontation of people of different status. In everyday life these people can be expected to harbour feelings of jealousy and resentment about their differential privileges . . . In brief, the ceremony says, 'We are all united', but it also says, 'We are all different'. And the element of difference contains another contradiction, for it makes two contrary communications. It says 'We are undifferentiated and interdependent', but it says, 'We are unequal' . . . Most people seemed to be more aware of feelings of unity and harmony. The feelings of antagonism showed themselves more in what people did than in what they said. (Bott 1972, p. 225)

The importance of this example is to illustrate that *even* in those social situations deliberately set up to foster a response of unity and harmony this is not completely successful and dissension if only at a practical level, as revealed through action, may be present. Through the passage of time this can, of course, result in open opposition and the collapse of legitimation through ceremonial forms. Social unity represented through the medium of ritual actions is torn apart and society split open.

We have seen during the TRB a development toward an increasing amount of social investment in ritual activities involving the ideological manipulation of material symbols. Ritual activities may move out of resonance with the social reality they serve to misrepresent, partly one could argue, as the result of the formalised premises of ritual communication precipitating, under specific circumstances, a change in social consciousness resulting in a transformation of the nature of social relations. The continued hierarchisation of lineage groups resulting in ever deepening contradictions between major structural principles, especially that between kin and political/power relations, discussed above, may have produced increasing strains on the elders to legitimate their authority. The increasing appropriation of prestige goods for consumption in ritual activities is likely to have put such strains on the social relations of production that they reached the limits of the conditions of their own existence. The endless conversion of economic surplus into symbolic capital or personal prestige would, ultimately, have provided the basis for the undermining of the position and authority of dominant individuals and/or groups leading to the social transformations manifested in the material-culture patterning of the BAC.

Conclusions

It has been argued that the need to legitimate the authority of dominant individuals and groups played a major axis structuring the material culture patterning of the TRB, which was ideologically manipulated to play an active role in the maintenance of social reproduction. Ultimately these practices became undermined leading to the transition to the BAC. Further detailed research is clearly required to assess more fully the value of the interpretative framework put forward. In this study a brief examination has been made of a number of disparate types of evidence and an attempt has been made to establish links between different aspects of the material-culture patterning. It is the demonstration of these links, and others yet to be firmly established, that lends some credibility to the arguments presented. It is the links that provide the meaning, and without them we are left with an uninterpretable mass of observations the significance of which is indeterminable, and the silence deafening. Two ways of proceeding would seem to be possible. The first is the unacceptable reduction of the meaningful, the symbolic, and the social significance of artifacts to the non-social, to grant our explanations of the past the veneer of a natural science. The other alternative, taken in this paper and in the other papers in this volume, is to *grasp the nettle* and attempt to explain social change in terms of social processes. Naturally our explanations will be underdetermined by the data but this is a problem faced to a greater or lesser extent in all areas of social science. It is only by accepting the challenge that the degree of indeterminacy can be reduced.

Notes

1. Detailed discussion of statistical techniques used, tables of figures etc. has been deliberately kept to a minimum because of space constraints. These will be presented in detail along with a large number of analyses not discussed in this paper in a forthcoming publication. For a detailed presentation of analyses dealing with BAC material see Tilley (1982a).
2. Diagram from the Ranviken bay, Lake Immeln in the extreme north-east of the study region.
3. 'The megalithic pottery is intensive, almost explosive, short-lived and internal.'
4. A more reliable picture would in fact be based on weighing quantities of sherd materials. This work is being carried out.
5. As a result of the manner in which the excavations were undertaken and the way in which the sherd materials had subsequently been arranged and stored it was not possible to take a random sample of the sherd material according to a constant sampling fraction. At most sites a systematic sample was taken working through the entire collections recording design attributes on individual sherds controlling, as far as was possible, that these came from different vessels or different areas of the profile of the same vessel. Only sherds where design-attributes could be accurately recorded at three or more levels of the classification system were taken into account.
6. Other infill types do occur but these are all quantitatively insignificant and were not recorded.
7. At level 3 of a classification system for BAC ceramics which was slightly different in form from the TRB classification because of the simplicity of BAC ceramics in which only three classificatory levels were distinguished for the entire set of design configurations (Tilley 1982a, Fig. 12).
8. There is only one possible exception to this rule; site no. 22 (Fig.

9). This dolmen with *c.* 28,000 sherds has only recently been discovered in connection with the industrial expansion of Malmö, the third largest city in Sweden. It seems very likely that this tomb formed part of a sub-regional group now totally destroyed.

Acknowledgements

I want to thank Danny Miller for comments on an earlier draft of this paper, Ian Hodder for discussions over the years which have clarified my thinking, Berta Stjernquist for her encouragement of my work in Sweden and Karin Nilsson for help in preparing the diagrams and support in innumerable ways.

References

Almgren, O. (1910) 'Stenåldersminnen i Hälsingborgstrakten', *Svenska Turistföreningens Årsskrift*

Ardener, S. (1981) *'Women and space: ground rules and social maps'* in S. Ardener Ed., *Women and Space*, Croom Helm, London

Asad, T. (1979) 'Anthropology and the analysis of ideology', *Man* (N.S.) 14, pp. 607–27

Bagge, A. and Kaelas, L. (1950) *Die Funde aus Dolmen und Ganggräbern in Schonen, Schweden*, Wahlström and Widstrand, Stockholm. Vol. I

  (1952) *Die Funde aus Dolmen und Ganggräbern in Schonen, Schweden*, Wahlström and Widstrand, Stockholm. Vol. II

Bakker, J. (1979) *The TRB West Group*, University of Amsterdam, Amsterdam

Barth, F. (1975) *Ritual and Knowledge among the Baktaman of New Guinea*, Yale University Press, New Haven, Conn.

Bartholin, T., Berglund, B. and Malmer, N. (1981) 'Vegetation and environment in the Gårdlösa area during the iron age', in B. Stjernquist Ed., *Gårdlösa: An Iron Age Community in its Natural and Social Setting*, 7: 1, Gleerups, Lund

Becker, C. (1954) 'Die mittel-neolithischen Kulturen in Südskandinavien', *Acta Archaeologica* XXV

Berglund, B. (1966) 'Late-Quaternary vegetation in eastern Blekinge, southeastern Sweden. II. Post-glacial time', *Opera Botanica* 12 (2), pp. 9–28

  (1969) 'Vegetation and human influence in south Scandinavia during prehistoric time', *Okios Suppl.* 12

Bloch, M. (1977) 'The past and the present in the past', *Man* (N.S.) 12, pp. 278–92

Boas, F. (1966) *Kwakiutl Ethnography*, H. Codere Ed., Chicago University Press, Chicago

Bott, E. (1972) 'Psychoanalysis and ceremony', in J.S. La Fontaine Ed., *The Interpretation of Ritual*, Tavistock, London

Bourdillon, M. (1978) 'Knowing the world or hiding it: a response to Maurice Bloch', *Man* (N.S.) 13, pp. 591–600

Brown, J. (1975) 'Iroquois women: an ethnohistoric note', in R. Reiter Ed., *Toward an Anthropology of Women*, Monthly Review Press, New York

Bruzelius, M. (1822) 'Nordiska fornlemningar från Skåne', *Iduna* 9

Burenhult, G. (1973) *En långdös vid Hindby Mosse, Malmö*, Malmö Museum, Malmö

Chapman, R. (1981) 'The emergence of formal disposal areas and the "problem" of megalithic tombs in prehistoric Europe', in R. Chapman, I. Kinnes and K. Randsborg Eds., *The Archaeology of Death*, Cambridge University Press

Clark, J.G. (1977) 'The economic context of dolmens and passage graves in Sweden', in V. Markotic Ed., *Ancient Europe and the Mediterranean*, Aris and Phillips, Warminster

Davidsen, K. (1974) 'Tragtbaegerkulturens slutfase, nye C14 dateringer', *Kuml*
 (1978) *The Final TRB Culture in Denmark*, Akademisk Forlag, Copenhagen
Digerfeldt, G. (1974) 'The post-glacial development of the Ranviken bay in lake Immeln', *Geologiska Föreningens i Stockholm Förhandlingar* 96, pp. 3–32
 (1975) 'A standard profile for Littorina transgressions in western Skåne, south Sweden', *Boreas* 4, pp. 125–42
Donnelly, K. (1978) 'Simulations to determine the variance and edge effect of total nearest-neighbour distance', in I. Hodder Ed., *Simulation Studies in Archaeology*, Cambridge University Press
Doran, J. and Hodson, F. (1975) *Mathematics and Computers in Archaeology*, Edinburgh University Press, Edinburgh
Douglas, M. (1970) *Natural Symbols*, Penguin, Harmondsworth
 (1978) *Cultural Bias*, Royal Anthropological Institute, London
Ebbesen, K. (1975) *Die jüngere Trichterbecherkultur auf den Dänischen Inseln*, Akademisk Forlag, Copenhagen
Edholm, F., Harris, O. and Young, K. (1977) 'Conceptualising women', *Critique of Anthropology* 9/10, pp. 101–30
Faron, L. (1962) 'Symbolic values and the integration of society among the Mapuche of Chile', *American Anthropologist* 64, pp. 1151–64
Flannery, K. (1976) 'Introduction: the village and its catchment area' (Ch. 4) in K. Flannery Ed., *The Early Mesoamerican Village*, Academic Press, London
Fleming, A. (1973) 'Tombs for the living', *Man* 8, pp. 177–93
Forge, A. (1973) 'Style and meaning in Sepik art', in A. Forge Ed., *Primitive Art and Society*, Oxford University Press, London
Forssander, J. (1930) Unpublished excavation report: Gillhög, Antikvarisk Topografiska Arkivet, Stockholm
 (1936) 'Skånsk megalitkeramik och kontinentaleuropeisk stenålder', *Meddelanden från Lunds Universitets Historiska Museum*, pp. 1–77
Friedman, J. (1975) 'Tribes, states and transformations', in M. Bloch Ed., *Marxist Analyses and Social Anthropology*, ASA, London
Friedman, J. and Rowlands, M. (1977) 'Notes towards an epigenetic model of the evolution of civilisation', in J. Friedman and M. Rowlands Eds., *The Evolution of Social Systems*, Duckworth, London
Friedrich, M. (1970) 'Design structure and social interaction: archaeological implications of an ethnographic analysis', *American Antiquity* 35, pp. 332–43
Fritz, J. (1978) 'Palaeopsychology today; ideational systems and human adaptation in prehistory', in C. Redman, M. Berman, E. Curtin, W. Langhorne, N. Versaggi and J. Wanser Eds., *Social Archaeology*, Academic Press, London
Gejvall, N.-G. (1973) 'Den osteologiska undersökningen', in G. Burenhult (1973) (appendix)
Gennep, A. Van (1909) *Les Rites de Passage*, Emile Noury, Paris
Goffman, E. (1959) *The Presentation of Self in Everyday Life*, Doubleday, Garden City, N.Y.
Gombrich, E. (1979) *The Sense of Order*, Phaidon, London
Gower, J. (1971) 'A general coefficient of similarity and some of its properties', *Biometrics* 27, pp. 857–74
Habermas, J. (1975) *Legitimation Crisis*, Beacon Press, Boston
 (1982) 'A reply to my critics', in J. Thompson and D. Held Eds., *Habermas: Critical Debates*, Macmillan, London
Halstead, P. (1981) 'Counting sheep in neolithic and bronze age Greece', in I. Hodder, G. Isaac and N. Hammond Eds., *Pattern of the Past*, Cambridge University Press
Hansen, F. (1918a) *Bidrag till kännedom om äldre Megalitkeramiken i Skåne och Danmark*, Lund
 (1918b) *En offerplats från Stenåldern*, Lund
 (1923) 'Gånggriftsundersökningar i Harjagers härad', *Historisk Tidskrift för Skåneland* 5, pp. 267–91
 (1923a) 'Undersökningen af gånggrift i Lackalänga', Unpublished

excavation report, Antikvarisk-Topografiska Arkivet, Stockholm
 (1924) 'Undersökning af gånggrift i Laxmans-Åkarp, Fjelie socken, Torna härad, Skåne', Unpublished excavation report, Antikvarisk-Topografiska Arkivet, Stockholm
 (1930) 'Gånggriften å Storegården i Barsebäck', *Meddelanden från Lunds Universitets Historiska Museum*, pp. 54–82
 (1938) *Stenåldersproblem*, Gleerups, Lund
Hårdh, B. (1982) 'The megalithic grave area round the Lödde/Kävlinge river. A research programme', *Meddelanden från Lunds Universitets Historiska Museum*, pp. 26–47
Harris, O. and Young, K. (1981) 'Engendered structures', in J. Kahn and J. Llobera Eds., *The Anthropology of Pre-Capitalist Societies*, Macmillan, London
Held, D. (1982) 'Crisis tendencies, legitimation and the state', in J. Thompson and D. Held Eds., *Habermas: Critical Debates*, Macmillan, London
Higgs, E. and Vita Finzi, C. (1970) 'Prehistoric economies in the Mount Carmel area of Palestine: site catchment analysis', *Proceedings of the Prehistoric Society* 36
Higham, C. (1969) 'The economic basis of the Danish funnel-neck beaker culture', *Acta Archaeologica* XL, pp. 200–8
Hindess, B. and Hirst, P. (1975) *Pre-Capitalist Modes of Production*, Routledge and Kegan Paul, London
Hjelmqvist, H. (1955) 'Die älteste Geschichte der Kulturpflanzen in Schweden', *Opera Botanica* 1 (3)
 (1962) 'Getriedeabdrücke in der Keramik der Schwedische-Norwegischen Streitaxkultur', in Malmer (1962) (appendix)
 (1964) 'Kulturväxter från Skånes forntid', *Ale*, pp. 23–35
 (1979) 'Beiträge zur Kenntnis der prähistorischen Nutzpflanzen in Schweden', *Opera Botanica* 47
 (1982) 'Economic plants from a middle neolithic site in Scania', Appendix I in Larsson (1982)
Hodder, I. (1982a) 'Sequences of structural change in the Dutch neolithic', in I. Hodder Ed., *Symbolic and Structural Archaeology*, Cambridge University Press
 (1982b) *Symbols in Action*, Cambridge University Press
Hodder, I. and Orton, C. (1976) *Spatial Analysis in Archaeology*, Cambridge University Press
Hulthén, B. (1977) 'On ceramic technology during the neolithic and bronze age', *Theses and Papers in North European Archaeology* 6, Stockholm
Jarman, M. (1972) 'A territorial model for archaeology', in D.L. Clarke Ed., *Models in Archaeology*, Methuen, London
Jarman, M., Bailey, G. and Jarman, H. Eds. (1982) *Early European Agriculture*, Cambridge University Press
Kaelas, L. (1953a) 'Den äldre megalitkeramiken under mellanneolitikum i Sverige', *Antikvariska Studier* V, pp. 9–77
 (1953b) 'Undersökning av gånggrifterna nr. 1 och 2, Viktorshög, Glumslövs sn., Rönneberga härad, Skåne', unpublished excavation report, Antikvarisk-Topografiska Arkivet, Stockholm
 (1967) 'The megalithic tombs in southern Scandinavia – migration or cultural influence?', *Palaeohistoria* 12, pp. 287–321
 (1981) 'Megaliths of the funeral beaker culture in Germany and Scandinavia', in J.D. Evans, B. Cunliffe and C. Renfrew Eds., *Antiquity and Man*, Thames and Hudson, London
Kahn, J. (1981) 'Marxist anthropology and segmentary societies: a review of the literature', in J. Kahn and J. Llobera Eds., *The Anthropology of Pre-Capitalist Societies*, Macmillan, London
Kjaerum, P. (1967) 'The chronology of the passage graves in Jutland', *Palaeohistoria* 12, pp. 323–33
Kus, S. (1982) 'Matters material and ideal', in I. Hodder Ed., *Symbolic and Structural Archaeology*, Cambridge University Press
La Fontaine, J. Ed. (1972) *The Interpretation of Ritual*, Tavistock, London
 (1977) 'The power of rights', *Man* (N.S.) 12, pp. 421–37

Larsson, L. (1979) 'Trollakistan – en dös i mellersta Skåne', *Fornvännen* 74, pp. 10–21

(1982) 'A causewayed enclosure and a site with Valby pottery at Stävie, western Scania', *Meddelanden från Lunds Universitets Historiska Museum*, pp. 65–115

Leach, E. (1976) *Culture and Communication*, Cambridge University Press

Lévi-Strauss, C. (1973) *Tristes Tropiques*, Penguin, Harmondsworth

Mackintosh, M. (1977) 'Reproduction and patriarchy: a critique of Claude Meillassoux, "Femmes, Greniers et Capitaux" ', *Capital and Class* 2, pp. 119–27

Madsen, T. (n.d.) 'The settlement system of the early agricultural societies in east Jutland, Denmark', to appear in *New Directions in Scandinavian Archaeology* Vol. II, Copenhagen

Malmer, M. (1962) 'Jungneolithische Studien', *Acta Archaeologica Lundensia*, octavo series, No. 2

(1975) *Stridsyxekulturen i Sverige och Norge*, Liber Läromedel, Lund

Malmros, C. and Tauber, H. (1975) 'Kulstof-14 dateringer af dansk enkeltgravskultur', *Aarbøger for Nordisk Oldkyndighed og Historie*, pp. 78–93

Marx, K. (1979) 'The Eighteenth Brumaire of Louis Napoleon', in K. Marx and F. Engels, *Collected Works*, Vol. 11, Lawrence and Wishart, London

Meillassoux, C. (1964) *Anthropologie Économique des Gouro de Côte d'Ivorie*, Mouton, Paris

(1972) 'From reproduction to production', *Economy and Society* 1, pp. 93–105

(1981) *Maidens, Meal and Money*, Cambridge University Press

Møhl, U. (1962) 'Übersicht über Knochenfunde aus Gräbern der Schwedisch-Norwegischen Streitaxkultur', in Malmer (1962) (appendix)

Molyneux, M. (1977) 'Androcentrism in Marxist Anthropology', *Critique of Anthropology* 9/10, pp. 55–82

Neilsen, P. (1977) 'De tyknakkede flintoksers kronologi', *Aarbøger for Nordisk Oldkyndighed og Historie*, pp. 5–66

Nilsson, T. (1948) 'On the application of the Scanian post-glacial zone system to Danish pollen diagrams', *Kongelige Danske Videnskabernes Selskab* V: 5

(1961) 'Ein neues Standardpollendiagramm aus Bjärsjöholmssjön in Schonen', *Lunds Univ. Årsskrift* N.F. 256: 18

(1964) 'Standardpollendiagramme und C14 Datierungen aus dem Ageröds mosse im mittleren Schonen', *Lunds Univ. Årrskrift* N.F. 259: 7

Persson, O. (1982) 'An osteological analysis of some bones from a settlement at Stävie 4: 1', in Larsson (1982) (appendix)

Petré, R. and Salomonsson, B. (1967) 'Gånggriften i Hög', *Ale*, pp. 36–9

Plog, S. (1980) *Stylistic Variation in Prehistoric Ceramics*, Cambridge University Press

Redman, C. (1977) 'The "Analytical individual" and prehistoric style variability', in J. Hill and J. Gunn Eds., *The Individual in Prehistory*, Academic Press, London

(1978) 'Multivariate artifact analysis: a basis for multidimensional interpretations', in C. Redman, M. Berman, E. Curtin, W. Langhorne, N. Versaggi and J. Wanser Eds., *Social Archaeology*, Academic Press, London

Renfrew, C. (1973a) 'Monuments, mobilisation and social organisation in neolithic Wessex', in C. Renfrew Ed., *The Explanation of Culture Change*, Duckworth, London

(1973b) *Before Civilisation*, Jonathan Cape, London

(1976) 'Megaliths, territories and populations', in S.J. De Laet Ed., *Acculturation and Continuity in Atlantic Europe*, De Tempel, Brugge

(1981) 'Introduction: the megalith builders of western Europe', in J.D. Evans, B. Cunliffe and C. Renfrew Eds., *Antiquity and Man*, Thames and Hudson, London

Rey, P.P. (1975) 'The lineage mode of production', *Critique of Anthropology* 3

(1979) 'Class contradiction in lineage societies', *Critique of Anthropology* 4, pp. 41–60

Rowley-Conwy, P. (1978) 'Forkullet fra Lindebjerg. En boplads fra aeldre bronzealder', *Kuml*

Rydbeck, O. (1932) 'Stenkammargravar i Barsebäck', *Arkeologiska studier tillägnade H.K.H. Kronprins Gustaf Adolf*, Stockholm

Sahlins, M. (1972) *Stone Age Economics*, Tavistock, London

Salomonsson, B. (1971) 'Malmötraktens förhistoria', in O. Bjurling Ed., *Malmö Stads Historia 1*, Malmö

SAS Institution (1979) *SAS User's Guide*, J. Helwig and K. Council Eds., Cary, North Carolina

Shanks, M. and Tilley, C. (1982) 'Ideology, symbolic power and ritual communication: a reinterpretation of neolithic mortuary practices', in I. Hodder Ed., *Symbolic and Structural Archaeology*, Cambridge University Press

Sherratt, A. (1981) 'Plough and pastoralism: aspects of the secondary products revolution', in I. Hodder, G. Isaac and N. Hammond Eds., *Pattern of the Past*, Cambridge University Press

Stjernquist, B. (1949) 'En nyfunnen raserad gånggrift i Gråmanstorp, Klippans socken', *Skånes Hembygdsförbunds Årsbok*, pp. 1–17

Strömberg, M. (1961) 'Eine siedlungsgeschichtliche Untersuchung in Hagestad, Südost-Schonen', *Meddelanden från Lunds Universitets Historiska Museum*

(1968) 'Der Dolmen Trollasten in St. Köpinge, Schonen', *Acta Archaeologica Lundensia*, octavo series, No. 7

(1971a) 'Die Megalithgräber von Hagestad', *Acta Archaeologica Lundensia*, octavo series, No. 9

(1971b) 'Hilleshög: undersökning kring en gånggrift i Borrby', *Ale*, pp. 1–14

(1977) *Bondesamhällen under Ingelstorps Forntid*, Lund

(1978) 'Three neolithic sites: a local seriation?', *Meddelanden från Lunds Universitets Historiska Museum*, pp. 68–97

(1980) 'Siedlungssysteme in südschwedischen Megalithgräbergebieten', *Funberichte Aus Hessen*, pp. 131–44

(1982) 'Specialised neolithic flint production with a hoard of scrapers at Hagestad as an example', *Meddelanden från Lunds Universitets Historiska Museum*, pp. 48–64

Tauber, H. (1972) 'Radiocarbon chronology of the Danish mesolithic and neolithic', *Antiquity* XLVI, pp. 106–10

Terray, E. (1975) 'Classes and class consciousness in the Abron kingdom of Gyaman', in M. Bloch Ed., *Marxist Analyses and Social Anthropology*, ASA, London

(1979) 'On exploitation: elements of an autocritique', *Critique of Anthropology* 4, pp. 29–40

Tilley, C. (1982a) 'An assessment of the Scanian battle-axe tradition: towards a social perspective', *Scripta Minora*, pp. 1–72

(1982b) 'Social formation, social structures and social change', in I. Hodder Ed., *Symbolic and Structural Archaeology*, Cambridge University Press

Tinz, T. and Wahlund Franck, K. (1980) 'Keramiken från Hindby Mosse', unpublished seminar paper, Lunds Universitets Historiska Museum

Tuan, Y.F. (1974) 'Space and place: humanistic perspective', *Progress in Geography* 6

Turner, V. (1967) *The Forest of Symbols*, Cornell University Press, Ithaca, N.Y.

(1969) *The Ritual Process*, Penguin, Harmondsworth

Wihlborg, A. (1976) 'Mellanneolithisk boplats Löddeköpinge, Löddeköpinge sn., Skåne', *Riksantikvarieämbetet Rapport* B34, Stockholm

Winge, G. (1976) *Gravfältet vid Kastanjegården*, Malmö Museum, Malmö

Zvulun, E. (1978) 'Multidimensional scalogram analysis: the method and its application', in S. Shye Ed., *Theory Construction and Data Analysis in the Behavioural Sciences*, Jossey-Bass, San Francisco

PART FOUR

Conclusions

Chapter 9

**Ideology, power and
long-term social change**
Daniel Miller and
Christopher Tilley

1. Ideology, power and long-term social change
    The introduction attempted to provide a background to the ideas and approaches that have been used in this volume. In this conclusion we wish to point out some of the ways in which the application of these approaches appears to present promising possibilities for the future, and also to deal more explicitly with the relationship between them and the study of prehistoric materials. The focus of this volume has been on diachronic analysis. Only the paper by Welbourn is synchronically conceived. Of the other papers in Part two, the periods under study, roughly half a century for Leone, and a century for Miller, may seem relatively short but these are periods of rapid and considerable change. The case studies of Part three are based on periods of around one millennium. This is a particular feature of archaeological synthesis and indeed one millennium is not an unduly long period by the standards of the discipline. Such a scope necessitates consideration of factors not generally encountered in other areas of the social sciences.
    For many archaeologists it has been precisely this long time-span that has been used to legitimate analyses founded on relatively mechanical and deterministic perspectives. The case studies presented here indicate that this need not be an inevitable result of archaeological analyses. Throughout the volume there is an emphasis on change as being predicated on a consideration of *social* factors inextricably linked with the form and nature of social totalities postulated for the segment of the past under

consideration. The kind of long-term change considered here is social change, which necessitates a particular conceptual framework. Where authors use such terms as 'adaptation' and 'function' these are descriptive rather than explanatory in intent. This focus on changes at specific temporal and spatial conjunctures may be characterised (as by Braithwaite and Tilley) in terms of a set of parallel and contingent developments, and may result in an effective structural transformation as in the case of Hodder's analysis or as a set of cycles as proposed by Parker Pearson.

No unitary model of change is adopted or subscribed to by the authors in this volume in the sense that change is always deemed to be derived from a single set of factors good for all times and places and cross-culturally valid. Rather the analysis of change is always seen as contingent upon the specific circumstance. The intention is to deal with the *variability* in the archaeological record, and not to subsume it under high-level generalisations.

Examined in the context of the analysis of long-term social change, ideology is not some autonomous comment on the social, but is part of attempts to produce, maintain or resist large-scale social changes, attempts which are always related to the existence of clashes of interest between different individuals and/or groups. A focus on ideology is very far from an attempt to reconstitute individual subjective intention or enter into the minds of individuals long since dead, it comprehends people only in relation to changing material conditions. Ideological practices are embedded in the materiality of the social, their relationship to economic practices is reciprocal and dialectical and cannot be conceived of in terms of either determination or dominance. Hodder focuses on the shift from an emphasis on the reproduction of labour to the control over material resources such as land. Braithwaite and Tilley emphasise changes from relatively closed social organisation based on kinship, alliance and genealogy, with communal and egalitarian *representations* of interest regulated by specific ceremonial expressions, to the development of more hierarchical or egalitarian, individualising societies. Parker Pearson demonstrates cycles between economic growth and depression dynamically interacting with the development of more egalitarian and more hierarchical sets of social relations. Several millennia later, the growth of science and a specific attitude towards technology are the background to further changes in the manner of production and the representation and manipulation of interest as analysed by Leone and Miller. The economic changes that appear to develop in tandem with social change are given emphasis, in particular by Parker Pearson and also in Hodder's analysis of the changing basis of power and control over resources.

A key concept underlying many of the studies in this volume is that of contradiction. Persistence and stability are not conceived of as a norm, hence requiring no explanation. Social production and reproduction are not in any primary sense to be related to a normative consensus occasionally upset by external factors or internal 'pathologies'. Society is not 'made possible' by an accepted social 'contract' but by the effects of the operation of

power in relation to different social strategies. Most of the studies concentrate on asymmetries of power and forms of social control and how these may be represented and misrepresented. The analyses are of how social reproduction and also transformation takes place under these conditions. Stability as much as change is produced, that is, made to happen, and equally requires explanation. Thus we do not see the contrast between past and present societies as that between 'cold' societies impotent to change and 'hot' societies characterised by change, but rather focus on the different forms of generating and legitimating asymmetrical power-relations. The production and representation of certain interests in society as being universal interests is a means of concealing such contradictions. Leone and Miller analyse stability and change to show how social contradictions and conflicts of interest may be concealed by ideological means. Welbourn and Hodder relate contradictions of interest to the negotiation for social position and social power in the form of gender differences. Braithwaite, Parker Pearson and Tilley emphasise conflicts of interests between different groups and individuals in the overall social totality leading to social transformations.

A debate on ideology has evident advantages over certain forms of anthropological analysis in terms of its own translation into archaeological research programmes. Unlike many social theories, it maintains a highly sceptical view on that which people interpret as underlying the workings of their own society. It is an approach frequently directed at what the informant does not say, but which is revealed by the analysis of the organisation and material production of a society, and which may contradict the stated model. Making the past human is not in this approach to be equated with taking the human outside of society, which would anyway be quite an implausible proposition for the analysis of the dead remains of past millennia.

The variety of applications in this volume leads to a diversity of approaches taken in the analysis of change. Parker Pearson uses the work of the Marxist economists Sweezey and Mandel and that of an anthropologist, Friedman as the model for his analysis of cyclical development in the iron age of Denmark. Braithwaite, Tilley and Welbourn are clearly influenced by developments in the analysis of gender asymmetry and its subtle reproduction in material differences in a manner that has emerged quite recently in anthropological theory. A different tradition, that developed in this century in Germany is used in Part two. One of the sources of inspiration for Leone are the writings of Lukács, who also influenced the Frankfurt school of critical theory, which, in turn, developed a model used by Miller. Hodder's analysis of change uses insights from the anthropological study by Goody of social production and reproduction, while Tilley discusses the work of the French Marxist anthropologists and also the critical theory of Habermas for his model of change. All of the contributions are influenced by Marx's original analysis of the notion of value but have used this in quite distinctive ways, the implications of which are often not compatible. Since the sources are so eclectic and based on their appropriateness for the specific analysis, there is less concern with the general question of the application of such models to pre- or non-capitalist societies. Only Parker Pearson addresses this question directly. It is important to underline the fact that Marx's own work is taken only as an example of critical analysis, and need not, therefore, be tied with its particular subject of analysis.

2. The application to an analysis of archaeological materials

An application of these ideas to archaeology means that there is a stress on particular kinds of information that would not be familiar in other disciplines. In this section we examine three elements that are focused upon as a result of the adoption of this approach and their advantages for archaeological reconstruction. These are the analysis of depositional context, the range of material evidence analysed, and the specificity of the analysis.

The archaeologist as excavator has always been sensitive to the precise nature of the deposition of the uncovered materials. Moore has shown how this feature may be used for the analysis of symbolic connotations of the depositional context, for example the equivalents to the term rubbish (Moore 1982). In this volume this theme is a recurrent one. Tilley notes not only differences in the place of deposition, as in the mass of pottery around the tombs compared to the settlement, but also that the material is treated in a different way, i.e. its structure is systematically broken down. Braithwaite shows how differences in the deposition of metal in the henge and burial areas, is used to differentiate the nature of the competing prestige systems represented in the two contexts. Both Parker Pearson and Braithwaite note examples that appear to indicate an explicit social concern with specific forms and contexts of deposition e.g. deposits in bogs and rivers as well as in burials. Parker Pearson relates changes in deposition not only to an implied relationship to the supernatural, but also to its material effects, such that the taking of this material out of circulation would of itself alter the economic base of these prestige goods.

A second and fundamental emphasis in Part three is the attempt to deal with a wide range of different types of evidence and show how in social terms these can be related to each other. This represents one of the significant shifts in interpretation in this volume. Instead of using each range of materials to affirm the patterns found in the other, the emphasis is often in the form of a playing off of one range of evidence against another. No longer do we assume, either that all sets of material equally represent and reflect the same basically homogeneous society, or that these representations will not be contextually dependent. One of the main ways in which we can learn about ideology is through a careful consideration of how far what is being represented in one body of material may be denied in another. Another step forward in analytical sophistication is the realisation, stressed in Tilley's study of site-orientation relations and the spatial patterning of design-attributes, that the same material form may be used both to represent and misrepresent particular social strategies, that is may be 'read' in different ways and, indeed, this is why it may prove successful as a form of ideological legitimation. For Parker Pearson a change in burial deposits may in itself suggest a decrease in the circulation of wealth, if it were not for the fact that

this is being simultaneously denied in the increase in wealth indicated by the analysis of contemporary settlements. Hodder uses a diachronic perspective to show how what is achieved through the elaboration of house forms at one stage is transformed in what is being represented by burials in a later phase. Braithwaite considers this dichotomy in terms of two competing systems, Tilley in terms of contradictions between fundamental structuring principles orientating the form and nature of the social totality. Hodder and Tilley place particular emphasis on links between different types of evidence which are seen as partial transformations of each other, linked to specific forms of ideological social practices. All this work stems from a realisation that material culture plays an active role in the production, reproduction and transformation of the social. Material culture is neither to be taken as a direct mirror of society, nor are different aspects of material culture necessarily compatible with each other in terms of what they represent, but rather material culture forms a complex series of related and interrelated elements that are nevertheless not unitary in their mode of expression but have to be analysed in relation to each other. Some readers may complain that such a conception makes archaeological analysis not only difficult but nearly impossible. That this is not so is borne out by the detailed case studies. Analytical tractability must not be substituted for a theoretical sophistication which fully recognises the complexity of that which we seek to understand.

This attitude towards the material evidence leads directly to the third characteristic of an approach using the critique of ideology. This is to the specificity of the analysis, which is directly addressed by Hodder. Because these are active manipulations we cannot suggest, *a priori*, what is represented by a particular set of objects. The emphasis is on material that shifts its meaning from one period to the next. We are therefore dependent upon a highly specific analysis of material in historically contingent circumstances, in which representations are played off against each other and against the background of social and economic changes analysed as taking place over the period discussed. This has the further advantage stressed by Hodder that we use the richness of the material record instead of simplifying it and reducing it to sets of law-like propositions based on *a priori* assumptions as to the nature of the symbolic process represented. Thus, far from failing to use the variability of the material, the facet of analysis that the new archaeology took great pride in, we see variability not as simply the statistical range held by an artifact form, but as the use and comparison of the great range of material evidence represented by the archaeological record especially over long periods of time.

3. The model of ideology applied

The introduction sought to present an excavation of the notion of ideology, an uncovering of the foundations upon which the various uses of the notion lie and its relationship with power. The specific application to both contemporary material culture and prehistory bring out certain foci of interest from the variety of that which might be uncovered. In this section we will comment upon four of these: the relationship between the individual and the supra-individual, the implications of the monumental form of some of the material evidence, the manner in which artifacts can be subject to recontextualisation and the opposition to the dominant ideology thesis.

There is a stress in nearly all the papers in this volume on the manner in which social relations are represented as relationships between the individual and the supra-individual, whether this be in the form of lineage, society, institutions or the supernatural. The manner in which these forms are represented in the material world is a leitmotiv of the volume. There is no theoretical discussion of the nature of reification (for which see Rose 1978, Chap. 3) but there are several examples that might come under such a term. A shift is noted by Hodder and Tilley towards the affirmation of the lineage represented in the megalithic tombs, which increases strongly through time. That this may be contrasted with the individuality represented in the single inhumations is stressed by Braithwaite. The megaliths serve to deny the individual in a naturalised form through collective representation and the precise manner in which this takes place, and how material culture manifests itself as part of the ideological process, is the core of the detailed analysis presented by Tilley.

The supernatural or the spirit world is taken to have formed the medium for much of this reification of the supra-individual. Parker Pearson, using Friedman's model shows how this has the direct result of creating debt relationships between individuals. This can be compared with the implications of the monumentality of the henges as communal representations analysed by Braithwaite. Miller points out at the end of his contribution how institutions in contemporary industrial societies act in a similar fashion to the reification of communal form as the supernatural in prehistory. In this case it is the modernist estate that is its material representation.

The monumental nature of many of the materials analysed becomes of itself part of the process of ideological representation and effect. The large-scale monuments may represent in a material form the previous generations but this is only part of their impact. As monuments remaining for a long period of time, they themselves survive the generations and are directly inherited by the given generation from their ancestors. The effect of this may be compared with the analysis by Lévi-Strauss (1972, pp. 237–44) of the Churinga, a wooden board used by some Australian aborigines. These boards are hidden in crevices and caves and are only taken out to be painted and repaired during major ceremonies by the males of the group. As such the young male experiences the act of discovery of objects left by previous generations, as a material objectification of the past. This is of particular importance in an area where the landscape itself is the only major material 'given', most other objects being relatively transient. They are thus part of the resolution of synchrony/ diachrony that plays a common role in the naturalisation of the present as tradition. On a larger scale the monuments attempt to make permanent an actually changing social formation by an appeal to the ancestral forces that created them. The manner in which this shifts the form of ideological naturalisation is brought out clearly in the contrast drawn by Hodder between that which is

represented in the houses and that which is effected through representation in the tomb.

This relationship of built form to the representation of time is stressed equally in the analysis of prehistory and the present. Leone, in particular, focuses on the manner by which new forms of construction could indicate new forms by which time itself is represented, and the notion of precedence developed within a juridical framework. For Miller, modernist style also speaks directly of time, in this case the future, which is appropriated by those forces that control that architectural form.

In contrast to the stress on the built environment as representing a more permanent fixture in the landscape as an ideological strategy, it is precisely the flexibility of portable artifacts that makes them so important in shifting relations of rank and prestige. In the case of Miller's analysis it is the inability of the subordinate groups to have access to the means of objectification that is symptomatic of their position. In contrast, where we come to consider portable artifacts there is the possibility of changes, of emulation and contradiction in systems, over a shorter period. These two may go in tandem as shifts in burial practice and the shifting form of artifacts represented in the burial provide a guide to the changing allegiances and alliances that indicate shifts in social forms. These themes are discussed by Parker Pearson, Braithwaite and Tilley.

Finally this use of a close analysis of artifacts and their changes allows for a concern in this volume, as against many other attempts to employ the notion of ideology, to stress the common failure of ideological practices (Abercrombie et al. 1980). It is only too easy to ascribe all major observed forms to a dominant group and assume that, because it can be shown to work as ideological mystification, it can also be assumed to work in a supplementary fashion to direct coercion for the reproduction of asymmetry in power. This is commonly a fault of synchronic analysis. It is perhaps one of the several advantages that have been pointed out with respect to the long time scale and emphasis on change in archaeological analysis, or in material culture studies inspired by archaeology, that there are clear examples of the failure of ideological practices and the need for representation and form to adapt, to abandon and to adopt where appropriate.

In several cases dominance can only be maintained by a radical shift in the form of representation as in the case of Hodder's analysis of a shift from house to tomb. Tilley represents such a failure of ideological control using Habermas' model of a legitimation crisis. This model was developed with respect to the situation in Europe today, and Miller shows how the implications of modernism have changed radically over the last two decades, now as often denigrated as it was once extolled, and that new forms such as the neo-vernacular have arisen that employ quite contrary ideological modes. Parker Pearson shows how systems of representation can break down when they result in changes that are incompatible with the productive possibilities of a given region at that stage in its economic development.

In many cases there is evidence of direct challenges or alternatives to dominant forms. Welbourn indicates the differences in interpretation of males and females with respect to what the pottery represents, Miller shows how control is maintained by the construction of both contrary and alternative modes within the same society by the same establishment. Leone indicates how an adaptation to change is represented in the development of the wilderness garden. Braithwaite shows how, over a range of time, an alternative form can grow, using at first the discourse of that which it seeks to challenge in order to legitimate itself, but in the end overthrowing and replacing that which it contested. The important qualifications addressed by Abercrombie et al. as to the manner in which the notion of ideology is commonly employed, have been well taken in these several examples.

4. Explanation

The contributions to this volume are intended to be explanatory but as the authors reject a positivist/empiricist conception of knowledge the work presented here cannot be adjudged in terms of whether or not it conforms with the canons of positivist criteria for explanation. A rejection of a positivist conception entails the rejection of the hypothetico-deductive method as a means of conceptualising the data/theory relationship. No attempt is made by the individual contributors to predict data sets or changes in these data sets in conformity with a set of theoretical premises which may then be 'validated' or 'falsified' as a result of these predictions. A supposed symmetry between prediction and explanation simply does not hold in the social sciences. An unsuccessful prediction can always be 'saved' by the contention that conditions or elements external to that being tested have not been met. We do not conceive theory as being ultimately parasitic on observation statements but rather the theory/data relationship is reflexive or dialectical in form; both are outcomes or products of knowledge. If the possibility of an atheoretical observation-language is denied there can be no logical basis for the belief that we are testing against a real, neutral reality that is not intersubjectively defined. Both archaeological evidence and the theoretical statements made which attempt to give meaning to that evidence are social creations. Concomitantly the primary logical relationship between theory and data is a conceptual one. Statements about the past are not therefore ultimately to be judged by whether or not they can be tested, or by the outcomes of such tests, but in terms of the conceptual, logical relationships presented between the data and its theorisation, i.e. the internal coherence of any particular study, which can only be criticised in terms of internal conceptual relations and not in terms of externally imposed standards or criteria for 'measuring' or 'determining' truth or falsity.

The explanations put forward in this volume can only be described as being contextual, committed, particularist, historical and structural. They are rooted in determinate social situations and are not meant to be generalisable to beyond the specific case under consideration. Apart from the papers by Hodder and Miller explanations for specific changes in the archaeological record are situated within a fairly small-scale regional framework of analysis. There is no rigid definition of the appropriate scale of analysis for archaeological studies. This is intimately related to that which is being studied. For example, Miller's study of mod-

ernist architecture as a world-wide phenomenon is related to its effects and the particular alternatives presented to that tradition in Britain, while Hodder considers the relationship between specific house and tomb forms within the context of diachronic developments in European prehistory as inextricably bound up with more localised developments at a smaller scale of analysis.

In this volume it is the establishment of detailed links between the disparate aspects of material culture patterning that lends strength and plausibility to the particular explanations given. these links, characterised by Tilley in terms of structural homologies, and their breadth in terms of the data base, are used as the basis for specific social contextualisations of the material evidence, as with Hodder's specific contention that megalithic tombs evoked houses. The links and transformations built up on the basis of perceived data sets are given their meaning by reference to the specific social and historical context. Determinate sets of social relations and structuring principles (the latter being observable but nevertheless ontologically privileged) underlie and give significance to the empirical relationships observed in the archaeological record.

Conclusions

The models developed and applied here do not constitute a 'school', in a formal sense, still less a 'paradigm', nor do they attempt to subsume all other approaches. Too many claims of this kind have been made for us to add another. There are clearly certain elements of archaeological practice that these ideas are incompatible with and do oppose, other elements they are in alignment with or irrelevant to. The papers are only examples of critical approaches which may take a multitude of forms, but they are part of a hope that our approaches to the analysis of past societies and present material culture will become increasingly critical in some form. We believe a critical approach can best be sustained by the close interconnection between the various kinds of studies illustrated in this volume, that is the construction of theoretical approaches, the analysis of material culture in contemporary societies, and the application to detailed and rich archaeological materials available to us, especially for research into long-term change.

This volume and its predecessor, *Symbolic and Structural Archaeology* (Hodder Ed. 1982) are aimed towards the development of certain forms of social archaeology, attempting to confer meaning and significance to a world of otherwise meaningless objects in terms of the social. Its particular foci and concerns are clearly selective and lie within more general trajectories in archaeology and general material-culture studies. The papers attempt to illustrate how shifts in theoretical perspectives can provide insights into the analysis of the sheer diversity of the materials uncovered by archaeologists and surrounding us in the contemporary world. Their value lies in the degree to which they can in fact provide such insights and also help integrate the particular discoveries and understandings thereby achieved within more general interests in the social sciences. For example it is hoped that a more adequate understanding of long-term change as the context for the study of relationships between social and material culture, ideology, power and social strategies, has a contemporary relevance as well as providing a more realistic and informative picture of the past. Equally it is hoped that a non-reductive social archaeology which respects the creators of the archaeological record as sentient beings can actively contribute to social sciences with similar aims for the general study of human society.

Acknowledgements

Thanks are due to Barbara Bender and Ian Hodder for comments on this text.

References

Abercrombie, N., Hill, S. and Turner, B. (1980) *The Dominant Ideology Thesis*, Allen and Unwin, London

Lévi-Strauss, C. (1972) *The Savage Mind*, Weidenfeld and Nicolson, London

Moore, H. (1982) 'The interpretation of spatial patterning in settlement residues', in I. Hodder Ed., *Symbolic and Structural Archaeology*, Cambridge University Press

Rose, G. (1978) *The Melancholy Science*, Macmillan, London

INDEX

For EU product safety concerns, contact us at Calle de José Abascal, 56–1°,
28003 Madrid, Spain or eugpsr@cambridge.org.

www.ingramcontent.com/pod-product-compliance
Ingram Content Group UK Ltd.
Pitfield, Milton Keynes, MK11 3LW, UK
UKHW030905150625
459647UK00025B/2882